Waging Peace

Waging Peace

The United Nations Security Council and Transnational Armed Conflicts

Max Hilaire

Logos Verlag Berlin

λογος

Bibliographic information published by the Deutsche Nationalbibliothek

The Deutsche Nationalbibliothek lists this publication in the Deutsche Nationalbibliografie; detailed bibliographic data are available in the Internet at http://dnb.d-nb.de .

ISBN 978-3-8325-4000-5

Logos Verlag Berlin GmbH
Comeniushof, Gubener Str. 47,
D-10243 Berlin
Germany
Tel.: +49 (0)30 42 85 10 90
Fax: +49 (0)30 42 85 10 92
INTERNET: http://www.logos-verlag.com

*This Book is Dedicated
to my Mom,
Ms. Benedict Thomas*

TABLE OF CONTENTS

PREFACE AND ACKNOWLEDGMENTS

A few years ago a book devoted exclusively to the role of the United Nations Security Council in restoring international peace and security by transnational armed groups would have been unthinkable. Since the end of the Cold War, and more recently, the situation concerning threats or breaches of international peace and security have taken on an added significance, as many of the threats or breaches of the peace are a direct result of transnational armed groups or non-state actors playing a direct role in armed conflicts, giving cause for concern by the international community. In order to remain relevant in light of these new kinds of threats, the Security Council must adapt to the changing international environment and recognize the new reality that now exists in the world. An impressive number of books and scholarly articles have been written about the Security Council and the need for reform to make it more democratic, transparent and more accountable to the United Nations. What we have not seen are books and scholarly articles about the ability or inability of the Security Council to respond to transnational armed conflicts involving states and non-state actors, or between two or more non-state actors or transnational armed groups. The agenda of the Security Council has expanded tremendously since 1989, and scholarly interest in the work of the agency has also accelerated. This book therefore joins a growing body of literature on the role of the Security Council, but unlike other works, this book looks exclusively at the role of the Security Council in maintaining or restoring international peace and security in situations involving transnational armed groups and non-state actors. My task here is to examine the role of the Security Council within the United Nations legal framework in order to determine how well the Security Council complies with United Nations law in discharging its responsibility in response to challenges involving transnational armed groups and non-state actors.

The Security Council is at the core of the United Nations regime for maintaining international peace and security. Unlike other agencies of the United Nations charged with advancing the mission of the organization, the Security Council has the primary responsibility for maintaining international peace and security, and is granted broad enforcement powers under Chapter VII of the Charter in order to do so. The Security Council can take whatever measures it deems necessary to carry out its responsibility, or to force states to comply with its demands. Decisions of the Security Council adopted under Chapter VII are binding and take precedence over all other obligations of member states (Article 103). This interpretation was affirmed by the International Court of Justice in its ruling on Libya's request for interim measures in two cases filed by Libya against the United Kingdom and the United States, in response to their demand for Libya to extradite two of its nationals to face trial in Britain or the United States for their involvement in the bombing of Pan Am Flight 103 over Lockerbie, Scotland.

As the principal organ of the United Nations charged with maintaining international peace and security, the Security Council has broad discretionary powers, and can act without restraint or oversight. No other United Nations body has the authority to review the decisions of the Security Council. All decisions of the Security Council are final, and cannot be subjected to legal challenges. Under Article 24, the Security Council is granted the authority to act on behalf of all states to maintain international peace and security. That authority is further articulated in Chapter VII of the Charter of the United Nations, which grants the Security Council the responsibility to determine a threat to the peace, a breach of the peace, or an act of aggression.

The Security Council is primarily a political body, and its decisions reflect the geopolitical interests of the five Permanent Members, each of whom has a veto over the decisions of the Council. The Security Council tends to act only when the vital interests of one or more of the Permanent Members are threatened, or when they are able to arrive at a consensus that a particular issue inevitably poses a threat to international peace and security. The Permanent Members must also have the assurance that a United Nations intervention will not lead to a realignment of existing arrangements. The Permanent Members of the Security Council act first in their own national interest, while the interest of the international community is secondary, and the decisions of the Security Council may not necessarily be in the best interests of the United Nations or of the international community. Although the Charter gives the Security Council broad powers to maintain international peace and security, it does require the Security Council to carry out its responsibilities in accordance with the purposes and principles of the Charter. The Security Council is also required to resolve disputes brought before it in conformity with the principles of justice and international law. The Security Council, therefore, has a legal obligation to comply with the laws of the Charter and customary international law, and cannot violate fundamental principles of international law (*jus cogens*). Moreover, since as individual states, members of the Security Council are required to comply with their obligations under the Charter and international law, the same principle applies to members of the Security Council as a collective body. However, actions taken by the Security Council under Chapter VII of the Charter are not subject to judicial review by the International Court of Justice. This leaves the Security Council with unchecked powers to exercise its responsibility.

During the Cold War, the Security Council had great difficulties in carrying out its responsibility under Chapter VII because of the ideological differences between the United States and the Soviet Union, and the fact that many of the conflicts during that period involved one or more of the Permanent Members of the Security Council or their close allies. However, with the end of the Cold War, the Security Council has become more actively engaged in managing transnational conflicts, which has raised questions about the extent to which the Security Council is complying with the law of the Charter or with fundamental principles of international law. The activities of the Security Council have generated tremendous controversy over issues of fairness, legitimacy, and transparency, due to the manner in which the Council arrives at its decisions regarding economic sanctions or other forms of enforcement measures.

In the early 1990s, with the onset of the conflicts in the former Yugoslavia and in Rwanda, the Security Council invoked Chapter VII to authorize economic sanctions and arms embargoes in response to over a dozen situations. It also authorized military measures against states and non-state actors in an unprecedented number of cases, some of which have been extremely controversial. These measures raised many questions about the Security Council's willingness to exceed its authority under Chapter VII, and also to overlook the restrictions imposed on the United Nations by Article 2 (7) of the Charter. The Security Council's decisions to classify the situation in northern Iraq in 1991, Somalia in 1993, and Haiti in 1994 as threats to regional or international peace and security, and then to authorize enforcement measures, led some observers to criticize the Security Council for exceeding its legal authority and of potentially having violated the Charter of the United Nations.

What constitutes a threat to international peace and security is whatever the Security Council deems it to be. There is no review of Security Council decisions adopted under Chapter VII. The Security Council has never defined a threat to the peace, nor established guidelines by which it determines what conflicts are international or non-international in nature. Increasingly, the lines between international and non-international conflicts are becoming blurred, making it more difficult to predict how the Security Council will respond. More importantly, domestic political unrest, economic disparity, and social issues now constitute principal causes of transnational conflicts. Threats to international peace and security are increasingly a result of issues related to severe food shortages, political instability, poverty and hopelessness, political repression, corruption, internal displacement of civilians, control over mineral resources, insurgent activity, terrorism, drug trafficking, and gross violations of human rights, to name a few. These issues, once considered matters within the domestic jurisdiction of states, now dominate the agenda of the Security Council.

Since the end of the Cold War, the international system has undergone a dramatic transformation; today's conflicts are arguably more fluid and unpredictable than conflicts during the Cold War. The Security Council has had to interpret its Chapter VII powers broadly and creatively in order to respond to new types of threats to international peace and security. The Security Council took unprecedented and extraordinary measures to maintain international peace and security in the former Yugoslavia and in Rwanda by establishing, for the first time, ad hoc tribunals. The International Criminal Tribunal for the Former Yugoslavia (ICTY), and the International Criminal Tribunal for Rwanda (ICTR), were created in response to the deliberate killings of civilians in Yugoslavia and Rwanda in order to bring those most responsible for violating international humanitarian law to justice. The Security Council also took other innovative steps to manage transnational conflicts, such as delegating its authority to individual states or regional organizations to intervene directly in transnational armed conflicts. Both of these steps were challenged for their unprecedented nature.

The following chapters will chronicle the work of the Security Council in managing transnational armed conflicts waged by states and non-state actors. They will examine the extent to which the Security Council is willing to stretch the law of the United Nations Charter to implement its mandate. The following chapters will also look at the challenges which transnational armed conflicts pose to the authority of the Security Council, and how in this new global environment, the Council is sometimes forced to grant itself expansive powers to respond appropriately and effectively to threats to international peace and security.

This book stems from a series of lectures I delivered at various universities in Africa and Central Europe in the immediate aftermath of the fall of the Berlin Wall, the end of state communism, and the demise of the Soviet Union, which paved the way for the Security Council to play a more pivotal role in managing various threats to international peace and security. My lectures coincided with the success of the United Nations Security Council in ending conflicts in Namibia, Mozambique, Cambodia, Afghanistan, and Central America, and with the beginning of new conflicts in the former Yugoslavia and in Rwanda. In retrospect, the immediate post-Cold War era can be considered a watershed in the history of the United Nations. New conflicts, such as those involving the Islamic State in Iraq and Syria (ISIS), al Shabaab in Somalia, and Boko Haram in Nigeria, pose serious challenges to the international community. Ongoing conflicts in the Democratic Republic of the Congo, in Libya, and in Syria have also all raised questions about the ability of the Security Council to find an effective mechanism to deal with these persistent situations. Hopefully, this exercise will inform policymakers, scholars, practitioners, and students of the United Nations and International Law of the activities of the Security Council, and will help them to arrive at their own conclusions about the Security Council's compliance with its obligations under the Charter of the United Nations and under international law.

M.H., December 2014
with special thanks to my wife, Anita, and to Elan and Elias

INTRODUCTION

THE SECURITY COUNCIL AND THE MAINTENANCE OF INTERNATIONAL PEACE AND SECURITY

Since its creation, the United Nations Security Council has helped to resolve a number of regional conflicts, or at least to defuse regional tensions. The Security Council was instrumental in bringing about a peaceful end to colonial rule in Africa, Asia, and the Caribbean; in finding a creative solution to the Suez Crisis, in which France, Britain, and Israel invaded Egypt; the Korean War; and the Congo and Cyprus crises. During the Cold War, the Security Council provided a platform for the United States and the Soviet Union to play out their ideological rivalry and to shield their satellites from international scrutiny. Crises in new states stemming from colonial rule, boundary disputes, and potential Cold War rivalries were quickly resolved by the Security Council. United Nations peacekeepers were deployed in a number of regional conflicts in newly independent states to prevent conflicts from escalating into major wars.[1]

The Korean War of 1950 and the Suez Crisis of 1956 were the first major conflicts to test the authority of the Security Council. In both cases, Permanent Members of the Security Council were either involved or had a stake in the outcome.[2] The Security Council was able to reach an agreement authorizing the deployment of U.S. troops in the Korean Peninsula due to the absence of the Soviet Union. Subsequent authorizations to extend the U.S. mandate were vetoed by the USSR. This forced the United States to take the matter before the General Assembly. The General Assembly was subsequently granted authority under the Uniting for Peace Resolution to debate issues concerning international peace and security when the Security Council was deadlocked, and to make recommendations to member states. In the Suez Crisis the Security Council could not condemn Britain, France, and Israel because of the threat of a veto by Britain and France. However, a Canadian compromise agreement was accepted, and the General Assembly was able to adopt a resolution which called for the withdrawal of British, French, and Israeli forces from Egyptian territory in exchange for the deployment of the United Nations Emergency Force (UNEF) peacekeeping force to serve as a buffer between Egyptian and Israeli forces. The success of the Suez experiment would later serve as a model for managing subsequent regional conflicts.

In the first decade of its existence, the Security Council supported the deployment of United Nations peacekeepers in transnational armed conflicts in order to prevent the United States or the Soviet Union from gaining a foothold in regions outside their respective spheres of influence. The conflicts were not overly complicated in themselves, but external involvement made them relatively difficult to resolve. The parties sought the assistance of the United Nations and were willing to cooperate with it to find a peaceful solution. These early transnational conflicts usually involved states and non-state actors such as liberation movements or groups fighting for self-determination; they were newly independent states that were still politically fragile and vulnerable to external interference. Many of these new states had weak political institutions, and groups that felt left out of the political process resorted to arms in order to be included, or to benefit from the spoils of power. The United Nations faced a very different situation in the post-Cold War era. The end of the Cold War led to a dramatic shift in the international system, including the demise of the Soviet Union, the end of communism, and the United States reigning supreme as the world's pre-eminent military power. The international security environment also changed drastically, with more conflicts occurring within states rather than between states, and the emergency of a range of non-state actors with the capacity to wage war.

The old ideological rivalry between East and West, in part responsible for many of the conflicts during the Cold War, disappeared with the collapse of communism. It was replaced by ethnic and religious rivalries which were more difficult to contain.[3] The attitude of the Permanent Members of the Security Council also changed; they were no longer as willing to respond to transnational conflicts as they were during the Cold War or in its immediate aftermath. Their response generally coincided with threats to their own economic or security interests, and was usually contingent on domestic politics and international public opinion.[4] The outcomes of these transnational conflicts no longer had the same impact on the international strategic balance as they did during the Cold War, and hence the major powers felt no urgency in rushing to intervene unless it was in their national interest.[5] Today's transnational conflicts tend to be more spontaneous, sporadic, unpredictable, and more difficult to contain. Military intervention by the international community does not guarantee results. Resolving these conflicts is far more complicated than was the case during the Cold War. Many of these transnational armed conflicts are rooted in long-standing political, social, religious, and ethnic rivalries, and cannot be solved by military intervention. In fact, military interventions tend to prolong or lead to an escalation of these conflicts.

Since the end of the Cold War, the United Nations has had to respond to several regional conflicts, which has overwhelmed the resources of the organization and has led to bad decisions during times of crisis.[6] The United Nations has rushed to intervene in many of these conflicts, often simultaneously, and without first carefully calculating an exit strategy or a formula for bringing about a permanent peace.[7] The disastrous results in some cases have forced the United Nations to reconsider when and how to intervene in future conflicts.[8] The United Nations was very successful in managing the conflicts in Cambodia, Namibia, and Mozambique, but less successful in Angola, Bosnia, Haiti, Rwanda, and Somalia.[9] Its missions in Sierra Leone, Kosovo, and East Timor encountered some initial difficulties, but the situation ultimately stabilized. More recent missions, such as those in the Democratic Republic of the Congo (DRC), Côte d'Ivoire, and Darfur have been plagued by controversy due to shortages of personnel, resources, and a lack of commitment from member states.

This book is an attempt to examine and critically appraise how United Nations law is applied in Security Council decision-making as regards the maintenance of international peace and security. Although several organs of the United Nations play a role in conflict management, including the Secretary General, the General Assembly, and the International Court of Justice, the text will concentrate primarily on the role of the Security Council, which the Charter of the United Nations gives exclusive responsibility for maintaining international peace and security. Unlike the other parts of the United Nations, the Security Council is the only organ whose resolutions, when adopted under Chapter VII, are binding on all states. The Security Council, therefore, is the only organ within the United Nations system with the ability to apply and enforce United Nations law.

Chapter I looks at the relevant laws of the United Nations as they relate to the maintenance of international peace and security, and the powers that these laws grant the Security Council. Chapter I also analyzes how consistently the Security Council has applied these laws to different conflict situations. Chapter II examines the evolution of the peacekeeping formula as a mechanism for managing international and regional or internal conflicts during the Cold War. Chapter III looks at peacekeeping operations in post-Cold War conflicts and the challenges posed by these conflicts to the traditional peacekeeping formula. Chapter IV examines cooperation between the United Nations and regional agencies or alliances in managing conflicts, and the challenges posed by alternative security regimes. Chapter V examines Security Council interventions in small-scale and limited transnational armed conflicts, while Chapter VI looks at a selection of inter-state conflicts since 1945 which the Security Council has seen to threaten international peace and security. Chapter VII examines the use of non-military enforcement measures, such as economic sanctions and arms embargoes. The final chapter makes some preliminary observations for improving the United Nations crisis response and management system.

CHAPTER I

UNITED NATIONS LAW FOR MAINTAINING INTERNATIONAL PEACE AND SECURITY

The basic legal foundation of the United Nations system can be found in Article 2 of the Charter, which spells out the legal obligations of member states and the organization. Article 2 (1) establishes the principle of sovereign equality of states, a premise that is at the core of the international system. Article 2 (3) calls on all member states to settle their disputes by peaceful means in such a manner that international peace and security, and justice, are not endangered.[1] Article 2 (4) requires all member states to refrain in their international relations from the threat or use of force against the territorial integrity or political independence of any state, or in any other manner inconsistent with the Purposes of the United Nations.[2] Article 2 (5) expects member states to give the United Nations every assistance in any action it takes in accordance with the present Charter, and to refrain from giving assistance to any state against which the United Nations is taking preventive or enforcement action. Article 2 (6) mandates that the United Nations ensures that states which are not members of the organization act in accordance with these Principles so far as may be necessary for the maintenance of international peace and security.[3] Article 2 (7) prohibits the United Nations from intervening in matters which are essentially within the domestic jurisdiction of any state, or shall require the members to submit such matters to settlement under the present Charter; but this principle shall not prejudice the application of enforcement measures under Charter VII.[4]

The actions of the United Nations and that of all member states are guided by the principles of the Charter. To further centralize decision making with respect to enforcing the obligations of the United Nations, the Charter grants the Security Council wide-ranging powers and a great deal of latitude to act on behalf of the entire organization. It calls on member states to comply with decisions of the Security Council adopted under Chapter VII for the maintenance of international peace and security.[5] Decisions of the Security Council adopted under Chapter VII are legally binding on all states, and all states are required to comply with them. This provision of the Charter gives the Security Council enormous discretionary power to circumvent principles of the Charter and customary international law. The Security Council can exercise such power without oversight or judicial scrutiny.[6] There are no provisions in the Charter for reviewing measures taken by the Security Council under Chapter VII for maintaining international peace and security. Occasionally decisions of the Security Council have raised questions about fairness, legitimacy and legality, but there is no formal mechanism for contesting them.

The Power of the Security Council under the Charter of the United Nations

Article 24 and Chapter VII of the United Nations Charter grant the Security Council exclusive responsibility for maintaining international peace and security. Under Article 24, member states confer on the Security Council primary responsibility for the maintenance of international peace and security, and agree that in carrying out its duties under this responsibility the Security Council acts on their behalf. However, Article 24 cautions the Security Council that in discharging these duties it shall act in accordance with the Purposes and Principles of the United Nations.[7] Article 25 requires member states to accept and carry out the decisions of the Security Council.[8] The specific powers granted to the Security Council for carrying out these duties are spelled out in Chapter VII of the Charter.

According to Chapter VII, 'Action with Respect to Threats to the Peace, Breaches of the Peace, and Acts of Aggression', Articles 39 to 51 contain the authority of the Security Council to maintain international peace and security. Under Article 39 the Security Council shall determine the existence of any threat to the peace, breach of the peace, or act of aggression and shall make recommendations, or decide what measures shall be taken in accordance with Articles 41 and 42, to maintain or restore international peace and security.[9] Article 40 provides for the Security Council, in order to prevent further aggravation of a situation, to call upon the parties concerned to comply with such provisional measures as it deems necessary or desirable, before making recommendations or deciding upon the measures specified in Article 39. Such provisional measures shall be without prejudice to the rights, claims, or positions of the parties concerned. The Security Council shall duly take account of failure to comply with such provisional measures.[10]

According to Article 41, the Security Council may decide what measures not involving the use of armed force are to be employed to give effect to its decisions, and it may call upon the Members of the United Nations to apply such measures.[11] These may include complete or partial interruption of economic relations and of rail, sea, air, postal, telegraphic, radio, and other means of communication, and the severance of diplomatic relations.[12] Article 42 calls on the Security Council, if measures provided for in Article 41 would be inadequate or have proved to be inadequate, to take such action by air, sea, or land forces as may be necessary to maintain or restore international peace and security. Such action may include demonstrations, blockades, and other operations by air, sea, or land forces of Members of the United Nations.[13] However, in order for the United Nations to act collectively, it must sign an Article 43 agreement with member states.

According to Article 43:

(1)   All Members of the United Nations, in order to contribute to the maintenance of international peace and security, undertake to make available to the Security Council, on its call and in accordance with a special agreement or agreements, armed forces,

assistance, and facilities, including rights of passage, necessary for the purpose of maintaining international peace and security.

(2)   Such agreement or agreements shall govern the numbers and types of forces, their degree of readiness and general location, and the nature of the facilities and assistance to be provided.

(3)   The agreement or agreements shall be negotiated as soon as possible on the initiative of the Security Council. They shall be concluded between the Security Council and Members or between the Security Council and groups of Members and shall be subject to ratification by the signatory states in accordance with their respective constitutional processes.[14]

Article 44 states that when the Security Council has decided to use force it shall, before calling upon a Member not represented on the Security Council to provide armed forces in fulfillment of the obligations assumed under Article 43, invite that Member, if the Member so desires, to participate in the decisions of the Security Council concerning the employment of contingents of that Member's armed forces.[15] Article 45 requires that Members hold immediately available national air force contingents for combined international enforcement action. The strength and degree of readiness of these contingents and plans for their combined action shall be determined, within the limits laid down in the special agreement or agreements referred to in Article 43, by the Security Council with the assistance of the Military Staff Committee.[16] Under Article 46, plans for the application of armed force shall be made by the Security Council with the assistance of the Military Staff Committee.[17]

Under Article 47:

(1)   There shall be established a Military Staff Committee to advise and assist the Security Council on all questions relating to the Security Council's military requirements for the maintenance of international peace and security, employment and command of forces placed at its disposal, the regulation of armaments, and possible disarmament.

(2)   The Military Staff Committee shall consist of the Chiefs of Staff of the Permanent Members of the Security Council or their representatives. Any Member of the United Nations not permanently represented on the Committee shall be invited by the Committee to be associated with it when the efficient discharge of the Committee's responsibilities requires the participation of that Member in its works.

(3)   The Military Staff Committee shall be responsible under the Security Council for the strategic direction of any armed forces placed at the disposal of the Security Council. Questions relating to the command of such forces shall be worked out subsequently.

(4)   The Military Staff Committee, with the authorization of the Security Council and after consultation with appropriate regional agencies, may establish regional subcommittees.[18]

Under Article 48, any action required to carry out the decisions of the Security Council for the maintenance of international peace and security shall be taken by all the Members of the United Nations or by some of them, as the Security Council may determine. Such decisions shall be carried out by the Members of the United Nations directly, and through their action in appropriate international agencies of which they are members.[19] Under Article 49 Members of the United Nations shall join in affording mutual assistance in carrying out the measures decided upon by the Security Council.[20] Article 50 gives any state confronted with special economic problems arising from the carrying out of preventive or enforcement measures the right to consult the Security Council with regard to a solution to those problems.[21]

Finally, Article 51 states that nothing in the present Charter shall impair the inherent right of individual or collective self-defense if an armed attack occurs against a Member of the United Nations, until the Security Council has taken the measures necessary to maintain international peace and security. Measures taken by Members in the exercise of this right of self-defense shall be immediately reported to the Security Council, and shall not in any way affect the authority and responsibility of the Security Council under the present Charter to take at any time such action as it deems necessary in order to maintain or restore international peace and security.[22]

From the above provisions of the Charter it is clear that the framers of the United Nations Charter gave broad authority to the Security Council for the maintenance of international peace and security. Chapter VII of the Charter does not define what specific incidents constitute a threat to the peace, breach of the peace, or an act of aggression. The Security Council can decide arbitrarily what matters threaten international peace and security and respond appropriately.[23] The Charter's complex formula proved unworkable soon after the United Nations Charter came into force. The Charter's security regime is predicated on the continuing consensus that existed amongst the great powers during the Second World War. That consensus broke down soon thereafter, and the ideological rivalry between the United States and the Soviet Union that followed paralyzed the ability of the Security Council to respond effectively to threats to the peace, breaches of the peace, or acts of aggression.[24] The Security Council also had great difficulty implementing the Charter security regime soon after the United Nations Charter came into effect, due to the involvement of one or more of the major powers or their allies in post-war conflicts.[25] The lack of a consensus in the Security Council on what constituted a threat to international peace and security led the Security Council to invent alternative formulas for maintaining international peace.[26]

THE SECURITY COUNCIL AND THE ENFORCEMENT OF CHAPTER VII

The Situation in the Korean Peninsula

The first test to the authority of the Security Council, and the first challenge for the new collective security regime of the Charter, came with the beginning of the Korean War in 1950.

Following North Korea's invasion of South Korea on June 25, 1950, the Security Council adopted resolution 82 (1950) on the same day, by which it condemned North Korea's action as a breach of the peace, and called on the government of Pyongyang to withdraw its forces to the 38th Parallel.[27] On June 27 the Security Council adopted resolution 83 (1950), by which it recommended that all Member States furnish such assistance to the Republic of Korea as may be necessary to repel the armed attack, and to restore international peace and security in the area.[28] On July 10 the Security Council adopted its third resolution on the situation in the Korean Peninsula. Under resolution 84 (1950) the Security Council recommended that all Member States providing military forces and other assistance make such forces and assistance available to a unified command under the United States of America.[29] Under resolution 84 (1950) the Security Council basically delegated its authority to the United States. The operation, therefore, was not a United Nations operation in the true meaning of Article 42 of the Charter, but rather an Article 51 measure; meaning it was a collective self-defense operation, not a collective security measure.[30] The United States was granted *carte blanche* to carry out a collective defense operation against North Korea. However, the United States manipulated the Security Council process in order to secure the approval of the mission in North Korea, such that it was a United Nations operation in name only.[31]

The Korean measure was approved in the absence of the Soviet Union, which was boycotting the Security Council to protest the failure of the Security Council to recognize communist China as the legitimate representative of the people of China.[32] Instead, the United Nations recognized the government of the breakaway province of Taiwan as the legitimate authority of China. This aggravated the Soviet leadership, who felt that the United Nations was too pro-Western. Once the Soviet Union returned to occupy its seat in the Security Council, it vetoed any further extension of the operation in Korea.[33] In response, the United States introduced a resolution in the General Assembly that would in principle amend the Charter of the United Nations, by giving the General Assembly authority to debate an issue related to peace and security in the event that the Security Council was unable to carry out its responsibility under Article 24 of the Charter due to a deadlock.[34]

The Uniting for Peace Resolution was adopted on November 3, 1950 by a vote of 52 to 5, with two abstentions. Section A, paragraph I of the resolution 'resolves that if the Security Council, because of lack of unanimity of the Permanent Members... fails to exercise its primary responsibility for the maintenance of international peace and security in any case when there appears to be a threat to the peace, breach of the peace or act of aggression, the General Assembly shall consider the matter immediately with a view to making appropriate recommendations to Members for collective measures, including in the case of a breach of the peace or act of aggression, the use of armed force where necessary, to maintain or restore international peace and security. If not in session at the time, the General Assembly may meet in emergency special session within twenty-four hours of the request. Such emergency special session shall be called if requested by the Security Council on the vote of any seven Members, or by a majority of the Members of the United Nations.'[35]

The Uniting for Peace Resolution provided the impetus for future United States military measures against North Korea. The General Assembly asserted its newly-won authority by approving the extension of the United States-led mission in the Korean Peninsula. The General Assembly subsequently invoked the Uniting for Peace Resolution to authorize the deployment of peacekeeping forces in the Suez Canal and in the Congo.[36] Both France and the Soviet Union refused to pay their assessed contributions for the operation, claiming that the General Assembly did not have the legal authority to authorize the deployment of peacekeepers under the command of the United Nations.[37] The General Assembly requested an Advisory Opinion from the International Court of Justice (ICJ). In its *Advisory Opinion in the Certain Expenses of the United Nations* case, the Court ruled that the General Assembly had the authority under Article 22 of the Charter to establish subsidiary organs such as the United Nations Organization for the Congo (ONUC); hence all states had a legal obligation to pay to support such organs.[38] Russia eventually paid its back dues, but to this day France has not accepted the legal opinion of the ICJ as an accurate interpretation of the Charter and it continues to insist that only the Security Council has the authority to authorize the deployment of forces such as ONUC.[39]

The Korean operation was a unilateral measure undertaken by the United States under the guise of the United Nations. The force was a United Nations force only in name. It had all the characteristics of a national army: the majority of the troops were American, with an American commander who reported directly to the President of the United States rather than to the Secretary General of the United Nations.[40] The United Nations had little or no control over the day-to-day activity of the force, and the Military Staff Committee played no role in advising the Security Council as required by Articles 46 and 47. This experience of the first application of the Charter regime for maintaining international peace and security further crippled an already paralyzed Security Council. It would be several years before the Security Council could authorize enforcement action against another state. Following the end of the Korean War the Cold War intensified, making reaching a consensus in the Security Council on the existence of a threat to the peace, breach of the peace, or act of aggression even more difficult.[41] The Security Council was faced with a number of disputes between 1950 and 1965, but failed to make a determination that a threat to the peace or a breach of the peace existed, and therefore did not authorize enforcement action.

The Situation in Rhodesia

Following Rhodesia's white minority government's Unilateral Declaration of Independence (UDI) on November 11, 1965, the Security Council convened an emergency meeting the next day on the request of Britain, the colonial power, to debate the situation. The Security Council adopted resolution 216 (1965) by which it condemned the UDI.[42] The Council called on all states to not recognize the illegal racist regime in Southern Rhodesia, and to refrain from rendering any assistance to the illegal regime.[43] On November 20, the Security Council met for a second time to debate the situation in Rhodesia. The Security Council adopted resolution 217 (1965), by which it determined that the situation resulting from the UDI was extremely grave, that the government of the United Kingdom should put an end to it, and that its continuance constituted a threat to international peace and security. The resolution imposed a limited set of voluntary economic and diplomatic sanctions on Rhodesia.[44] The resolution further called on all states to refrain from any action which would assist and encourage the illegal regime, and to do their utmost to break all economic relations with it.[45] The failure of resolution 217 (1965) to force the white minority regime to rescind the UDI led the Security Council to adopt resolution 221 (1966), by which it imposed mandatory sanctions on Rhodesia under Chapter VII of the Charter.[46] The Security Council made its determination on the grounds that the situation in Southern Rhodesia constituted a threat to international peace and security. The adopted measures included an arms embargo, an embargo on imports of oil and motor vehicles, and a ban on Rhodesian imports. Resolution 221 (1966) called upon the government of the United Kingdom to prevent, by the use of force if necessary, the arrival at Bier (Mozambique) of vessels reasonably believed to be carrying oil destined for Southern Rhodesia.[47]

Under resolution 232 (1966), the Security Council further expanded the sanctions imposed under resolution 221 (1966) to include a ban on commodity imports and restrictions on economic relations with the minority regime in Southern Rhodesia.[48] The sanctions had a limited impact on the white minority regime, as some states continued to trade with Rhodesia in violation of the sanctions. The sanctions therefore did not accomplish their objective of bringing an end to white minority rule in Southern Rhodesia. On May 29 the Security Council adopted resolution 253 (1968) by which it further tightened the sanctions regime on Rhodesia. The Security Council also established a committee to (a) examine and report on the implementation of the resolution, and (b) to seek further information from Member States and specialized agencies as to any potential breach of the sanctions.[49] The sanctions on Southern Rhodesia remained in place until white minority rule ended in 1979, following implementation of the Lancaster House Agreement, which led to the independence of Zimbabwe in December 1979.[50]

The Situation in South Africa

South Africa was the third and only other country to have Chapter VII measures invoked against it. In response to South Africa's racial policy of apartheid, the Security Council took the extraordinary step on November 4, 1977, of imposing mandatory sanctions on South Africa to force it to change its internal policies. Acting under Chapter VII of the Charter of the United Nations, the Security Council adopted resolution 418 (1977), by which it imposed an arms embargo against South Africa.[51] In 1963 the Security Council had imposed a voluntary arms embargo on South Africa on the recommendation of the General Assembly, but some members of the Security Council continued to trade in weapons with South Africa.[52] The Security Council mandatory sanctions under Chapter VII were designed to close this loophole. The measures taken had a limited impact on South Africa's economy, and it was not until private companies doing business in South Africa began to divest their assets from that country as a result of mass protest by anti-apartheid groups in the United States and Europe that the regime agreed to negotiate with the black majority population. Municipalities in the United States also withdrew their pension funds from companies doing business with South Africa. These measures had an adverse effect on the South African economy and forced the white minority regime to modify its policies and to adopt reform measures that ultimately led to multi-party elections and to black majority rule. The arms embargo and other restrictions were lifted by Security Council resolution 919 (1994), following majority rule in South Africa.[53]

The three cases of enforcement measures cited above were the only instances in which the Security Council invoked its authority under Chapter VII to maintain international peace and security during the Cold War. However, since the end of the Cold War, the Security Council has invoked Chapter VII on numerous occasions to authorize an unprecedented number of enforcement measures against states and non-state actors. The Security Council authorized Chapter VII enforcement measures against Iraq, under resolutions 661, 665, and 678 (1990);[54] against the former Yugoslavia, under resolutions 713 (1991), 770 (1992), 827 (1993), 1031 (1995), and 1088 (1996);[55] against Somalia, under resolutions 733 (1992), 794 (1992), and 814 (1993);[56] against Libya, under resolutions 731 (1992), 748 (1992), and 883 (1993);[57] against Liberia, under resolution 788 (1992);[58] against Haiti, under resolutions 841 (1993), 875 (1993), and 940 (1994);[59] against the UNITA rebels of Angola, under resolution 864 (1993);[60] against Rwanda, under resolution 929 (1994);[61] against Sudan, under resolution 1054 (1996);[62] against rebels in Eastern Zaire, under resolution 1080 (1996);[63] against the Revolutionary United Front of Sierra Leone, under resolutions 1162 and 1171 (1998);[64] in Kosovo, under resolution 1244 (1999);[65] in East Timor, under resolution 1264 (1999);[66] in the Democratic Republic of the Congo, under resolution 1304 (2000);[67] and against Ethiopia and Eritrea, under resolution 1298 (2000).[68] These Chapter VII measures, including the military actions against Iraq in 1991, have not always been applied consistently, and in the manner specified under Chapter VII. In some instances the Security Council over-extended its authority, and was in violation of United Nations law by doing so.[69] Despite criticisms of the Security Council's actions, no state or institution was able to successfully challenge the authority of the Security Council to impose these measures. More importantly, the Charter makes no provision for judicial review of Security Council measures adopted under Chapter VII of the Charter. None of the above sanction measures met their stated objectives. Instead, several of the sanctions regimes were deemed to have been unfairly applied, with serious consequences for the civilian populations of the target states.[70]

The mere fact that the Security Council has been able to adopt these measures with greater frequency does not make the actions in and of themselves legitimate. The international community may appreciate the fact that the Security Council can now carry out its responsibilities under the Charter in the current international climate, as opposed to the period during the Cold War, but the basis for some of its actions raises serious questions about the legitimacy and fairness of Security Council sanctions.[71] The operation against Iraq, like the one against North Korea, was a collective self-defense measure authorized by the Security Council under Chapter VII.[72] It was not an Article 42 operation, for it did not satisfy the specific requirements for collective enforcement measures specified in Article 42 of the Charter.[73] In both cases, the United States used the Security Council framework to win international legitimacy and neutralize domestic political opposition for its military operations. The United States was able to persuade a majority of Security Council members to go along with its plans. However, neither of these operations can be considered true United Nations operations. In fact, once the Security Council had given its approval for military action it no longer had influence over the day-to-day conduct of the operations. Both operations may have violated the spirit of the Charter, if not the laws of the United Nations.[74]

The above cases underscore the difficulty of implementing Chapter VII measures in conflict situations. The major powers continue to resist signing an Article 43 agreement, which would place their forces under United Nations command.[75] They prefer retaining full control over their troops and to manage operations unilaterally, rather than through the complex United Nations bureaucracy. Moreover, the process for implementing the United Nations Chapter VII enforcement regime can be extremely slow and uncertain. The process of signing an Article 43 agreement would subject the United Nations to serious partisan political bickering in the national parliaments of member states, further delaying any rapid response to a crisis situation.[76]

The Legality of Peacekeeping Operations

During the Cold War the Security Council had great difficulty in imposing Chapter VII measures on states because one or more Permanent Members vetoed the resolution.[77] This made the Security Council ineffective and incapable of discharging its responsibility under the Charter. The Security Council initially overcame the threat of the veto by granting the General Assembly authority to act in emergency situations under the Uniting for Peace Resolution.[78]

In 1956 the Security Council was faced with a very peculiar situation that was clearly a breach of international peace and security, in the form of the Suez Crisis. British, French, and Israeli forces invaded Egyptian territory in response to President Nasser's decision to nationalize the Suez Canal. The threat of a British and French veto was likely to paralyze the Security Council and leave it unable to confront the challenge. To break the impasse, Canada proposed a compromise that would require Britain, France, and Israel to withdraw their troops from Egyptian territory in exchange for the deployment of a United Nations peacekeeping force. The operation would be fundamentally different from the measures specified in Chapter VII of the Charter, but it would serve as a face-saving device for a disabled Security Council, and for Britain and France. As part of that agreement, the United Nations created the United Nations Emergency Force (UNEF I), to be deployed as an observer force, with the consent of the Egyptian government. It was a novel concept intended to address a unique situation.[79] The General Assembly invoked its authority under the Uniting for Peace Resolution and adopted resolution 998 (ES-I), by which it established UNEF I.[80] UNEF I was mandated to secure and supervise the cessation of hostilities, including the withdrawal of the armed forces of France, Britain, and Israel from Egyptian territory, and after the withdrawal, to serve as a buffer between Egyptian and Israeli forces.[81] UNEF I was withdrawn in 1967 on the request of the Egyptian government.[82]

The concept of peacekeeping was significantly different from enforcement measures under Chapter VII of the Charter. Under the UNEF I formula, troops would deploy between hostile armies to keep them separated but would not take part in any fighting. They were to remain neutral at all times and were only authorized to use force in self-defense. The force was to be deployed on the consent of the parties involved, and only after a ceasefire agreement had been signed between the parties.[83] As a precautionary measure, only troops from non-aligned states were invited to participate in the mission, to insulate the conflict from the Cold War. UNEF I, unlike a force under Chapter VII, was authorized by the General Assembly, with the Secretary General placed in charge of the daily activities of the force.[84] The Security Council had the authority to terminate the mission, but the Secretary General was responsible for its day-to-day operation.

Since the United Nations Charter made no mention of peacekeeping, members of the Security Council had to scramble to find a provision in the Charter to legally justify the existence of UNEF I. Some states argued that peacekeeping was justified under the implied powers of the Security Council to maintain international peace and security, which it can delegate to the General Assembly or the Secretary General. The concept therefore can be justified under either Chapter VI or Chapter VII of the Charter.[85] Other observers have maintained that neither Chapter VI nor VII provide a convincing legal basis for peacekeeping, and have placed it in a grey area, referring to it as Chapter VI and a half.[86] The International Court of Justice in its 'Advisory Opinion on the Special Expenses' case upheld the rights of the Security Council and the General Assembly to establish peacekeeping missions. With peacekeeping now a permanent aspect of the United Nations conflict management regime, no one any longer questions its legality. The success of UNEF I led the United Nations to make peacekeeping a permanent mechanism for resolving disputes between states. The UNEF I model has since been applied in a number of regional conflicts, both during and after the Cold War.

The specific powers granted to the Security Council under Chapter VII of the Charter are also supported by Chapter VI, Articles 33 to 38. Article 33 calls for the parties to any dispute which is likely to endanger the maintenance of international peace and security to first seek a solution by negotiation, enquiry, mediation, conciliation, arbitration, judicial settlement, resort to regional agencies or arrangements, or other peaceful means of their choice.[87] The Security Council shall, when it deems necessary, call upon the parties to settle their dispute by such means. Under Article 34, the Security Council may investigate any dispute, or any situation which might lead to international friction or give rise to a dispute, in order to determine whether the continuance of the dispute or situation is likely to endanger the maintenance of international peace and security.[88] Under Article 35, any Member of the United Nations may bring to the attention of the Security Council or the General Assembly any dispute to which it is a party, if it accepts in advance, for purposes of the dispute, the obligation to peaceful settlement provided in the Charter.[89]

Under Article 36 of the Charter of the United Nations, the Security Council may, at any stage of a dispute of a nature referred to in Article 33, or a situation of a like nature, recommend appropriate procedures or methods of adjustment.[90] The Security Council should take into consideration any procedures for the settlement of the dispute which have already been adopted by the parties. In making recommendations under this Article, the Security Council should also take into consideration that legal disputes should as a general rule be referred by the parties involved to the International Court of Justice, in accordance with the provisions of the Statutes of the Court.[91] Article 37 states that should the parties to a dispute of a nature referred to in Article 33 fail to settle it by the means indicated in that Article, they shall refer it to the Security Council. If the Security Council deems that the continuance of the dispute is in fact likely to endanger the maintenance of international peace and security, it shall decide whether to take action under Article 36, or to recommend such terms of settlement as it may consider appropriate.[92] Article 38 states that without prejudice to the provisions of Articles 33 and 37, the Security Council may, if all the parties to any dispute so request, make recommendations to the parties with a view to a peaceful settlement of the dispute.[93]

Chapter VI of the Charter of the United Nations addresses itself to Member States that are parties to a dispute and gives them broad discretionary authority in settling their dispute. The Security Council has limited authority to enforce its will under Chapter VI.[94] The Security Council can call on the parties to settle their dispute through the peaceful means specified in Article 33; however, it cannot force the parties to comply.[95] The Security Council is granted the authority under Chapter VI to make recommendations to the parties; its power is more one of persuasion rather than compulsion. Unlike Chapter VII, Chapter VI calls on the Security Council to act only after the parties have failed to reach a peaceful solution to their dispute.[96]

Peacekeeping as a means of settling disputes between parties has occasionally been linked to Chapter VI of the Charter. However, Chapter VI makes no mention of peacekeeping as a peaceful means for settling disputes between states. Given the emphasis on peaceful settlement in Article 33, the Security Council would be acting within its powers by creating new means of peaceful settlement of disputes in the event the means mentioned in Article 33 have failed or proved inadequate.[97] The Security Council did not exceed or abdicate its authority under Chapters VI and VII by allowing the General Assembly to authorize the deployment of a peacekeeping force on Egyptian territory in response to the Suez Crisis. The Security Council can exercise broad powers under Article 24, and Chapters VI and VII, to maintain international peace and security. The power to authorize the deployment of peacekeeping forces can be justified under three different types of powers: the substantive powers of both the Security Council and to a certain extent that of the General Assembly, that is, power to deal with certain emergency situations; formal powers, that is, the power to adopt certain types of decisions; and the power to create subsidiary organs or to assign functions to the Secretary General under Articles 22, 29, and 98.[98]

The Role of Regional Arrangements and Agencies

Chapter VIII, Articles 52 to 54 of the Charter of the United Nations, speaks of Regional Arrangements through which the Security Council can maintain international peace and security. Article 52 states:

(1)   Nothing in the present Charter precludes the existence of regional arrangements or agencies for dealing with such matters relating to the maintenance of international peace and security as are appropriate for regional action, provided that such arrangements or agencies and their activities are consistent with the Purposes and Principles of the United Nations.[99]

(2)   Members of the United Nations entering into such arrangements or constituting such agencies shall make every effort to achieve pacific settlement of local disputes through such regional arrangements or by such agencies before referring them to the Security Council.[100]

(3)   The Security Council shall encourage the development of pacific settlement of local disputes through such regional arrangements or by such regional agencies either on the initiative of the states concerned or by reference from the Security Council.[101]

(4)   This Article in no way impairs the application of Articles 34 and 35.

Under Article 53:

(1)   The Security Council shall where appropriate utilize such regional arrangements or agencies for enforcement action under its authority. But no enforcement action shall be taken under regional arrangements or agencies without the authorization of the Security Council, with the exception of measures against enemy states, as defined in paragraph 2 of this Article, provided for pursuant to Article 107 or in regional arrangements directed against renewal of aggressive policy on the part of any such state, until such time as the Organization may, on request of the government

concerned, be charged with the responsibility for preventing further aggression by such state.[102]

(2)   The term enemy state as used in paragraph 1 of this Article applies to any state which during the Second World War has been an enemy of any signatory of the present Charter.

Article 54 states that the Security Council shall at all times be kept informed of activities undertaken by or under contemplation by regional arrangements or regional agencies for the maintenance of international peace and security.[103]

Chapter VIII does not define a local dispute, nor does it give exclusive authority to regional agencies for managing local disputes. Similarly, a party to a regional dispute is not legally obligated to refer its dispute to a regional agency first before bringing the matter to the attention of the Security Council.[104] Regional agencies have limited capacity to resolve local disputes and in some instances may inflame the dispute. As a result of the Cold War, regional agencies never quite evolved in the manner anticipated by the framers of the Charter.[105] The few regional arrangements that were created remained relatively weak and ineffective. Their ability to manage regional disputes was dictated by one or another of the major powers, who manipulated these organizations to further their own ideological and strategic objectives.[106]

As an alternative, states established regional alliances and defense pacts, whose authority fell under Article 51 of the Charter instead of Chapter VIII.[107] The concept of regional arrangements or agencies never fully evolved under the United Nations system, and the few that were created never subjected their authority to the Security Council.[108] The few times that regional arrangements intervened in regional conflicts they did so without the authorization of the Security Council and their actions violated provisions of Chapter VIII of the Charter.[109] During the Cold War, regional disputes in the Western Hemisphere and in Eastern Europe were managed exclusively by military alliances or regional arrangements dominated by the United States and the Soviet Union, respectively.[110] The United Nations was only allowed to manage colonial disputes and disputes outside the spheres of influence of the two super-powers.

During the Cold War era, the Security Council was unable to arrive at a consensus on the existence of a threat to the peace because many regional disputes had a direct link to the Cold War, or involved one or more permanent members of the Security Council or their allies.[111] Both the United States and the Soviet Union exercised their veto power in the Security Council to prevent the United Nations from intervening in their respective regions and spheres of influence. The United States and the Soviet Union opposed United Nations intervention in Latin American and Eastern Europe, and tried to convince other members of the Security Council that the dispute was regional in nature and should be referred to the appropriate regional agency instead: the Organization of American States (OAS) for the Western Hemisphere and the Warsaw Pact for Eastern Europe.[112] At different times the two major powers gave conflicting interpretations to the regional arrangement provisions of the Charter.[113] They argued that states had a legal obligation to seek a regional solution to their dispute first before referring the matter to the Security Council. United Nations intervention was limited to colonial conflicts in Africa. However, the attitudes of the two major powers changed toward the end of the Cold War, paving the way for the United Nations to intervene in several regional conflicts.[114]

One of the major issues to confront the United Nations was the question of what qualifies as a regional arrangement or agency. Since the Charter does not define what a regional arrangement is, it was left to states to determine their geographic nature and membership.[115] More importantly, it was not quite clear whether the member state of a regional arrangement must exhaust all local or regional remedies before taking its dispute to the United Nations. In the 1950s Guatemala attempted to bypass the Organization of American States and take its dispute with the United States directly to the Security Council.[116] The United States opposed Guatemala's request on the grounds that Guatemala had not sought a solution through the OAS. The Security Council never definitively determined what the procedure was for taking a dispute to it without first going to a regional agency. Similarly, Cuba sought the same protection from the Security Council in its dispute with the United States and was blocked by the United States. Cuba also tried to get the International Court of Justice to issue an advisory opinion on the issue, but this measure was also dismissed.[117]

It appears that states do have a choice of forum for settling their disputes and can select either the Security Council or a regional arrangement, whichever suits them best. The Charter preference for regional solutions seems logical, given the fact that at the regional level member states may be more familiar with the issue and more inclined to find a regional solution.[118] However, given the domination by the major powers of regional organizations and the influence of the Cold War in regional disputes, it is not surprising that some states chose the Security Council instead of the regional organization.[119] Regional arrangements can also prejudice the outcome of a conflict because of member states' vested interest in a preferred outcome. The legal obligation of states to settle their disputes by peaceful means allows states broad latitude in the choice of forum and the mechanism which they can apply. A choice of forum in Chapter VIII of the Charter is consistent with Article 33 of the Charter.

Another important issue to confront the United Nations with respect to regional arrangements was whether regional arrangements can engage in peacekeeping activities without the authorization of the Security Council. Both the United States and the Soviet Union insisted that their actions in the Dominican Republic and in Czechoslovakia, respectively, were peacekeeping measures not subject to Security Council approval.[120] The rationale for such an argument is that if the Security Council can call on regional arrangements to perform peacekeeping duties, regional arrangements on their own can engage in these activities without authorization from the Security Council.[121] The issue is not whether regional arrangements can engage in peacekeeping activities, but whether their actions are in fact peacekeeping or enforcement actions, and who makes the determination, the Security Council or the regional organization itself.[122] That issue was never settled, and it has come to haunt the United Nations in the post-Cold War era.

Recent enforcement measures taken by ECOWAS in Liberia and Sierra Leone were taken without the authorization of the Security Council. The measures were initially deemed to be peacekeeping, but subsequently changed to enforcement actions after the conflicts intensified.[123] In Security Council resolution 788 (1992), the Council endorsed ECOWAS's peace initiatives, and exempted it from the sanctions imposed on rebel-controlled territory in Liberia.[124] Similarly, the Security Council did not condemn NATO military actions against Yugoslavia during the Kosovo crisis. The Security Council later approved resolution 1244 (1999) to authorize the deployment of the NATO-led Kosovo Force (KFOR).[125]

CHAPTER II

THE SECURITY COUNCIL AND TRANSNATIONAL ARMED CONFLICTS

Conflict Management during the Cold War: Phase I

The political atmosphere during the Cold War was detrimental to great power cooperation in the United Nations Security Council. The Cold War adversely affected the ability of the Security Council to manage conflicts in the manner envisioned by the framers of the Charter. Except for the Korean War in 1950 and the limited authorization granted to the United Kingdom in Rhodesia in 1966, the Security Council was unable to authorize further enforcement action under Chapter VII of the Charter. The Security Council had to resort to other means to manage regional conflicts. As an alternative to the failed collective security system, the United Nations introduced the new peacekeeping formula, which was fundamentally different from what the framers of the Charter had hoped for. The new formula, which required the consent of the parties before United Nations forces could be deployed, also withheld making a determination as to who was the aggressor.[1] The formula was first tested in Egypt, following the British, French, and Israeli invasion of Egyptian territory.

The Suez Canal Crisis

In 1956 the United Nations was confronted with a peculiar situation when two permanent members of the Security Council, Britain and France, along with Israel, invaded Egypt. Britain and France used their veto to block the Security Council from taking action against them. However, the General Assembly invoked its authority under the Uniting for Peace Resolution and accepted the Canadian Foreign Minister Lester Pearson's peace initiative, which called for a ceasefire and the deployment of a peacekeeping force under the command of the Secretary General, who was granted authority to prepare a plan for an international emergency force.[2] Under the plan, the United Nations would deploy a peacekeeping force under a restricted mandate with the consent of the parties involved and after a ceasefire had been agreed upon.[3]

The peacekeeping formula worked out during the Suez Crisis was very different from the Charter regime for maintaining international peace and security. Under the Suez formula the Secretary General was given a pivotal role in managing the conflict.[4] It further required that troops be drawn solely from neutral countries, and that they would carry light arms for use only in self-defense. The troops were to be deployed after a ceasefire agreement had been signed and the mandate was limited solely to monitoring the ceasefire agreement and keeping the hostile armies disengaged.[5] The troops were to be deployed on the consent of the parties involved, and the United Nations had to withdraw the troops on the request of the host country.[6]

The Suez formula was flawed in several respects: the deployment of the peacekeeping force was contingent on the consent of the parties and only after a ceasefire agreement had been reached. It was a voluntary force that relied on the goodwill of certain states. Finally, the troops had to be withdrawn on the request of the host country even if their withdrawal would lead to a resumption of hostilities. The United Nations was blamed for withdrawing UNEF from Egypt on the request of the Egyptian government, although by so doing it was pretty clear that Egypt and Israel would go to war.[7] Despite UNEF's flaws, peacekeeping became a permanent feature of the United Nations formula for settling small-scale conflicts between states, and it was invoked in several other regional conflicts in the ensuing Cold War years.

The Congo Crisis

In 1961 the United Nations received a request from Prime Minister Patrice Lumumba of the newly independent Congo for military assistance to prevent his country from disintegrating into civil war.[8] Following the granting of independence by Belgium and the withdrawal of its troops from the Congo, ethnic violence, rioting and a mutiny in the army threatened to destabilize the new state and its fragile regime. The war later intensified when the province of Katanga, with the help of Belgian mercenaries, tried to secede from the Congo and become a part of Belgium.[9] After a lengthy debate on the issue, the Security Council authorized the Secretary General to prepare a plan for military and technical assistance, and subsequently approved his plan for the deployment of a peacekeeping force in the Congo under his authority.[10] The United Nations Operation in the Congo (ONUC) was authorized with a vague mandate and without carefully calculating the risk involve or the prospects of a quick diplomatic solution. The Congo mission, which was billed as 'preventive diplomacy', tried to insulate the conflict from the Cold War by excluding troops from the United States and the Soviet Union from participating in the operation.[11] However, both the United States and the USSR indirectly influenced the course of the conflict to suit their ideological and strategic objectives.

Secretary General Dag Hammarskjold's attempt to prevent the conflict from becoming a Cold War battle alienated both the United States and the USSR and it drove a wedge between the United Nations and the major powers. Both the United States and the Soviet Union saw Hammarskjold's strategy of establishing an independent role for the United Nations in regional conflicts as a challenge to their own authority. They feared it would create a dangerous precedent that could undermine their strategic interests in various regions.[12] In the midst of the confusion surrounding the role of the United Nations, and the disagreement between the United States and the USSR about the proper role of the organization, Hammarskjold died in a plane crash. One of the key players in the crisis, Patrice Lumumba, was subsequently assassinated in the presence of ONUC. Lumumba's death stirred a great deal of controversy and it raised some suspicion about the involvement of the United Nations in the Congo.[13] ONUC gradually became more involved in the conflict and was forced to take sides. ONUC's involvement compromised its neutrality and led to a crisis at the United Nations.[14] For the first time, the United Nations was involved in a civil war, fighting on behalf of the national government. This raised questions about the legal authority of the United Nations to get involved in a civil war, a right denied to states under international law. According to Thomas Franck, the United Nations was violating international law by authorizing its troops to fight on behalf of the government of the Congo in the absence of a specific determination from the Security Council that the conflict in the Congo was a threat to international peace and security and then invoking Chapter VII to authorize enforcement measures.[15]

France and the Soviet Union also challenged the legality of the United Nations action in the Congo. Both France and the USSR refused to pay their peacekeeping dues in protest at United Nations policy, both objecting to ONUC siding with the government of the Congo in the civil war. The Soviet Union was critical of the role of the United Nations and called for the reconfiguration of the Office of the Secretary General into a Troika.[16] Many African states were also critical of the United Nations, blaming it for Lumumba's death. ONUC finally withdrew from the Congo in 1963 after a new government headed by Mobutu came into power. Despite its many setbacks, the United Nations managed to prevent a potentially devastating colonial conflict from becoming a major Cold War battle between the United States and the USSR. The United Nations lost much of its legitimacy after the Congo crisis, which led to a re-examination of the role of the United Nations in regional conflicts.[17]

The Crisis in West Irian

The United Nations Congo operation was followed by two new missions: in West Irian and Cyprus. The United Nations Security Force (UNSF) in West Guinea (West Irian) and the United Nations Peacekeeping Force in Cyprus (UNFICYP) were both authorized while the Congo mission was still in progress. Although the two operations relied heavily on the precedents established during the Suez and Congo crises, they were slightly modified to suit the unique situations in each country.

UNSF was established in 1962 as a result of a prior agreement between the government of the Netherlands and the government of Indonesia over the withdrawal of Dutch sovereignty over West Irian.[18] The agreement provided for the Dutch to hand over control of the territory to a United Nations Temporary Executive Authority (UNTEA) which would in turn transfer governmental authority to Indonesia within a year. UNSF was intended to maintain the authority of UNTEA and to assist the local police in maintaining law and order.[19]

The Situation in Cyprus

The Cyprus situation was much more complicated than West Irian. Cyprus was ruled by Britain from 1878 to 1960. In 1960 Britain granted Cyprus independence after consultation with Greece, Turkey, and the local Cypriot leaders.[20] The constitutional arrangement accepted by all sides proved unworkable soon after independence. The Greek Cypriot majority subsequently attempted to amend the constitution without consulting the Turkish Cypriot minority.[21] The political stalemate soon led to violence and political unrest, which brought Greece and Turkey almost to the brink of war. On Britain's request, the Security Council authorized the deployment of a 6,000-strong United Nations Peacekeeping Force in Cyprus (UNFICYP) in 1964. UNFICYP's mandate required it to maintain internal order and prevent external intervention.[22]

UNFICYP's mandate also called for the creation of a buffer zone between the two Cypriot communities, but to not impede the free movement of people throughout the island. In 1974 a military government took power in Cyprus and brought the island into a closer military alliance with Greece.[23] Turkey retaliated by invading Cyprus and establishing a de facto territorial division in favor of the Turkish Cypriot community.[24] Cyprus remains divided between the Turkish north and the Greek south, with United Nations peacekeepers juxtaposed as a buffer between the two antagonists.

In 1983 the Turkish Cypriot part of the island declared itself an independent Turkish Republic of Northern Cyprus, but only Turkey has recognized it as a separate state.[25] The international community continues to recognize the Greek Cypriot government based in Nicosia as the legitimate government of Cyprus. UNFICYP has done remarkably well in fulfilling its mandate, and the Security Council continues to extend its duration. UNFICYP has prevented an escalation of hostilities between Greece and Turkey and has kept the two Cypriot communities in check.[26] Efforts by successive United Nations Secretaries General over the last three decades to find a political settlement to the Cyprus crisis have been unsuccessful.[27] The prospects for a permanent settlement in Cyprus in the immediate future remain extremely gloomy, particularly with tension still very high between Greece and Turkey over their outstanding territorial disputes. A solution to the Greek-Turkish dispute will have to be found before either side can agree to a formula for settling the Cyprus dispute. A recent round of peace talks under the auspices of Secretary General Kofi Annan's Special Representative, Richard Holbrooke, failed to break the deadlock. The patience of the international community may begin to wane if no solution is found soon.

The Conflict in Kashmir

Following the independence of India and Pakistan in 1947, Kashmir was free to accede to either India or Pakistan. Its accession to India was a matter of dispute between the two countries. Fighting between India and Pakistan broke out soon thereafter. In January 1948, the Security Council adopted resolution 39 (1948) by which it established the United Nations Commission for India and Pakistan (UNCIP) to investigate and mediate the dispute.[28] In April 1948 the Security Council adopted resolution 47 (1948) by which it decided to enlarge the membership of UNCIP and recommend various measures, including the use of observers to stop the fighting.[29] In July 1949, India and Pakistan signed the Karachi Agreement to establish a ceasefire line to be supervised by observers. On March 30, 1951, following the termination of UNCIP, the Security Council adopted resolution 91 (1951) by which it established the United Nations Military Observer Group in India and Pakistan (UNMOGIP) to continue to supervise the ceasefire in Kashmir. UNMOGIP was required to observe and report, investigate complaints of ceasefire violations, and submit its findings to each party and to the Secretary General.[30]

In 1971 India and Pakistan went to war over Kashmir. In 1972 both sides signed a ceasefire agreement defining the Line of Control in Kashmir which, with minor changes, followed the same course as the 1949 Karachi Agreement. India took the position that the mandate of UNMOGIP had expired, since it related specifically to the ceasefire line under the Karachi Agreement. Pakistan continued to recognize the mandate of UNMOGIP.[31] Given the disagreement between the two parties about UNMOGIP's mandate and functions, the Secretary General took the position that UNMOGIP could be terminated only by a decision of the Security Council. The military authorities of Pakistan continue to submit complaints to UNMOGIP about ceasefire violations. The Indian military authorities have lodged no complaints since 1972 and have restricted the activities of the observers on the Indian side of the ceasefire line. India, however, continued to provide accommodation, transportation and other facilities to UNMOGIP.[32]

The Civil War in Lebanon

The Security Council also deployed a number of small peacekeeping missions in various countries during the Cold War period in response to emerging regional conflicts. In 1958 the United Nations authorized the deployment of the United Nations Observation Group in Lebanon (UNOGIL) to stop the flow of weapons from Syria to Lebanese rebels.[33] UNOGIL's authority was later usurped by U.S. troops, deployed to deter an exaggerated external communist threat in Lebanon brought about by the violent pro-Soviet coup in Iraq.[34] UNOGIL withdrew in December 1958 after a new president assumed power in Lebanon.

Following Israel's invasion of Lebanon in March 1978, the Security Council adopted resolution 425 (1978) by which it authorized the deployment of the United Nations Interim Force in Southern Lebanon (UNIFIL) for the purpose of confirming the withdrawal of Israeli troops from Lebanese territory, restoring international peace and security, and assisting the government of Lebanon in ensuring the return of its effective authority over the area.[35] On

May 3, in response to a request from the Secretary General, the Security Council adopted resolution 427 (1978) by which it increased the troop level from 4,000 to 6,000.[36] UNIFIL had great difficulty implementing its mandate due to sporadic fighting between Israeli forces and Hezbollah. Israel withdrew its forces from the self-declared security zone in southern Lebanon in 2000.[37] UNIFIL entered the zone to fill the security vacuum left by the Israelis.

The Civil War in Yemen

In July 1963, the United Nations established the United Nations Yemen Observation Mission (UNYOM) to monitor a military disengagement agreement between the parties in the Yemeni civil war.[38] The likelihood of the war posing a serious threat to regional peace and security intensified after Egyptian and Saudi Arabian troops intervened on opposite sides in the conflict. UNYOM was unable to fulfill its mandate because it was too small to monitor repeated violations of the agreement by the involved parties. The United Nations withdrew its troops from Yemen in September 1964 and did not authorize another peacekeeping operation in the Middle East until the end of the 1973 Arab-Israeli War.[39]

The Situation in the Middle East after the 1973 Arab-Israeli War

Following the end of the Six Days War between Israel and its Arab neighbors in 1973, the Security Council authorized the deployment of two peacekeeping missions in the region. The Security Council authorized the deployment of the United Nations Emergency Force (UNEF II) in Egypt to supervise the ceasefire agreement and troop disengagement, and to control the buffer zone between Egypt and Israel.[40] In 1974 the Security Council authorized the deployment of the United Nations Disengagement Observer Force (UNDOF) on the Golan Heights in Syria to monitor the ceasefire agreement, patrol the border area of Israel and Syria, and serve as a buffer between the two hostile armies. UNEF II successfully implemented its mandate and created a stable political climate that contributed to a peace agreement between Egypt and Israel. UNEF II withdrew in 1979 after Egypt and Israel signed the Camp David Accords.[41] UNDOF continues to patrol the border area between Syria and Israel. Its presence has helped to diffuse tensions between the two warring parties. Although Israel has since annexed the Golan Heights, UNDOF's presence has neutralized a very volatile border region and has prevented a war between Israel and Syria. Peace between Israel and Syria remains elusive, despite efforts by the United States to get both sides to the negotiating table.

Conflict Management after the Cold War: Phase II

The end of the Cold War had a positive impact on the Security Council's ability to carry out its responsibilities under Chapter VII of the Charter. There were also dramatic developments in the international system that led to a change in the attitudes of member states of the

Security Council. The revival of United Nations peacemaking and peacekeeping activities was caused in part by the change in attitudes in the Soviet Union brought about by the new Soviet leader, Mikhail Gorbachev.[42] Gorbachev saw the United Nations as a centerpiece of his foreign policy, playing a more effective role in managing regional conflicts. The idea was part of his overall strategy to bring about a reduction in tension between the United States and the USSR and to become partners in peace instead adversaries. This new Soviet attitude led to a renaissance in United Nations peacekeeping activities and to a renewal in confidence in the ability of the organization to manage regional conflicts. With the Cold War no longer an obstacle, the United Nations was being asked to manage many both new and long-standing regional conflicts that had their origins in the Cold War rivalry between the United States and the Soviet Union. The revival of the Security Council led to United Nations involvement in a number of regional conflicts.[43] The United Nations had some immediate successes resolving regional conflicts that gave reason for optimism.

The Iran-Iraq War

In 1988 the United Nations Secretary General mediated an end to the ten-year Iran-Iraq war. The Security Council later authorized a small peacekeeping mission to monitor these agreements. The United Nations Iran-Iraq Military Observer Group (UNIIMOG) was established by the Security Council under resolution 619 (1988).[44] UNIIMOG's mandate called for it to verify, confirm, and supervise the ceasefire agreement and the withdrawal of all forces to the internationally recognized boundaries. UNIIMOG was also required to patrol the 850-mile border between Iran and Iraq.[45] UNIIMOG withdrew in 1991 after Iran and Iraq signed a formal peace treaty, coincidentally on the eve of the Gulf War between Iraq and the United States-led coalition. A number of issues were left outstanding in that peace agreement, including the repatriation of prisoners of war.

The Afghanistan Conflicts

The Secretary General negotiated the Geneva Agreement which led to the withdrawal of Soviet troops from Afghanistan, and a temporary halt in the fighting between Afghan government troops and Mujahedeen guerrillas.[46] However, differences between the various factions prevented the agreement from being fully implemented. Following the signing of the peace agreement, the Security Council adopted resolution 622 (1988) by which it established the United Nations Good Offices Mission in Afghanistan and Pakistan (UNGOMAP) to assist the Personal Representative of the Secretary General to assist (indeed, to lend his good offices) to the parties in ensuring the implementation of the Agreements on the Settlement of the Situation Relating to Afghanistan, and in this context, to investigate and report violations of any of the provisions of the Agreements.[47]

UNGOMAP was charged with supervising Soviet troop withdrawal from Afghan territory and monitoring military activities in the Afghan-Pakistani border area.[48] Pakistan had served as a haven for Afghan rebels fighting the Soviet-backed government in Kabul, and with United States support, funneled military aid to the rebels. UNGOMAP withdrew in 1990, but the internal strife between the various Afghan factions continued.

In 1992 the Mujahedeen guerrillas overthrew the Soviet-backed regime; however, the fractious Mujahedeen regime which had split along factional lines was in turn later overthrown by the Taliban. The Taliban advocated an extremely conservative brand of Islam which forced women to stay at home and required all men to grow long beards. It carried out a number of public executions and floggings of those who opposed its rule. The Taliban regime was not officially recognized as the legitimate government of Afghanistan because of Western dissatisfaction with its policies and its continuing support for terrorism. In addition, the Taliban never gained full control of all of Afghanistan. Remnants of the Mujahedeen controlled the northern part of the country and waged war against the Taliban. In October 2001, the United States began a bombing campaign against the Taliban regime and al Qaeda terrorists for their involvement in the September 11 attacks on the United States. The Taliban regime collapsed within weeks of the bombing campaign, and a pro-Western government was installed for a six month transition period. The situation in Afghanistan remains very volatile and unpredictable.

These early peacekeeping successes significantly enhanced the stature of the United Nations as a conflict management organization capable of carrying out the responsibility it was initially charged with when the organization was created in 1945. The role of the Security Council was being taken more seriously by member states, and more disputes were referred to the Security Council for resolution.[49] With its new-found confidence, the United Nations tackled several regional conflicts that were far more complex and more difficult to resolve. However, the United Nations' involvement in some of these new regional conflicts severely damaged its reputation and permanently compromised its ability to manage future conflicts.[50] The United Nations suffered serious setbacks in Somalia and Bosnia, which forced it to re-examine its involvement in future regional conflicts. Some of the Permanent Members of the Security Council also reviewed their policy toward United Nations peacekeeping. The new policies adopted by the Security Council came on the eve of a major conflict in Rwanda, in which close to a million civilians were killed in one of the century's worst cases of genocide. Fresh from its failures in Bosnia and Somalia, some members of the Security Council refused to authorize a new United Nations mission in Rwanda or to expand the mandate of the existing mission.[51] The failure of the United Nations to act in Rwanda led to international condemnation of the way in which the United Nations handles certain regional conflicts. Early intervention by the United Nations could have saved the lives of thousands of Rwandan civilians.

Conflict Management after the Cold War: Phase III

The United Nations began its post-Cold War peacekeeping activities with the deployment of large peacekeeping missions, comprising both military and civilian personnel, in Namibia, Cambodia, the former Yugoslavia, and Mozambique.[52] The Security Council authorized the deployment of the United Nations Transition Assistance Group (UNTAG) in Namibia in 1989 to oversee the colony's transition from South African rule to independence, following the signing of a peace accord between South Africa and SWAPO, the rebel movement that was fighting South Africa for independence for Namibia. As part of that agreement the Security Council also deployed a small observer force, the United Nations Angola Verification Mission (UNAVEM), to monitor the withdrawal of Cuban forces from Angola.[53]

Following the signing of the Paris Accords by all the parties in the Cambodia conflict, the Security Council authorized the deployment of United Nations Transitional Authority in Cambodia (UNTAC) in 1990 to supervise the implementation of that agreement, designed ultimately to bring peace to Cambodia.[54] The Security Council adopted resolution 743 (1992) to authorize the deployment of United Nations Protection Force (UNPROFOR) in Croatia in 1992 to monitor the ceasefires in Croatia.[55] Its mandate was later expanded to include monitoring the ceasefires in Bosnia-Herzegovina, oversee the border area between Macedonia and Albania, and to protect relief workers.[56] In 1992 the Security Council authorized the creation of the United Nations Operation in Mozambique (ONUMOZ) to supervise the internal peace accord between the government of Mozambique and the rebel movement RENAMO,[57] disarm combatants, organize elections, and resettle internally displaced persons. Also in December 1992, the Security Council adopted resolution 794 (1992) by which it authorized the deployment of the United Nations Operation in Somalia (UNOSOM I) to monitor a ceasefire agreement between the warring factions in Somalia and to protect shipments and distribution of relief supplies.[58]

These new peacekeeping missions were very ambitious undertakings by the United Nations. Their mandates comprised multiple missions, combining both civilian and military duties. They included ceasefire monitoring and separating hostile armies, distributing humanitarian relief supplies, organizing national elections, monitoring human rights, disarming, demobilizing and integrating combatants into civilian life, social and economic rehabilitation, nation-building, and political reconciliation.[59] In addition, the missions were also required to monitor the post-conflict implementation of the peace process. The missions were very different from any of the missions previously undertaken by the United Nations. These conflicts were more complicated than previous conflicts, and for the first time the United Nations had to negotiate with both states and non-state actors.[60] Below is a detailed analysis of the various peacekeeping missions, and an assessment of how well the United Nations performed.

The Namibia Conflict

After decades of fighting a bush war and resisting efforts by the United Nations to find a peaceful settlement for the Namibia issue, the South African government accepted a joint United States-Soviet Union peace agreement that provided for its withdrawal from Namibia, a ceasefire between its forces and that of the South-west African People's Organization (SWAPO), and for the territory to be administered by the United Nations during the transitional period leading to independence.[61] Under resolution 632 (1989) the Security Council approved the peace agreement and authorized the deployment of the United Nations Transitional Assistance Group (UNTAG) in Namibia[62] in February 1989. UNTAG's tasks included overseeing complete implementation of the peace agreement.

The 1988 United States-Soviet Union 'Joint Declaration of Principles for a Peaceful Settlement in South Africa' called for the independence of Namibia under the terms of Security Council resolution 435 (1978).[63] The agreement called for the decommissioning of SWAPO forces, the withdrawal of South African troops from the territory, the abolition of apartheid laws in Namibia, the election of a constituent assembly, and the deployment of a United Nations peacekeeping force to oversee the implementation of the agreement.[64] UNTAG would prepare Namibia for independence from South Africa by conducting a voter registration drive and establishing the security conditions necessary for the holding of free and fair elections. The joint declaration was part of a comprehensive agreement which linked South African troop withdrawal from Namibia with the withdrawal of Cuban troops from Angola.[65]

At its peak UNTAG consisted of 4,500 troops and 1,500 civilians. Its mission lasted thirteen months and it was a remarkable success. Except for a border skirmish between SWAPO and South African forces at the beginning of the operation, the mission was trouble-free. Namibia gained its independence on March 21, 1990 and was admitted to the United Nations immediately thereafter. UNTAG forces withdrew from Namibia at the end of March 1990. The success of UNTAG's mission proved that the United Nations was capable of managing complex regional conflicts. It gave added momentum to the Security Council to tackle other regional conflicts.

The Angolan Civil War

As part of the comprehensive agreement under the United States-Soviet Union joint declaration, the Security Council adopted resolution 626 (1988) to authorize the deployment of a much smaller peacekeeping mission in neighboring Angola.[66] The United Nations Angola Verification Mission (UNAVEM I) was established in Angola to verify the redeployment of Cuban troops to the north of the country and their phased and final withdrawal from Angolan territory in accordance with the timetable agreed upon by Angola and Cuba.[67] Cuban troops withdrew a month ahead of schedule. The Secretary General then informed the Security Council that UNAVEM I had accomplished its mission within the time frame established by the parties and that UNAVEM I had fully and effectively implemented the mandate entrusted to it. However, instead of withdrawing UNAVEM I, the Security Council adopted resolution 696 (1991) on May 31, 1991, by which it authorized UNAVEM I to be integrated into a new mission called UNAVEM II.[68] UNAVEM II was established by the Security Council to verify the implementation of the Bicesse Peace Accords, signed on May 31, 1991 by the government of Angola and UNITA.[69]

UNAVEM II's mandate required it to verify the arrangements between the Angola parties under the Gbadolite Accords. The Gbadolite Accords were supposed to end the civil war in Angola and to establish a government of national unity, followed by the holding of national elections.[70] UNAVEM II was charged with monitoring that process. In its initial deployment UNAVEM II comprised 350 military observers and 126 police monitors. The Security Council later increased the troop level by an additional 400 election observers to monitor the general election of September 1992.[71] The elections were held as scheduled and were certified by the United Nations as generally free and fair. However, UNITA contested the results and refused to recognize the outcome. UNITA abandoned the peace process and resumed the civil war.[72] To avoid a complete breakdown of the peace process in Angola, the Security Council adjusted the mandate of UNAVEM II in October 1992, in order to assist the two parties to reach an agreement on the modalities for completing the peace process, including implementation of the ceasefire agreements.[73]

In November 1994 the government of Angola and UNITA signed the Lusaka Protocol, which called for an end to the civil war, the creation of a government of national unity, the decommissioning of UNITA troops, and their integration into the Angolan army.[74] Under resolution 966 (1994) the Security Council endorsed the peace accord, and subsequently authorized the establishment of UNAVEM III under resolution 976 (1995), to monitor the implementation of the new agreement.[75]

The main provisions of UNAVEM III's mandate included the following: to provide good offices and mediation to the Angolan parties; to monitor and verify the extension of the State administration throughout the country and the process of national reconciliation; to supervise, control and verify the disengagement of forces and to monitor the ceasefire; to verify information received from both sides regarding their forces, as well as all troop movements; to assist in the establishment of quartering areas; to verify the withdrawal, quartering and demobilization of UNITA forces; to supervise the collection and storage of UNITA armaments; to verify the movement of government forces (*Forças Armadas de Angola*, or FAA) to barracks; to verify the free circulation of persons and goods; to verify and monitor the neutrality of the Angolan National Police, disarming of civilians, quartering of the rapid reaction police, and security arrangement for UNITA leaders; to coordinate, facilitate and support humanitarian activities directly linked to the peace process, as well as participating in mine-clearance activities; to declare formally that all essential requirements for holding of the second round of presidential elections had been fulfilled; and to support, verify and monitor the electoral process.[76]

Within a few months after it took effect, the Lusaka Protocol ran into difficulties after UNITA failed to carry out in good faith its obligations under the agreement. Jonas Savimbi, UNITA's leader, refused to disarm his forces completely or to join the government of national unity in Luanda. In frustration with UNITA, the Security Council, acting under Chapter VII of the Charter, imposed additional sanctions on UNITA-controlled territory in Angola.[77] Those sanctions were imposed on UNITA for its refusal to comply with its international obligations under the Lusaka Protocol. New sanctions were also imposed in 1997 and again in June 1998, including a travel ban on UNITA officials, the freezing of UNITA's overseas assets, and a ban on imports of diamonds from UNITA-held territory.[78] Both the government of Angola and UNITA abandoned the peace process and engaged in full-scale fighting. UNAVEM III was withdrawn from Angola following the failure of the peace process. The Security Council, however, authorized the establishment of the United Nations Observer Mission in Angola (MONUA) to continue contact with the parties and to assist in the distribution of humanitarian assistance.[79]

In December 1998 and in January 1999, UNITA shot down two United Nations aircraft, killing all the passengers and crew. UNITA refused to cooperate with the international rescue efforts to locate the victims. In February 1999 the Security Council adopted resolution 1229 (1999) to endorse the report of the Secretary General on the situation in Angola.[80] The report called for the immediate withdrawal of MONUA from Angola due to the security situation and the failure of the peace process. Security Council resolution 1229 (1999) criticized UNITA for restarting the war, and it threatened to take more drastic action against UNITA if the fighting continued. The Secretary General based his recommendation for the withdrawal of MONUA on the failure of UNITA to comply with its obligations under the 'Acordos de Paz' (Peace Accords), the Lusaka Protocol and relevant Security Council resolutions, and the fact that the political and security situation in Angola prevented MONUA from fully carrying out its mandated role.[81] The Secretary General's decision to withdraw MONUA was seen as a blow to the peace process in Angola, and many observers called on the United Nations to reconsider its decision.

On May 7 the Security Council adopted another resolution on the situation in Angola, resolution 1237 (1999), in which it held UNITA responsible for the crisis in Angola due to its refusal to comply with its obligations under the 'Acordos de Paz', the Lusaka Protocol, and relevant Security Council resolutions.[82] The Security Council also determined that, as a result of UNITA's refusal to comply with its obligations under the above-mentioned agreements and relevant Security Council resolutions, the situation in Angola continued to constitute a threat to international peace and security in the region. The Security Council deplored the deteriorating situation in Angola and condemned the continued, indiscriminate attacks by

UNITA against the civilian population of Angola, particularly in the cities of Huambo, Kuito, and Malange.[83]

Fighting intensified in Angola in the months following the withdrawal of MONUA. On October 15 the Security Council adopted resolution 1268 (1999) by which it accused UNITA of resuming the conflict in Angola because of its failure to comply with its obligations under the 'Acordos de Paz', the Lusaka Protocol, and relevant Security Council resolutions.[84] The Security Council expressed its concern for the humanitarian effects of the conflict on the civilian population in Angola, and reaffirmed its view that a continued presence of the United Nations in Angola could contribute greatly to the promotion of peace, national reconciliation, human rights, and regional security. Based on these two critical factors, the Security Council authorized the establishment, for a period of six months until April 15, 2000, of the United Nations Office in Angola (UNOA), staffed with the personnel necessary to liaise with the political, military, police, and other civilian authorities.[85] UNOA was given a mandate to explore effective measures for restoring peace, assisting the Angolan people in the area of capacity-building, humanitarian assistance, the promotion of human rights, and coordinating other activities.[86]

Fighting soon intensified in Angola, with UNITA initially making significant territorial gains. However, the Angolan military recaptured much of the lost territory and regained the military advantage by cutting off supplies to UNITA through the Democratic Republic of the Congo.[87] International efforts to curb the sale of Angolan diamonds and the freezing of UNITA's overseas assets reduced UNITA's weapons supply, but did not significantly alter the strategic balance. UNITA continued to launch attacks on government-held areas and to make life difficult for the civilian population. Also, pressure from South Africa, the United States, and the European Union, and a more vigorous effort by the international community to tighten the ban on diamond exports from rebel-controlled areas, did not weaken Savimbi's ability to wage war. Several UNITA officials abandoned the war and joined the national government, but Savimbi continued to be defiant. In March 2002, Savimbi was ambushed and killed by government troops. His death gave new hope for ending the thirty-five year war, but ultimately, the international community did not do enough to help Angola find a solution to its long-running war.

The peace process failed in Angola for a number of reasons, not least among them being the lack of political will between the two main adversaries to commit themselves to stopping the war. Both sides had an incentive for continuing the war, and the United States-USSR-Portuguese brokered peace agreement was fundamentally flawed: it left no room for compromise after the election. The elections were to determine a winner and loser, with the loser supposedly disappearing. Responsibility for implementation of the agreement was given to the parties themselves, with the United Nations given a limited mandate to monitor the implementation process.[88] The United Nations did not participate in the peace talks and it had no influence on the timetable for implementing the agreement, or to modify it once it became quite clear that the elections could not go on as scheduled. UNAVEM II operated on very meager resources, with far fewer staff than were deployed in neighboring Namibia, or in Cambodia. Given the nature of the Angola conflict and the limited commitment of the United Nations, UNAVEM II was destined to fail.

The Situation in Cambodia

The United Nations undertook its most ambitious post-Cold War peacekeeping challenge in Cambodia. The Cambodia mission was the largest United Nations peacekeeping operation since the end of the Congo operation some three decades previously. Following the signing of the Paris Peace Accords in 1991 between all the parties involved in the Cambodian conflict and the Contact Group, the United Nations was given the difficult task of implementing the agreement.[89] The Security Council adopted resolution 717 (1991), by which it authorized the deployment of the United Nations Advance Mission in Cambodia (UNAMIC), with a staff of 380 military and civilian personnel.[90] On October 31, 1991 the Security Council adopted resolution 718 (1991), by which it recognized that the agreement called for the United Nations to establish a transitional authority in Cambodia.[91] UNAMIC's initial mandate required it to prepare Cambodia for the eventual deployment of a huge United Nations peacekeeping contingent, to commence in March 1992. It was also responsible for monitoring the ceasefire and for maintaining lines of communication between the factions.[92] In January 1992 the Security Council adopted resolution 728 (1992), by which it enlarged and expanded UNAMIC's mandate to include de-mining and conducting a mine awareness campaign for the local population[93]. UNAMIC was terminated in March 1992 and its mandate absorbed by the United Nations Transitional Authority in Cambodia (UNTAC).[94]

After a decade of civil war, and a reign of terror perpetrated by the Khmer Rouge regime a few years before the Vietnamese invasion, all sides in the Cambodian civil war accepted a peace agreement mediated by the United Nations Secretary General and the Contact Group (the United States, Russia, France, and China). The Paris Peace Accords called for the withdrawal of Vietnamese troops from Cambodia, an end to the Khmer Rouge's guerrilla war, and the deployment of a United Nations peacekeeping force of 16,000 military and civilian personnel to implement the accord.[95] Under the terms of the Agreements, the Supreme National Council was 'the unique legitimate body and source of authority in which, throughout the transitional period, the sovereignty, independence and unity of Cambodia are enshrined'. The SNC, which comprised the four Cambodian parties to the Agreements, delegated to the United Nations 'all powers necessary' to ensure the implementation of the Agreements.[96] UNTAC was established by the Security Council under resolution 745 (1992) for a period of 18 months. UNTAC was granted a broad mandate, including the complete administrative responsibility and governmental authority for Cambodia. UNTAC was responsible for promoting and monitoring respect for human rights, maintaining law and order, organizing and conducting free and fair elections, decommissioning the rebel army, facilitating the repatriation and resettlement of Cambodian refugees and displaced persons, and rehabilitating Cambodia's infrastructure during the transitional period.[97]

During the first phase of its mandate, UNTAC encountered few difficulties in carrying out its mission. However, a few months before the general elections were held the peace process was thrown into chaos following the Khmer Rouge decision not to participate in the elections. The Security Council condemned the actions of the Khmer Rouge, and acting under Chapter VII of the Charter imposed a ban on deliveries of weapons and other military equipment, or strategic supplies such as petroleum products, destined for territory under Khmer Rouge control.[98] Democratic elections went ahead as scheduled in April 1993. UNTAC's mandate was terminated following the promulgation of a new constitution and the formation of a government of national unity in September 1993.

Following the withdrawal of UNTAC, Cambodia reverted to a period of instability. UNTAC's sudden and probably premature departure left a security vacuum in Cambodia, and it made the country's fragile transition to democracy even more unpredictable. The Khmer Rouge resumed its jungle war, and the national unity government collapsed in the wake of Hun Sen's increasingly dictatorial tendencies.[99] Cambodia held its second democratic elections in 1998, the outcome of which was disputed by opposition candidates. With the death of Pol Pot, the Khmer Rouge leader, and the surrender of several of his followers, the Khmer Rouge no longer posed a threat to Cambodia's new democracy. The United Nations and the government of Cambodia agreed on a mechanism for establishing an international criminal tribunal to try the remaining Khmer Rouge officials for their involvement in the genocide perpetrated against the Cambodian people in the 1970s. Life in Cambodia has returned to normal but the political situation remains volatile.

The Civil War in Mozambique

Following the signing of the General Peace Agreement between the government of Mozambique and the Resisténcia Nacional Mozambicana (RENAMO) on October 4, 1992, in Rome, the Security Council adopted resolution 782 (1992), by which it welcomed the agreement.[100] The Security Council also took note of the Joint Declaration of August 7, 1992 of the president of Mozambique and the president of RENAMO, in which the two sides accepted the role of the United Nations in monitoring and guaranteeing the implementation of the General Peace Agreement.[101] The Security Council further approved the appointment of the Secretary General's interim Special Representative, and it dispatched a team of 25 military observers to Mozambique. The General Peace Agreement brought to an end 19 years of civil war, which neither side could win. The war took a great toll on the civilian population and created tremendous hardship for an already very impoverished country.

In December 1992 the Security Council adopted resolution 797 (1992) by which it authorized the deployment of the United Nations Operations in Mozambique (ONUMOZ) to oversee the implementation of the peace accord.[102] ONUMOZ's mandate included: to facilitate impartially the implementation of the Agreement; to monitor and verify the ceasefire, the separation of forces, and their demobilization; the collection, storage and destruction of weapons; to monitor and verify the complete withdrawal of foreign forces and to provide security in the transport corridors; to monitor and verify the disbanding of private and irregular armed groups; to authorize security arrangements for vital infrastructure; and to provide security for United Nations and other international activities in support of the peace process; to provide technical assistance and monitor the entire electoral process; and to coordinate and monitor humanitarian assistance operations, in particular those relating to refugees, internally displaced persons, demobilized military personnel, and the affected local population.[103]

Except for one major incident in which RENAMO sought to withdraw from the general elections shortly before the conduct of the vote began, ONUMOZ had little difficulty implementing its mandate. All aspects of the mandate were successfully completed on schedule. All sides were committed to the peace process and they cooperated fully with ONUMOZ. The ruling FRELIMO party won the presidency, but RENAMO made significant gains in the legislature. A new democratically elected President and Parliament were inaugurated in Mozambique in December 1994, and ONUMOZ's mission was terminated in January 1995.[104]

The remarkable success of the Mozambique mission was in part due to the commitment of the parties, the support of neighboring states, and the will of the international community. Mozambique demonstrated how successfully the international community can resolve long-standing conflicts if there is a commitment from all sides. The success of the United Nations missions in Namibia, Cambodia, and Mozambique would give the Security Council the encouragement to tackle more difficult regional conflicts. However, unlike the conflicts in Namibia, Cambodia, and Mozambique, the new generation of conflicts proved more difficult to resolve, and required the Security Council to invoke Chapter VII measures in order to get the parties to comply with its demands.[105]

This new generation of regional conflicts would test the will of the international community and seriously challenge the ability of the Security Council to manage regional conflicts in the post-Cold War era. Many of the post-Cold War regional conflicts stemmed in part from the collapse of the Soviet Union, the end of the Cold War, and the improvement in Russian-American relations. The conflicts were basically internal in character and posed little or no threat to world peace.[106] However, this new breed of conflicts was extremely violent and affected large segments of the civilian population. The United Nations was forced to intervene, in part on humanitarian grounds, and to prevent these conflicts from spilling over into neighboring states. With the Cold War over, the major powers had no incentive to intervene unilaterally to keep these conflicts in check. The United Nations reluctantly assumed responsibility for resolving these conflicts but was not given adequate resources or a proper mandate to do so.[107]

CHAPTER III

TRANSNATIONAL ARMED CONFLICTS AND THE DELEGATION OF AUTHORITY BY THE SECURITY COUNCIL

The third category of conflicts confronting the Security Council in the post-Cold War era were conflicts stemming from the collapse of states or governments. They included ethnic violence, humanitarian crises, and efforts by rebel organizations to overthrow fragile regimes.[1] The majority of the victims in these conflicts were civilians, and many were forced to flee their homes and take refuge in neighboring states. These conflicts posed a serious challenge to the traditional peacekeeping formula employed by the United Nations in previous conflicts. Consequently the Security Council had to devise new means of managing these complex conflicts. It delegated its powers to individual states and to the Secretary General in all of these conflicts, and combined the traditional peacekeeping formula with more robust methods of conflict management, including peacemaking and enforcement measures.[2] The new forces deployed in these conflict situations had to perform multiple missions, including the distribution of humanitarian relief supplies, the protection of relief workers and United Nations personnel, monitoring human rights, resettling refugees, supervising ceasefire agreements, organizing and conducting elections, negotiating political settlements and helping to rehabilitate political institutions, and rebuilding the economic and social structures of the states in crisis.[3] This new approach would bring United Nations forces into direct confrontation with the warring factions, and in some instances it proved difficult for the United Nations to negotiate permanent political settlements to the conflicts. This chapter examines the role of the Security Council in the conflicts in Somalia, the former Yugoslavia, Haiti, and Rwanda.

The Somalia Conflict

Somalia was one of the first casualties of the end of the Cold War and the first test for the Secretary General's new Agenda for Peace, which called for a more vigorous approach to managing regional conflicts.[4] Somalia was a long-time pawn in the United States-Soviet Union Cold War rivalry. It switched from pro-Soviet to pro-United States during its war with Ethiopia in the mid-1970s. In 1991 Somalia's longtime dictator, Siad Barre, lost his United States backing and was overthrown in a coup. Soon thereafter a power struggle ensued among various warlords vying for control of the government. Meanwhile, Somalia was left with no legitimate government or anyone with effective authority over the entire country. Different warring factions controlled different parts of the country and battled for control of the capital, Mogadishu. A severe drought in Somalia led to serious food shortages, which if left unattended would lead to mass starvation in the country. The warring factions used food supply as a means of warfare, and within months the shortage resulted in a serious humanitarian crisis.[5] Fighting in Mogadishu made it extremely difficult to unload food at the port and to distribute emergency supplies to the civilian population. By mid-1992 the humanitarian situation in Somalia had deteriorated to such an extent that it posed a serious threat to international peace and security.[6] The political situation in Somalia was also in a virtual state of anarchy.

The United Nations was slow to respond to requests from aid agencies to intervene in Somalia to avert the impending humanitarian crisis. The Permanent Members of the Security Council were reluctant to authorize United Nations intervention in Somalia for fear that the organization would be intervening in the internal affairs of a state in violation of Article 2 (7) of the Charter.[7] The United States, France, and Britain were also reluctant to authorize United Nations intervention in a conflict as remote as Somalia, and China and Russia feared a Security Council authorization to intervene would set a dangerous precedent. However, after repeated requests from aid agencies and a personal intervention by the Secretary General, the Security Council adopted resolution 733 (1992) to impose an arms embargo on all deliveries of weapons and military equipment to Somalia.[8] However, as the humanitarian situation deteriorated further, the Security Council was forced to take more drastic measures.

On April 24 the Security Council reluctantly adopted resolution 751 (1992) to launch a major humanitarian assistance operation.[9] The United Nations Operation in Somalia (UNOSOM I) was protected by 500 peacekeepers. They were to monitor the ceasefire in the capital, provide security to aid convoys, and guard food depots. The peacekeepers, comprising mostly Pakistani troops, arrived several months later but proved ill-equipped to carry out the mission. The Pakistanis quickly became the target of attacks by the warring factions. In August 1992 the Security Council adopted resolution 775 (1992) by which it expanded the mandate of UNOSOM I to enable it to protect humanitarian convoys and distribution centers throughout Somalia.[10] UNOSOM I was not well-organized, and its mandate was dubious. It could not contain the violence or halt Somalia's decline into a state of violent anarchy. UNOSOM was authorized only after the Security Council was severely criticized by the Secretary General, African governments, and aid agencies for its double standards. They accused the Security Council of assisting the Bosnian Muslims, who were in far less danger at the time, but not helping the people of Somalia. The Secretary General later responded to international criticism of the United Nations' handling of the situation in Somalia by calling for the deployment of a much larger force with a different mandate, adopted under Chapter VII of the Charter.[11]

By late 1992 the humanitarian situation in Somalia was growing steadily worse. Secretary General Boutros Ghali accepted, with some reservations, a United States request to lead a multi-national force into Somalia. He restricted the strategic goals of the mission, and asked that the force report to the Security Council on a regular basis.[12] On December 3, 1992, the Security Council, acting under Chapter VII of the Charter, adopted resolution 794 (1992), by which it authorized the Secretary General and any cooperating Member States to 'use all necessary means to establish as soon as possible a secure environment for humanitarian relief operations in Somalia'.[13] Operation Restore Hope was led by the United States, which provided the majority of the 36,000 troops that made up the United Task Force (UNITAF). UNITAF's mandate required that it establish a secure environment for the delivery of humanitarian assistance in Somalia. The Security Council made its determination to deploy UNITAF under Chapter VII on the basis that 'the magnitude of the human tragedy caused by the conflict in Somalia, further exacerbated by the obstacles being created to the distribution of humanitarian assistance, constitutes a threat to international peace and security.'[14]

Unlike previous peacekeeping missions, UNITAF was authorized under Chapter VII, and given broad authority to implement its mandate, including using force if necessary. UNITAF was to cooperate with UNOSOM I, which would resume its mission after UNITAF had established a secure environment for the distribution of relief supplies.[15] This was the first time the Security Council had authorized such a mission under Chapter VII of the Charter in response to a humanitarian crisis. The operation was relatively successful, as humanitarian supplies began reaching those in need. However, by the time UNITAF withdrew in March 1993, a secure environment had not been established throughout Somalia.

On March 26, 1993 the Security Council accepted the recommendation of the Secretary General to deploy a peacekeeping force in Somalia to replace UNITAF. Acting under Chapter VII of the Charter of the United Nations, the Security Council adopted resolution 814 (1993) by which it authorized the deployment of UNOSOM II as a replacement to UNITAF.[16] Security Council resolution 814 (1993) 'request[ed] the Secretary General, through his Special Representative, to direct the Force Commander of UNOSOM II to assume responsibility for the consolidation, expansion and maintenance of a secure environment throughout Somalia… in accordance with the recommendations contained in his report of 3 March 1993, and in this regard to organize a prompt, smooth and phased transition from UNITAF to UNOSOM II'.[17]

The mandate of UNOSOM II required that it take appropriate action, including enforcement measures, to establish throughout Somalia a secure environment for humanitarian assistance.[18] UNOSOM II was to complete, through disarmament and reconciliation, the task begun by UNITAF for the restoration of peace, stability, law and order. Its primary responsibilities included monitoring the cessation of hostilities, preventing resumption of violence, seizing unauthorized small arms, maintaining security at ports, airports, and lines of communication required for delivery of humanitarian assistance, continuing mine-clearing, and assisting in repatriation of refugees in Somalia.[19] UNOSOM II was also required to assist the people of Somalia in rebuilding their economy and social and political life, re-establishing the country's political institutional structure, achieving national political reconciliation, recreating a Somali state based on democratic principles of governance, and rehabilitating the country's economic infrastructure.[20]

Within months of its deployment UNOSOM II engaged in several violent clashes with forces loyal to General Aidid. In one incident 23 peacekeepers were killed. The Security Council responded by adopting resolution 837 (1993) by which it condemned the killings.[21] The resolution further stated: 'Acting under Chapter VII of the Charter of the United Nations… [the Security Council] reaffirms that the Secretary General is authorized under resolution 814 (1993) to take all necessary measures against all those responsible for the armed attacks…, to establish the effective authority of UNOSOM II throughout Somalia, including to secure the investigation of their actions and their arrest and detention for prosecution, trial and punishment.'

Resolution 837 (1993) gave new and expanded authority to UNOSOM II to take additional military enforcement action in pursuit of those responsible for killing the peacekeepers. A warrant was issued for the arrest of General Aidid, and a bounty of $10,000 was posted for his capture.[22] United States Marines and Special Forces returned to Somalia to join the manhunt. The attack on UNOSOM II and the warrant for the capture of General Aidid drastically transformed the political climate and security environment in Somalia. Several U.S. Marines were later ambushed and killed when they attempted to capture General Aidid.[23] This incident was played repeatedly on American television, and was later turned into a popular movie called *Black Hawk Down*. The incident and movie turned public opinion against further United States participation in United Nations peacekeeping missions. It also led to calls from the U.S. Congress for the United States to withdraw from Somalia.[24] Public feuding between Secretary General Boutros-Ghali and President Clinton over who should be blamed for the fiasco further aggravated an already tense situation. In light of this controversy, President Clinton announced an early withdrawal of American troops from Somalia and called for the United Nations to terminate the operation by March 31, 1995.[25] The United States also intensified its efforts at finding a diplomatic solution to the Somalia crisis.

The Somalia operation was a unique experience in United Nations peacekeeping. First, Somalia had no functioning government which could give its consent to the deployment of a United Nations peacekeeping force.[26] The United Nations, therefore, had to intervene under a Chapter VII mandate for fear of violating provisions of its own Charter and Somalia's sovereignty. Hence, UNOSOM II was an occupying army. A second feature of UNOSOM II was that several of the units operating in Somalia were not directly under its command. These forces took their orders directly from their national commanders instead of from the United Nations headquarters in New York. This led to a serious breakdown in the command structure and weakened UNOSOM II's ability to implement its mandate effectively.[27] Thirdly, by giving UNOSOM II a combined mandate of peacekeeping and authorization to use all necessary means to implement its mandate, the Security Council compromised the neutrality of the UNOSOM II, a principle upon which all previous peacekeeping missions had been predicated.[28] More importantly, the Security Council's delegation of Chapter VII powers to the Secretary General led him to believe that the Somalia mission was a test case for proving that his 'Agenda for Peace' was workable. The mission failed, and so did his hopes for getting member states to approve the 'Agenda for Peace'. Finally, the breakdown of communications between United Nations headquarters staff and field commanders, and the feuding between the Secretary General and the President of the United States over the timetable for the withdrawal of United States forces from Somalia, further undermined the effectiveness of UNOSOM II.[29]

In spite of these difficulties, the humanitarian aspect of the operation was a relative success. UNOSOM II quickly restored order in Mogadishu and provided the necessary security guarantees to aid workers to allow them to continue distributing humanitarian assistance.[30] However, it was the political mandate given to UNOSOM II that destroyed the mission. In this respect, the Security Council grossly over-stepped its legal bounds in making a determination that the situation in Somalia was a threat to international peace and security, and then authorizing the Secretary General and Member States to take all necessary measures under Chapter VII of the Charter to establish a secure environment for the distribution of humanitarian assistance. The Security Council's delegation of Chapter VII powers to the Secretary General's Special Representative in Somalia is a questionable legal authorization under the Charter.[31]

The Somalia operation was a turning point in the Security Council's active involvement in regional conflicts. The reputation of the United Nations was severely tarnished as a result of the failure of UNOSOM II to resolve the political crisis in Somalia. The Somalia fiasco forced the Security Council to reassess the way it dealt with transnational armed conflicts. After the military disaster in Somalia, the Secretary General's power to manage regional conflicts was sharply curtailed. The Secretary General's 'Agenda for Peace' was shelved, and the debacle cost him a second term in office. The situation in Somalia forced the Permanent Members of the Security Council to reconsider authorizing new peacekeeping missions. Two decades after the United Nations prematurely withdrew from Somalia, the country remains mired in a protracted conflict involving al Shabaab, a terrorist group linked to al Qaeda.

In the wake of the Somalia fiasco the Clinton Administration decided to review its participation in future United Nations peacekeeping missions. The President Clinton issued his now famous Presidential Decision Directive 25 (PDD 25), which called for restricting the United States' participation in future peacekeeping missions.[32] The President's new peacekeeping initiative established a set of preconditions under which the United States would participate in future United Nations peacekeeping operations. PDD 25 demanded that all future peacekeeping operations state clearly the goals of the mission, a timetable for completion, and an exit strategy before the operation can be authorized.[33] Congress also reduced the United States' financial contribution to United Nations peacekeeping operations. This new U.S. policy would have major implications for future United Nations peacekeeping operations in Bosnia and Rwanda.

The Conflicts in the Former Yugoslavia

The conflict in the former Yugoslavia presented yet another major challenge for the United Nations in the post-Cold War era. Following the death of President Tito, the Yugoslav Federation began showing signs of disintegration. In separate referenda, Slovenia, Croatia, and Bosnia voted to secede from the Serbian-dominated Yugoslav Federation.[34] This left many ethnic Serbs scattered throughout the various new republics as minorities with limited political power. The Serbs in both Bosnia and Croatia opposed living under Muslim or Croat-dominated governments and instead wanted to create their own independent republics linked to Serbia.[35] With the support of President Milošević of Serbia and the Yugoslav Army (JNA), the Serbs of Bosnia and Croatia launched separate offensives against the two new states with the goal of creating a greater Serbia. Bosnian Serbs later began a campaign of 'ethnic cleansing' in Serb-held areas of Bosnia in order to drive the Muslim population out.[36]

The United Nations was slow to intervene in the conflicts in the former Yugoslavia. The conventional view was that the conflicts were internal, and that the United Nations had no jurisdiction to intervene.[37] The United Nations took a 'wait and see' approach, and deferred to the European Union and the OSCE to find a peaceful solution to the conflicts. The EU negotiated a ceasefire on September 17, 1991, but the parties immediately violated the terms of the agreement and resumed fighting. However, as fighting intensified, the Security Council convened an emergency session to review the situation. The Security Council was concerned that the continuation of the conflicts in the former Yugoslavia would constitute a threat to international peace and security, and urged the parties to seek a peaceful settlement to the conflicts.[38] Acting under Chapter VII of the Charter, the Security Council adopted resolution 713 (1991) on September 25 by which it imposed a general and complete arms embargo on the entire Yugoslav federation. The Security Council also called on the parties to the various conflicts to adhere to the September 17 ceasefire agreement.[39]

On November 27 the Security Council convened a meeting to consider Yugoslavia's request for the deployment of a peacekeeping force. However, in resolution 721 (1991), the Security Council refused to authorize the peacekeeping force until the parties complied fully with the ceasefire agreements signed in Geneva.[40] On December 15 the Security Council convened a meeting to consider the situation and to review the Secretary General's report on the conditions for the establishment of a peacekeeping force. Under resolution 724 (1991) the Security Council endorsed the report of the Secretary General that the conditions did not exist for the deployment of a peacekeeping force.[41] Instead, the Security Council endorsed his offer to send to Yugoslavia a small group of personnel, including military personnel, to prepare for the possible deployment of a peacekeeping force.[42] Acting under Chapter VII of the Charter, the Security Council further requested that all states report to the Secretary General within 20 days on the measures they had instituted for meeting the obligations under Resolution 713 (1991), to implement a general and complete embargo on the deliveries of weapons and military equipment to Yugoslavia.[43] On January 8, 1992, the Security Council adopted resolution 727 (1992), by which it endorsed the signing, under the Secretary General's Personal Envoy, of the January 2 Implementation Accord at Sarajevo, concerning modalities for implementing the November 23, 1991 ceasefire agreement.[44] The Security Council also sent 50 military personnel to observe the maintenance of the ceasefire.

On February 8 the Security Council adopted resolution 740 (1992), by which it strengthened the force by an additional 25 officers. The Security Council recalled the provisions of Chapter VIII of the Charter of the United Nations and expressed its concern at indications that the arms embargo established under resolution 713 (1991) was not being fully complied with.[45] The Security Council called on all states to take all appropriate steps to ensure that the Yugoslav parties implement their unqualified acceptance of the United Nations peacekeeping plan, fulfill their commitments in good faith, and cooperate fully with the Secretary General. It also called on the Yugoslav parties to cooperate fully with the Conference on Yugoslavia in its aim of reaching a political settlement consistent with the principles of the Conference on Security and Cooperation in Europe.[46]

On February 15 the Secretary General submitted another report to the Security Council on the situation in the former Yugoslavia. The Secretary General confirmed in his report that the conditions permitting the deployment of a United Nations Protection Force (UNPROFOR) had been met.[47] The Security Council approved the Secretary General's report and adopted resolution 743 (1992) by which it authorized the deployment of the United Nations Protection Force (UNPROFOR) in Croatia for a period of twelve months to monitor a ceasefire agreement between Croats and Serbs.[48] On May 5 the Security Council adopted resolution 752 (1992) in which it called for a cessation of hostilities in Bosnia and for the withdrawal of units of the Yugoslav People's Army (JNA), as well as the Croatian army. The Security Council also demanded that all irregular forces in Bosnia be disbanded and disarmed, and further called for a halt to forcible expulsion of civilians and attempts by the Serbs to change the ethnic composition of the population in the former Yugoslavia.[49] Both Yugoslavia and Croatia refused to comply with resolution 752 (1992). In response, the Security Council adopted resolution 757 (1992) in which it deplored the parties' noncompliance with its demands in resolution 752 (1992).[50]

Those demands included an end to the fighting, an end to all external interference, respect for the territorial integrity of Bosnia, and the withdrawal of JNA forces from Bosnia. The Security Council also deplored the fact that its call for the immediate cessation of forcible expulsions and attempts to change the ethnic composition of the population had not been heeded, and reaffirmed in this context the need for the effective protection of human rights and fundamental freedoms, including those of ethnic minorities.[51] The Security Council further rejected the claim by the Federal Republic of Yugoslavia (Serbia and Montenegro) to continue automatically the membership of the former Socialist Federal Republic of Yugoslavia in the United Nations and said that the FRY had to reapply as a new state.[52]

Acting under Chapter VII of the Charter of the United Nations, the Security Council:

(1) Condemns the failure of the authorities in the Federal Republic of Yugoslavia, including the Yugoslav People's Army (JNS), to take effective measures to fulfill the requirements of resolution 752 (1992);

(2) Demands that any elements of the Croatian Army still present in Bosnia and Herzegovina act in accordance with paragraph 4 of resolution 752 (1992) without further delay;

(3) Decides that all States shall adopt the measures set out below, which shall apply until the Security Council decides that the authorities in the Federal Republic of Yugoslavia, including the JNA, have taken effective measures to fulfill the requirements of resolution 752 (1992);

(4) Decides that all States shall prevent:

   (a) The import into their territories of all commodities and products originating in the Federal Republic of Yugoslavia exported therefrom after the date of the present resolution;

   (b) Any activities by their nationals or in their territories which would promote or are calculated to promote the export or trans-shipment of any commodities or products originating in the Federal Republic of Yugoslavia; and any dealing by their nationals or their flag vessels or aircraft or in their territories in any commodities or products originating in the Federal Republic of Yugoslavia and exported therefrom after the date of the present resolution, including in particular any transfer of funds to the Federal republic of Yugoslavia for the purpose of such activities or dealings;

   (c) The sale or supply by their nationals or from their territories or using their flag vessels or aircraft of any commodities or products, whether or not originating in their territories, but not including supplies intended strictly for medical purposes and foodstuffs notified to the Committee established pursuant to resolution 724 (1991), to any person or body in the Federal Republic of Yugoslavia or to any business carried on in or operated from the Federal Republic of Yugoslavia, and any activities by their nationals or in their territories which promote or are calculated to promote such sale or supply of such commodities or products.[53]

Resolution 757 (1992) further imposed a ban on flights to and from Yugoslavia, on maintenance servicing of Yugoslav aircraft, and urged member states to prevent Yugoslav nationals from participating in sporting activities. It also suspended scientific and technical cooperation and cultural exchanges with Yugoslavia, and reduced the level of staff at Yugoslavia's diplomatic missions.[54]

The Security Council's comprehensive economic and diplomatic sanctions on Yugoslavia did not deter the Serbs or the JNA. In June the Security Council adopted resolution 758 (1992) by which it deplored the continuation of fighting in Bosnia-Herzegovina.[55] The Security Council condemned the violations of the ceasefire that had been reaffirmed in the June 5 agreement, and decided to enlarge the mandate and strength of UNPROFOR. The resolution further called on all parties to the conflict to cooperate fully with UNPROFOR. It also demanded that all parties create immediately the necessary conditions for the unimpeded delivery of humanitarian supplies to Sarajevo and other destinations in Bosnia and Herzegovina, including the establishment of a security zone encompassing Sarajevo and its airport.[56]

In a series of resolutions, the Security Council condemned the continuing violation of humanitarian law, repeated violations of the ceasefire agreements, and ethnic cleansing and atrocities committed in detention camps.[57] The Security Council also authorized the enlargement of UNPROFOR's mandate and strength in Bosnia to include the protection of convoys of released detainees if requested by the International Committee of the Red Cross.[58] In resolution 777 (1992) the Security Council reaffirmed its rejection of the claim of the Federal Republic of Yugoslavia to continue automatically the membership of the former Socialist Federal Republic of Yugoslavia.[59] In light of the continuing violations of international humanitarian law, including grave breaches of the Geneva Conventions, committed in the territory of the former Yugoslavia, the Security Council requested that the Secretary General establish an impartial Commission of Experts to examine and analyze such allegations and report back to it.[60] This was the Security Council's first step in the establishment of an International Criminal Tribunal for the Former Yugoslavia to try those responsible for violations of international humanitarian law.

By early October the Security Council was running out of options in Bosnia. On October 9 the Council adopted resolution 781 (1992) to impose a ban on military flights in the airspace of Bosnia.[61] That ban was later reaffirmed in resolution 786 (1992).[62] The Security Council strengthened UNPROFOR's mandate and authorized it to enforce the ban on military flights in the airspace of Bosnia and Herzegovina. On November 16 the Security Council, acting under Chapter VII of the United Nations Charter, adopted resolution 787 (1992) to impose an embargo on crude oil, petroleum products, coal, energy-related equipment, iron, steel, other metals, chemicals, rubber, tires, vehicles, aircraft, and motors of all types on the Federal Republic of Yugoslavia.[63] The Security Council called on member states to take all necessary steps to ensure that none of their exports were diverted to the Federal Republic of Yugoslavia in violation of resolution 757 (1992). Acting under Chapters VII and VIII of the Charter of the United Nations, the Security Council called upon states acting nationally or through regional agencies or arrangements 'to use such measures commensurate with the specific circumstances as may be necessary under the authority of the Security Council to halt all inward and outward maritime shipping in order to ensure strict implementation of the provisions of resolutions 713 (1991) and 757 (1992).'[64]

The Security Council also took the precautionary steps necessary to prevent the conflict in Bosnia and Herzegovina from spreading into neighboring Macedonia. The Security Council adopted resolution 795 (1992) on December 11 to authorize the Secretary General to establish a presence of UNPROFOR in the former Yugoslav Republic of Macedonia as recommended in his report (S/24923), and to inform the authorities in Albania and those in the Federal Republic of Yugoslavia.[65] UNPROFOR was responsible for monitoring and reporting any developments in the border areas of Macedonia that would undermine confidence and stability in that Republic and threaten its territory. UNPROFOR patrolled Macedonia's borders in cooperation with the Organization on Security and Cooperation in Europe (OSCE), which had previously deployed a small observer mission in Macedonia.

On March 31, 1995, the Security Council restructured UNPROFOR and replaced it with three separate interlinked units. It extended the mandate for UNPROFOR in Bosnia and Herzegovina, established the United Nations Confidence Restoration Operation in Croatia (UNCRO), and decided UNPROFOR in the former Yugoslav Republic of Macedonia would be known as the United Nations Preventive Deployment Force (UNPREDEP). Under resolution 983 (1995) the Security Council established UNPREDEP, with a mandate as specified in the report of the Secretary General of March 22, 1995. UNPREDEP was established for a period terminating on November 30, 1995.[66] UNCRO was later succeeded by the United Nations Transitional Administration for Eastern Slavonia, Baranja and Western Sirmium (UNTAES), and established by the Security Council under resolution 1037 (1996).[67]

Despite the many resolutions adopted by the Security Council, the war in Bosnia continued unabated. In fact, the atrocities against civilians, including reports of massive, organized, and systematic detention and execution of Bosnian men, and rape of Muslim women, intensified. In February 1993 the Security Council accepted the recommendation of the Commission of Experts, which called for the establishment of an ad hoc international tribunal to investigate events in the territory of the former Yugoslavia, including reports of mass killings and the continuance of the practice of 'ethnic cleansing'.[68] The Security Council adopted resolution 808 (1993) by which it determined that 'this situation constitutes a threat to international peace and security', and that it was determined to put an end to such crimes and take effective measures to bring to justice the persons responsible for them.[69] The Security Council further decided that an international tribunal would be established for the prosecution of persons responsible for serious violations of international humanitarian law committed in the territory of the former Yugoslavia since 1991. It called on the Secretary General to submit a report within 60 days on all aspects of the matter.[70]

The Security Council took further steps to expand and enforce the flight ban it had established over Bosnia in resolution 781 (1992), to cover flights by fixed-wing and rotary-wing aircraft. The Security Council also gave NATO the authorization to take all necessary measures to ensure compliance with the ban on flights.[71] However, NATO's ability to use force was restricted by the requirement to consult with UNPROFOR and the Secretary General's Special Representative prior to launching attacks against Serbian aircraft.[72] The Serbs exploited the loophole in the arrangement under which NATO could attack Serb aircraft, and continued waging the war with ever-greater intensity.

The new threat of air strikes against the Serbs did not deter subsequent attacks against Bosnian civilians by Serb paramilitary units. A major offensive against Bosnian civilians led to a tragic humanitarian situation in Srebrenica and its surrounding areas. The attack on Srebrenica was the worst of the atrocities committed by Serb paramilitary forces, resulting in the death of 8,000 Bosnian Muslim men and boys. The atrocity was a turning point in the war. The incident occurred in the presence of the Dutch battalion attached to UNPROFOR. The Dutch battalion did not have the military means nor the mandate to defend the safe area against a Serbian attack. The United Nations and the Dutch government were later criticized for their inaction.[73]

The Security Council condemned the attack on Srebrenica, and recalling the provisions of Chapter VIII of the Charter, the Security Council determined that the grave situation in the Republic of Bosnia and Herzegovina continued to be a threat to international peace and security.[74] Acting under Chapter VII of the Charter, the Security Council:

(1)   Decides to extend the ban established by resolution 781 (1992) to cover flights by all fixed-wing and rotary-wing aircraft in the airspace of the Republic of Bosnia and Herzegovina, this ban not to apply to flights authorized by UNPROFOR in accordance with paragraph 2 below;

(2)   Requests UNPROFOR to modify the mechanism referred to in paragraph 3 of resolution 781 (1992) so as to provide for the authorization, in the airspace of the Republic of Bosnia and Herzegovina, of humanitarian flights and other flights consistent with relevant resolutions of the Security Council;

(3)   Requests UNPROFOR to continue to monitor compliance with the ban on flights in the airspace of the Republic of Bosnia and Herzegovina, and called on all parties urgently to cooperate with UNPROFOR in making practical arrangements for the close monitoring of authorized flights and improving the notification procedures;

(4)   Authorizes Member States, seven days after the adoption of this resolution, acting nationally or through regional organizations or arrangements, to take, under the authority of the Secretary General and UNPROFOR, all necessary measures in the airspace of the Republic of Bosnia and Herzegovina, in the event of further violations to ensure compliance with the ban on flights referred to in paragraph 1 above, and proportionate to the specific circumstances and the nature of the flights.[75]

The Serbs continued to violate the airspace of Bosnia, despite the new measures the Security Council authorized in resolution 816 (1993). On April 16 the Security Council adopted resolution 819 (1993), in which it condemned all violations of international humanitarian law, including, in particular, the practice of 'ethnic cleansing', the pattern of hostilities by Bosnian Serb paramilitary units against towns and villages in eastern Bosnia, and further reaffirmed that the taking or acquisition of territory by the threat or use of force, including through the practice of 'ethnic cleansing', was unlawful and unacceptable.[76] The Security Council said it was deeply alarmed with the rapid deterioration of the situation in Srebrenica and its surrounding areas, as a result of the continued deliberate armed attacks and shelling of innocent civilian populations by Bosnian Serb paramilitary units. The Security Council strongly condemned the deliberate interdiction by Serb paramilitary units of humanitarian assistance convoys, attacks against UNPROFOR, and their refusal to guarantee the safety and freedom of movement of UNPROFOR personnel.[77]

The Security Council recalled the provisions of resolution 815 (1993) on the mandate of UNPROFOR and in that context acting under Chapter VII of the Charter, the Security Council:

(1)   Demands that all parties and others concerned treat Srebrenica and its surroundings as a safe area which should be free from any armed attack or any other hostile act;

(2)   Demands also to that effect the immediate cessation of armed attacks by Bosnian Serb paramilitary units against Srebrenica and their immediate withdrawal from the areas surrounding Srebrenica;

(3)   Demands that the Federal Republic of Yugoslavia immediately cease supply of military arms, equipment and services to the Bosnian Serb paramilitary units in the Republic of Bosnia and Herzegovina;

(4)   Requests the Secretary General, with a view to monitoring the humanitarian situation in the safe area, to take immediate steps to increase the presence of UNPROFOR in Srebrenica and its surroundings;

(5)   Reaffirms that any taking or acquisition of territory by threat or use of force, including through the practice of 'ethnic cleansing', is unlawful and unacceptable;

(6)   Condemns and rejects the deliberate actions of the Bosnian Serb party to force the evacuation of the civilian population from Srebrenica and its surrounding areas as well as from other parts of the Republic of Bosnia and Herzegovina as part of its overall abhorrent campaign of 'ethnic cleansing'.[78]

On April 17 the Security Council adopted resolution 820 (1993), by which it approved the reports of the Secretary General on the peace talks held by the Co-Chairmen of the Steering Committee of the International Conference on the Former Yugoslavia. The Security Council commended the peace plan for Bosnia and Herzegovina in the form agreed to by two of the Bosnian parties and spelled out in the report of the Secretary General of March 26, 1993. The Security Council welcomed the fact that the plan was accepted in full by two of the Bosnian parties, and it called on the other parties to accept the peace plan in full.[79] Acting under Chapter VII of the Charter, the Security Council decided to strengthen the implementation of the sanction measures imposed in its earlier relevant resolutions against the Federal Republic of Yugoslavia, within nine days, unless the Secretary General inform the Security Council that the Bosnian Serb party had joined the other parties in signing the peace plan and had ceased their military attacks. The Security Council also rebuked the Federal Republic of

Yugoslavia by rejecting its request to be automatically recognized as the successor state to the former Socialist Republic of Yugoslavia.[80]

In May 1993 the Security Council moved to expand the safe areas. Under resolution 824 (1993), the Security Council, pursuant to Chapter VII of the Charter:

(1) Welcomes the report of the Mission of the Security Council established pursuant to resolution 819 (1993), and in particular its recommendations concerning safe areas;

(2) Demands that any taking of territory by force cease immediately;

(3) Declares that the capital city of the Republic of Bosnia and Herzegovina, Sarajevo, and other such threatened areas, in particular the towns of Tuzla, Zepa, Gorazde, Bihac, as well as Srebrenica, and their surroundings shall be treated as safe areas by all the parties concerned and should be free from armed attacks and from any other hostile act;[81]

(4) Further declares that in these safe areas the following shall be observed:

    (a) The immediate cessation of armed attacks or any hostile acts against these safe areas, and the withdrawal of all Bosnian Serb military or paramilitary units from these towns to a distance wherefrom they cease to constitute a menace to their security and that of their inhabitants to be monitored by United nations military observers;

    (b) Full respect by all parties of the rights of the United Nations Protection Force (UNPROFOR) and the international humanitarian agencies to free and unimpeded access to all safe areas in the Republic of Bosnia and Herzegovina and full respect for the safety of the personnel engaged in these operations.[82]

UNPROFOR was not given the means to adequately defend the safe areas, and as a result Serb paramilitary units overran them and committed great atrocities. The Serbs exploited the division between the United States and its European allies over how to proceed with air strikes in the event the safe areas were violated. Serb paramilitary units strengthened their defensive positions by taking United Nations peacekeepers hostage and holding them as human shields to prevent possible NATO air strikes.[83]

UNPROFOR's inability to defend the safe areas was complicated by Serbian military superiority and by the nature of its mandate. UNPROFOR was deployed under Chapter VII of the Charter but functioned like a traditional peacekeeping force. Its mandate was expanded several times as the security situation in Bosnia deteriorated; however, the Member States of the Security Council were unwilling to authorize more drastic military measures against Serb paramilitary units. Both China and Russia opposed military action by NATO. The United States did not want to intervene because domestic public opinion was not in favor of United States intervention. Britain and France, with troops on the ground, did not want to take any military action that would jeopardize the safety of their troops.[84]

Meanwhile, the Vance-Owen Peace Plan was submitted to the parties for consideration. The plan called for dividing Bosnia into ten provinces, three provinces for each ethnic group and one province jointly controlled by all three.[85] The Serbs and Croats accepted the plan, but the Bosnian Muslims delayed their decision on acceptance of the plan in anticipation that a new president in the United States, President Clinton, would submit a plan more favorable to their political objectives.[86] Upon taking office in January 1993, President Clinton submitted no new plan, and his administration refused to endorse the Vance-Owen Plan in the form that it then took.[87]

Following another Serb attack on the safe areas, the Security Council adopted resolution 836 (1993) on June 4 to condemn the attack. Acting under Chapter VII of the Charter, the Security Council decided that Member States, acting nationally or through regional arrangements, could take, under the authority of the Security Council and subject to close coordination with the Secretary General and UNPROFOR, all necessary measures, through the use of air power, in and around the safe areas in the Republic of Bosnia and Herzegovina, to support UNPROFOR in the performance of its mandate, set out in paragraphs 5 and 9 of the resolution.[88] It took another shelling of the Sarajevo market for NATO to issue an ultimatum to the Serbs. Following the February 4 attack on the Sarajevo market, which killed scores of civilians, NATO decided to authorize air strikes within ten days if the Bosnian Serb forces and the government of Bosnia did not withdraw or regroup and place under the control of UNPROFOR all heavy weapons located in an exclusion zone within 20 kilometers of the center of Sarajevo. This ultimatum was given under the authority granted NATO in resolutions 824 and 836 (1993).[89]

The threat of force and the various other measures adopted by the Security Council failed to bring an end to the fighting in Bosnia, or to stop the atrocities against the civilian populations in the safe areas. It took another Serbian shelling of the Sarajevo market in August 1995 to force NATO to take a more vigorous military stand against Serbian paramilitary units. NATO used air strikes to force the Serbs to accept a ceasefire and to withdraw their heavy weapons from the vicinity of the center of Sarajevo.[90] The United States Balkan Envoy, Richard Holbrooke, negotiated a permanent ceasefire, and under the threat of further NATO air strikes, all the parties to the war in Bosnia were invited to a peace conference in Dayton, Ohio.[91]

On November 5 the conference on Bosnia began in Dayton. After two weeks of difficult negotiations, the parties reached an agreement on November 21, 1995.[92] The Republic of Bosnia and Herzegovina, the Republic of Croatia, the Federal Republic of Yugoslavia (which represented the Bosnian Serbs), and other parties signed the Peace Agreement, which brought an end to the wars in the former Yugoslavia. At the Paris Peace Conference on December 14, the parties formally signed the General Framework Agreement for Peace in Bosnia and Herzegovina and the Annexes thereto (known as the Dayton Agreement).[93] The parties to the Agreement recognized the role of outside parties in restoring peace and implementing the

Agreement. In Annex 1-A (the Agreement on Military Aspects of the Peace Settlement) of the Dayton Agreement, the parties invited the Security Council to adopt a resolution that would authorize Member States or regional organizations and arrangements to establish a multinational military Implementation Force (IFOR). The parties also agreed that NATO would establish such a force, and that it would begin operation upon the transfer of authority from UNPROFOR to IFOR.[94]

On November 22, the Security Council, under resolution 1022 (1995), welcomed the initialing of the General Framework Agreement for Peace in Bosnia and Herzegovina. Acting under Chapter VII of the Charter, the Security Council suspended indefinitely the sanctions imposed on the Federal Republic of Yugoslavia under the relevant resolutions.[95] On November 30, the Security Council adopted resolution 1026 (1995), by which it renewed its support for the Peace Agreement. Acting under Chapter VII of the Charter, the Security Council reaffirmed its determination to ensure the security and freedom of movement of personnel of the United Nations peacekeeping forces in the territory of the former Yugoslavia, and it extended the mandate of UNPROFOR to January 31, 1996.[96]

On December 15 the Security Council adopted resolution 1031 (1995) by which it formally approved the Peace Agreement for Bosnia and Herzegovina. The Security Council also formally transferred the authority of UNPROFOR to IFOR.[97] The Security Council reaffirmed its commitment to a negotiated settlement of the conflicts in the former Yugoslavia, welcomed the signing on December 14, 1995 at the Paris Peace Conference of the General Framework Agreement for Peace in Bosnia and Herzegovina, the Dayton Agreement on the Federation of Bosnia and Herzegovina of November 10, and the Peace Implementation Conference held in London on December 8 and 9 (the London Conference).[98] Acting under Chapter VII of the Charter, the Security Council authorized the creation of the multinational Implementation Force (IFOR), authorized participating states to use all necessary measures to effect implementation and ensure compliance with the Peace Agreement, to ensure compliance with the rules and procedures established by the commander of IFOR, and to defend IFOR or assist it in carrying out its mission.[99] The resolution further called for the termination of UNPROFOR on the date the Secretary General reported to the Security Council that the transfer of authority from UNPROFOR to IFOR had been completed The Security Council authorized participating states to use all necessary measures to assist in the withdrawal of UNPROFOR.

On December 21, 1995, the Security Council approved the Secretary General's report and the proposals for the United Nations' involvement in the implementation of the Peace Agreement. Under resolution 1035 (1995) the Security Council established for one year a United Nations civilian police force known as the International Police Task Force (IPTF) and a United Nations civilian office to oversee civilian-related issues in Bosnia, in accordance with the Dayton Peace Agreement and the General Framework Agreement.[100] The United Nations operation became known as the United Nations Mission in Bosnia and Herzegovina

(UNMIBH). The IPTF and the United Nations civilian office were placed under the authority of the Secretary General, but subjected to the coordination and guidance of the European Union High Representative for Bosnia. UNMIBH was expected to cooperate closely with IFOR. The IPTF tasks included:

(1)   Monitoring, observing and inspecting law enforcement activities and facilities, including associated judicial organizations, structures and procedures;

(2)   Advising law enforcement personnel and forces;

(3)   Training law enforcement personnel;

(4)   Facilitating within the IPTF mission of assistance, the parties' law enforcement activities;

(5)   Assessing the threats to public order and advising on the capability of law enforcement agencies to deal with such threats;

(6)   Advising government authorities in Bosnia and Herzegovina on the organization of effective civilian law enforcement agencies;

(7)   Assisting by accompanying the parties' law enforcement personnel as they carry out their responsibilities, as the Task Force deems appropriate. The Task Force can also consider requests from the parties or law enforcement agencies for assistance to ensure the existence of conditions for free and fair elections.[101]

IFOR was deployed in December 1995 to assume full responsibility for implementing the provisions of the Dayton peace accords. IFOR was required to enforce the ceasefire agreement, facilitate the return of refugees to their original areas of residence, and remove heavy weapons from the region. The High Representative was granted extraordinary power to implement the civil and political provisions of the agreement. He was responsible for making sure that the Bosnia-Croatia federation succeeded, that the Bosnian Serb Parliament was integrated into the Bosnian government, and that national elections were held on schedule. The Higher Representative was also required to oversee the reconstruction of Bosnia and facilitate the return of refugees to their original places of residence. The High Representative was given broad authority to remove any Bosnian elected official who undermined the peace process.[102]

The most contentious issue of the Bosnian Peace Agreement was how to arrest indicted war criminals, whose presence in Bosnia threatened the implementation of the peace process. The Dayton accords deliberately left that responsibility vague. IFOR commanders objected to pursuing accused Bosnian Serb war criminals, whose cooperation IFOR needed to successfully implement the peace agreement. The International Criminal Tribunal for the Former Yugoslav did not receive the full cooperation of IFOR, and only a few of the suspected war criminals were captured by IFOR. Although the Dayton accords and Security Council resolution 1031 (1995) called on all parties to cooperate fully with the Tribunal and to surrender suspected war criminals, the parties stopped short of fulfilling their obligation under the agreement and the resolution. IFOR made little effort to capture the major suspected war criminals.[103]

United States officials were reluctant to require IFOR to pursue war criminals for fear of repeating the Somalia debacle, in which several American servicemen were killed in a failed operation to capture General Aidid. The incident, broadcast live on American television, angered members of Congress and led to a shift in public opinion toward American participation in United Nations peacekeeping operations. The incident led to a drastic change in American policy regarding the role of the military in peacekeeping. United States forces would not participate in the apprehension of suspected war criminals.

IFOR commanders were also reluctant to use the military to pursue war criminals, believing that it was beyond the scope of IFOR's mission to pursue war criminals. IFOR feared that if the military was used to carry out what it considered the responsibility of civilian police, it would complicate an already fragile peace process. Despite its reluctance, IFOR carried out several successful arrest missions, but the important indicted war criminals remained at large.

IFOR's overall mission in implementing the Dayton accords was partly successful. It managed to bring peace to Bosnia, or at least to prevent a new outbreak of hostilities. However, it did not fulfill the main goals of the mission, which was to facilitate the return of all refugees to their original places of residence, and to integrate all of Bosnian territory into the Muslim-Croat federation. The Bosnian Serb Republic (Republika Srpska) continued to exist as a *de facto* independent republic. Efforts to create a rotating presidency for Bosnia were not very successful, and elections in the republic actually served to complicate efforts to create a multi-ethnic state. IFOR had little choice but to legitimize the *de facto* ethnic divisions that were created by the war.[104] In 1996 IFOR was transformed into the Stabilization Force (SFOR). SFOR's mission was to stabilize the existing situation in Bosnia instead of trying to change it. The goal of creating a multi-ethnic state in Bosnia as envisioned by the Dayton accords seemed unrealistic under the prevailing circumstances.

The United Nations involvement in the former Yugoslavia will be remembered for its failure to stop ethnic cleansing, protect the safe areas, enforce its resolutions, and most importantly, to protect Bosnia's independence and territorial integrity. UNPROFOR was ill-conceived, and was deployed with the wrong mandate. The Security Council acted on the recommendation of the Secretary General to deploy UNPROFOR, but did not carry out a thorough study of the situation to determine whether the timing was appropriate to deploy the force. The Security Council's rush to impose an arms embargo on all of the former Yugoslavia, including the Republic of Bosnia and Herzegovina, may have undermined Bosnia's right to self-defense, in light of the fact that the Security Council did not authorize collective action against the Serbs and the Yugoslav Army, who had the superior military capacity to continue to execute the war in defiance of Security Council demands.[105]

The Security Council adopted numerous resolutions dealing with the war in Bosnia, but did not back up its words with deeds. Many of these resolutions were unenforceable, as UNPROFOR did not have the means to implement them, and the Bosnian Serbs violated the resolutions with impunity. It took NATO's intervention in Bosnia to bring the war to a halt. It also took the threat of further force from NATO to force the parties to attend the Dayton Peace Conference. The United Nations was not a negotiating party at the Dayton Peace Conference. The agreement was basically handed to the Security Council as a *fait accompli* for its approval. The United Nations' failure in Bosnia brought many recriminations about the role of the United Nations in regional conflicts. The Bosnian fiasco would force the United Nations to again take a hard look at how it managed regional conflicts. In the aftermath of the Bosnian war, the United Nations was confronted with another humanitarian crisis in Rwanda, and the United Nations' failure to intervene early enough led to the deaths of 800,000 civilians.

The situation in Bosnia gradually returned to normal. However, the ethnic divisions remained intact, the majority of refugees were not able to return to their original places of residence, and the ethnic hatreds that initially started the war continue to be prevalent in Bosnian society. Efforts to build political institutions and to rebuild Bosnia's economy were slow. The major suspected war criminals remained at large, and continued to exert tremendous influence on their subordinates. SFOR appeared likely to remain in Bosnia far longer than originally anticipated in the Dayton Accords. Bosnia certainly became by far a safer place than it was before the Dayton Accords, but hopes for a unified Bosnia continued to appear unlikely.

The Situation in Haiti

The United Nations became involved in Haiti following a request from Haiti's interim civilian president, Madame Trouliott, a former high court judge who was appointed to the presidency by the Haitian military after a transition to civilian rule ended in violence and planned elections were canceled.[106] Haiti has been under one form of authoritarian rule or another since independence. The Duvalier family (first François 'Papa Doc', and then his son, Jean-Claude 'Baby Doc') ruled Haiti with an iron fist from 1957 to 1986, during which time they employed a paramilitary force, popularly known as the Tontons Macoutes, to terrorize and murder their opponents.[107] In 1986, Baby Doc Duvalier was forced out of power in a military coup after growing dissatisfaction with his rule led to popular unrest. Duvalier was forced into exile and replaced by a civilian-military regime. The post-Duvalier era was marked by political instability and successive military coups and counter-coups.[108] In a desperate last-ditch effort, the military appointed an interim civilian regime headed by a high court judge, Ertha Pascal-Trouillot. President Trouillot called on the United Nations to assist in establishing the conditions for credible elections in Haiti.[109]

The request from Haiti's interim president was transmitted to the Security Council, but the matter was referred to the General Assembly for consideration because it fell outside the scope of the Security Council's jurisdiction.[110] The request was unusual, for it was only the second time in the history of the United Nations that a sovereign state was requesting assistance to organize national elections. The previous request came from Nicaragua; however, given the war in Nicaragua, the Security Council broadly construed the situation in Nicaragua as a threat to international peace and security and thus authorized the deployment of the United Nations Observer Mission to Verify the Electoral Process in Nicaragua (ONUVEN).[111]

Following a review of the request from the president of Haiti, the General Assembly adopted resolution 45/2 (1990) by which it authorized the Secretary General to establish the United Nations Observer Group for Verification of Elections in Haiti (ONUVEH).[112] Pursuant to General Assembly resolution 45/2 (1990), the Secretary General dispatched a small group of election experts to assist the government of Haiti in organizing democratic elections. The measure was adopted against a back-drop of opposition from several states, including Cuba and Mexico. Both countries were concerned that the Haitian mission would establish a dangerous precedent and warned that the United Nations should not use this as a pretext to interfere in the internal affairs of sovereign states.[113] Mexico was concerned that a similar mission could one day be deployed on its territory to calm fears of election irregularities. Cuba maintained that national elections could never be regarded as affecting international peace and security, and so cannot involve a breach of the Charter leading to collective action. Mexico likewise argued that sending such a mission to Haiti would not set a precedent in respect of the domestic jurisdiction of states: 'Electoral Processes lie within the domain in which domestic legislation in each State is sovereign'.[114]

ONUVEH's mandate required that it participate in all aspects of the electoral process, including voter education, ensuring that all candidates receive equal access, organizing a voter registration drive, and monitoring the election process. The mission faced a difficult task, as Haiti had no tradition of democratic politics, and political institutions were non-existent. In the past, Haitians had used violence to settle political scores and select leaders. The idea of a democratic election was quite unfamiliar and foreign. Despite these daunting challenges, ONUVEH fulfilled its mandate very successfully and democratic elections were held in Haiti in December 1990.[115] Father Jean-Bertrand Aristide received an overwhelming majority of the votes and was declared the new president. Within weeks of the election results, supporters of former President Duvalier staged an unsuccessful coup against president-elect Aristide. The January coup was crushed by the military, and Aristide was sworn in, in February 1991, as Haiti's first democratically elected president. However, that experience of democracy was short-lived; in September the Haitian army staged a successful coup and unseated Aristide. Aristide fled the country to avoid execution.[116]

Following the coup in Haiti, the Organization of American States (OAS) convened a meeting of Foreign Ministers in Washington on October 13 and declared that the coup 'represent[ed] disregard for the legitimate government of Haiti, which was constituted by the will of the people freely expressed in a free and democratic electoral process under international observation'.[117] The OAS Foreign Ministers resolved, *inter alia*:

(1)   To recognize the representatives of the government of President Jean-Bertrand Aristide as the only legitimate representatives of the government of Haiti to the organs, agencies and entities of the inter-American system;

(2)   To recommend, with due respect for the policy of each member state on the recognition of states and governments, action to bring about the diplomatic isolation of those who hold power illegally in Haiti;

(3)   To recommend to all states that they suspend their economic, financial, and commercial ties with Haiti and any aid and technical cooperation except that provided for strictly humanitarian purposes;

(4)   To adopt in accordance with the Charter and international law, any additional measures that may be necessary and appropriate to ensure the immediate reinstatement of President Jean-Bertrand Aristide to the exercise of his legitimate authority.

In a follow-up meeting a few days later, the Foreign Ministers resolved:

(1)   To declare that no government that may result from this illegal situation will be accepted and, consequently, to declare that no representative of such government will be accepted;

(2)   To urge the Member States to proceed immediately to freeze the assets of the Haitian State and to impose a trade embargo on Haiti, except for humanitarian aid. All humanitarian assistance must be channeled through international agencies or non-governmental organizations.[118]

The OAS dispatched a diplomatic mission to Haiti to try to negotiate with the junta on the restoration of civilian rule, but that mission failed when the regime refused to relinquish power. The Security Council debated the issue of the coup in Haiti and heard a passionate plea from President Aristide for help in restoring democracy to his country, but the Security Council took no action.[119] China and some Third World states on the Security Council opposed the involvement of the Council in what they considered a domestic matter. On the request of the government of Haiti, the General Assembly debated the issue, and on October 11 it adopted resolution A/Res/46/7 (1991).[120] The resolution welcomed resolutions MRE/RES.1/91 and MRE/RES.2/91 adopted on 3 and 8 October 1991, respectively, by the Ministers of Foreign Affairs of the member countries of the Organization of American States, which:

(1)   Strongly condemns as unacceptable the attempted illegal replacement of the Constitutional President of Haiti, the use of violence and military coercion and the violation of human rights in that country;

(2)   Affirms as unacceptable any entity resulting from that illegal situation and demanded the immediate restoration of the legitimate government of President Jean-Bertrand Aristide, together with the full application of the National Constitution and hence the full observance of human rights in Haiti;

(3)   Requests the Secretary General of the United Nations, in accordance with his function, to consider providing support sought by the Secretary General of the OAS in implementing the mandates arising from resolutions MRE/RES.1/91 and MRE/RES.2/91 adopted by the organization;

(4)   Appeals to the Member States of the United Nations to take measures in support of the resolutions of the OAS referred to in paragraph 3 above.[121]

The General Assembly requested the Secretary General to report on the situation at its 47th Session, and it continued to recognize the government of President Aristide as the legitimate government of Haiti and denied all rights of membership to the military regime.[122] Pursuant to the General Assembly's request, the Secretary General appointed Dante Caputo as his Special Representative to Haiti, in an attempt to help mediate between the parties. Caputo's diplomatic efforts got nowhere. The OAS sanctions also proved ineffective, as non-members of the OAS continued to trade with Haiti. Meanwhile, the situation in Haiti deteriorated. Human rights abuses and politically motivated violence escalated and a general feeling of lawlessness permeated the capital.[123] Thousands of civilians fled the country in unsafe vessels, seeking refuge in the United States and in neighboring Caribbean countries. The General Assembly later adopted several resolutions condemning the human rights situation in Haiti.[124]

On June 16 the Security Council held a session to discuss the situation in Haiti. The Security Council was brief on the general deterioration in the human rights situation in Haiti and the escalation in political violence, particularly against supporters of President Aristide. At the end of the debate the Security Council adopted resolution 841 (1993), by which it determined that the situation in Haiti threatened international peace and security in the region.[125] Acting explicitly under Chapter VII of the Charter, the Security Council imposed mandatory economic sanctions on Haiti. The Security Council gave the following justifications for its action:

(1)   Recognizing the urgent need for an early, comprehensive and peaceful settlement of the crisis in Haiti in accordance with the provisions of the Charter of the United Nations and international law;

(2)   Recalling its [prior statement noting] with concern the incidence of humanitarian crises, including mass displacements of population, becoming or aggravating threats to international peace and security;

(3)   Deploring the fact that, despite the efforts of the international community, the legitimate government of President Jean-Bertrand Aristide has not been reinstated;

(4)   Concerned that the persistence of this situation contributes to a climate of fear of persecution and economic dislocation, which could increase the number of Haitians seeking refuge in neighboring Member States, and convinced that a reversal of this situation is needed to prevent its negative repercussions on the region;

(5)   Considering that the above-mentioned request of the representative of Haiti, [i.e. of its legitimate government], made within the context of [previous OAS and UN General Assembly actions], defines a unique and exceptional situation warranting extraordinary measures by the Council in support of efforts undertaken within the framework of the [OAS];

(6)   Determining that, in these unique and exceptional circumstances, the continuation of this situation threatens international peace and security in the region.[126]

Soon after the Security Council resolution took effect, the military junta agreed in principle to participate in peace talks with President Aristide to be held in New York. Dante Caputo, the Special Representative of the United Nations Secretary General, brokered the talks on New York's Governors Island. The parties signed the Governors Island Agreement on July 3, 1993, and agreed to abide by its terms. The Agreement called for the military regime to relinquish power and allow for the return of President Aristide to resume his term in office. The Agreement further called for the lifting of sanctions in August and for the deployment of a joint United Nations-OAS International Civilian Mission in Haiti (MICIVIH) to monitor the human rights situation throughout the country. A peacekeeping force was also to be deployed in order to establish a secure environment for President Aristide's return.[127] On the eve of the accord taking effect, the military junta reneged on the agreement and refused to relinquish power. Supporters of the junta also blocked Haiti's port to prevent the landing of a Canadian peacekeeping contingent as part of the United Nations Mission in Haiti (UNMIH). MICIVIH staff were later declared undesirable and expelled by the junta.[128]

With the collapse of the Governors Island Agreement and the New York Pact, the Security Council adopted resolution 873 (1994) by which it condemned the military regime for its continuing failure to comply with the terms of the agreements. Acting under Chapter VII of the Charter, the Security Council further tightened the economic sanctions on the regime to include an oil embargo, a ban on air travel, and a freeze on the assets of members of the junta.[129] The Security Council also adopted resolution 875 (1993), by which it imposed a naval blockade on Haiti. Acting under Chapter VII of the Charter, the Security Council called on member states 'to use such measures commensurate with the specific circumstances as may be necessary under the authority of the Secretary General to ensure strict implementation of the provisions of resolutions 841 (1993) and 873 (1993) relating to the supply of petroleum or petroleum products or arms and related materiel of all types, and in particular to halt inward maritime shipping as necessary in order to inspect and verify their cargoes and destinations.'[130] This was the first time the Security Council had taken such unusual measures in an attempt to reinstate a democratically elected government and to force a military regime to relinquish power.

On June 30 the Security Council convened a meeting to review the Secretary General's report on UNMIH. The Security Council adopted, by unanimously vote, resolution 933 (1994). It condemned the recent escalation of violations of international humanitarian law and the naming of the so-called '*de facto* III government'. The Security Council decided to extend the mandate of UNMIH for an additional month and strongly deplored the refusal of the military authorities to implement the Governors Island Agreement.[131]

In July 1994 the Security Council reconvened to review the report of the Secretary General, as required by resolution 933 (1994). The Secretary General's report called for an expanded UNMIH under three possible scenarios:

(1)   a very large international force would be deployed for a period of unforeseeable duration;
(2)   the Security Council would turn to like-minded states or to the OAS, and authorized them to establish a multinational or inter-American force to help create a secure and stable environment and implement the Governors Island Agreement;
(3)   the Security Council would divide the work between a multinational force or inter-American force and UNMIH.[132]

UNMIH would replace the former once a stable environment was created for it to carry out its original mandate. On the request of President Aristide and the recommendation of the Secretary General, the Security Council adopted resolution 940 (1994) by which it accepted the Secretary General's second scenario. The Security Council condemned the military junta and authorized the use of force to restore President Aristide to power.[133]

Acting under Chapter VII of the Charter, the Security Council 'authorized Member States to form a multinational force under unified command and control and, in this framework, to use all necessary means to facilitate the departure from Haiti of the military leadership, consistent with the Governors Island Agreement, the prompt return of the legitimately elected President and the restoration of the legitimate authorities of the government of Haiti, and establish and maintain a secure and stable environment that will permit implementation of the Governors Island Agreement.'[134] The Haitian military authorities were given a grace period of one month to comply with resolution 940 (1994) or face military action.

Within weeks of the passage of resolution 940 (1994), the United States began mobilizing its forces in anticipation of a military invasion of Haiti. However, hours before United States troops landed in late September, former President Jimmy Carter led an eleventh-hour diplomatic mission to persuade the military junta that a military invasion was imminent and that they should leave office to avoid defeat and being arrested and tried for human rights crimes.[135] The Carter mission secured a commitment from the Haitian military junta that it would leave office in exchange for a general amnesty. The Carter agreement granted amnesty to General Raul Cedras, the coup leader, Brigadier General Biamby, and Lieutenant-Colonel Michel François, providing they left Haiti by October 15. The agreement also required that the regime cooperate with United States forces in creating a smooth transition and a secure environment for the restoration of the democratically-elected government of President Aristide. The agreement paved the way for the peaceful deployment of United States forces in Haiti with the full cooperation of the Haitian army.[136]

United States forces landed in Haiti with no incident or opposition and they received a warm welcome from the general public. United States forces immediately secured the Port-au-Prince airport and port facility and established a secured environment in and around the Haitian capital.[137] The force also captured Cap Haitien, Haiti's second largest city, in a relatively short period of time. A weapons control program was initiated, and a joint police patrol with the Haitian police was established to reduce unrest and build trust among the Haitian people. A program to professionalize a new police force to replace the hated Haitian police began in Puerto Rico. The multinational force also coordinated several civic operations, such as water purification, sanitation, and medical care that improved the quality of life of the people of Haiti.[138]

In response to the events in Haiti, the Security Council adopted resolution 944 (1994) on September 29 by which it welcomed the peaceful deployment of the multinational force. The Security Council also called for the termination of all sanction measures imposed on Haiti in resolutions 841 (1993), 873 (1993) and 875 (1993) on the day after President Aristide returned to Haiti.[139] On October 15 the Security Council adopted resolution 948 (1994) by which it welcomed the return of President Aristide to Haiti. It formally lifted all sanctions in accordance with resolution 944 (1994). On November 29 the Security Council adopted resolution 964 (1994) to strengthen the advance team of UNMIH to 500 troops in anticipation of the withdrawal of the multinational force.[140] United States forces gradually withdrew from Haiti once UNMIH reached its full capacity. In July 1995 the Security Council adopted resolution 1007 (1995) by which it expanded UNMIH's mandate for an additional seven months, with the hope of concluding the mission in that time.[141]

Following President Aristide's return to Haiti the political climate and the human rights situation improved significantly. The United Nations scaled back UNMIH's troop level in February 1996 and then terminated the mission in June 1996 by resolution 1063 (1996). UNMIH was later replaced with the United Nations Support Mission in Haiti (UNSMIH) until November 1996, in order to assist the government of Haiti in the professionalization of the police and the maintenance of a secure and stable environment conducive to the success of efforts to establish and train an effective national police force.[142] The Security Council also called for support for the role of the Special Representative of the Secretary General in coordinating the activities by the United Nations system to promote institution-building, national reconciliation, and economic rehabilitation in Haiti.

In November 1996 the Security Council adopted resolution 1085 (1996) by which it reaffirmed the provisions of resolution 1063 (1996), and it extended UNSMIH's mandate for an additional period terminating on December 5, 1996.[143] On the request of the government of Haiti, in December 1996 the Security Council decided for a final time to extend the mandate of UNSMIH until May 31, 1997, with 300 civilian police personnel and 500 troops. UNSMIH was terminated on July 31, 1997 and was replaced with the United Nations Transition Mission in Haiti (UNTMIH) with a mandate limited to a single four-month period ending on November 30, 1997. UNTMIH's mandate called for it to assist the government of Haiti by supporting and contributing to the professionalization of the Haitian National Police.[144]

UNTMIH's mission was terminated on November 30, 1997 in accordance with resolution 1123 (1997). However, given the success of UNTMIH in professionalizing the Haitian National Police, the government of Haiti requested additional assistance from the United Nations in that regard. The Security Council took note of the success of UNTMIH in resolution 1141 (1997), and decided to establish for one year a United Nations Civilian Mission in Haiti (MIPONUH), comprising about 300 civilian police.[145] MIPONUH succeeded UNTMIH and continued to assist the government of Haiti by supporting and contributing to the professionalization of the Haitian National Police in accordance with the reports of the Secretary General. Prior to the termination of MIPONUH's mandate on November 30, 1997, the government of Haiti requested an extension of the mission. The Security Council honored that request in resolution 1212 (1998) by extending MIPONUH's mandate until November 30, 1999.[146]

Since the landing of the United States-led multinational force in Haiti in September 1995, the human rights situation and political environment improved significantly. The United Nations contribution to political stability and national reconciliation in Haiti was tremendous, and the Haitian people began to enjoy a degree of law and order and respect for human rights unknown in Haiti's history. Haiti held presidential elections in December 1995 and a new President took office in February 1996. Presidential elections were also held in November 2000, which Aristide won overwhelmingly.

Haiti's experiment with democracy has not been free of violence and political stalemate. As a result of a dispute with outgoing President Preval over his choice of Prime Minister, the Haitian Parliament did not function for over two years. Political violence in Haiti also saw an increase. The newly formed civilian police was in part responsible for the political violence and a drug-related crime wave. Poverty and economic stagnation continue to be a serious threat to Haiti's political future.

The measures adopted by the Security Council to restore democracy in Haiti were quite extraordinary and unprecedented. Never before in the organization's history had the Security Council authorized the use of force to restore a democratically-elected government. Nor did resolution 940 (1994) make the restoration of democracy its primary legal basis for authorizing the use of force. The preamble of resolution 940 (1994) stated that the Security Council was 'gravely concerned by the significant further deterioration of the humanitarian situation in Haiti, in particular the continuing escalation by the illegal *de facto* regime of systematic violations of civil liberties, the desperate plight of Haitian refugees and the recent expulsion of the International Civilian Mission'.[147] The restoration of democracy was only one of a series of justifications given for the Security Council's unprecedented action. The Security Council also relied on the invitation from exiled President Aristide, who was still recognized by the United Nations and the international community as a whole as the legitimate president of Haiti.[148] However, the question that needs to be answered is whether such justifications provide a legal basis for the Security Council to authorize Chapter VII measures against a state.

The use of force for humanitarian reasons had previously been approved by the Security Council in Somalia, Bosnia, and Rwanda, and could therefore provide the legal basis for similar measures in Haiti. However, the humanitarian situation in Haiti was not of the magnitude of the cases cited above, and therefore the argument is not convincing. Secondly, to say that the actions of the military junta in Haiti constituted a threat to international peace and security in the region is also not a convincing argument. The military regime posed no genuine threat to Haiti's neighbors, nor did its actions threaten international peace and security. By determining the legitimate government of Haiti, the Security Council exceeded its authority.[149] Finally, to base resolution 940 (1994) on the invitation of President Aristide also raises certain concerns, as the military junta was in firm control of the country and President Aristide was in exile.

Under customary international law, intervention by invitation is legal if the invitation comes from the legitimate authority within the state.[150] President Aristide was in exile and hence had no control over the country. A foreign state is in violation of international law if it intervenes in another state on the request of a government in exile.[151] The Security Council, therefore, could not rely solely on the invitation of President Aristide to intervene in Haiti, given his lack of effective control over the territory. The military junta may not have been internationally recognized as the legitimate government of Haiti, but it had effective control over the country. The Security Council can only intervene in a foreign state if it determines that the situation within the state threatens international peace and security. On the other hand, the United Nations was a party to the Haiti crisis since it was invited to participate in the electoral process by the government of Haiti. The United Nations was also a party to the Governors Island Agreement, under which all parties agreed to comply with their obligations. The military junta reneged on the agreement, and as such the United Nations credibility would have been severely damaged had it not enforced the terms of the agreement. On that basis the

Security Council acted within its legal authority to approve military measures against the junta.

There are those in the legal community who argued against the actions of the Security Council and felt that the Security Council exceeded its powers in authorizing the use of force in Haiti, and in so doing may have established a dangerous precedent for the United Nations.[152] The legitimacy of a government has traditionally been considered a matter within the domestic jurisdiction of a state, and should be determined by the people of that state. Article 2 (7) of the Charter prohibits the United Nations from interfering in matters essentially within the domestic jurisdiction of Member States. In the past, the General Assembly condemned overwhelmingly the intervention by the United States in Grenada and Panama on grounds of restoring democracy. In the Haiti situation, the Security Council legitimized United States use of force in its sphere of influence to establish a government consistent with the policies of the United States.

On its surface, the Haitian situation fell within the definition of a matter that was traditionally considered to be within the domestic jurisdiction of a state. However, when one takes a deeper look at the issues, including gross violations of human rights, the invitation from the Haitian government for the United Nations to participate in the political process, and the conduct of the military junta, the situation in Haiti can be considered an international issue. The Security Council may have also based its decision on the growing trend in Latin America and Europe to recognize the democratic will of the people as a fundamental human right. Both the OSCE and the OAS had previously adopted measures to strengthen democratically elected governments.[153] Haiti may very well be the exception to the rule, but it established a precedent that undemocratic regimes are illegitimate.

The Conflict in Rwanda

Rwanda has been plagued by ethnic violence throughout its modern history. In 1959 Belgium instituted democratic reforms in Rwanda under pressure from the United Nations General Assembly.[154] Rwanda was a trust territory of Belgium under United Nations auspices. The democratization process was strongly supported by the Hutu majority, but fiercely contested by the Tutsi minority, who retained control over Rwanda despite constitutional changes that gave the Hutus greater representation. The Tutsi minority had enjoyed tremendous privileges under Belgian rule and was determined to retain control after independence. In the immediate post-independence period, Hutus rebelled against Tutsi domination, killing hundreds and forcing thousands to flee into neighboring Uganda. As a result of that rebellion, the Hutus gained political control and formed the government at the time of independence in 1961. Many Tutsis were forced into long-term exile in Uganda, where they began a military campaign against the Hutu-dominated government in Rwanda.[155]

In 1973 General Habyarimana seized power in a successful military coup and became president. Habyarimana governed Rwanda for the next two decades through his National Republican Movement for Democracy and Development (MRND), the country's sole political party.[156] President Habyarimana maintained a tight grip on power and refused to allow the exiled Tutsis back into Rwanda. In 1990 the Rwanda Patriotic Front (RPF), comprising exiled Tutsis, invaded Rwanda from bases in Uganda. Hundreds of civilians were killed and thousands were displaced. The Organization for African Unity (OAU) and United Nations High Commissioner for Refugees (UNHCR) convinced President Habyarimana to enter a dialogue with the opposition on reforming Rwanda's political system.[157] Peace talks resumed in October 1990, but the process ended without a significant breakthrough. President Habyarimana instigated a campaign of hatred and fear of Tutsis among the Hutu majority. Tutsis inside Rwanda were suspected of being accomplices of the RPF and subjected to persecution. While advocating reform, President Habyarimana was also inciting ethnic hatred among Hutus and Tutsis.[158] Between 1990 and 1993, the RPF intensified its military campaign against the Rwandan Army. Under pressure from the war, President Habyarimana began peace talks with the RPF under the auspices of the OAU and the United Nations.

In March 1993 the government of Rwanda and the RPF signed a ceasefire agreement in Dar-es-Salaam, Tanzania, that began a process of political reconciliation with the prospect of genuine political reform.[159] On March 12 the Security Council adopted resolution 812 (1993) by which it recognized the agreement and called on the parties to respect the ceasefire agreement and to honor the obligations they accepted in their joint communiqué.[160] The Security Council called on the Secretary General to examine what contribution the United Nations could make toward strengthening the peace process in Rwanda, in particular through the establishment of an international peacekeeping force under the aegis of the OAU and the United Nations.[161] The Security Council also invited the Secretary General to examine the request from Rwanda and Uganda for the deployment of observers on their common border. On June 22, 1993 the Security Council convened to review the interim report of the Secretary General. On the recommendation of the Secretary General and a request from the government of Rwanda and the RPF, the Security Council adopted resolution 846 (1993) by which it authorized the deployment of the United Nations Observer Mission Uganda Rwanda (UNOMUR) on the Uganda side of the border for an initial period of six months, in order to monitor the Uganda-Rwanda border and verify that no military assistance reached Rwanda.[162]

On August 4 the government of Rwanda and the RPF signed the Arusha Peace Agreement to permanently end the conflict.[163] The Agreement called for the United Nations to play a significant role in supervising its implementation, under what the agreement termed the Neutral International Force (NIF), during a transitional period which was expected to last for 22 months.[164] Both the government of Rwanda and the RPF jointly requested the establishment of such a force, and asked the Secretary General to send a reconnaissance team to Rwanda to plan the force. The parties agreed to integrate the existing OAU Neutral Monitoring Group (UMOG) into the NIF. In a statement, the Security Council welcomed the signing of the Arusha Peace Agreement and urged full compliance from the parties involved.[165]

Under the Arusha Peace Agreement, the NIF was required to assist in the implementation of the Peace Agreement, in particular the supervision of the protocol on the integration of the armed forces of the parties. The NIF was assigned wide security tasks, including to guarantee the overall security of the country and verify the maintenance of law and order, ensure the security of the delivery of humanitarian assistance, and to assist in catering to the security of civilians. The NIF was also asked to assist in tracking arms caches and in the neutralization of armed gangs throughout the country, to undertake mine clearance operations, assist in the recovery of all weapons distributed to or illegally obtained by civilians, and monitor the observance of the cessation of hostilities.[166] In addition, the NIF was expected to assume responsibility for the establishment and preparation of assembly and cantonment points, and determine security parameters for Kigali, with the objective of making it a neutral zone. Finally, the NIF was required to supervise the demobilization of those servicemen and gendarmes who were not going to be integrated into the armed forces. The NIF was to be informed of any violations of the ceasefire and to track down the perpetrators.[167]

On the request of the parties, the Secretary General dispatched a reconnaissance mission to Rwanda from August 19-31, 1993, to study the possible functions of the NIF and the resources needed for such a peacekeeping operation. The Secretary General also met with a joint government-RPF delegation on September 15 in New York. The delegation argued for a rapid deployment of the international force and the rapid establishment of the transitional institutions. The Secretary General cautioned the delegation about the length of time it would take to deploy the force and the need for the parties to make every effort to respect the ceasefire. The Secretary General advised the parties of the demands on the United Nations for troops in Somalia and Bosnia, and the impact the organization's financial crisis was having on its ability to undertake new peacekeeping missions.[168]

On October 5 the Security Council adopted resolution 872 (1993) by which it established the United Nations Assistance Mission for Rwanda (UNAMIR) for a period of six months. UNAMIR was given the following mandate:

(1)   To continue to maintain the security of the city of Kigali... within a secure area established by the parties in and around the city;

(2)   To monitor observance of the ceasefire agreement, which calls for the establishment of cantonment and assembly zones and the demarcation of the new demilitarized zone and other demilitarized procedures;

(3)   To monitor the security situation during the final period of the transitional government's mandate, leading up to the elections;

(4)   To assist with mine clearance, primarily through training programs;

(5)   To investigate at the request of the parties or on its own initiative instances of alleged non-compliance with the provisions of the Arusha Peace Agreement relating to the integration of the armed forces, and pursue any such instances with the parties responsible and report thereon as appropriate to the Secretary General;

(6)   To monitor the process of repatriation of Rwandan refugees and resettlement of displaced persons to verify that it is carried out in a safe and orderly manner;

(7)   To assist in the coordination of humanitarian assistance activities in conjunction with relief operation;

(8)   To investigate and report on incidents regarding the activities of the gendarmerie and police.[169]

In January 1994 the Security Council adopted resolution 893 (1994) by which it welcomed the conclusion of an agreement on the status of UNAMIR and its personnel in Rwanda. The Security Council also noted with concern the incidents of violence in Rwanda and their consequences for the country; the Security Council also took note of the situation in Burundi.[170] The Security Council further reaffirmed its approval of the Secretary General's proposal concerning the deployment of a second battalion of UNAMIR troops. In spite of the Security Council's action and its further expansion of UNAMIR's mandate, developments in Rwanda began to derail the fragile peace accord.

On April 6, 1994, the political situation in Rwanda took a turn for the worse following the death of President Habyarimana, and the President of Burundi, Cyprien Ntaryamira, who died in a plane crash while approaching Kigali airport *en route* from peace talks in Dar-es-Salaam, Tanzania.[171] Their death led to widespread violence by members of the Presidential Guard and other Hutu extremists, who blamed the RPF for the death of the two presidents. Members of the Presidential Guard, the Interahamwe militia, and members of the Rwandan Army carried out a search and kill mission of members of President Habyarimana's government, including the Prime Minister and other high-ranking political figures.[172] The United Nations peacekeepers guarding the house where the Prime Minister took refuge were disarmed and severely beaten. A contingent of Belgian peacekeepers were taken away and later executed by Rwandan soldiers.[173] Hutu extremists went on the rampage and began killing en masse ethnic Tutsis and moderate Hutus. The massacre of Tutsis was unprecedented in Rwanda's post-independence history. In the next hundred days over 800,000 Tutsis and moderate Hutus were killed.[174] The genocide in Rwanda shattered any hopes for peace in that troubled country, and raised serious questions both in Africa and elsewhere about the ability of the United Nations to manage regional conflicts. The magnitude of the violence in Rwanda went far beyond the capacity of UNAMIR to deal with. UNAMIR personnel were also at risk, and the mission could not adequately protect the civilian population without an expanded mandate and an increase in resources and manpower.[175]

The killing of the Belgian peacekeepers led Belgium to withdraw its contingent from UNAMIR. The Belgian Foreign Minister met with the Secretary General in Bonn and informed him that the requirements to pursue a peacekeeping operation in Rwanda were no longer met, the Arusha peace plan was dead, and there were no means for a dialogue between the parties; consequently, the UN should suspend UNAMIR.[176] Belgium also campaigned vigorously to get members of the Security Council to withdraw UNAMIR. In response to the developments in Rwanda, the Department of Peacekeeping Affairs (DPKO) proposed two options for the future of UNAMIR, which were sent to UNAMIR and the Secretary General for comments: (1) to keep UNAMIR, minus the Belgian contingent, for a period of three weeks, providing the following conditions were met: the existence of an effective ceasefire, each side accepting responsibility for law and order and the security of civilians in areas under their control, declaring Kigali airport a neutral territory and concentrating UNAMIR at the airport. The parties would be warned that unless an agreement was secured by May 6, UNAMIR would be withdrawn; or (2) to immediately reduce UNAMIR and maintain only a small political presence of the Special Representative, advisers, some military observers and a company of troops.[177] Both General Dellaire, the commander of UNAMIR, and the Secretary General opted for option one.

The Security Council reacted strongly to the death of presidents Habyarimana and Ntaryamira, the outbreak of violence against the civilian population, and the collapse of the peace process. The Security Council also expressed deep regret at the failure of the parties to implement fully the provisions of the Arusha Peace Agreement, particularly the provisions relating to the ceasefire. However, resolution 912 (1994) did not strongly condemn, or even acknowledge, that the crime of genocide had been committed in Rwanda.[178] The Security Council expressed its deep concern for the safety and security of UNAMIR and other international protected personnel, and it condemned the ongoing violence in Rwanda and the attacks against UNAMIR and other United Nations personnel that led to several deaths and injuries among UNAMIR personnel.[179] The Security Council called upon all concerned to end the violence and to respect fully international humanitarian law. The Security Council further demanded an immediate cessation of hostilities between the forces of the government of Rwanda and the Rwandan Patriotic Front, and for an end to the mindless violence and carnage which were engulfing Rwanda.[180] In light of the developments in Rwanda, the Security Council decided to adjust the mandate of UNAMIR to reflect the following:

(1)   To act as an intermediary between the parties in an attempt to secure their agreement to a ceasefire;
(2)   To assist in the resumption of humanitarian relief operations to the extent possible;
(3)   To monitor and report on developments in Rwanda, including the safety and security of the civilians who sought refuge with UNAMIR.[181]

The Security Council decided to keep the situation in Rwanda under constant review and indicated its readiness to consider promptly any recommendations the Secretary General made concerning the force level and mandate of UNAMIR in light of new developments.

Despite the passing of resolution 912 (1994), in which the Security Council condemned the violence in Rwanda and called for its immediate halt, the violence escalated. In response, the Security Council adopted resolution 918 (1994), by which it once again strongly condemned the ongoing violence in Rwanda. It condemned, in particular, the numerous killings of civilians which had taken place, and the impunity with which armed individuals had been able to operate and continued to operate.[182] The Security Council expressed its deep concern that the situation in Rwanda had resulted in the deaths of thousands of innocent civilians, including women and children, and had led to the internal displacement of a significant percentage of the Rwandan population. The Security Council also said that this situation, coupled with the massive exodus of refugees to neighboring countries, constituted a humanitarian crisis of enormous proportions.[183] For the first time since the violence began, the Security Council warned that the killing of members of an ethnic group with the intention of destroying such a group, in whole or in part, constituted a crime punishable under international law.[184] It strongly urged all parties to cease forthwith any incitement, especially through the mass media, to violence or ethnic hatred.

In a further sign of how seriously it was taking the situation in Rwanda, the Security Council indicated that the magnitude of the human suffering caused by the conflict and its continuation would constitute a threat to regional peace and security.[185] The Security Council also decided to expand the mandate given to UNAMIR under resolution 912 (1994) to include the following additional responsibilities:

(1)   To contribute to the security and protection of displaced persons, refugees and civilians at risk in Rwanda, including through the establishment and maintenance of secure humanitarian areas;

(2)   To provide security and support for the distribution of relief supplies and humanitarian relief operations.

The Security Council in this context authorized an expansion of the UNAMIR force level up to 5,500 troops.[186]

By resolution 918 (1994), the Security Council further determined that the situation in Rwanda constituted a threat to peace and security in the region.[187] Acting under Chapter VII of the Charter of the United Nations, the Security Council:

(1)   Decides that all states shall prevent the sale or supply to Rwanda by their nationals or from their territories or using their flag vessels or aircraft of arms and related materiel of all types, including weapons and ammunition, military vehicles and equipment, paramilitary police equipment and spare parts;

(2)   Decides also to establish, in accordance with rule 28 of the provisional rules of procedure of the Security Council, a Committee of the Security Council consisting of

all the members of the Council, to undertake the following tasks and to report on its
work to the Council with its observations and recommendations:

    (a) To seek from all States information regarding the actions taken by them
    concerning the effective implementation of the embargo imposed by paragraph
    1 above;

    (b) To consider any information brought to its attention by States concerning
    violations of the embargo, and in that context to make recommendations to the
    Council on ways of increasing the effectiveness of the embargo;

    (c) To recommend appropriate measures in response to violations of the embargo
    imposed by paragraph 1 above and provide information on a regular basis to
    the Secretary General for general distribution to Member States.[188]

On June 8 the Security Council adopted resolution 925 (1994) by which it approved the
Secretary General's proposals on the deployment of UNAMIR under its expanded mandate,
and it extended the mission's mandate until December 9.[189] The Security Council also called
on Member States to respond promptly to the Secretary General's request for resources,
including additional forces. More importantly, the Security Council acknowledged for the first
time that 'acts of genocide' had occurred in Rwanda.[190] However, despite its recognition that
genocide had occurred in Rwanda, the Security Council did not invoke Chapter VII of the
Charter to authorize immediate action to stop the violence.[191]

The Security Council met on June 21 to debate a French proposal for the deployment of a
Temporary International Presence in Rwanda (codenamed Operation Turquoise), to be led by
France. The magnitude of the humanitarian situation in Rwanda had reached crisis
proportions, with thousands of refugees fleeing the violence and taking refuge in neighboring
Zaire. On June 22 the Security Council adopted resolution 929 (1994), by which it voiced
serious concern for the continuation of the systematic and widespread killings of civilians in
Rwanda.[192] The Security Council recognized that 'the situation in Rwanda constitutes a
unique case which demands an urgent response by the international community'.[193] The
Security Council further determined that 'the magnitude of the humanitarian crisis in Rwanda
constitutes a threat to peace and security in the region'.[194] The Security Council welcomed the
offer by Member States to cooperate with the Secretary General in order to achieve the
objectives of the United Nations in Rwanda through the establishment of a temporary
operation under international command and control aimed at contributing, in an impartial
way, to the security and protection of displaced persons, refugees, and civilians at risk in
Rwanda. Acting under Chapter VII of the Charter of the United Nations, the Security Council:

(1)   Authorizes Member States cooperating with the Secretary General to conduct
    [Operation Turqoise]… using all necessary means to achieve the humanitarian
    objectives set out in subparagraphs 4 (a) and (b) of resolution 929 (1994). The
    Security Council further decides that 'Operation Turquoise' will be limited to two
    months, unless the Secretary General determined at an earlier date that the expanded

UNAMIR was able to carry out its mandate. The French-led multinational force was subsequently replaced by UNAMIR after the two-month period specified under resolution 929 (1994);

(2)   Decides that the mission of Member States cooperating with the Secretary General would be limited to a period of two months following the adoption of the present resolution, unless the Secretary General determines at an earlier date that the expanded UNAMIR is able to carry out its mandate;

(3)   Commends the offers already made by Member States of troops for the expanded UNAMIR;

(4)   Calls upon all Member States to respond urgently to the Secretary General's request for resources, including logistical support, in order to enable expanded UNAMIR to fulfill its mandate effectively as soon as possible, and requested the Secretary General to identify and coordinate the supply of the essential equipment required by troops committed to the expanded UNAMIR;

(5)   Demands that all parties to the conflict and others concerned immediately bring to an end all killings of civilian populations in areas under their control and allow Member States cooperating with the Secretary General to implement fully the mission set forth in paragraph 3 above.[195]

The deployment of the Temporary International Force in Rwanda may have come too late to stop the genocide. By the time the force landed in Rwanda, the scale of the violence had declined significantly. However, the flow of Hutu refugees into Zaire increased as the conflict between the RPF and the Hutu-dominated Rwandan Army intensified. The RPF subsequently captured the capital, Kigali, and declared itself the new government of Rwanda. The RPF government was immediately recognized by the United Nations, and it was asked to participate in Security Council debates regarding the situation in Rwanda. The RPF government opposed the deployment of the new Temporary International Force because of France's previous support for the Hutu-led government. Against RPF opposition, the force landed in the southern part of Rwanda and established a safe haven for refugees.

On July 1, 1994, the Security Council adopted resolution 935 (1994) by which it authorized the Secretary General to establish an impartial Commission of Experts to advise him 'on the evidence of grave violations of international humanitarian law committed in the territory of Rwanda, including the evidence of possible acts of genocide'.[196] Upon submission of the Commission's report, the Security Council adopted resolution 955 (1994) by which it expressed its grave concern at the reports 'that genocide and other systematic, widespread and flagrant violations of international humanitarian law have been committed in Rwanda', and further determining that 'this situation continues to constitute a threat to international peace and security'.[197] The Security Council also stated that it was determined to put an end to such crimes and would take effective measures to bring to justice the persons responsible. Acting under Chapter VII of the Charter of the United Nations, the Security Council:

(1)   Decides hereby, having received the request of the government of Rwanda (S-1994-
        1115), to establish an international tribunal for sole purpose of prosecuting persons
        responsible for genocide and other serious violations of international humanitarian law
        committed in the territory of Rwanda and Rwandan citizens responsible for genocide
        and other such violations committed in the territory of neighboring States, between 1
        January and 31 December 1994 and to this end to adopt the Statute of the International
        Criminal Tribunal for Rwanda annexed hereto;

(2)   Decides that all States shall cooperate fully with the International Tribunal and its
        organs in accordance with the present resolution and the Statute of the International
        Tribunal and that consequently all States shall take any measures necessary under their
        domestic law to implement the provisions of the present resolution and the Statute,
        including the obligation of States to comply with requests for assistance or orders
        issued by the Trial Chamber under Article 28 of the Statute, and request States to keep
        the Secretary General informed of such measures.[198]

The International Criminal Tribunal for Rwanda (ICTR) was the second war crimes tribunal
the Security Council had established in recent years in response to violations of international
humanitarian law in internal conflicts. The ICTR was modeled on the International Criminal
Tribunal for the Former Yugoslavia (ICTY), and the Chief Prosecutor and the Appeals
Chamber of the ICTY had jurisdiction over the ICTR. Like the ICTY, the ICTR was
established under Chapter VII of the Charter of the United Nations as a means of maintaining
international peace and security. The Security Council established the tribunal after much
criticism from NGOs and other human rights observers over its handling of the Rwanda crisis.
The Security Council was criticized for not intervening earlier to stop the genocide in
Rwanda, and for doing too little too late in light of the magnitude of the humanitarian
situation. African states accused the Security Council of operating under a double standard.
They accused the Security Council of being more concerned about the plight of the civilian
population in the former Yugoslavia than in Rwanda.[199]

By late November 1994, the security and humanitarian situation in the refugee camps had
improved significantly. The international force withdrew and was replaced by UNAMIR. On
November 30, 1994, the Security Council adopted resolution 965 (1994) by which it extended
the mandate of UNAMIR until June 9, 1995. The resolution called on UNAMIR to:

(1)   Contribute to the security and protection of displaced persons, refugees and civilians at
        risk in Rwanda including through the establishment and maintenance, where feasible,
        of secure humanitarian areas;

(2)   Provide security and support for the distribution of relief supplies and humanitarian
        relief operations;

(3)   Exercise its good offices to help achieve national reconciliation within the frame of
        reference of the Arusha Peace Agreement.[200]

The Security Council also decided to expand UNAMIR's mandate to include the following additional responsibilities within the limits of the resources available to it:

(1)   To contribute to the security in Rwanda of personnel of the International Tribunal for Rwanda and human rights officers, including full-time protection for the Prosecutor's Office, as well as details for missions outside Kigali;
(2)   To assist in the establishment and training of a new, integrated, national police force.[201]

On June 9 the Security Council reviewed the Secretary General's report on UNAMIR. The Security Council later adopted resolution 997 (1995) by which it extended UNAMIR's mandate until December 8, 1995. The Security Council also authorized a reduction of the force level to 2,330 troops within three months of the adoption of the resolution and to 1,800 troops within four months.[202] The Security Council decided to maintain the current level of military observers and civilian police personnel, and adjusted the mandate of UNAMIR to allow it to:

(1)   Exercise its good offices to help achieve national reconciliation within the frame of reference of the Arusha Peace Agreement;
(2)   Assist the government of Rwanda in facilitating the voluntary and safe return of refugees and their reintegration in their home communities, and to that end, to support the government of Rwanda in its ongoing efforts to promote a climate of confidence and trust through the performance of monitoring tasks throughout the country with military and police observers;
(3)   Support the provision of humanitarian aid, and of assistance and expertise in engineering, logistics, medical care and de-mining;
(4)   Assist in the training of a national police force;
(5)   Contribute to the security in Rwanda of personnel and premises of United Nations agencies, of the International Tribunal for Rwanda, including full-time protection for the Prosecutor's Office, as well as those of human rights officers, and to contribute also to the security of humanitarian agencies in case of need.[203]

The situation in Rwanda remained on the agenda of the Security Council for much of 1995. In July 1995 the Security Council adopted resolution 1005 (1995) in which it addressed the issue of land mines in Rwanda. Acting under Chapter VII of the Charter of the United Nations, the Security Council decided to lift the restrictions imposed in paragraph 13 of resolution 918 (1994) to allow an appropriate amount of explosives to enter Rwanda to be used exclusively for humanitarian de-mining programs.[204] A month later, on August 16, the Security Council noted the destabilizing effect of uncontrolled circulation of arms in the Great Lakes sub-region. The Security Council adopted resolution 1011 (1995), by which it welcomed Zaire's proposal to establish an international commission under the auspices of the United Nations to investigate reports of arms supplies to former Rwandan government forces.[205] The Security

Council also took note of military preparations and increasing incursions into Rwanda by elements of the former regime, and underlined the need to prevent Rwandan nationals in camps in neighboring countries from undertaking military activities aimed at destabilizing Rwanda or receiving arms supplies for use in Rwanda.[206]

Acting under Chapter VII of the Charter of the United Nations, the Security Council decided, effective immediately, and until September 1, 1996, to lift the restrictions on the sale of arms in paragraph 13 of resolution 918 (1994), to allow the government of Rwanda to import arms and related materiel through designated points of entry.[207] The Security Council decided that the restrictions on the sale of arms to the government of Rwanda would be terminated after September 1, 1996, but would continue to apply to non-governmental forces fighting against the government of Rwanda.

In December 1995 the Security Council adopted resolution 1029 (1995) by which it extended the mandate of UNAMIR for a final period until March 8, 1996. The Security Council also decided, in light of efforts to restore peace and stability through the voluntary and safe repatriation of Rwandan refugees, to adjust the mandate of UNAMIR to allow it to:

(1)   Exercise its good offices to assist in achieving the voluntary and safe repatriation of Rwandan refugees within the frame of reference of the recommendations of the Bujumbura Conference and the Cairo Summit of the Heads of State of the Great Lakes Region, and in promoting genuine national reconciliation;

(2)   Assist the government of Rwanda in facilitating the voluntary and safe return of refugees and, to this end, to support the government of Rwanda in its ongoing efforts to promote a climate of confidence and trust through the performance of monitoring tasks;

(3)   Assist the United Nations High Commissioner for Refugees and other international agencies in the provision of logistical support for the repatriation of refugees;

(4)   Contribution, with the agreement of the government of Rwanda, to the protection of the International Tribunal for Rwanda as an interim measure until alternative arrangements agreed with the government of Rwanda can be put in place.[208]

The Security Council also authorized the Secretary General to reduce the force level of UNAMIR to 1,200 troops in order to allow it to fulfill its mandate. The Security Council decided to withdraw UNAMIR on March 8, 1996.[209]

Relations between the United Nations and the Patriotic Front-led government of Rwanda never really improved. The government of Rwanda blamed the United Nations, and UNAMIR in particular, for not doing more to stop the genocide. In fact, once the new government gained control of the entire country, it signaled its intention to ask UNAMIR to leave. Further friction developed between the United Nations and Rwanda over the issue of humanitarian assistance provided to Hutu refugees in camps in Goma, Zaire (now the Democratic Republic of Congo), some of whom the government of Rwanda accused of carrying out the genocide and of continuing to launch armed incursions into Rwanda. Soon after the RPF consolidated its power, it began concentrating its efforts on driving Hutu extremists out of Rwanda and neighboring Zaire. The RPF government supported the civil war in Zaire, which led to the overthrow of Mobutu. The RPF also carried out a military campaign in Zaire that led to the massacre of thousands of Hutu extremists. Other Hutu refugees in camps in Goma were forcibly repatriated. Discovery of the massacres led to a further deterioration in relations between Rwanda and the United Nations.

The situation in Rwanda eventually stabilized, but a political settlement between Hutus and Tutsis was not realized. Rwandan refugees were ultimately all repatriated, and the humanitarian situation in Rwanda has improved significantly. Despite these gains, Rwanda remains a country with tremendous problems. The conditions in Rwanda's jails are appalling, and suspects must wait indefinitely to be tried. Some high-level Hutu extremists were tried and convicted, including a Catholic priest, but the vast majority of those suspected of taking part in the genocide, young men and boys, were still awaiting their day in court years after the killings. Rwanda simply did not have the means to carry out speedy trials for all those who were being held in detention. Serious concerns have been raised by international jurists about the fairness of trials in Rwanda, and the consequent prospects for political reconciliation.[210]

The ICTR got off to a slow start and was plagued by controversy. However, since the appointment of a new administrator, the ICTR moved quickly to try those under its jurisdiction. The ICTR secured indictments and convictions of a number of former Rwandan government officials. In September 1998, the ICTR convicted the former mayor of a small town, Jean-Paul Akayesu, of genocide, for his role in the deaths of 2,000 people and the rape of dozens of Tutsi women.[211] He became the first person ever convicted of genocide, a remarkable achievement for the tribunal. Following a decision by the tribunal to dismiss charges against Jean-Bosco Barayagwiza because of the length of time he was detained without being notified of the charges against him, the government of Rwanda launched a protest and threatened to stop cooperating with the ICTR. However, the new prosecutor, Carla Del Ponte, appealed the decision to the tribunal's Appeals Chamber, and the decision was reversed.[212]

The role of the United Nations in Rwanda has been severely criticized, and it generated tremendous controversy. Kofi Annan, who was head of the Department of Peacekeeping Operations (DPKO) during the Rwanda genocide and later became Secretary General, was granted permission by the Security Council to establish a commission of inquiry to determine what the United Nations could have done to stop the genocide in Rwanda.[213] Mr Annan was personally accused by the authorities in Rwanda of giving the orders that prevented UNAMIR from intervening to stop the genocide. Whether or not history vindicates Mr Annan, the people of Rwanda will never forgive the United Nations for not doing more to help them during their time of desperate need.

On December 16 the commission issued its report 'Independent Inquiry into the Actions of the United Nations During the 1994 Genocide in Rwanda'. The commission blamed both the United Nations and certain members of the Security Council for failing to heed the advice of UNAMIR field commander General Dallaire that Hutu extremists were in the process of exterminating the Tutsi minority, and that UNAMIR's mandate should be augmented to allow it to play a more assertive and preventive role in Rwanda.[214] The commission faulted the United Nations, particularly member states which had pressured the Secretariat to limit the proposed number of troops for UNAMIR. The report also criticised the United States for its attitude toward United Nations peacekeeping operations, in light of the deaths of Pakistani and United States peacekeepers in Somalia.[215] The report said that the incidents in Somalia were a watershed in United States policy toward United Nations peacekeeping.

Prior to the commencement of the genocide in Rwanda in May 1994, President Clinton had enacted his Presidential Decision Directive 25 (PDD 25), a directive which placed strict conditions on United States participation in future United Nations peacekeeping missions. It called for a precisely defined mandate and an exit strategy. The Somalia incidents also had a chilling effect on the United Nations Secretariat regarding risks that could be assumed during peacekeeping operations, and the interpretation of mandates.[216] The report maintained that the legacy of Somalia was of particular importance to the conduct of UNAMIR. Overall, the report faulted the great majority of member states for their unwillingness to send troops or materiel to Rwanda. The Secretary General accepted the report of the commission and expressed deep remorse on behalf of the United Nations. The government of Rwanda initially requested a formal apology from the United Nations, but received only an acknowledgement from the Security Council that mistakes had been made.

The crisis in Rwanda raised several questions about the role of the Security Council in managing complex humanitarian situations. First, the Security Council had been slow to recognize that genocide was occurring in Rwanda. Secondly, the Security Council had refused to expand UNAMIR's mandate, even given the deterioration of the humanitarian situation; instead, the Security Council had reduced the number of troops and later withdrew UNAMIR. Even when the Security Council finally decided to act, it delegated its Chapter VII authority to the Secretary General and certain member states, instead of carrying out the responsibility duly assigned to it under the Charter. The Security Council not only violated international law by ignoring the genocide in Rwanda, but it also violated United Nations law by delegating to the Secretary General and certain member states its responsibility for maintaining international peace and security in Rwanda.

CHAPTER IV

REGIONAL ORGANIZATIONS AND TRANSNATIONAL ARMED CONFLICTS

In the conflicts to be examined below, the Security Council deferred to regional organizations to find peaceful solutions to disputes before becoming involved. In fact, the absence of Security Council leadership, or a delay in its involvement, led to deterioration of the security situation, and may have contributed to prolonging of the conflicts in question. Regional organizations did have a role to play but were over-burdened by the intensity of the conflicts, and in most cases did not have the resources to resolve them. The Security Council managed these conflicts by simply issuing resolutions, but it did not get involved until well after the regional organizations had either failed to settle the disputes, or had negotiated settlements which called on the Security Council's help for implementation. This chapter focuses on the conflicts in the states of Central America, Liberia, Sierra Leone, and the provinces of Kosovo and East Timor. It looks at the role played by regional organizations and determines whether these were consistent with the provisions of Chapter VIII of the Charter, which deals with the relationship between the Security Council and regional arrangements and agencies. It also examines the reasons why the Security Council has had difficulty in working closely with regional organizations to resolve regional disputes.

The Conflicts in Central America

After a decade of civil war, human rights abuses, political assassinations, extra-judicial killings, and the disappearance and displacement of thousands of civilians, the five Central American governments of Costa Rica, El Salvador, Guatemala, Honduras, and Nicaragua signed the Esquipulas II Peace Plan in 1987 to formally end the conflicts in the region.[1] Thereafter the United Nations undertook a major peace initiative in Central America to implement the various provisions of the plan. Two years after the foreign ministers of the five countries signed the agreement, new developments in the region and the world at large made it possible for the accord to take effect. The civil wars in El Salvador and Nicaragua had wreaked havoc on the economies of both countries and left a large percentage of their populations displaced and desperately poor. Neither the rebels nor government troops appeared to be any closer to a military victory. Then President Reagan, who had fueled the conflicts by supplying arms and financial backing to the rebels in Nicaragua and the government in El Salvador, left office in 1989, making it possible for third-party mediation of the disputes. The new Bush administration also took a different approach to the conflicts in the wake of the Iran-Contra scandal, which had implicated several high-level Reagan administration officials.[2]

The Congress of the United States also asserted its authority in foreign affairs and began playing a stronger role in U.S. policy in Central America after it was revealed that the Reagan

Administration had violated the Boland Amendment, in which Congress banned the export of weapons to the Contra rebels in Nicaragua. The Bush administration was also pressed to seek a diplomatic solution to the conflict in Nicaragua in light of the International Court of Justice ruling against the United States in the case brought before it by Nicaragua.[3]

Under the Esquipulas II Agreement the parties were required to negotiate ceasefire agreements with their adversaries and enter a political dialogue that would lead to political reconciliation. Restrictions on civil liberties were to be lifted, and National Reconciliation Commissions were to be established to facilitate the peace-building process.[4] The agreement further committed the parties to hold national elections that would be free and fair and pluralistic in character, and held under international supervision. Although the agreement experienced some difficulty, the overall political climate in the signatory states improved significantly.

In March 1989 the government of Nicaragua took a decisive step in implementing the election provision of the agreement by issuing a formal request to the United Nations and the Organization of American States (OAS) to establish a group of international election observers to monitor the electoral process in Nicaragua.[5] This was an unusual request; it was the first time such a request came from a sovereign state. Since the General Assembly had adopted a resolution previously authorizing the Secretary General to assist the parties in Central America to implement the agreement, the Secretary General immediately established the United Nations Observer Mission to Verify the Electoral Process in Nicaragua (ONUVEM).[6] The Security Council later endorsed the creation of ONUVEM in resolution 637 (1989) as part of a broader plan for restoring peace and security in the Central American region.[7] The resolution therefore called for completion of the various agreements signed by the five countries, and a halt to all support for guerrillas in the region. The Security Council also gave its strong backing to the Secretary General's efforts in the peace process.[8]

ONUVEM's mandate required it to:

(1)   Verify that political parties are equitably represented in the Supreme Electoral Council and its subsidiary bodies (nine regional electoral councils and 4,100 electoral boards);
(2)   Verify that political parties enjoy complete freedom of organization and mobilization, without hindrance or intimidation by anyone;
(3)   Verify that all political parties have equitable access to State television and radio in terms of both the timing and length of broadcasts;
(4)   Verify that electoral rolls are properly drawn up.[9]

ONUVEM was not merely an observer mission, but became a fully-fledged election monitoring team. It was responsible for supervising all aspects of the electoral process and making certain that the process was free and fair. Elections were held in Nicaragua in 1989 and a new president, Violeta Chamorro, was elected and sworn in in 1990. The Sandinistas accepted the outcome of the elections and stepped down peacefully.[10] ONUVEM completed its mission in February 1990, at which time it ceased to exist.

In November 1989 the Security Council adopted resolution 644 (1989) by which it established the United Nations Observer Group in Central America (ONUCA) to help verify implementation of the Esquipulas II Agreement, which formally ended the conflicts affecting the five Central American countries. ONUCA's responsibilities included the decommissioning of the Contras, supervising the release of political detainees, registering voters, and making sure that the election process was free and fair. ONUCA was also responsible for checking border violations affecting the neighboring Central American states caused by the civil wars in Nicaragua and El Salvador.[11] With the defeat of the Sandinistas in the general elections, a new era of peace began in Nicaragua. Following the successful implementation of the peace agreement in Nicaragua, ONUCA's mission was terminated in 1992.

In May 1991 the Security Council adopted resolution 693 (1991), by which it established the United Nations Observer Mission in El Salvador (ONUSAL).[12] ONUSAL was responsible for monitoring the agreement between the government of El Salvador and the Frente Farabundo Marti para Liberacion Nacional (FMLN) rebel movement. ONUSAL's initial staff of 135 civilians was responsible for helping improve the human rights situation in El Salvador.[13] In January 1992 the Security Council adopted resolution 729 (1992) by which it expanded ONUSAL to include 372 military personnel and 631 police officers. ONUSAL was also given an additional mandate to monitor a ceasefire agreement to take effect on February 1, 1992, and the more difficult task of professionalizing a new national police force that would assume responsibility for maintaining law and order among former adversaries.[14] The Security Council enlarged ONUSAL's mandate in May 1993 to allow it to observe the electoral process that culminated in the general elections of March 1994. ONUSAL's mandate was extended on three subsequent occasions to accommodate El Salvador's difficult transition from a war-torn country to a civil society with democratic institutions and governed by the rule of law, instead of by violence and intimidation by right-wing death squads.

The United Nations missions in both Nicaragua and El Salvador were very successful in bringing peace to a region that had not known peace for over a decade. For years the United States deliberately kept the United Nations out of Latin American conflicts for fear that United Nations involvement would open the region to unnecessary meddling by the Soviet Union. The United States' attitude changed following the end of the Cold War and the demise of the Soviet Union. The civil wars in both Nicaragua and El Salvador have since ended, and human rights abuses have declined sharply. Insurgents in both countries put down their weapons to become actively involved in civilian politics. This is a remarkable accomplishment for the United Nations.[15]

In addition to the missions in Nicaragua and El Salvador, the Security Council established the United Nations Human Rights Verification Mission in Guatemala to monitor implementation of the peace accord between the rebels and the Guatemalan government, and to oversee the government's compliance to human rights standards.[16] The Guatemalan army was responsible for numerous human rights atrocities over a thirty-year period. Its involvement in extra-judicial killings, disappearances, and torture had fueled the conflict in Guatemala.[17] The United Nations human rights team was to create mechanisms that would prevent future rights violations. In 1997 China vetoed a resolution that would have authorized the deployment of a military component to the United Nations Human Rights Verification Mission. China's action was in retaliation against Guatemala's diplomatic recognition of the government of Taiwan as the legitimate government of China. The presence of the United Nations human rights mission in Guatemala helped reduce human rights violations in Guatemala, and fostered a climate of peace in which political life could return to normal.

The Conflict in Liberia

The war in Liberia had been in progress for two years before the Security Council placed the issue on its agenda. The civil war in Liberia caught the attention of the international media in 1989 after rebels from the National Patriotic Front of Liberia (NPFL) stormed the capital, Monrovia, and engaged government troops in close-quarters combat. By the time the Economic Community of West African States (ECOWAS) negotiated a cease fire, thousands of civilians had died in the war, and hundreds of thousands had taken refuge in neighboring countries. Following the death of several Nigerian nationals, ECOWAS agreed to deploy a peacekeeping force to the capital to protect the civilian population.[18] Initially, ECOMOG, the peacekeeping wing of ECOWAS, operated within the traditional boundaries of a peacekeeping force. ECOMOG was deployed on the invitation of the host government, although the issue of when the invitation was issued is disputed. During the struggle for control of Monrovia, President Samuel Doe was captured and later tortured and executed in the presence of ECOMOG troops. Liberia was in a state of anarchy, with three warring factions vying for control of the government. Meanwhile, Liberia had no legitimate authority which could negotiate the deployment of additional forces. Western states withdrew their essential diplomatic personnel and nationals from Monrovia in anticipation of further violence.

Initially, the Security Council ignored the conflict in Liberia and basically treated it as another internal conflict over which it had no jurisdiction. The Security Council deferred to the Organization of African Unity (OAU) and ECOWAS, which already had a 'peacekeeping' force (ECOMOG) in Liberia, to find a diplomatic solution to the conflict.[19] In August 1990, when ECOWAS intervened in Liberia, the Security Council was preoccupied with a more serious threat to international peace resulting from Iraq's invasion of Kuwait.[20] ECOWAS took the unprecedented step of authorizing the deployment of the Economic Community

Military Observer Group (ECOMOG) in Liberia's capital, Monrovia, on humanitarian grounds. However, within a few months of its deployment, ECOWAS amended the mandate of ECOMOG and authorized it to use force to enforce the ceasefire and to secure the cooperation of the various warring factions.[21] ECOWAS did not consult with the Security Council before it changed ECOMOG's mandate to include an authorization to use force in Liberia. Although the measure violated provisions of Chapter VIII of the Charter of the United Nations, the Security Council did not issue a statement to that effect.[22]

In November 1992 six American nuns were brutally murdered by NPFL rebels. The Security Council soon thereafter placed the situation in Liberia on its agenda and later adopted resolution 788 (1992) by which it condemned the killing and called on the warring parties to settle their dispute by peaceful means.[23] Acting under Chapter VII of the Charter of the United Nations, the Security Council determined that the situation in Liberia constituted a threat to international peace and security, particularly in West Africa, and took the unusual step of imposing a general and complete arms embargo on all deliveries of weapons and military equipment to rebel-held territory in Liberia.[24] The Security Council condemned the repeated violations of the ceasefire agreement and called on the parties to implement the Yamoussoukro IV Accord. The Security Council condemned continuing attacks against the peacekeeping forces of ECOWAS. The Security Council decided within that same framework to exempt weapons destined for ECOMOG. Under resolution 788 (1992) the Security Council commended ECOWAS for its efforts to restore peace, security, and stability in Liberia. The Security Council did not contest the legality of ECOWAS's military activities in Liberia without Security Council authorization. Some observers later argued that the Security Council, by not condemning ECOWAS, gave its tacit endorsement to the ECOWAS peace initiative and legitimized its intervention in Liberia.[25]

In March 1993 the Security Council convened to consider the report of the Secretary General on the situation in Liberia. The Security Council adopted resolution 813 (1992) by which it condemned the parties to the conflict for failing to comply with the Yamoussoukro IV Accords and the ceasefire agreement. The Security Council further recalled the provisions of Chapter VIII of the Charter of the United Nations and determined that the deterioration of the situation in Liberia constituted a threat to international peace and security, particularly in the West African region.[26] The Security Council condemned the violation of the November 20, 1990 ceasefire by the opposing parties; condemned the continuing armed attacks against the peacekeeping forces of ECOWAS; demanded that all parties cooperate fully with the Secretary General and with ECOWAS; reiterated its full support for the Yamoussoukro IV Accords; and declared its readiness to consider appropriate measures in support of ECOWAS if any party was unwilling to cooperate in implementing the provisions of the Yamoussoukro IV Accords, in particular the encampment and disarmament provisions.[27] The Security Council also called on all parties to the conflict to refrain from any action that would obstruct the delivery of humanitarian assistance and put the safety of humanitarian or peacekeeping personnel at risk. Finally, the Security Council requested the Secretary General to discuss with ECOWAS the contribution of the United Nations in implementing the peace agreement, including the deployment of United Nations observers.[28]

On July 25, 1993 the various parties to the conflict in Liberia signed a Peace Agreement in Cotonou, Benin: the Interim government of National Unity of Liberia (IGNU), the National Patriotic Front of Liberia (NPFL), and the United Liberation Movement for Democracy (ULIMO).[29] The parties called on the United Nations and ECOWAS to assist in the implementation of the agreement. The Security Council convened a meeting on August 10 to consider the agreement and to review the report of the Secretary General. The Security Council adopted resolution 856 (1993), by which it formally endorsed the Peace Agreement, and it approved the dispatch of thirty military observers to participate in the work of the Joint Ceasefire Monitoring Committee.[30]

In September 1993 the Security Council approved the report of the Secretary General, which called for the establishment of the United Nations Observer Mission in Liberia (UNOMIL). In resolution 866 (1993) the Security Council recognized the uniqueness of the mission as the first peacekeeping mission undertaken by the United Nations in cooperation with a peacekeeping mission already established by a regional organization.[31] The resolution stressed the importance of full cooperation and close coordination between UNOMIL and ECOMOG in implementing their respective mandates. The Security Council established UNOMIL under its authority and under the direction of the Secretary General through his Special Representative for a period of seven months. The Security Council further decided that UNOMIL would comprise military observers, as well as medical, engineering, communications, transportation, and electoral components. UNOMIL was given the following mandate:

(1) To receive and investigate all reports of alleged incidents of violations of the ceasefire agreement;

(2) To monitor compliance with other elements of the Peace Agreement, including at points of Liberia's borders with Sierra Leone and other neighboring countries, and to verify its impartial application, and in particular to assist in the monitoring of compliance with the embargo on delivery of arms and military equipment to Liberia and the cantonment, disarmament and demobilization of combatants;

(3) To observe and verify the election process, including the legislative and presidential elections to be held in accordance with the provisions of the Peace Agreement;

(4) To assist in the coordination of humanitarian assistance activities in the field in conjunction with the existing United Nations humanitarian relief operation;

(5) To develop a plan and assess financial requirements for the demobilization of combatants;

(6) To report on the major violations of international humanitarian law to the Secretary General;

(7)   To train ECOMOG engineers in mine clearance and, in cooperation with ECOMOG, coordinate the identification of mines and assist in the clearance of mines and unexploded bombs;

(8)   Without participation in enforcement operations, to coordinate with ECOMOG in the discharge of ECOMOG's responsibilities both formally and informally through the Violations Committee.[32]

The Security Council also called on the transitional government to conclude expeditiously a Status of Mission Agreement with the United Nations, to facilitate the full deployment of UNOMIL. The Security Council further urged all the parties to finalize the composition of the Elections Commission in order to undertake promptly the necessary preparation for legislative and presidential elections by March 1994.

Between 1994 and 1996 the Security Council adopted a series of resolutions concerning the situation in Liberia. In light of continued fighting, the Security Council extended the mandate of UNOMIL several times to give the parties more time to implement the peace agreement. The Security Council also condemned the widespread killings of civilians and other violations of international humanitarian law by the warring factions in Liberia, and the detention and maltreatment of UNOMIL observers, ECOMOG soldiers, humanitarian relief workers, and other international personnel.[33]

On June 30, 1995 the Security Council adopted resolution 1001 (1995) by which it called on the parties to make serious progress toward implementation of the Akosombo and Accra Agreements, and specifically accomplish the following steps:

(1)   Installation of the Council of State;

(2)   Reestablishment of a comprehensive and effective ceasefire;

(3)   Disengagement of all forces;

(4)   Creation of an agreed timetable and schedule for the implementation of all other aspects of the agreements, in particular the disarmament process.[34]

On August 19, 1995 the parties to the Liberian conflict signed the Abuja Agreement, which amended the Cotonou and Akosombo Agreements.[35] The Security Council adopted resolution 1014 (1995), by which it welcomed the new agreement and efforts by the parties to implement the provisions of the Akosombo and Accra Agreements.[36] The Security Council also extended the mandate of UNOMIL until January 31, 1996. Under resolution 1020 (1996) the Security Council recognized the progress the parties had made toward peace, and adjusted UNOMIL's mandate as follows:

(1)   To exercise its good offices to support the efforts of ECOWAS and the Liberian National Transitional government (LNTG) to implement the peace agreements and to cooperate with them for this purpose;

(2)   To investigate all allegations of violations of the cease fire reported to the Cease fire Violation Committee, to recommend measures to prevent the recurrence of such violations and to report to the Secretary General accordingly;

(3)   To monitor compliance with the other military provisions of the peace agreements including disengagement of forces, disarmament and observance of the arms embargo and to verify their impartial application;

(4)   To assist, as appropriate, in the maintenance of assembly sites agreed upon by ECOMOG, the LNTG and other factions, and in the implementation of a program for demobilization of combatants, in cooperation with the LNTG, donor agencies and non-governmental organizations;

(5)   To support, as appropriate, humanitarian assistance activities;

(6)   To investigate and report to the Secretary General on violations of human rights and to assist local human rights groups, as appropriate, in raising voluntary contributions for training and logistic support;

(7)   To observe and verify the election process, in consultation with the Organization of African Unity and ECOWAS, including the legislative and presidential elections to be held in accordance with provisions of the peace agreements.[37]

By the middle of 1996 the parties to the Liberian conflict were gradually moving closer to ending the civil war. The Security Council acknowledged the progress made thus far by further extending the mandate of UNOMIL. The Security Council reminded the parties that continued support of the international community for the peace process in Liberia, including the participation of UNOMIL, was contingent on the Liberian factions' demonstrating their commitment to resolve their differences peacefully and to achieve national reconciliation in accordance with the agreement reached in Abuja in August 1996. The Security Council further condemned all attacks on international personnel and the practice of recruiting, training, and deploying children for combat by some of the factions.[38]

Liberia held democratic elections in 1997, supervised by ECOWAS, the OAU and UNOMIL. Charles Taylor, the principal rebel leader, was elected president. Taylor's victory ended all fears of a resumption of the conflict. It brought to a close a very violent chapter in Liberia's history, and some degree of normal life gradually returned to Liberia. However, the security situation remained precarious: rebel forces continued to occupy parts of the country, and some of Taylor's opponents attempted to assassinate him. Liberia was accused of being the main conduit for the shipment of weapons to rebels fighting the civil war in neighboring Sierra Leone. Liberia also served as the transit point for the illicit trade in diamonds from Sierra Leone, which the rebels used to purchase weapons, and the Security Council accused Liberia of fueling the conflict in Sierra Leone by facilitating the sale of so-called 'blood diamonds'.[39]

The Security Council did not violate United Nations law by not intervening in the Liberian conflict. However, by refusing to condemn ECOWAS for violating fundamental norms of the Charter of the United Nations, the Security Council violated its obligations under the Charter, and encouraged future violations by regional organizations. ECOWAS violated both Articles 2 (7) and 53 of the Charter of the United Nations. Its intervention was a violation of Liberia's sovereignty. Secondly, by not receiving prior authorization from the Security Council to intervene in Liberia, ECOWAS violated Article 53 of the Charter, which requires regional arrangements to receive prior Security Council authorization before carrying out enforcement actions. By not condemning ECOWAS, the Security Council set a dangerous precedent which other regional organizations may invoke in the future. In fact, NATO's military measures against Yugoslavia in 1998 may have been based on the precedent ECOWAS established in Liberia.

The Conflict in Sierra Leone

On May 25, 1997, disgruntled former soldiers of the national army of Sierra Leone overthrew the democratically elected government of President Akmed Tejan Kabbah and forced him into exile in neighboring Guinea. They seized control of government buildings, and freed and armed prisoners from the central prison in Freetown, the capital, including Major Johnny Koromah, head of the Revolutionary United Front (RUF).[40] Koromah, who later declared himself president, suspended the constitution and banned all political parties. The OAU Council of Ministers condemned the coup and called on all African states and the international community at large to refrain from recognizing the new military regime. ECOWAS also issued a statement in which it condemned the coup, and called on the military junta to immediately reinstate the democratically elected government.[41] ECOWAS issued an ultimatum to the military junta to comply with its demands or be removed by force. For the next several months, the military standoff continued, and the junta refused to leave office. Nigerian naval vessels later bombarded targets in Freetown, but Nigerian forces were beaten back by the rebel army. Sporadic fighting between Nigerian troops and the rebel army continued for several months. In the spring of 1998, ECOMOG launched a final offensive and succeeded in expelling the military junta from power.[42] The rebel army retreated into the jungles of Sierra Leone and tried to regroup. President Kabbah was thereafter reinstated to power. ECOMOG's action was unprecedented, as it was the first time military force had been used to reinstate a democratically elected government in Africa. What was more interesting was that the measure was led by the military government of Nigeria, which previously had prevented an elected government from assuming power in Nigeria. ECOWAS action violated both the OAU and United Nations Charters. However, neither the Security Council nor the OAU condemned ECOWAS.

For the first two decades of its independence, Sierra Leone had been ruled by autocratic rulers. Thereafter military rulers took turns at running the country, until 1996. In March 1996, Kabbah was voted in as the first democratically elected leader of Sierra Leone. His election brought to an end a five-year civil war between government troops and the RUF rebel organization. In November 1996 the new government signed the Abidjan Accord with the

RUF.[43] The Accord called for an immediate end to the armed conflict and the demobilization of RUF forces, and set forth political provisions whereby the RUF would register and function as a political party. The Accord further called for the deployment of neutral international observers and a capable security presence to deter undisciplined elements from interrupting the peace process.[44] President Kabbah requested assistance from the United Nations in implementing the Accord. Secretary General Kofi Annan agreed to assist, and he later proposed to the Security Council a plan to authorize the deployment of a peacekeeping force in Sierra Leone to aid in implementing the agreement.[45] Within months of signing the agreement, the RUF stopped complying with key provisions of the plan, and soon thereafter seized power in a military coup.

The Security Council was slow to respond to the situation in Sierra Leone. The President of the Security Council issued three statements in May, July, and August of 1997, in which he condemned the military coup, but the Security Council as a body did not adopt a resolution condemning the coup.[46] In October 1997 the Security Council adopted its first resolution on the situation in Sierra Leone. Under resolution 1132 (1997), the Security Council condemned the coup and determined that the situation in Sierra Leone constituted a threat to international peace and security in the West Africa region.[47] The Security Council acknowledged the sanctions imposed on the military junta by ECOWAS at its August 28-29, 1997 summit in Abuja, Nigeria, and expressed its support for ECOWAS mediation efforts. The Security Council deplored the fact that the military junta had not taken steps to allow the restoration of the democratically elected government and a return to constitutional order.[48] The Security Council did not rule on the legality of the military measures taken by ECOWAS.

Acting under Chapter VII of the Charter, the Security Council:

(1)   Demands that the military junta take immediate steps to relinquish power in Sierra Leone and make way for the restoration of the democratically elected government and a return to constitutional order;

(2)   Reiterates its call upon the junta to end all acts of violence and cease all interference with the delivery of humanitarian assistance to people of Sierra Leone;

(3)   Expresses its strong support for the efforts of the ECOWAS Committee to resolve the crisis in Sierra Leone and encouraged it to continue to work for a peaceful restoration of the constitutional order, including through the resumption of negotiations;

(4)   Encourages the Security General, through his Special Envoy, in cooperation with the ECOWAS Committee, to assist in the search for a peaceful resolution and the peaceful restoration of the constitutional order, including through the resumption of negotiation;

(5)   Decides that all States shall prevent the entry into or transit through their territories of members of the military junta and adult members of their families... provided that the entry into or transit through a particular State of any such person may be authorized... for verified humanitarian purposes or purposes consistent with paragraph 1 above, and

provided that nothing in this paragraph shall oblige a State to refuse entry into its territory to its own nationals.[49]

The Security Council also acted under Chapter VIII of the Charter to authorize ECOWAS, in cooperation with the democratically elected government of Sierra Leone, to ensure strict implementation of the provisions of the resolution relating to supply of petroleum and petroleum products, and arms and related materiel of all types, including, where necessary and in conformity with applicable international standards, by halting inward maritime shipping in order to inspect and verify their cargoes and destinations, and called upon all states to cooperate with ECOWAS in this regard.[50] The Security Council did not specifically authorize ECOWAS to use military force to implement provisions of resolution 1132 (1997), nor did it endorse ECOWAS military intervention in Sierra Leone. However, it is safe to say that by authorizing ECOWAS to enforce the embargo, the Security Council had acquiesced to the military actions of ECOWAS.[51] The Security Council's action can be construed as a *post facto* authorization.

ECOWAS continued to negotiate with the RUF on the conditions for the reinstatement of President Kabbah. In October 1997 representatives of Koromah and President Kabbah signed a peace agreement in Conakry, Guinea.[52] The Conakry Agreement outlined a peace plan for Sierra Leone and established a six-month timetable for its implementation. Under the agreement, the RUF would begin demobilization and disarming immediately, and President Kabbah would be reinstated no later than April 22, 1998.[53] A few months after the signing of the Conakry Agreement, the RUF reneged. The military junta refused to disarm and continued its military activities in the countryside. Guerrilla activities against the junta also increased. An organization known as the Komajors and traditional village-based fighters escalated their activities against the junta. The fighting had a serious impact on the humanitarian situation in the rural areas, particularly around the southern town of Bo. The deteriorating humanitarian situation in Sierra Leone was subsequently documented in the Secretary General's third report on the situation in Sierra Leone to the Security Council.[54]

In February 1998, two months before the six-month deadline established in the Conakry Agreement expired, Nigerian troops stormed the capital, Freetown, and within nine days ousted the military junta and captured the capital.[55] Major Koromah fled the country into neighboring Guinea, but several of his associates were captured and jailed. Both the OAU and the United Nations Security Council welcomed Nigeria's action. The President of the Security Council issued a statement welcoming 'the fact that the military junta has been brought to an end' and commended 'the important role' that ECOWAS played in the 'peaceful resolution' of the crisis.[56] The President of the Security Council did not address the issue of the legality of the ECOWAS action.

Following the return of President Kabbah to Sierra Leone on March 10, the Security Council adopted resolution 1156 (1998) acknowledging the new developments in Sierra Leone. Acting under Chapter VII of the Charter, the Security Council welcomed the return to Sierra Leone of the democratically-elected President, and decided to terminate, with immediate effect, the prohibition on the sale and supply to Sierra Leone of petroleum and petroleum products referred to in paragraph 6 of resolution 1132 (1997).[57] On April 17 the Security Council adopted resolution 1162 (1998) by which it endorsed the efforts made by the democratically-elected President of Sierra Leone since his return on March 10 and by the government of Sierra Leone to restore peaceful and secure conditions in the country, to re-establish effective administration and the democratic process, and to embark on the task of reconstruction and rehabilitation.[58] The Security Council also commended ECOWAS and its Military Observers (ECOMOG) deployed to Sierra Leone on the important role they played in support of the objectives related to the restoration of peace and security set out in paragraph 1 of the resolution. The Security Council emphasized the need to promote national reconciliation in Sierra Leone, and encouraged all parties in the country to work together toward this objective.[59]

In accordance with the recommendations contained in the March 18 report of the Secretary General, the Security Council authorized the immediate deployment of up to ten United Nations military liaison and security advisory personnel to Sierra Leone for a period of up to 90 days.[60] The officers were to work under the authority of the Special Envoy of the Secretary General, in close coordination with the government of Sierra Leone and ECOMOG, to report on the military situation in the country, to ascertain the state of and to assist in the finalization of planning by ECOMOG for future tasks, such as the identification of the former combatant elements to be disarmed and the design of a disarmament plan, as well as to perform other related security tasks as identified in paragraphs 42, 45, and 46 of the Secretary General's report.[61]

On June 5 the Security Council convened to review the situation in Sierra Leone. The Security Council adopted resolution 1171 (1998) by which it welcomed the efforts of the government of Sierra Leone to restore peaceful and secure conditions in the country, to re-establish effective administration and the democratic process, and to promote national reconciliation.[62] The Security Council deplored the continued resistance to the authority of the legitimate government of Sierra Leone and stressed the urgency for all rebels to put an end to atrocities, cease their resistance, and lay down their arms. Acting under Chapter VII of the Charter of the United Nations, the Security Council decided to terminate the remaining prohibitions imposed by paragraphs 5 and 6 of resolution 1132 (1997).[63] The Security Council further decided, with a view to preventing the sale and supply of arms and related materiel to non-governmental forces in Sierra Leone, that all States should prevent the sale or supply, by their nationals or from their territories, or using their flag vessels or aircraft, of arms and related materiel of all types, including weapons and ammunition, military vehicles and equipment, paramilitary equipment and spare parts for the aforementioned, to Sierra Leone other than to the government of Sierra Leone, through named points of entry, and a list to be supplied by that government to the Secretary General, who would promptly notify all Member

States of the United Nations of the list.[64] The Security Council also decided that the arms ban would not apply to ECOMOG.

In addition to the weapons ban, the Security Council decided that all States should prevent the entry into or transit through their territories of leading members of the former military junta and of the RUF, as designated by the Committee established by resolution 1132 (1997), provided that the entry into or transit through a particular State of any such person may be authorized by the same Committee, and provided that nothing in this paragraph shall oblige a State to refuse entry to its territory to its own nationals.[65]

Within months of his return to power, President Kabbah's authority was being challenged by the RUF. The security situation deteriorated after remnants of the ousted junta and members of the RUF retreated to the bush and began a campaign of terror against the civilian population.[66] The rebels also launched attacks on government-controlled areas near the capital, Freetown, which threatened to reverse the peace process. On July 13, 1998 the Security Council adopted resolution 1181 (1998) by which it condemned the continuing resistance of remnants of the ousted junta and members of the RUF to the authority of the legitimate government, and the violence they were perpetrating against the civilian population of Sierra Leone.[67] The Security Council demanded that the rebels lay down their arms immediately. On the recommendation of the Secretary General, contained in his June 9 report, the Security Council also decided to establish the United Nations Observer Mission in Sierra Leone (UNOMSIL) for an initial period of six months until January 13, 1999.[68] UNOMSIL would comprise 70 military observers as well as a small medical unit, with the necessary equipment and civilian support staff. UNOMSIL's mandate required it to perform the following tasks:

(1)   To monitor the military and security situation in the country as a whole, as security conditions permit, and provide the Special Representative of the Secretary General with regular information thereon in particular with a view to determining when conditions are sufficiently secure to allow subsequent deployments of military observers;

(2)   To monitor the disarmament and demobilization of former combatants concentrated in secure areas of the country, including monitoring of the role of ECOMOG in the provision of security and in collection and destruction of arms in those secure areas;

(3)   To assist in monitoring respect for international humanitarian law, including at disarmament and demobilization sites, where security conditions permit;

(4)   To monitor the voluntary disarmament and demobilization of members of the Civilian Defense Forces (CDF), as security conditions permit.[69]

The Security Council further decided that UNOMSIL would be led by a Special Envoy of the Secretary General, who would be designated Special Representative for Sierra Leone. UNOMSIL was also required to subsume the office of the Special Envoy and its civilian staff, and that the augmented civilian staff, as recommended by the Secretary General in his report, would perform, *inter alia*, the following tasks:

(1)   To advise, in accordance with other international efforts, the government of Sierra Leone and local police officials on police practice, training, re-equipment and recruitment, in particular on the need to respect internationally accepted standards of policing in democratic societies, to advise on the planning of the reform and restructuring of the Sierra Leone police force, and to monitor progress in that regard;

(2)   To report on violations of international humanitarian law and human rights in Sierra Leone, and, in consultation with the relevant United Nations agencies, to assist the government of Sierra Leone in its efforts to address the country's human rights needs.[70]

Meanwhile efforts to find a diplomatic solution to the crisis in Sierra Leone continued, with the rebels attacking government positions and ECOMOG forces. They also torched villages and amputated the limbs of thousands of innocent civilians to revenge their ouster from the government.

On January 12, 1999 the Security Council adopted resolution 1220 (1999) by which it expressed its deep concern over the deteriorating situation in Sierra Leone, and encouraged the parties to redouble their efforts to resolve the conflict and restore lasting peace and stability. On the recommendation of the Secretary General, contained in his Third Progress Report and Special Report on UNOMSIL of January 7, 1999, the Security Council decided to extend the mandate of UNOMSIL until March 13, 1999. The Security Council also noted the intention of the Secretary General in his Special Report to reduce the number of military observers in UNOMSIL and retain in Conakry a small number who would return to Sierra Leone when conditions permitted, together with the necessary civilian substantive and logistical support staff under the leadership of his Special Representative.[71]

With the situation in Sierra Leone rapidly deteriorating, the Security Council adopted resolution 1231 (1999) by which it expressed concern over the fragile situation in Sierra Leone. The Security Council called on all states to respect the sovereignty, political independence, and territorial integrity of Sierra Leone.[72] On the recommendation of the Secretary General contained in his fifth report on the situation in Sierra Leone, the Security Council extended the mandate of UNOMSIL until June 13, 1999. The Security Council condemned the atrocities perpetrated by the rebels on the civilian population of Sierra Leone, including in particular those committed against women and children. The Security Council further deplored all violations of human rights and international humanitarian law which had occurred in Sierra Leone during the recent escalation of violence referred to in the Secretary General's report, including the recruitment of children as soldiers.[73] The Security Council urged the appropriate authorities to investigate all allegations of such violations with a view to bringing the perpetrators to justice. The Security Council called upon all parties to the conflict to fully respect human rights and international humanitarian law and the neutrality and impartiality of humanitarian workers, and to ensure full and unhindered access for humanitarian assistance to affected populations. The Security Council also expressed its grave concern that supplies of arms and mercenaries were being channeled to the rebels from the territory of Liberia. The Security Council affirmed the obligation of all States to comply strictly with the provisions of the embargo on the sale or supply of arms and related materiel imposed by resolution 1171 (1998) of June 5, 1998.[74]

The international community soon began showing signs of fatigue with the situation in Sierra Leone. The rebels attacked civilian areas close to Freetown, and were determined to terrorize the population unless their demands were met by the government. Realizing that they could not win the war, the rebels were basically disrupting the peace process in order to retain control of the diamond-producing regions. The government of Sierra Leone, ECOWAS and the United Nations later agreed to include the rebels in future peace negotiations in exchange for a commitment from them to observe a ceasefire.

In early June 1999 an all-party peace conference was convened in Lomé, Togo under the auspices of the United Nations and the President of Togo. On June 11, while the peace talks were in progress, the Security Council adopted resolution 1245 (1999), by which it extended the mandate of UNOMSIL until December 1999.[75] The Security Council stressed that an overall political settlement and national reconciliation were essential to achieving a peaceful resolution of the conflict in Sierra Leone, and welcomed the holding of talks in Lomé between the government of Sierra Leone and representatives of the rebels.[76] The Security Council called upon all parties to remain committed to the process of negotiation and to demonstrate flexibility in their approach to the process. The Security Council further underlined its strong support for those involved in the mediation efforts of the United Nations within the Lomé process, in particular the work of the Special Representative of the Secretary General to facilitate dialogue, and for the key role being played by the President of Togo as Chairman of ECOWAS. The Security Council further emphasized the strong commitment of the international community to support a sustainable peace settlement in Sierra Leone.[77]

On July 7 the parties to the conflict signed the Lomé Peace Agreement to bring an end to the war.[78] Under the terms of the agreement, the rebels would receive four cabinet seats, including the Mines and Resources Ministry, which allowed them to retain control of the diamond industry; they were granted amnesty for crimes committed during the war; and the death penalty imposed on the rebel leader, Sankoh, who was convicted of treason for his involvement in the coup that overthrew President Kabbah in 1997, was lifted.[79] The United Nations supported the agreement, but opposed the amnesty for those who committed war crimes, crimes against humanity, genocide, and other serious violations of human rights. The United States, the EU and human rights organizations also objected to the amnesty, and they called for the prosecution of those responsible for serious violations of human rights and international humanitarian law.[80]

In August 1999 the Security Council adopted resolution 1260 (1999), by which it endorsed the Peace Agreement between the government of Sierra Leone and the Revolutionary United Front (RUF) in Lomé on July 7, 1999, and commended the President of Togo, the Special Representative of the Secretary General, ECOWAS, and all those involved in facilitating the negotiations in Lomé on their contributions to this achievement.[81] The Security Council authorized the provisional expansion of UNOMSIL to up to 210 military observers along with the necessary equipment and administrative and medical support to perform the tasks set out in paragraph 38 of the report of the Secretary General. The Security Council further decided that all additional military observers were to be deployed as security conditions permitted, and would operate for the time being under security provided by ECOMOG as indicated in paragraph 39 of the report. The Security Council authorized the strengthening of the political, civil affairs, information, human rights, and child protection elements of UNOMSIL as set out in paragraphs 40 to 52 of the report of the Secretary General, including through the appointment of a deputy Special Representative of the Secretary General and the expansion of the Office of the Special Representative of the Secretary General.[82]

During the conflict in Sierra Leone a large number of children were recruited as child combatants. They committed serious offences including murder and rape against the civilian population. These children had to be rehabilitated. The Security Council recognized the commitment of the government of Sierra Leone to work with the United Nations Children's Fund and the Office of the Special Representative of the Secretary General for Children and Armed Conflict and other international agencies to give particular attention to the long-term rehabilitation of child combatants in Sierra Leone. The Security Council encouraged those involved also to address the special needs of all children affected by the conflict in Sierra Leone, including through disarmament, demobilization, and reintegration programs and the Truth and Reconciliation Commission, and through support to child victims of mutilation, sexual exploitation, and abduction, to the rehabilitation of health and education services, and to the recovery of traumatized children and the protection of unaccompanied children.[83]

Two weeks following the signing of the Sierra Leone Peace Agreement, members of the RUF took several United Nations aid workers hostage to protest the accord. The hostages were released after the rebel leader, Foday Sankoh, intervened to assure the rebels that they would have a significant role in the government. RUF rebels resisted efforts to give up their weapons and comply with the disarmament provisions of the Lomé Agreement. Some of the rebels retreated to the interior of the country and into neighboring Liberia, where they regrouped and received training and equipment. The United Nations mission initially experienced a series of setbacks because of the complexity of the Sierra Leone situation, which the mission was ill-equipped to handle. On September 27 the Secretary General submitted a report on Sierra Leone to the Security Council, as requested in resolution 1260 (1999). The Secretary General recommended the deployment of a 6,000-strong peacekeeping force for Sierra Leone, made up largely of ECOMOG forces.[84]

The Secretary Council met on October 22 to reassess the situation in Sierra Leone. The Security Council adopted resolution 1270 (1999) in which it approved the Secretary General's recommendation for the deployment of a large peacekeeping force in Sierra Leone. The Security Council determined that the situation in Sierra Leone continued to constitute a threat to international peace and security in the region, and it deplored the taking of hostages, including UNOMSIL and ECOMOG personnel, by rebel groups.[85] The Security Council called upon those responsible to end such practices immediately. The Security Council decided to establish the United Nations Mission in Sierra Leone (UNAMSIL) with immediate effect for an initial period of six months and with the following mandate:

(1)   To cooperate with the government of Sierra Leone and the other parties to the Peace Agreement in the implementation of the Agreement;

(2)   To assist the government of Sierra Leone in the implementation of the disarmament, demobilization and reintegration plan;

(3)   To that end, to establish a presence at key locations throughout the territory of Sierra Leone, including at disarmament/reception centers and demobilization centers;

(4)   To ensure the security and freedom of movement of United Nations personnel;

(5)   To monitor adherence to the ceasefire in accordance with the ceasefire agreement of May 18, 1999 through the structures provided for therein;

(6)   To encourage the parties to create confidence-building mechanisms and support their functioning;

(7)   To facilitate the delivery of humanitarian assistance;

(8)   To support the operations of United Nations civilian officials, including the Special Representative of the Secretary General and his staff, human rights officers and civilian affairs officers;

(9)   To provide support, as requested, to the elections, which are to be held in accordance with the present constitution of Sierra Leone.[86]

The Security Council further decided that UNAMSIL would comprise a maximum of 6,000 military personnel, including 260 military observers. The Security Council also decided that UNAMSIL would absorb the substantive civilian and military components and functions of UNOMSIL as well as its assets, and decided to terminate the mandate of UNOMSIL immediately following the establishment of UNAMSIL.[87] Acting under Chapter VII of the Charter of the United Nations, the Security Council authorized UNAMSIL to take the necessary action to ensure the security and freedom of movement of its personnel and, within its capabilities and areas of deployment, to afford protection to civilians under imminent threat of physical violence.[88]

The new United Nations Mission in Sierra Leone (UNAMSIL) was required to integrate the current regional force into its structure. The new Obasanjo government of Nigeria informed the United Nations of its intention to withdraw Nigerian troops from Sierra Leone because of the financial burden it imposed on Nigeria. Nigeria's withdrawal would paralyze the peacekeeping mission in Sierra Leone. Under a new agreement the United Nations agreed to retain the troops under the command of UNAMSIL. The government of Sierra Leone and the RUF welcomed the decision of the United Nations to deploy a peacekeeping force, and they agreed to cooperate with UNAMSIL.

On February 7, 2000, the Security Council adopted resolution 1289 (2000) by which it approved the recommendation of the Secretary General to increase the military contingent of UNAMSIL to a maximum of 11,100 military personnel, including the 260 military observers already deployed. The Secretary General made the request based on an assessment of a new security threat from the RUF, who had taken United Nations peacekeepers hostage and were continuing their attacks on civilians.[89] Acting under Chapter VII of the Charter of the United Nations, the Security Council decided to revise the mandate of UNAMSIL to include the following additional tasks, to be performed by UNAMSIL within its capabilities and areas of deployment and in light of conditions on the ground:

(1)   To provide security to key locations and government buildings, in particular in Freetown, important intersections and major airports, including Lungi airport;

(2)   To facilitate the free flow of people, goods and humanitarian assistance along specified thoroughfares;

(3)   To provide security in and at all sites of the disarmament, demobilization and reintegration program;

(4)   To coordinate with and assist, in common areas of deployment, the Sierra Leone law enforcement authorities in the discharge of their responsibilities;

(5)   To guard weapons, ammunition and other military equipment collected from ex-combatants and to assist in their subsequent disposal or destruction.[90]

Resolution 1289 (2000) further authorized UNAMSIL to take all necessary action to fulfill its new responsibilities. The Security Council also affirmed that, in the discharge of its mandate, UNAMSIL could take the necessary action to ensure the security and freedom of movement of its personnel, and within its capabilities and areas of deployment, to afford protection to civilians under imminent threat of physical violence.[91] On the recommendation of the Secretary General, as spelled out in his January 11 report, the Security Council increased the civilian affairs, civilian police, administrative, and technical personnel of UNAMSIL. The Security Council endorsed the proposal of the Secretary General for the establishment within UNAMSIL of a land mine action office responsible for awareness training of UNAMSIL personnel, and for the coordination of mine action activities of non-governmental organizations and humanitarian agencies operating in Sierra Leone.[92]

In his January 11 report to the Security Council on the situation in Sierra Leone, the Secretary General outlined the role of UNAMSIL in the peace process in Sierra Leone. The Secretary General sounded a note of cautious optimism about the pace of the peace process in Sierra

Leone, but cited the slow progress made so far in the disarmament program in the northern and eastern parts of the country and highlighted repeated rebel interference with humanitarian activities and UNAMSIL patrols, and their harassment of civilians in those areas.[93] In addition, the Secretary General accused the RUF and its leader Foday Sankoh of making several hostile public statements against UNAMSIL. The report also accused Sankoh of violating the travel ban imposed on him in resolution 1171 (1998), by traveling to Côte d'Ivoire and South Africa on February 14, 2000.[94] In response to that incident, the Security Council sanctions committee convened an emergency session on February 18 and urged Mr Sankoh to return immediately to Sierra Leone, which he did on February 28. The Secretary General further documented other activities by the RUF in the northern and eastern provinces that impeded the peace process. RUF violations of the ceasefire included ambushes against civilians, maintaining illegal roadblocks, and obstructing the peacekeeping operation.

Other incidents involving the RUF included a January 10 incident in which RUF elements seized a large number of weapons, ammunition, and vehicles from convoys of Guinean troops moving to join UNAMSIL. Additionally, members of the UNAMSIL Kenya battalion were ambushed and forced to surrender their weapons to former soldiers of the Sierra Leone Army and RUF rebels. RUF rebels also disarmed and detained 14 soldiers of ECOMOG, who were providing escort for a humanitarian non-governmental organization on its way to collect child combatants at Kabala on January 18.[95] On February 23, a convoy consisting of an Indian battalion moving from Kenema to Daru was stopped by a large contingent of well-armed RUF fighters, who refused to allow the UNAMSIL convoy to proceed, despite repeated assurances from the RUF leadership that UNAMSIL's freedom of movement would be respected. Other isolated incidents included an exchange of gunfire between rebels and a patrol unit of UNAMSIL, and a standoff between RUF fighters and UNAMSIL at Magburaka, in which a United Nations helicopter was prevented from landing.[96]

The Secretary General concluded his report by voicing concern about the negative and confusing approach taken by Mr Sankoh to key provisions of the peace process and the role entrusted to the United Nations. The RUF's hostile remarks about UNAMSIL and its mandate, he said, had increased tension between RUF fighters and UNAMSIL troops.[97] The Secretary General also questioned Mr Sankoh's and the RUF's commitment to implementing the Peace Agreement in good faith. In short, the Secretary General underscored some key problem areas with the United Nations mission in Sierra Leone. The Secretary General said that the international community was showing sign of growing frustration with the RUF leader and his refusal to fully disarm his rebels, and his intention to resume fighting if his party lost the general election scheduled for 2001.[98]

On May 1, 2000, the peace process in Sierra Leone suffered a serious setback, following RUF failure to comply with key provisions of the Lomé Agreement. RUF forces refused to disarm and enter the reintegration program, as required by the Lomé Agreement. They launched a series of attacks on UNAMSIL and took 500 peacekeepers hostage. The incident was planned to coincide with the withdrawal of the remaining Nigerian contingent of ECOMOG. The RUF resisted efforts by UNAMSIL to disarm and staged demonstrations in opposition to the plan. The attack on UNAMSIL disrupted the United Nations operation and cast doubt on the United Nations' ability to learn from its mistakes. Similar attacks on United Nations missions in Somalia and Bosnia were supposed to have led to improvements in United Nations peacekeeping operations. Sierra Leone underscored the inadequacy of United Nations peacekeeping initiatives, and the experience calls for a fundamental overhaul of the way peacekeeping missions are organized and deployed.

The hostage incident led to a resumption of the war in Sierra Leone and further exacerbated the crisis in United Nations peacekeeping operations. Former Sierra Leone Army (SLA) soldiers and Civil Defense Forces combatants took up arms against RUF forces. Civilians also organized a huge demonstration in front of Mr Sankoh's residence and attacked his security force. Several civilians and a few of Sankoh's security men were killed in the exchange of gunfire. Sankoh evaded arrest and was on the run for several days before he was captured by ex-SLA troops and turned over to the government. United Nations peacekeepers were later released after Charles Taylor of Liberia intervened and persuaded the RUF to release the hostages.[99] This episode led to a review of UNAMSIL's mandate and an increase in troop strength.

During the crisis, British troops intervened to evacuate British nationals from Sierra Leone. British troops seized the airport and guarded checkpoints leading to and from the airport and key locations in Freetown. The British presence gave a boost to pro-government forces, which prevented the RUF from launching a major offensive on Freetown.[100] The RUF continued their illicit export of diamonds through Liberia and used the proceeds to purchase additional weapons. The Security Council imposed a ban on the export and sale of Sierra Leonean diamonds and established a diamonds certification regime to determine the origin of all diamonds.[101]

On May 19 the Security Council adopted resolution 1299 (2000) by which it expanded UNAMSIL to a maximum of 13,000 military personnel, including the 260 military observers already deployed. The Security Council expressed its appreciation to all states who, in order to expedite the rapid reinforcement of UNAMSIL, accelerated the deployment of their troops to UNAMSIL, made available additional personnel, and offered logistical, technical, and other forms of military assistance. Acting under Chapter VII of the Charter of the United Nations, the Security Council decided to lift the restrictions set in paragraph 2 of resolution 1171 (1998) regarding the sale and supply of arms and related materiel for use in Sierra Leone for those states cooperating with UNAMSIL and the government of Sierra Leone.[102]

The taking of United Nations peacekeepers hostage in Sierra Leone was the worst crisis to hit the organization since the crises in Somalia and Bosnia. The Security Council reacted negatively to the situation, but took no drastic measures to warn other rebel organizations that such actions would be met by a strong show of force by the international community. With the exception of Britain, other Permanent Members of the Security Council refused to send troops to Sierra Leone. The United States, in light of its previous experience in Somalia, refused to even consider using force to extricate United Nations peacekeepers. Instead, the United States offered to train a contingent of Nigerian troops to be deployed alongside UNAMSIL but operating under different rules of engagement.[103]

The crisis in Sierra Leone underscores the vulnerability of United Nations peacekeepers, who are inadequately trained and ill-equipped to carry out such dangerous missions. The majority of the troops in Sierra Leone were drawn from developing countries, whose presence was strictly for the cash payment their governments received, instead of for their ability to enforce a peace agreement. These soldiers have little or no training and carry inferior weapons and ammunition. The RUF was better trained and carried more sophisticated weapons than United Nations forces. The refusal of the major powers to participate in the Sierra Leone mission sent the wrong message to the RUF, who was able to undermine the peace process with impunity. More importantly, UNAMSIL was given a mandate, but not the means to implement it. This placed UNAMSIL at a disadvantage and made its position extremely vulnerable. Relative stability was subsequently restored throughout Sierra Leone. UNAMSIL was able to exert a greater degree of control over the entire country, and with the support of British troops, was able to provide a sense of security that made it possible for political activities to resume.

International Legal Issues Related to the Conflict in Sierra Leone

The Sierra Leone conflict raised some serious legal concerns regarding intervention by regional arrangements. ECOWAS initially authorized the deployment of a peacekeeping force in Sierra Leone, but later augmented the mandate to allow for ECOMOG to carry out enforcement measures.[104] ECOWAS did not request prior authorization from the Security Council, and did not report to the Security Council after its intervention. As a regional organization, ECOWAS is restricted by Article 53 of the Charter of the United Nations from using force against another state without the consent of the Security Council. The Security Council initially supported the ECOWAS peace-making effort in Sierra Leone, but it stopped short of deciding whether ECOWAS was in violation of the United Nations Charter. Some scholars have argued that by the Security Council not condemning the ECOWAS intervention as illegal, it tacitly approved the organization's action *post facto*.[105] However, the Security Council made no clear declaration to that effect and its statement cannot be interpreted as such.

ECOWAS followed a precedent it previously established in Liberia, when it intervened without the authorization of the Security Council and was not sanctioned for its action.[106] Instead, the Security Council subsequently endorsed the ECOWAS peace-making initiative in Liberia and exempted ECOWAS from the arms embargo imposed on Liberia.[107] In the same resolution, the Security Council called on member states to provide assistance to ECOWAS in its effort to bring peace to Liberia. ECOWAS also acted on the realization that the international community was indifferent to African conflicts and was generally reluctant to intervene. Had ECOWAS not intervened, the conflict in Sierra Leone could have spread to other neighboring states and destabilized the entire region.

ECOWAS initially claimed that it intervened in Sierra Leone on the invitation of the government of Sierra Leone, which was in exile in Guinea but still recognized by the international community as the legitimate government of Sierra Leone.[108] ECOWAS also justified its intervention on grounds of self-defense, restoring democracy, stopping atrocities committed against the civilian population, the threat to regional peace and security, and to prevent possible genocide by the military junta.[109]

It is disputable whether a government has a legitimate right to invite foreign forces onto its territory to quash a rebellion or coup. External intervention would deprive the population of its legitimate right to self-determination. A state supplying arms to the rebels would be in violation of international law.[110] Similarly, the government would also be violating international law if it invited foreign troops onto its soil to put down a rebellion. The fact that the government of Sierra Leone was in exile and did not have effective control over its territory would make reliance on its invitation less convincing. A government which is not in full control of its national territory does not have the right to invite foreign troops into a state it does not control. Notwithstanding the fact that the international community continued to recognize President Kabbah's government as the legitimate government of Sierra Leone, this did not give him the right under international law to invite foreign forces into Sierra Leone to overthrow the military government. By inviting foreign troops to intervene in Sierra Leone to restore him to power, President Kabbah raised questions about his legitimacy. Previous attempts to justify intervention in internal conflicts by the invitation of the host government have been condemned by the international community as illegal.[111]

The second issue is whether ECOWAS had a right to self-defense under international law and Article 51 of the Charter of the United Nations. Under Article 51 a state has an inherent right to individual or collective self-defense if an armed attack occurs. In the Sierra Leone situation, no member state of ECOWAS had been attacked by the military junta. Nigeria, the leading member of ECOWAS, claimed that it was the victim of an armed attack after RUF forces fired on its troops which were stationed in Sierra Leone as part of ECOMOG. To the contrary, Nigeria may have acted in violation of Article 2 (4) of the Charter of the United Nations after its naval forces bombarded rebel bases in Freetown. Nigeria also used excessive force against the military junta in violation of the laws and customs of war. Nigeria's actions were inconsistent with Article 2 (4) of the United Nations Charter and the ECOWAS treaty. Its actions violated Sierra Leone's territorial integrity and political independence.[112]

A more controversial claim made by ECOWAS was that it intervened in Sierra Leone to restore democracy. The doctrine of democratic intervention has not been recognized under international law. The majority of the Member States of the United Nations are not democratic, and nor is Nigeria, which led the intervention. Nigeria was under military rule at the time the democratic government of Sierra Leone was overthrown. The Nigerian military regime came to power by intervening in the electoral process to prevent Moshood Abiola, the man who allegedly won the election, from taking office. The Abacha regime had the worst human rights record in Africa, and was by far one of the most undemocratic regimes in the world. Nigeria, therefore, had no moral authority to lead a military expedition to restore a democratic government in Sierra Leone, when it could not comply with the will of its own people, as manifested in a free and fair democratic electoral process.[113]

During the Cold War the United States intervened in Guatemala, Cuba, the Dominican Republic, Grenada, and Panama on the basis of restoring democracy to those countries. However, none of these claims were recognized as a legitimate exception to Article 51 of the Charter of the United Nations.[114] The United States' actions were condemned by an overwhelming majority of states in the United Nations General Assembly as flagrant violations of international law. The United States also invoked the intervention by invitation doctrine in the cases of the Dominican Republic, Grenada, and Panama, but this claim was equally rejected. Similar attempts by the Soviet Union to use the intervention by invitation doctrine in Hungary, Czechoslovakia, and Afghanistan were condemned by the General Assembly as violations of international law and the sovereignty of those states.[115]

Since the end of the Cold War there has been a gradual shift in the attitude of states toward intervention to restore democracy. Some scholars have even argued that such a right is legitimate under international law.[116] In 1994 the Security Council authorized military intervention in Haiti to remove the military junta and restore the democratically elected government of President Aristide. Both the OAS and the OSCE have adopted declarations to recognize the democratic process as supreme. The Copenhagen Charter and the Santiago Declaration call on member states not to recognize regimes that come into power through undemocratic or unconstitutional means. Both measures call on member states to impose sanctions on such regimes.[117] The right of peoples to participate in the governments of their states is recognized as a fundamental human right under the Universal Declaration of Human Rights, and the Covenant on Civil and Political Rights. A majority of states are parties to these agreements and recognize this right as inalienable. Every state constitution recognizes the right of its citizens to participate in their government. A regime that comes to power through undemocratic or unconstitutional means cannot invoke international law to insulate itself from international condemnation or expulsion. Such a regime would be considered illegitimate; however, there is no consensus on the use of force to remove the regime from power.[118]

The ECOWAS action was consistent with the post-Cold War shift in attitude toward undemocratic regimes. It was based on the precedent established by the United Nations in the Haitian situation. Although ECOWAS was not authorized by the Security Council to intervene in Sierra Leone, it acted on the request of the internationally-recognized government of Sierra Leone, which was still recognized as the legitimate government. The Security Council had previously condemned the coup in Sierra Leone and called for the immediate restoration of the elected government.[119] The OAU had also condemned the coup and called on the international community not to recognize the military junta. From an international standpoint the military regime in Sierra Leone was an illegal regime that violated international law. Kabbah's government was still recognized as the legitimate government of Sierra Leone; hence, an invitation from Kabbah to ECOWAS was perfectly legal under international law.

ECOWAS also based its intervention in Sierra Leone on the issue of human rights violations and the threat of genocide. Humanitarian intervention has been a practice of states since the 18th century; however, it was never considered legal under customary international law.[120] Since the coming into force of the Charter of the United Nations, all such practices have been banned under Article 2 (4) of the Charter. In the few instances in which states invoked humanitarian intervention, such as India in Bangladesh, Tanzania in Uganda, and the United States in the Dominican Republic, Grenada, and Panama, the international community condemned these claims as a violation of international law and the sovereignty of the targeted states.[121] Since the end of the Cold War states have been more receptive to the idea of humanitarian intervention.

In 1991 the Security Council adopted resolution 688 (1991) by which it authorized humanitarian intervention in northern and southern Iraq to protect Kurdish and Shi'ite refugees, respectively. In 1992 the Security Council invoked Chapter VII of the Charter of the United Nations to establish several civilian safe havens in Bosnia, and authorized NATO to use air power to protect these safe areas.[122] The Security Council also authorized UNPROFOR to use force to protect aid convoys trying to deliver humanitarian relief supplies to the safe areas (resolution 770).[123] In 1993 the Security Council authorized intervention in Somalia (resolution 794) to protect humanitarian aid convoys and safeguard food distribution to the civilian population.[124] The Security Council also authorized intervention in Rwanda (resolution 929), and Haiti (resolution 940) to protect human rights.[125]

Human rights have gained prominence in international law, and states can no longer invoke sovereignty to shield their treatment of their nationals from international scrutiny. There is an emerging consensus that intervention to protect human rights is perfectly legitimate under international law and the Charter of the United Nations. The real question is whether intervention to protect human rights must be authorized by the Security Council for it to be considered legal. Nothing in the Charter of the United Nations gives the Security Council the sole authority to protect human rights, unless the human rights situation constitutes a threat to international peace and security. Given the circumstances under which human rights abuses take place and the need for an urgent response to prevent further atrocities, it seems appropriate that states or regional organizations closest to the event have a responsibility to act. Deliberations in the Security Council on such issues take too long and are too unpredictable to rely on. The Security Council does not have a monopoly over the use of force to protect human rights. Human security is a global responsibility and every state is entitled to act when a government is unwilling or unable to protect the human rights of its citizens. Hence, the ECOWAS intervention in Sierra Leone to protect human rights was consistent with emerging human rights norms and state practice in the post-Cold War era.

The restoration of the government of President Kabbah was welcomed by the Security Council, and the sanctions imposed on the military junta were lifted soon thereafter. The actions of the Security Council were an endorsement of the ECOWAS military action in Sierra Leone, albeit late. The Security Council later approved the deployment of a peacekeeping force for Sierra Leone to help with the implementation of the Lomé Peace Agreement. The intransigence of the Security Council in handling the Sierra Leone situation is the topic of the following section.

The Security Council and the Conflict in Sierra Leone

The failure of the Security Council to address the crisis in Sierra Leone may have precipitated ECOWAS to intervene to reverse a deteriorating human rights situation. The Security Council initially ignored the situation in Sierra Leone, hoping it would go away or would be resolved by a regional organization. ECOWAS, which had previously intervened in Liberia without the authorization of the Security Council, assumed it could take similar action in Sierra Leone without consulting the Security Council. The Security Council violated United Nations law by not specifically faulting ECOWAS for its failure to consult the Security Council before using force in Sierra Leone. The Security Council also abdicated its responsibility by not taking the necessary measures to halt the deterioration of the security situation in Sierra Leone. The lack of interest in Sierra Leone by the Security Council meant that a state or group of states had the right to act to save lives.

In the past the Security Council has paid lip service to African conflicts, leaving the OAU and ECOWAS to assume responsibility for restoring peace and security in African states.[126] In recent years individual states and regional organizations have assumed a greater role in maintaining regional stability. The Security Council has also encouraged such developments. It is wrong to assume that the Security Council can and will intervene in every regional conflict. ECOWAS acted out of necessity to save lives in Sierra Leone. The Security Council did not provide the global leadership necessary for managing the conflict in Sierra Leone; hence, it cannot blame a regional organization for acting. The Security Council's failure to act early in Sierra Leone was a violation of its responsibility under Chapter VII of the Charter of the United Nations.

The Establishment of the Special Court for Sierra Leone

In the wake of UNAMSIL's hostage crisis and the death of several peacekeepers, the Security Council condemned the violence against UNAMSIL and warned members of the RUF that they would be held individually responsible for violating international humanitarian law.[127]

On the request of the Security Council, the Secretary General concluded an agreement with the government of Sierra Leone to establish a Special Court for Sierra Leone to prosecute those persons most responsible for serious violations of international humanitarian law and Sierra Leonean law committed in the territory of Sierra Leone since November 30, 1996.[128] The Special Court was granted the power to prosecute crimes against humanity, the commission or ordering of violations of Article 3 common to the Geneva Conventions for the Protection of War Victims and Additional Protocol II thereto, and serious violations of international humanitarian law, including abduction and forced recruitment into armed forces of children under 15 for their active participation in hostilities.[129] The Special Court was to hold persons committing such crimes individually responsible, regardless of their official position. The Special Court would also have the power to prosecute certain crimes under Sierra Leonean law related to the abuse of girls or the wanton destruction of property.[130] The Special Court would have jurisdiction over accused persons who were 15 years old or older at the time of the alleged crime's commission.

The Special Court in Sierra Leone was to have concurrent jurisdiction, although the Special Court would have primacy, and may formally request a national court to defer its competence at any stage of procedure.[131] No person tried by the Special Court could be tried before a Sierra Leonean national court for the same acts. The Special Court shall have its seat in Sierra Leone and consist of two Trial Chambers and an Appeals Chamber.[132] The Appeals Chamber's deliberations were to be guided by decisions of the Appeals Chamber of the International Criminal Tribunals for the Former Yugoslavia and Rwanda. The Rules of Procedure and Evidence of the International Criminal Tribunal for Rwanda would be applicable, *mutatis mutandis*, to the Special Court proceedings.[133]

The situation in Sierra Leone gradually began returning to normal and the country prepared for elections, which were scheduled for May 2002. The RUF cooperated with UNAMSIL and registered itself as a legitimate political party. UNAMSIL also regained control of a majority of Sierra Leonean territory that was previously under RUF control. Regular meetings between UNAMSIL and the RUF helped to improve relations between the two sides. On March 28, the Security Council adopted resolution 1400 (2002) by which it extended the mandate of UNAMSIL for a period of six months from March 30. However, events in Liberia and Guinea threatened the peace process in Sierra Leone, and made a long-term presence for UNAMSIL in Sierra Leone seem inevitable.

The Security Council, NATO, and the Situation in Kosovo

Kosovo was an integral part of the Federal Republic of Yugoslavia (FRY), but populated with a majority ethnic Albanian population. Under the revised Yugoslav Constitution of 1974, Kosovo was granted significant autonomy. However, in 1989, with the collapse of the Socialist Republic of Yugoslavia, President Milošević abolished Kosovo's autonomy.[134] President Milošević stripped ethnic Albanians of all basic political, social, and cultural rights, and their jobs in the provincial government were given to ethnic Serbs. He also abolished the use of the Albanian language in schools and in official government activities in the province. Serb repression of the ethnic Albanian population increased under Milošević. In response to the crackdown, ethnic Albanians organized an armed resistance under the Kosovo Liberation Army (KLA), an umbrella organization comprising several groups. They launched sporadic attacks against targets under the control of the Serbian security forces, with the initial goal of driving the Serbs out. However, as the conflict intensified, the Albanians began advocating secession from the FRY.[135] In 1998, Yugoslav authorities launched a major military offensive against the KLA and their civilian supporters. Many Albanian villages were destroyed and hundreds of civilians were killed. Over two hundred thousand civilians were displaced from their homes, and many took refuge in neighboring Albania and Macedonia.[136]

On March 9 and 25, 1998, the Security Council heard statements from the Foreign Ministers of France, Germany, Italy, the Russian Federation, the United Kingdom, and the United States (the Contact Group), including a proposal on a comprehensive arms embargo on the Federal Republic of Yugoslavia, to include Kosovo.[137] On March 31 the Security Council adopted resolution 1160 (1998) by which it condemned the use of excessive force by Serbian police forces against civilians and peaceful demonstrators in Kosovo, as well as acts of terrorism by the Kosovo Liberation Army or any other group or individual.[138] It called for a halt to all external support for terrorist activity in Kosovo, including finance, arms, and training.

Acting under Chapter VII of the Charter, the Security Council further called upon the Federal Republic of Yugoslavia to immediately take the necessary measures to achieve a political solution to the issue of Kosovo through dialogue, and to implement the actions indicated in the Contact Group statements of March 9 and 25, 1998.[139] The Security Council called upon the Kosovar Albanian leadership to condemn all acts of terrorism, and it emphasized that all elements in the Kosovar Albanian community should pursue their goals by peaceful means only. The Security Council also called on the authorities in Belgrade to offer the Kosovar Albanian community a genuine political process. The Security Council further called upon the authorities in Belgrade and the Kosovar Albanian community urgently to enter, without preconditions, into a meaningful dialogue on political status issues. The Security Council indicated the readiness of the Contact Group to facilitate such a dialogue and expressed its support for an enhanced status for Kosovo, to include a substantially greater degree of autonomy and meaningful self-administration.[140]

Additionally, the Security Council decided that all states shall prevent the sale or supply to the Federal Republic of Yugoslavia, including Kosovo, by their nationals or from their territories or using their flag vessels and aircraft, of arms and related materiel of all types, such as weapons and ammunition, military vehicles and equipment and spare parts for the aforementioned, and shall prevent arming and training for terrorist activities there. Finally, the Security Council urged the Office of the Prosecutor of the International Tribunal established pursuant to resolution 827 (1992) of May 25, 1992, to begin gathering information related to the violence in Kosovo that was potentially within its jurisdiction.[141] The Security Council also noted that the authorities of the Federal Republic of Yugoslavia had an obligation to cooperate, and that the Contact Group countries would make available to the Tribunal substantiated relevant information in their possession.

The Security Council resolution had little effect on the fighting in Kosovo. Instead, fighting intensified, and the humanitarian situation further deteriorated. Yugoslav security forces continued their campaign of destroying Albanian villages and indiscriminately killing Albanian civilians. On September 23, 1998 the Security Council convened a session on the situation in Kosovo. The Security Council adopted resolution 1199 (1998), in which it indicated its concern at the recent escalation in fighting in Kosovo, and in particular, the excessive and indiscriminate use of force by Serbian security forces and the Yugoslav Army.[142] The renewed fighting resulted in numerous casualties and, according to estimates of the Secretary General, displacement of over 23,000 persons from their homes.[143] The Security Council further expressed its deep concern over the flow of refugees into northern Albania, as well as the increasing numbers of displaced persons within Kosovo and other parts of the FRY. The United Nations High Commissioner for Refugees estimated that over 50,000 civilians were without shelter and other basic necessities. The Security Council reaffirmed the right of the refugees and displaced persons to return to their homes in safety, and underlined the responsibility of the FRY for creating the conditions necessary for their return.[144]

In resolution 1199 (1998) Security Council condemned all acts of violence by any party, as well as terrorism in pursuit of political goals by any group or individual. The resolution placed a ban on all external support for such military activities in Kosovo, including the supply of arms and training for terrorist activities in Kosovo, and it expressed concern at the reports of continuing violations of the prohibitions imposed by resolution 1160 (1998).[145] The Security Council warned of the deteriorating humanitarian situation in Kosovo and the increasing violations of human rights. The Security Council further affirmed that the deterioration of the situation in Kosovo constituted a threat to peace and security in the region.[146] Acting under Chapter VII of the Charter, the Security Council demanded that all parties, groups and individuals immediately cease hostilities and maintain a cease fire in Kosovo, in order to enhance the prospects for a meaningful dialogue between the authorities of the Federal Republic of Yugoslavia and the Kosovo Albanian leadership and reduce the risks of a humanitarian catastrophe.[147] The Security Council also demanded that the authorities of the FRY and the Kosovo Albanian leadership take immediate steps to improve the humanitarian situation and to avert an impending humanitarian disaster.

The Security Council called on the authorities of the FRY and the Kosovo Albanian leadership to enter into a meaningful dialogue without preconditions and with international involvement, and to establish a clear timetable leading to an end of the crisis and to a negotiated political solution on the issue of Kosovo. The Security Council endorsed current efforts aimed at facilitating such a dialogue. The Security Council further demanded that the FRY, in addition to the measures called for under resolution 1160 (1998), implement immediately the following concrete measures toward achieving a political solution to the situation in Kosovo as contained in the Contact Group statement of June 12, 1998:

(1)   Cease all action by the security forces affecting the civilian repression;
(2)   Enable effective and continuous international monitoring in Kosovo by the European Community Monitoring Mission and diplomatic missions accredited to the FRY, including access and complete freedom of movement of such monitors to, from, and within Kosovo unimpeded by government authorities, and expeditious issuance of appropriate travel documents to international personnel contributing to the monitoring;
(3)   Facilitate an agreement with the UNHCR and the International Committee of the Red Cross (ICRC) on the safe return of refugees and displaced persons to their homes and allow free and unimpeded access for humanitarian organizations and supplies to Kosovo;
(4)   Make rapid progress to a clear timetable in the dialogue referred to in paragraph 3 with the Kosovo Albanian community called for in resolution 1160 (1998), with the aim of agreeing confidence-building measures and finding a political solution to the problems in Kosovo. The Security Council decided that unless the concrete measures demanded in this resolution and resolution 1160 (1998) are taken that it would consider further action and additional measures to maintain and restore peace and stability in the region.[148]

In his October 3 report, Secretary General Kofi Annan confirmed to the Security Council the impact of the fighting on the civilian population in Kosovo and the human toll the fighting was inflicting on ethnic Albanian communities. The Secretary General made a very bleak assessment of the humanitarian situation in Kosovo. He accused Serbian security forces of using terror and violence against civilians to force them to flee their homes or the places where they had sought refuge. He also said that the disproportionate use of force and actions of the Serbian security forces were designed to subjugate the population; a form of collective punishment to teach the ethnic Albanian civilians the price of supporting the Kosovo Albanian paramilitary units.[149]

In anticipation of the Secretary General's report to the Security Council, the FRY announced an end to its military offensive in Kosovo and ordered the withdrawal of tanks and other heavy armor from the province. The FRY also withdrew its forces from certain parts of Kosovo.[150] The withdrawals, however, did not fulfill the requirements of Security Council resolution 1199 (1998). Attacks against civilians, including massacres in villages west of the capital, Pristina, continued unabated. Many nations were outraged by the continuing violence, and some called for air strikes against FRY military units and installations unless President Milošević complied with the demands of the Security Council.[151] Russia and China opposed United Nations authorization for use of force in Kosovo and threatened to use their veto if the matter came up for a vote in the Security Council. China continued to insist that the conflict in Kosovo was an internal matter that fell outside the jurisdiction of the Security Council. China was also concerned that an authorized United Nations intervention in Kosovo would set a dangerous precedent that could be invoked against its occupation of Tibet. Russia opposed a United Nations-authorized intervention in Kosovo for fear it would legitimize NATO's hegemony in the Balkans. Russia was also concerned that the Security Council would condemn its actions in Chechnya.[152]

Diplomatic efforts to end the conflict in Kosovo were initiated separately by the European Union, the United States and Russia. United States Special Envoy Richard Holbrooke went to Belgrade in early October to try to negotiate an agreement with President Milošević to end the conflict in Kosovo. After eight days of talks the negotiations reached a deadlock, and brought Yugoslavia one step closer to a confrontation with NATO. On October 13, NATO approved an 'activation order' authorizing NATO military commanders to conduct limited air strikes and an air campaign in the FRY no later than ninety-six hours after issuance of the order.[153] This was the first time in the history of the alliance that NATO had authorized the use of military strikes against another state on humanitarian grounds without the authorization of the Security Council.[154] NATO's activation order raised some controversial legal issues, for it was authorized against a non-member of the organization that had not previously attacked a member state of NATO. Some NATO members felt it was necessary for NATO to act, given the urgency of the humanitarian situation in Kosovo and the danger of relying on the Security Council, in light of the threat of the Chinese and Russians to veto any resolution that authorized the use of force. NATO acted out of concern for protecting the ethnic Albanian civilian population and preserving order in Europe.

NATO's threat of force expedited the conclusion of an agreement between Richard Holbrooke and President Milošević. That agreement called for a ceasefire, the withdrawal of FRY military forces and heavy artillery from Kosovo, to be verified from the air by NATO, and from the ground by two thousand unarmed OSCE observers.[155] The agreement also provided for OSCE observers to monitor relief groups assisting ethnic Albanian refugees, for elections to be held in Kosovo, and for setting up a political framework for addressing Kosovo's future.[156] On October 15 the Chief of General Staff of the FRY and the Supreme Allied Commander of NATO signed an agreement providing for the establishment of an air verification mission over Kosovo to complement the OSCE mission.[157] On October 16 the Minister of Foreign Affairs of the FRY and the Chairman-in-Office of the OSCE signed an agreement providing for the OSCE to establish a verification mission in Kosovo, including the undertaking of the FRY to comply with resolutions 1160 (1998) and 1199 (1998).[158]

The KLA reacted negatively to the accord in protest at not being consulted by Richard Holbrooke during the negotiations. The KLA said its forces would continue fighting until the FRY withdrew its forces from Kosovo. The FRY initially showed signs of complying with the accord by withdrawing some of its forces and weaponry from Kosovo, as required by the agreement. However, observers reported continued violence by the security forces against ethnic Albanian civilians and attacks on FRY forces by the KLA.

The Security Council welcomed the efforts to bring peace to Kosovo through the agreement signed between Richard Holbrooke and President Milošević, and the implementation agreements between the FRY, NATO, and the OSCE. On October 24 the Security Council adopted resolution 1203 (1998), by which it reaffirmed the authority granted to the Security Council under the Charter of the United Nations for maintaining international peace and security.[159] The Security Council reiterated its support for a peaceful resolution of the Kosovo problem, which would include an enhanced status for Kosovo, a substantially greater degree of autonomy, and meaningful self-determination.[160] In addition, the Security Council condemned all acts of violence by any party, as well as terrorism in pursuit of political goals by any group or individual. The Security Council reiterated its ban on all external support for such activities in Kosovo, including the supply of arms and training for terrorist activities in Kosovo, and expressed concern at the reports of continuing violations of the prohibitions imposed by resolution 1160 (1998).[161]

Acting under Chapter VII of the Charter of the United Nations, the Security Council:

(1)   Endorses and supports the agreements signed in Belgrade on October 15 and 16 between the FRY and NATO and the FRY and the OSCE, concerning the verification of compliance by the FRY and all others concerned in Kosovo with the requirements of its resolution 1199 (1998), and demands the full and prompt implementation of these agreements by the FRY;

(2)   Notes the endorsement by the government of Serbia of the accord reached by the President of the FRY and the United States Special Envoy, and the public commitment of the FRY to complete negotiations on a framework for a political settlement by November 2, 1998, and called for the full implementation of these commitments;

(3)   Demands that the FRY complies fully with resolutions 1160 (1998) and 1199 (1998) and cooperate fully with the OSCE Verification Mission in Kosovo and the NATO Verification Mission over Kosovo, according to the terms of the agreements referred to in paragraph 1 above;

(4)   Demands also that the Kosovo Albanian leadership and all other elements of the Kosovo Albanian community comply fully and swiftly with resolutions 1160 (1998)

and 1199 (1998) and cooperate fully with the OSCE Verification Mission in Kosovo.[162]

In late 1998 the prosecutor for the ICTY was prevented from entering Kosovo to investigate possible acts of genocide committed by Yugoslav security forces in the deaths of several ethnic Albanians. The president of the ICTY called on the Security Council to condemn the Federal Republic of Yugoslavia for its failure to cooperate with the Tribunal, as required under Security Council resolution 827 (1993).[163] At the urging of the Tribunal, the Security Council adopted resolution 1207 (1998) by which it deplored the failure of the Federal Republic of Yugoslavia to cooperate with the Tribunal.[164] Acting under Chapter VII of the Charter of the United Nations, the Security Council:

(1)   Reiterates its decision that all states shall cooperate fully with the Tribunal and its organs in accordance with resolution 827 (1993) and the Statute of the Tribunal, including the obligation of states to comply with requests for assistance or orders issued by a Trial Chamber under Article 29 of the Statute, to execute arrest warrants transmitted to them by the Tribunal, and to comply with its requests for information and investigations;

(2)   Calls again upon the Federal Republic of Yugoslavia, and all other states which have not already done so, to take any measures necessary under their domestic law to implement the provisions of resolution 827 (1993) and the Statute of the Tribunal, and affirms that a state may not invoke provisions of its domestic law as justification for its failure to perform binding obligations under international law;

(3)   Condemns the failure to date of the Federal Republic of Yugoslavia to execute the arrest warrants issued by the Tribunal against the three individuals referred to in the letter of September 1998, and demands the immediate and unconditional execution of those arrest warrants, including the transfer to the custody of the Tribunal of those individuals;

(4)   Reiterates its call upon the authorities of the Federal Republic of Yugoslavia, the leaders of the Kosovo Albanian community and all others concerned to cooperate fully with the Prosecutor in the investigation of all possible violations within the jurisdiction of the Tribunal.[165]

The presence of OSCE observers on the ground in Kosovo and NATO's air verification mission over Kosovo did little to stop the violence. Following a deadly attack on ethnic Albanian civilians in an open market in Kosovo by Serb security forces, NATO Foreign Ministers intensified their search for a peaceful solution.[166] The KLA also regrouped and increased its attacks on Serb forces. At a NATO Ambassadors' meeting in Brussels, the Ministers strongly condemned the killing of ethnic Albanian civilians, and dispatched its two top generals, General Wesley Clark and General Klaus Nauman, to warn President Milošević of the consequences if the violence continued. NATO called the killings 'a flagrant violation of international humanitarian law'.[167] Acting to prevent a repeat of the Bosnian war, the

United States Secretary of State, Madeleine K. Albright, and the Foreign Ministers from five European states and Russia met in London in late January 1999 to outline a peace initiative for Kosovo. The peace plan called on the Belgrade government and the Kosovo Albanians to approve the interim accord within a fixed deadline.[168]

In early February 1999 the government of the FRY and the various ethnic Albanian factions were invited to Rambouillet, France, to negotiate a peace agreement for Kosovo. The delegations were given little flexibility to change the basic tenets of the plan. They were required to basically approve the peace plan, with minor modifications. The Kosovo peace plan called for granting the ethnic Albanians significant political autonomy, including control of the legislature, police, judiciary, and other functions of regional government, but not independence, as the KLA wanted.[169] Kosovo would remain under Serbian rule for at least three years, after which time a referendum would be held to determine the province's future political status. NATO would deploy a peacekeeping force to monitor the ceasefire and to verify compliance with the agreement.[170] Yugoslavia objected strongly to the presence of foreign troops on its soil and refused to sign the agreement. The sponsors of the talks set a deadline of February 19, 1999 for both sides to approve the agreement without significant modifications. The sponsors issued an ultimatum to President Milošević, calling on him to sign the final document or face NATO air strikes. The Albanian rebels would face severe sanctions on the flow of weapons and money if they rejected the accord.[171]

President Milošević declined to attend the conference, but sent his subordinates to represent the government of Yugoslavia. Milošević refused to negotiate with the KLA, who he considered to be terrorists. He also objected to the deployment of NATO peacekeepers in Kosovo. The KLA and the other ethnic Albanian factions accepted NATO's conditions for participating in the Rambouillet peace talks. Milošević dismissed NATO's threat to use force if his government did not participate. A week after the three-week deadline for concluding the agreement had passed, the parties reached an agreement. The parties returned home to their respective constituents to sell them the plan. The Kosovo Albanian delegation approved the agreement, but the Yugoslav Parliament rejected it. The sponsors gave President Milošević a grace period to reconsider his decision, after which time NATO would use force to against Yugoslavia to halt the war.[172] A Russian envoy attempted to persuade President Milošević to accept the Kosovo plan and avoid an imminent NATO bombing campaign, but President Milošević refused to capitulate. The United States Balkan envoy, Richard Holbrooke, also attempted a last-minute diplomatic mission to Belgrade to persuade President Milošević to accept the peace plan, but he refused. The OSCE withdrew its observers in anticipation of NATO air strikes. With international observers out of the province, FRY security forces committed some of the worst atrocities in the Balkans since the Bosnian war.[173]

The diplomatic strategy employed by the EU and the United States to force President Milošević to accept a negotiated settlement to the Kosovo conflict gave rise to serious concerns. President Milošević was given an ultimatum that required him to attend the

Rambouillet conference and approve the final document, or face NATO air strikes. Article 52 of the Vienna Convention on the Law of Treaties prohibits states from using force or coercion to force another state to sign a treaty or international agreement. The ultimatum given to President Milošević was a clear violation of the Vienna Convention and Yugoslavia's rights as a sovereign state, and President Milošević was right to reject NATO's ultimatum for approving the final document. Article 2 (4) of the United Nations Charter prohibits the threat of use of force in international relations against the territorial integrity or political independence of a Member State of the United Nations, or actions in any manner inconsistent with the Purposes and Principles of the United Nations. The ban on the use of force is a fundamental norm in international law and forms the basis upon which international relations are predicated. The International Court of Justice upheld such a ban as a fundamental norm in its Nicaragua decision.[174] Yugoslavia, therefore, acted within its sovereign rights under international law in rejecting NATO's ultimatum. Had Yugoslavia complied with NATO's demands it would have established a dangerous precedent for international relations.

On March 25 NATO began a bombing campaign against Yugoslav targets in Belgrade. NATO acted without the authorization of the Security Council. The seventy-six day bombing campaign destroyed several of Yugoslavia's bridges, power stations, telecommunication units, and military installations in Belgrade and Kosovo.[175] Initially, President Milošević remained defiant and refused to accept a ceasefire. However, he later agreed to a ceasefire to avoid further damage to his country's economy.[176]

Soon after the air campaign began, Yugoslavia intensified its campaign of expelling ethnic Albanians from Kosovo. The forcible expulsion of ethnic Albanians from their homes in Kosovo into neighboring Albania, Macedonia, Bosnia, and the Republic of Montenegro by Serb security forces led to an unforeseen humanitarian crisis which overwhelmed the resources of UNHCR and other international aid agencies.[177] Serb security forces burned ethnic Albanian villages and killed Albanian men suspected of collaborating with the KLA. The deteriorating humanitarian situation in Kosovo led to criticism of the air campaign and to calls for a ground invasion to halt further expulsion of ethnic Albanians.[178] NATO member states were divided on the issue of a ground invasion. Public opinion in the United States and Western Europe opposed a ground invasion.

Alarmed by the growing humanitarian crisis in Kosovo, the Security Council convened a meeting on May 14, 1999 to review the situation in Kosovo. The Security Council adopted resolution 1239 (1999) by which it expressed its grave concern at the humanitarian catastrophe in and around Kosovo caused by the continuing conflict.[179] The Security Council also expressed its deep concern over the enormous influx of Kosovar refugees into Albania, the former Yugoslav Republic of Macedonia, Bosnia and Herzegovina, and other countries, as well as the increasing numbers of displaced persons within Kosovo, the Republic of Montenegro, and other parts of the Federal Republic of Yugoslavia.[180] The Security Council invited UNHCR and other international humanitarian relief organizations to extend relief assistance to internally displaced persons in Kosovo, the Republic of Montenegro, and other parts of the Federal Republic of Yugoslavia, as well as to other civilians being affected by the ongoing crisis. In a separate development, the ICTY issued a statement saying that it would hold President Milošević personally responsible for the atrocities in Kosovo.[181] The ICTY subsequently indicted President Milošević for crimes against humanity and genocide for the violence committed by Yugoslav forces in Kosovo.[182]

Several meetings between the Russian Balkan Envoy, Viktor Chernomyrdin, and President Milošević failed to bring about an agreement to end the air strikes. Following a flurry of diplomatic initiatives between the United States, Russia, and the EU, it was decided that the EU Special Envoy, Martti Ahtisaari, should go to Belgrade to meet with Milošević to spell out NATO's conditions for suspending the bombing campaign. Russia's Special Envoy Viktor Chernomyrdin accompanied the EU envoy to Belgrade to persuade Milošević to accept NATO's terms for halting the war, or face the possibility of a prolonged air campaign and a possible ground invasion.[183] NATO's terms for ending the air campaign called for an end to the violence and repression against ethnic Albanians, the withdrawal of all Yugoslav forces from Kosovo, the introduction of an international security presence with NATO troops at its core, the safe return of all refugees to their homes, and the start of a political process that would restore self-government to ethnic Albanians in Kosovo.[184]

On June 3 President Milošević accepted NATO's conditions for ending the air campaign.[185] Milošević gave no indication as to why he was accepting NATO's terms for ending the conflict now, seventy-eight days after the bombing began, instead of sooner. Nor is it clear whether NATO made any concessions to Milošević for his acceptance of a ceasefire. However, a few events may have influenced President Milošević's decision. The ICTY indicted President Milošević on May 27, at the peak of NATO's bombing campaign. The Tribunal also issued warrants for the arrest of President Milošević and four of his top associates, including Milan Milutinovic, the Serbian President, Dragoljub Ojdanic, the Chief of Staff of Yugoslav armed forces and former commander of an army corps active in eastern Bosnia, Nikola Sainovic, the Deputy Prime Minister of Yugoslavia, and Vlajko Stojilkovi, the Minister of Internal Affairs.[186] The charges against President Milošević and his associates included the forced deportation of 740,000 ethnic Albanians from Kosovo in 1998, and the murder of more than 340 identified Albanians.[187] President Milošević and his supporters dismissed the charges as politically motivated, and they accused the Chief Prosecutor, Louise Arbour, of misleading the world community.[188]

In addition to his indictment by the Tribunal, President Milošević suffered a major setback before the International Court of Justice (ICJ). On June 2 the ICJ issued its decision on Yugoslavia's request for interim measures to halt the bombing campaign by the participating NATO member states. Yugoslavia had previously instituted proceedings against Belgium, Canada, France, Germany, Italy, the Netherlands, Portugal, Spain, the United Kingdom, and the United States for violating its sovereignty and territorial integrity.[189] In its application,

Yugoslavia maintained that the above states had violated a series of international legal norms, including the Genocide Convention of 1948.[190] The ICJ rejected Yugoslavia's request for interim measures on the basis that it lacked subject matter jurisdiction.[191] The ICJ also dismissed the cases against the United States and Spain. The ICJ further determined that its lack of *prima facie* jurisdiction in the cases against the other states prevented it from issuing provisional measures of protection.[192] The ICJ delayed a final ruling on the jurisdictional phase for a later date.

Yugoslavia also suffered serious physical damage to its bridges, power plants, and communications systems, and the country's economy, which was in already in ruins as a result of several years of international sanctions, was further devastated. President Milošević's ability to wage war and threaten his neighbors was drastically curtailed. More importantly, Yugoslavia's principal ally, Russia, was growing increasingly impatient with Milošević's intransigence. President Yeltsin pressured Milošević to accept NATO's terms for ending the war or face further isolation. Finally, Serb civilians in Belgrade and elsewhere in Yugoslavia were beginning to feel the economic hardship of the bombing campaign and were growing increasingly worried about the impact of a prolonged military campaign that would continue into the winter months.[193]

The international peace proposal President Milošević accepted for ending the conflict in Kosovo called for:

(1) Immediate and verifiable end of the violence and repression in Kosovo;

(2) Verifiable withdrawal from Kosovo of all military, police and paramilitary forces according to a rapid timetable;

(3) Deployment in Kosovo under United Nations auspices of an effective international civil and security presence, acting under Chapter VII of the Charter, capable of guaranteeing the achievement of common objectives;

(4) The international security presence with substantial NATO participation must be deployed under unified command and control and authorized to establish a safe environment for all people in Kosovo and to facilitate the safe return to their homes of all displaced persons and refugees;

(5) Establishment of an interim administration of Kosovo as a part of the international civil presence under which the people of Kosovo can enjoy substantial autonomy within the FRY to be decided by the Security Council of the United Nations. Interim administration to provide transitional administration while establishing and overseeing the development of provisional democratic self-governing institutions to insure conditions for a peaceful and normal life for all inhabitants in Kosovo;

(6) After withdrawal, an agreed number of Yugoslav and Serbian personnel will be permitted to return to perform the following functions:

    (a) Liaison with international civil mission and international security presence.

    (b) Marking/clearing minefields.

(c)   Maintaining a presence at Serb patrimonial sites.

(d)   Maintaining a presence at key border crossings.

(7)   Safe and free return of all refugees and displaced persons under the supervision of the UNHCR and unimpeded access to Kosovo by humanitarian aid organizations;

(8)   A political process towards the establishment of an interim political framework agreement providing for substantial self-government for Kosovo, taking full account of the Rambouillet accords and the principles of sovereignty and territorial integrity of the Federal Republic of Yugoslavia and the other countries of the region, and the demilitarization of the UCK [Kosovo Liberation Army]. Negotiations between the parties for the settlement should not delay or disrupt the establishment of democratic self-governing institutions.

(9)   Comprehensive approach to the economic development and stabilization of the crisis region. This will include the implementation of a Stabilization Pact for South-Eastern Europe with broad international participation in order to further promotion of democracy, economic prosperity, stability and regional cooperation.

(10)   Suspension of military activity will require acceptance of the principles set forth above in addition to agreement to other, previously identified, required elements, which are specified in the footnote below. A military-technical agreement will then be rapidly concluded that would, among other things, specify additional modalities including the roles and function of Yugoslav/Serb personnel in Kosovo.[194]

Following the agreement in Belgrade between the EU Special Envoy and President Milošević, NATO and Yugoslav military officials met on the border of Kosovo to finalize the agreement and begin its implementation. After five hours of negotiations the talks stalled, as Yugoslav military officials asked for time to consult with officials in Belgrade before finally approving the agreement. General Jackson, the head of the NATO delegation, was not sure what aspects of the terms of the withdrawal troubled the Yugoslavs, but was clearly surprised by the delay.[195] The Yugoslavs returned two days later and signed the agreement without objections. Serb forces immediately began their withdrawal, as specified under the terms of the agreement. NATO in return announced a suspension of the bombing campaign on June 9, 1999.[196] The agreement was then submitted to the Security Council for its approval.

On June 10, 1999 the Security Council adopted resolution 1244 (1999) by which it formally approved the peace accord for Kosovo. The resolution condemned all acts of violence against Kosovo's population, as well as all terrorist acts by any party.[197] The Security Council emphasized its determination to resolve the grave humanitarian situation in Kosovo, and provide for the safe and free return of all refugees and displaced persons to their homes. The Security Council reaffirmed its call in previous resolutions for substantial autonomy and meaningful self-administration for Kosovo. The Security Council also determined that the situation in the region continued to constitute a threat to international peace and security.[198]

Acting under Chapter VII of the Charter of the United Nations, the Security Council:

(1) Decides that a political solution to the Kosovo crisis shall be based on the general principles of Annex 1 and as further elaborated in the principles and other required elements in Annex 2;

(2) Welcomes the acceptance by the Federal Republic of Yugoslavia of the principles and other required elements referred to in paragraph 1 above, and demanded the full cooperation of the Federal Republic of Yugoslavia in their rapid implementation;

(3) Demands in particular that the Federal Republic of Yugoslavia put an immediate and verifiable end to violence and repression in Kosovo, and begin/complete verifiable phased withdrawals from Kosovo of all military, police and paramilitary forces according to a rapid timetable, with which the deployment of the international security presence in Kosovo will be synchronized;

(4) Confirms that after the withdrawal an agreed number of Yugoslav and Serb military and police personnel will be permitted to return to Kosovo to perform the functions in accordance with Annex 2;

(5) Decides on the deployment in Kosovo, under United Nations auspices, of civil and security presence, with appropriate equipment and personnel as required, and welcomes the agreement of the Federal Republic of Yugoslavia to such presences;

(6) Requests the Secretary General to appoint, in consultation with the Security Council, a Special Representative to control the implementation of the international civil presence, and further requests the Secretary General to instruct this Special Representative to coordinate closely with the international security presence to ensure that both presences operate towards the same goals and in mutually supportive manner;

(7) Authorizes Member States and relevant international organizations to establish the international security presence in Kosovo as set out in point 4 of Annex 2 with all necessary means to fulfill its responsibilities under paragraph 9 below;

(8) Affirms the need for the rapid early deployment of effective international civil and security presences to Kosovo, and demands that the parties cooperate fully in their deployment;

(9) Decides that the responsibilities of the international security presence to be deployed and acting in Kosovo will include:

    (a) Deterring renewed hostilities, maintaining and where necessary enforcing a ceasefire, and ensuring the withdrawal and preventing the return into Kosovo of Federal and Republic military, police and paramilitary forces, except as provided in point 6 of Annex 2;

    (b) Demilitarizing the Kosovo Liberation Army (KLA) and other armed Kosovo Albanian groups as required in paragraph 15 below;

    (c) Establishing a secure environment in which refugees and displaced persons can return home in safety, the international civil presence can operate, a transitional administration can be established, and humanitarian aid can be delivered;

(d)   Ensuring public safety and order until the international civil presence can take responsibility for this task;

(e)   Supervising de-mining until the international civil presence can, as appropriate, take over responsibility for this task;

(f)   Supporting, as appropriate, and coordinating closely with the work of the international civil presence;

(g)   Conducting border monitoring duties as required;

(h)   Ensuring the protection and freedom of movement of itself, the international civil presence, and other international organizations.[199]

Resolution 1244 (1999) authorized the Secretary General, with the assistance of the relevant international organizations, to establish an international civil presence in Kosovo in order to provide an interim administration for Kosovo under which the people could enjoy substantial autonomy within the Federal Republic of Yugoslavia.[200] The United Nations transitional administration would establish and oversee the development of provisional democratic self-governing institutions in the province to ensure conditions for a peaceful and normal life for all inhabitants of Kosovo.[201] The main responsibilities of the international civil administration would include:

(1)   Promoting the establishment, pending a final settlement, of substantial autonomy and self-government in Kosovo, taking full account of Annex 2 and of the Rambouillet accords;

(2)   Performing basic civilian administrative functions there and as long as required;

(3)   Organizing and overseeing the development of provisional institutions for democratic and autonomous self-government pending a political settlement, including the holding of elections;

(4)   Transferring, as these institutions are established, its administrative responsibilities while overseeing and supporting the consolidation of Kosovo's local provisional institutions and other peace-building activities;

(5)   Facilitating a political process designed to determine Kosovo's future status, taking into account the Rambouillet accords;

(6)   In a final stage, overseeing the transfer of authority from Kosovo's provisional institutions to institutions established under a political settlement;

(7)   Supporting the reconstruction of key infrastructure and other economic reconstruction;

(8)   Supporting, in coordination with international humanitarian organizations, humanitarian and disaster relief aid;

(9)   Maintaining civil law and order, including establishing local police forces, and meanwhile through the deployment of international police personnel to serve in Kosovo;

(10)   Protecting and promoting human rights;

(11)   Assuring the safe and unimpeded return of all refugees and displaced persons to their homes in Kosovo.[202]

Within days of the adoption of Security Council resolution 1244 (1999) the NATO-led multinational force (Kosovo Force, or KFOR) began preparation for its deployment in Kosovo. However, the deployment was interrupted by the premature movement of Russian troops from Bosnia to Kosovo without informing NATO officials. Russian troops occupied the Pristina airport and other strategic locations and refused to allow NATO access. The presence of Russian troops in Kosovo before NATO had worked out the modalities of their deployment under NATO command created tremendous confusion for NATO and the KFOR commander, General Jackson. The confrontation between Russian troops and KFOR almost brought the two forces to the brink of war.[203] Diplomatic consultations between Secretary of State Albright, Secretary of Defense Cohen, and their Russian counterparts, and assurances from Russian officials that Russian troops would withdraw, failed to break the standoff. Russian troops later relinquished control of the airport after they were ordered to do so by President Yeltsin, who met with President Clinton in an attempt to break the impasse. An agreement specifying the terms under which Russian forces would operate within an integrated command structure with the multinational force was later signed between NATO and Russia. Russian troops were subsequently assigned to the German sector, with the remaining sectors divided between the United States, Britain, France, and Italy.[204]

Following the deployment of the NATO-led KFOR, the United Nations Secretary General took the necessary steps to establish a United Nations Interim Administration Mission in Kosovo (UNMIK). UNMIK was vested with broad authority in Kosovo, including legislative, executive, and judicial powers.[205] This new United Nations mission undertaken in Kosovo is by far one of the most ambitious peace-building efforts undertaken by the organization since Cambodia. However, unlike Cambodia, the future political status of Kosovo was not clearly defined. Yugoslavia retained sovereignty over Kosovo under the peace agreement and Security Council resolution 1244 (1999).[206] The United Nations mission in Kosovo was also complicated by the obvious conflict between the goals of the Kosovo Albanian population, Yugoslavia, and of the international community. The United Nations mandate required it to administer Kosovo for a three year interim period, after which time the future political status of the province would be determined. UNMIK did not have a mandate to prepare Kosovo to become an independent state. The ethnic Albanian population saw UNMIK's mission differently; they assumed that UNMIK would ultimately bring about an independent Kosovo.

There was also uncertainty about Kosovo's future status within the Yugoslav Republic. The United Nations Secretary General voiced his opposition to attempts by his Special Representative to convey the impression that the role of the United Nations was to establish an independent Kosovar state. UNMIK established a number of political institutions in Kosovo, and had implemented its mandate by the end of the three-year period. Security Council resolution 1244 (1999) did not specifically address the future political status of Kosovo.[207] It basically postponed the issue to a later date. This led Bernard Kouchner to call on the Security Council to begin considering the issue as UNMIK prepared to implement phase two of its mandate.

On July 12, 1999 the Secretary General submitted his report to the Security Council, detailing the operational framework for the United Nations administration of Kosovo. The Secretary General appointed Dr Bernard Kouchner of France as his Special Representative. Kouchner succeeded Mr Sergio Vieira de Mello, who led the United Nations advance team to Kosovo immediately after the war. Mello established a United Nations presence on the ground, assessed the situation, and finalized an operational concept for the United Nations Mission in Kosovo. Dr Kouchner was to preside over four sectors involved with implementing the civilian aspects of rehabilitating and reforming Kosovo. Those sectors, known as the four pillars, were:

- Civilian administration, under the United Nations itself;
- Humanitarian assistance, led by the Office of the UN High Commissioner for Refugees;
- Democratization and institution-building, led by the Organization of Security and Cooperation in Europe;
- Economic reconstruction, managed by the European Union.[208]

The work of UNMIK was to proceed in five integrated phases, outlined as follows:

Phase I — The Mission will set up administrative structures, deploy international civilian police, provide emergency assistance for returning refugees and displaced people, restore public services and train local police and judiciary. It will also develop a phased economic recovery plan and seek to establish a self-sustaining economy.

Phase II — The focus will be on administration of social services and utilities, and consolidation of the rule of law. Administration of such sectors as health and education could be transferred to local and possibly regional authorities. Preparation for elections will begin.

Phase III — UNMIK will finalize preparations and conduct elections for a Kosovo Transitional Authority.

Phase IV — UNMIK will help Kosovo's elected representatives organize and set up provisional institutions for democratic and autonomous self-government. As these are established, UNMIK will transfer its remaining administrative responsibilities while supporting the consolidation of Kosovo's provisional institutions.

Phase V — This concluding phase will depend on a final settlement of the status of Kosovo. UNMIK will oversee the transfer of authority from Kosovo's provisional institutions to institutions established under a political settlement.[209]

The United Nations Mission in Kosovo got off to a slow start and was overwhelmed by a number of problems it inherited from Yugoslavia. The United Nations was criticized by NATO for not moving quickly to establish an administrative presence in Kosovo, including the deployment of a civilian police force to halt the violence and ethnic retribution that followed the departure of Yugoslav security forces.[210] KFOR, with its focus on securing

Kosovo's borders with Yugoslavia and verifying the departure of Yugoslav security forces from Kosovo, had little time to concentrate on maintaining order among the two ethnic groups in all sectors of the province. The United Nations countered by blaming KFOR for not establishing a security environment conducive to the deployment of United Nations policemen. The United Nations also complained that it had not received the funds member states had pledged for the reconstruction of Kosovo.[211] The United Nations mission was eventually deployed, but the mission was strapped for cash and was paralyzed in carrying out some of its mandate. The complexity of the Kosovo situation made KFOR's and UNMIK's missions extremely difficult.

Kosovo ultimately came under complete international control, with KFOR and UNMIK providing the necessary security and administrative support, respectively, to allow the province to begin to regain some of its past glory. Ethnic violence continued to be of major concern for the international community, as ethnic Albanians and Serbs continued the cycle of violence against each other.[212] The situation remained tense in some communities. The majority of ethnic Albanian refugees who fled their homes during the conflict have since returned to Kosovo, while the majority of Serbs, who made up a fraction of the pre-war population, have mainly fled to Belgrade. The small number of Serbs who remained became the target of retribution by ethnic Albanians, and their homes were torched or occupied by Albanians. Similarly, ethnic Albanians were barred from returning to their homes in the predominantly Serbian town of Metrovica.[213] This resulted in violent confrontations between KFOR and ethnic Albanians. Ethnic Albanians also blocked Russian peacekeepers from entering their towns to patrol, accusing the Russians of siding with the Serbs during the conflict.

The Serbian minority population refused to participate in the provisional council established by UNMIK and asked for permission to establish their own security force in Kosovo to protect Serbs.[214] The United Nations and KFOR acknowledged the continuing ethnic violence in Kosovo and the targeting of non-Albanian minorities, but rejected the proposed Serb Kosovo security force. Kosovo remains a *de facto* partitioned province, with Serbs living behind barbed wire fences in one section of the city and ethnic Albanians occupying the rest of Kosovo. Efforts by UNMIK to reassure Serbs that they can live a normal life in Kosovo without fear of violence were not successful. A grenade attack on an UNMIK bus, which was transporting ethnic Serbs to the main part of Kosovo to conduct business, strengthened Serb opposition to the idea of a multi-ethnic Kosovo.[215]

The KLA completed the terms of its disarmament agreement on schedule and accepted the KFOR-UNMIK proposal to transform itself into a Kosovo Corps, which would perform basic emergency services, but not carry out law-enforcement duties.[216] The KLA established *de facto* political institutions and assumed civic duties in areas where UNMIK did not establish full legal control. Despite the international presence in Kosovo, the province remains very volatile. Criminal elements took control of the economy, and smuggling, prostitution, and gang violence continue to be rampant, with a serious breakdown of law and order in the province. According to an OSCE report in 2000, the courts in Kosovo were corrupt and failed to administer a minimum standard of justice consistent with international standards[217]; in this regard, little has changed. UNMIK lacked the manpower or resources to successfully administer Kosovo.

The international community did not articulate the future political arrangement it envisioned for Kosovo after the expiry of UNMIK's mandate in 2002. Whereas resolution 1244 (1999) provided for a three-year transitional administration for Kosovo, it did not address the province's future political status. It appeared inconceivable, however, that Kosovo would revert to Yugoslav rule, given the bitter divide between the ethnic Albanian and Serb communities.

The Kosovo mission, like most post-Cold War peacekeeping operations, posed a serious dilemma for the international community. United Nations peacekeepers have generally monitored ceasefire agreements and served as buffers between armies. The Kosovo situation required the United Nations to keep two hostile civilian communities apart and to build trust and reconciliation between them. The United Nations also had the difficult task of serving as the legitimate government of Kosovo until such time as the province's future political status could be determined. This new experiment in United Nations peacekeeping, which combined maintaining peace where no peace existed and building new political structures, seemed nearly certain to lead to a very different outcome than originally intended. Kosovo's problems were socio-political in nature and required a new kind of peacekeeping arrangement.

The Legal Aspects of NATO's Intervention in Kosovo

NATO military strikes against Yugoslavia in response to Serb mistreatment of ethnic Albanians raised a series of concerns about the unauthorized use of force by regional arrangements or organizations in humanitarian crisis situations. The primary concern was whether NATO violated international law and the Charter of the United Nations by using military force against Yugoslavia without the authorization of the Security Council. NATO's decision to bypass the Security Council was a strategic decision to avoid being constrained by China or Russia exercising their veto to block the Security Council from adopting a resolution authorizing the use of force against Yugoslavia.[218] The veto would have prevented the United Nations or member states from using force against Yugoslavia to stop the atrocities in Kosovo.

The second concern raised by NATO's use of force against Yugoslavia was whether NATO or any regional organization needs the authorization of the Security Council to use force to stop gross violations of human rights or crimes against humanity being committed against innocent civilians. The human rights situation in Kosovo was appalling, and despite repeated warnings from the international community, including from the Security Council, the violence against civilians continued.[219] NATO had exhausted all diplomatic means to settle the conflict, including by giving President Milošević a grace period to find a peaceful solution to the conflict. In the interim, Yugoslav forces intensified their attacks on civilians and committed some of the worst atrocities. Given Milošević's involvement in atrocities committed against civilians in Bosnia and his refusal to accept a diplomatic solution, NATO had to act in order to avert a repeat of the humanitarian catastrophe that had occurred in Bosnia.

In his address to the nation to announce the commencement of the air strikes against Yugoslavia, President Clinton invoked human rights to justify NATO's action. The President stated:

> We act to protect thousands of innocent people in Kosovo from a mounting military offensive. We act to prevent a wider war, to defuse a powder keg at the heart of Europe that has exploded twice in this century with catastrophic results. And we act to stand united with our allies for peace. By acting now, we are upholding our values, protecting our interests, and advancing the cause of peace.

> We have seen innocent people taken from their homes, forced to kneel in the dirt and sprayed with bullets; Kosovar men dragged from their families, fathers and sons together, lined up and shot in cold blood. This is not a war in the traditional sense. It is an attack by tanks and artillery on a largely defenseless people whose leaders already have agreed to peace.[220]

The United States also raised the issue of Yugoslavia's failure to comply with previous ceasefire agreements endorsed by the Security Council in resolution 1203 (1998), and humanitarian and security considerations in the Balkans.[221] The State Department spokesman, James P. Rubin, also criticized Yugoslavia for failing to comply with previous ceasefire agreements. In one of his daily press briefings, he said: 'The Serbs have failed to comply with the Organization of Security and Cooperation in Europe and NATO verification agreements. They've violated UN Security Council agreements. They're in violation of the requirements of the International Criminal Tribunal and its own unilateral commitments.'[222]

Many states shared the United States' position that the air strikes were justified on the basis of the magnitude of the humanitarian crisis.[223] At a March 26 meeting, the Security Council voted 12 to 3 against a Russian-sponsored resolution condemning the attack as a 'threat to international peace' and a 'flagrant violation' of the United Nations Charter.[224] In a comment to the press, Argentina's representative stated: 'A large majority of nations have acted together to say that no longer will you be able to violate human rights massively over a long period of time without evoking reaction.' He went on to say that 'while not a United Nations endorsement of the NATO attacks, the vote bolstered the legitimacy of what NATO is doing.'[225] The United Nations Secretary General, although critical of NATO for acting without Security Council authorization, implicitly endorsed the air strikes by stating that 'there are times when the use of force may be legitimate in the pursuit of peace.'[226]

The failure of NATO to receive Security Council authorization before launching the air strikes against Yugoslavia was cited by many states, including member states of NATO and the OSCE, as a violation of international law and the Charter of the United Nations.[227] Austria closed its air-space to NATO aircraft, citing the lack of a United Nations mandate for the strikes.[228] Russia recalled its ambassador to NATO and condemned the NATO attacks.[229] Russia argued that regional alliances may act to restore peace and security only upon specific authorization by the Security Council; Belarus, China, India, and Ukraine also condemned the air strikes for similar reasons.[230]

Under Chapter VII of the Charter of the United Nations, the Security Council has the sole responsibility for maintaining international peace and security. Article 51 preserves the inherent right of states to self-defense, if an armed attack occurs. All collective enforcement measures short of self-defense must be authorized by the Security Council.[231] However, states and regional organizations have not always consulted with the Security Council before carrying out collective enforcement measures. States and regional organizations have relied on other justifications, such as an invitation from the government or collective self-defense provisions of a treaty to justify their interventions. In the post-Cold War era, regional organizations are increasingly resorting to collective enforcement measures without the authorization of the Security Council. The Economic Commission of West African States (ECOWAS) intervened in Liberia and Sierra Leone without the authorization of the Security Council[232]; the Security Council did not object to ECOWAS's action.

Since the end of the Cold War the Security Council has authorized collective enforcement measures to protect human rights or for other humanitarian reasons, but the Security Council has been slow to respond to every humanitarian situation, leaving states no choice but to take unilateral measures to protect civilian populations. The inability of the Security Council to respond quickly to stop the atrocities in Rwanda and Bosnia left many observers to question the need to rely on the Security Council when the need to save lives is compelling. The human rights and humanitarian situation in Kosovo was one of those cases which required an immediate response which the Security Council could not provide because of the threat of a veto by China and Russia. NATO military actions against Yugoslavia may have violated Article 2 (4) of the Charter of the United Nations, but it was a temporary breach intended to save the lives of innocent civilians. The sanctity of life should take precedence over state sovereignty in humanitarian situations. NATO acted out of sheer humanitarian consideration, and its actions were consistent with emerging norms of humanitarian intervention to protect human rights.[233]

The Situation in East Timor

East Timor was first placed on the United Nations agenda in 1960, when the General Assembly included the territory on its list of Non-Self-Governing Territories.[234] East Timor was a colony administered by Portugal until 1974, at which time Portugal sought to establish a provisional government and a popular assembly in East Timor to determine its future political status.[235] Portugal's decision led to an outbreak of civil war between pro-independence and pro-Indonesian forces. Unable to halt the unrest, Portugal simply abandoned the territory. Indonesia, which had previously claimed East Timor, invaded the territory, and in 1975 annexed East Timor as its 27th province.[236] The United Nations did not recognize Indonesia's annexation of East Timor, and both the Security Council and the General Assembly called for Indonesia's withdrawal.

On December 12, 1975, the General Assembly adopted resolution 3485, by which it called for the withdrawal of Indonesian troops from East Timor. The General Assembly requested the Special Committee on the Situation with Regard to the Implementation of the Declaration on the Granting of Independence to Colonial Countries and Peoples to send a fact-finding mission to East Timor. On December 22, 1975, the Security Council adopted resolution 384 (1975), by which it reaffirmed the inalienable right of the people of East Timor to self-determination and independence in accordance with the principles of the Charter of the United Nations and the Declaration on the Granting of Independence to Colonial Countries and Peoples, contained in General Assembly resolution 1514 of December 14, 1960.[237] The Security Council called on the government of Indonesia to withdraw, without further delay, all of its forces from East Timor. The General Assembly also reaffirmed East Timor's right to self-determination.[238] From 1982, on the request of the General Assembly, successive Secretaries General held frequent consultations with the governments of Indonesia and Portugal in an attempt to resolve the status of East Timor.[239]

A majority of East Timorese resisted efforts by Indonesia to impose its rule over the territory. The East Timorese organized armed resistance against the Indonesian military for the next 25 years. During the ensuing years, Indonesian troops carried out a reign of terror against the East Timorese people and committed serious human rights abuses. In 1991 the Indonesian military massacred hundreds of innocent civilians who were observing the anniversary of a previous massacre.[240] The incident received widespread international condemnation and brought renewed attention to the situation in East Timor. The Indonesian authorities rebuffed all attempts by the United Nations to find a peaceful solution to the East Timorese conflict.

The New York Agreements on East Timor

In 1998 developments in Indonesia led to the downfall of President Suharto, who had ruled Indonesia for thirty years. Suharto had defied international criticism to keep East Timor under

Indonesian rule. The appointment of a new government in Indonesia headed by B.J. Habibie, and the political turmoil that preceded his appointment, provided a new opportunity to revisit the situation in East Timor.[241] In June 1998 President Habibie proposed limited autonomy for East Timor within Indonesia. He also indicated in a subsequent statement that if the East Timorese rejected his proposal, Indonesia might be faced with losing the territory.[242] In light of this proposal, peace talks began between Indonesia and Portugal under the auspices of the Secretary General and his Personal Representative. The talks made rapid progress, and within weeks a series of agreements were signed between Indonesia and Portugal, and between Indonesia, Portugal, and the United Nations. The New York Agreements entrusted the Secretary General with the authority to organize and conduct a 'popular consultation' in order to ascertain whether the East Timorese people, both inside and outside the territory, accepted or rejected a special autonomy for East Timor within the unitary Republic of Indonesia.[243]

On May 7, 1999 the Security Council adopted resolution 1236 (1999) by which it endorsed the May 5 agreement between the governments of Indonesia and Portugal, and separate agreements between the United Nations and the governments of Indonesia and Portugal.[244] The Security Council endorsed the intention of the Secretary General to establish a United Nations presence in East Timor to implement the agreements, in particular through:

(1)   Conducting a popular consultation of the East Timorese people on the acceptance or rejection of a constitutional framework for an autonomy for East Timor, scheduled for August 8, 1999, in accordance with the General Agreement;

(2)   Making available a number of civilian police officers to act as advisers to the Indonesian Police in the discharge of the duties in East Timor and, at the time of the consultation, to supervise the escort of ballot papers and boxes to and from the polling sites.[245]

Pursuant to resolution 1236 (1999), the Secretary General submitted his report on the situation in East Timor to the Security Council on May 22, 1999, in which he proposed the establishment of the United Nations Mission in East Timor (UNAMET), to organize and conduct a popular consultation in order to ascertain whether the East Timorese people accepted or rejected the proposed constitutional framework providing for a special autonomy for East Timor within the unitary Republic of Indonesia.[246] The Secretary General's proposed mission for East Timor would compromise 241 international staff members and 420 United Nations volunteers, up to 280 civilian police, and 4,000 local staff. UNAMET would have two components: a political unit and an electoral unit. The political unit would monitor the overall implementation of the May 5 Agreements, including responsibility for monitoring the fairness of the political environment and ensuring the freedom of all political and other non-governmental organizations to carry out their activities peacefully. The electoral unit would be responsible for all activities related to registration and voting.[247]

The Deployment of UNAMET

On June 11 the Security Council adopted resolution 1246 (1999) by which it endorsed the Secretary General's proposed mission for East Timor, and established until August 31, 1999 the United Nations Mission in East Timor (UNAMET) for the purpose of organizing and conducting a popular consultation, scheduled for August 8, 1999.[248] The Security Council also authorized until August 31, 1999 the deployment within UNAMET of up to 280 civilian police officers to act as advisers to the Indonesian Police in the discharge of their duties and, at the time of the consultation, to supervise the escort of ballot papers and boxes to and from the polling sites.[249] In addition to the civilian police, the Security Council authorized the deployment within UNAMET of 50 military liaison officers to maintain contact with the Indonesian Armed Forces in order to allow the Secretary General to discharge his responsibilities under the General Agreement and the Security Agreement.[250] The Security Council emphasized the responsibility of the government of Indonesia to maintain peace and security in East Timor, in particular in the context of the security situation referred to in the report of the Secretary General. It called on Indonesia to ensure the security of East Timor in order to ascertain that the popular consultation was carried out in a fair and peaceful way and in an atmosphere free of intimidation, violence, or interference from any side, and to ensure the safety and security of United Nations and other international staff and observers in East Timor.[251]

The United Nations mission in East Timor got off to a slow start. Security and logistical concerns delayed both the voter registration process and the actual voting, which was initially scheduled for August 8.[252] The voter registration process began in mid-July instead of late June, and the referendum was rescheduled for August 22, instead of August 8. Indonesian security forces initially cooperated with UNAMET, but as the voting period drew closer, they ignored threats by anti-independence militia to disrupt the referendum.[253] In the weeks leading up to the referendum, violence escalated against pro-independence supporters and United Nations personnel. The Secretary General postponed the referendum for a second time to August 30. However, despite further threats of violence and intimidation of voters by Indonesian-backed militias, the referendum went ahead as scheduled. Ninety-eight percent of the electorate turned out to vote, and an overwhelming majority of the people voted for independence.[254] The conduct of the referendum was a victory for the people of East Timor and the United Nations.

Post-Referendum Violence in East Timor

Shortly after the result of the referendum was announced, Indonesian-backed militias went on a violent rampage. They burned villages and attacked East Timorese suspected of voting for independence.[255] On September 7 the Security Council dispatched a five-man delegation to Jakarta to confer with the Indonesian government regarding the violence in East Timor and the concrete steps it ought to take to implement the May 5 Agreement. During its four-day visit, the Security Council delegation met with various Indonesian officials, and visited Dili, the capital of East Timor, to survey the violence. On its visit to Dili, the mission stated that it was shocked at the destruction which had taken place in Dili, at the severe loss of confidence in the security provided by local forces, and expressed its distress at the desperate state of the displaced population.[256] The delegation indicated in its report that the Indonesian Armed Forces (or TNI) had done little to stop the violence in East Timor, and in many instances had encouraged and participated in it.[257] The report further stated that the declaration of martial law had not succeeded in stabilizing the situation. Finally, the report stated that tens of thousands of East Timorese who had fled to the Falintil cantonment sites and elsewhere in East Timor were perilously close to starvation.[258]

The mission made the following additional observations: (a) the account given by the government of Indonesia of events in East Timor and action taken by Indonesia to carry out its responsibilities under the May 5 Agreement did not tally with the briefings provided by United Nations staff and senior diplomatic representatives in Jakarta and Dili; (b) the involvement of large elements of the Indonesian military and police in East Timor in organizing and backing the unacceptably violent actions of the militias had become clear to any objective observer and was publicly acknowledged by the Minister of Defense on September 11; (c) the situation of the majority of the population in East Timor and the refugee population in West Timor was extremely grave; (d) there was strong evidence of abuses of international humanitarian law committed since the announcement of the ballot result on September 4 ; (e) Indonesia did not carry out its security responsibility to UNAMET, instead, the authorities allowed UNAMET's situation to deteriorate during the mission's stay; and (f) preparation of United Nations actions to fulfill its responsibilities under phase III of the May 5 Agreement could dovetail with the enhanced security to be provided by international security cooperation in phase II.[259]

The mission made the following recommendations:

(1)　The grave humanitarian crisis in East Timor should be given the utmost priority by the United Nations, in terms both of supply of basic needs to the displaced population, including in West Timor, and of insistence that the government of Indonesia provide access and security to the United Nations and international humanitarian organizations;

(2)　The Security Council should welcome the decision of the president of Indonesia to invite an international peacekeeping force to cooperate with Indonesia in restoring peace and security in East Timor and should adopt a resolution without delay to provide a framework for the implementation of that proposal;

(3)　The Secretary General, advised by his Special Representative in East Timor, should consider reducing to a minimum, or if necessary evacuating, the UNAMET deployment in Dili before the arrival of an international security presence, provided that the safety and welfare of the IDPs in the UNAMET compound has been satisfactorily arranged;

(4)   The Security Council should consider authorizing an advance party of the international security presence to undertake urgent and essential tasks in and around Dili related to UNAMET and the provision of humanitarian supplies;

(5)   The Secretary General should be invited to submit plans for the advance preparation of United Nations action in phase III in ways which contribute to the more effective implementation of phase II under the new circumstances;

(6)   The Security Council should hold the government of Indonesia to its obligations under phase II of the May 5 Agreement, both before and after the arrival of an international security presence, with particular insistence on the proper care of IDPs and on curtailing the role of the militias and preventing any clashes between the militias and Falintil;

(7)   The Security Council should institute action for the investigation of apparent abuses of international humanitarian law on the ground in East and West Timor since September 4.[260]

Following the departure of the United Nations mission from East Timor, the violence escalated. In the wake of the escalation in violence, the United Nations evacuated the majority of its personnel from the territory to Australia. The United Nations reminded the government of Indonesia of its obligation under the May 5 Agreement. Thousands of East Timorese fled their homes and villages to take refuge in the hills or in neighboring West Timor. The humanitarian crisis in East Timor closely paralleled the humanitarian crisis in Kosovo, for which NATO invaded Yugoslavia. Human rights groups condemned the atrocities in East Timor and called for United Nations intervention to stop the violence against civilians.[261] The Security Council refused to authorize the deployment of an international force to stop the violence unless Indonesia gave its consent. Under the New York Agreement, Indonesia had the responsibility for guaranteeing the security of the province; however, its forces failed to do so. As a party to that agreement, the United Nations had a legitimate right to ensure that all the parties complied with their obligations under the terms of the agreement. The complicity of Indonesian security forces in the violence and Indonesia's failure to halt the violence were clear indications that the United Nations could no longer rely on Indonesia and should have had a contingency plan in place in anticipation of further violence. The United Nations should have assumed immediate responsibility for East Timor soon after the outcome of the referendum which rejected Indonesian rule.

Both the Secretary General and the Security Council continued to oppose United Nations intervention to stop the violence.[262] Indonesia also rejected any attempt by the international community to force it to accept an international force in East Timor until its Parliament had ratified the referendum. The United States and the EU suspended military cooperation with the Indonesian military until the violence in East Timor stopped and Indonesia cooperated with the international community in finding a peaceful settlement to the conflict.[263] At its

September 10 meeting in New Zealand, the leaders of the Asian Pacific Economic Conference (APEC) called on Indonesia to cooperate with the international community to end the violence. President Clinton also pressured President Habibie to allow the deployment of a United Nations peacekeeping force in East Timor to stop the violence. On September 12, President Habibie bowed to international pressure and invited the United Nations to deploy a peacekeeping force to join the Indonesian military in restoring order to East Timor.[264]

On September 15 the Security Council held a meeting to review the situation in East Timor. The Security Council adopted resolution 1264 (1999), by which it once again welcomed the successful conduct of the popular consultation of the East Timorese people of August 30 and took note of the outcome, which it regarded as an accurate reflection of the views of the East Timorese people.[265] The Security Council voiced its deep concern regarding the deterioration in the security situation in East Timor, and in particular for the continuing violence against the civilian population. The Security Council also raised concerns about the large-scale displacement and relocation of East Timorese civilians to the western half of the island, which was under Indonesian rule.[266] The Security Council also condemned attacks on the staff and premises of UNAMET. The Security Council affirmed the right of refugees and displaced persons to return in safety and security to their homes. The Security Council welcomed the statement by the President of Indonesia on September 12, expressing the readiness of Indonesia to accept a United Nations-authorized international peacekeeping force in East Timor. Finally, the Security Council determined that the situation in East Timor constituted a threat to peace and security.[267] Acting under Chapter VII of the Charter of the United Nations, the Security Council:

(1) Condemns all acts of violence in East Timor, calls for their immediate end, and demands that those responsible for such acts be brought to justice;

(2) Emphasizes the urgent need for coordinated humanitarian assistance and the importance of allowing full, safe, and unimpeded access by humanitarian organizations, and called upon all parties to cooperate with such organizations so as to ensure the protection of civilians at risk, the safe return of refugees and displaced persons, and the effective delivery of humanitarian aid;

(3) Authorizes the establishment of a multinational force under a unified command structure, pursuant to the request of the government of Indonesia conveyed to the Secretary General on September 12 with the following tasks: to restore peace and security in East Timor, to protect and support UNAMET in carrying out its tasks and, within force capabilities, to facilitate humanitarian assistance operations, and authorized the States participating in the multinational force to take all necessary measures to fulfill this mandate;

(4) Welcomes the expressed commitment of the government of Indonesia to cooperate with the multinational force in all aspects of the implementation of its mandate and looked forward to close coordination between the multinational force and the government of Indonesia;

(5)   Underlines the government of Indonesia's continuing responsibility under the May 5 Agreement, taking into account the mandate of the multinational force set out in paragraph 3 above, to maintain peace and security in East Timor in the interim phase between the conclusion of the popular consultation and the start of the implementation of its result and to guarantee the security of the personnel and premises of UNAMET;

(6)   Welcomes the offers by Member States to organize, lead and contribute to the multinational force in East Timor, called on Member States to make further contributions of personnel, equipment and other resources, and invited Member States in a position to contribute to inform the leadership of the multinational force and the Secretary General;

(7)   Stresses that it was the responsibility of the Indonesian authorities to take immediate and effective measures to ensure the safe return of refugees to East Timor;

(8)   Notes that Article 6 of the May 5 Agreement stated that the governments of Indonesia and Portugal and the Secretary General shall agree on arrangements for a peaceful and orderly transfer of authority in East Timor to the United Nations, and requested that the leadership of the multinational force cooperate closely with the United Nations to assist and support those arrangements;

(9)   Stresses that the expenses for the force would be borne by the participating Member States concerned and requested the Secretary General to establish a trust fund through which contributions could be channeled to the States or operations concerned;

(10)   Agrees that the multinational force should collectively be deployed in East Timor until replaced as soon as possible by a United Nations peacekeeping operation, and invited the Secretary General to make prompt recommendations on a peacekeeping operation to the Security Council;

(11)   Invites the Secretary General to plan and prepare for a United Nations transitional administration in East Timor, incorporating a United Nations peacekeeping operation, to be deployed in the implementation phase of the popular consultation (phase III) and to make recommendations as soon as possible to the Security Council;

(12)   Requests the leadership of the multinational force to provide periodic reports on progress toward the implementation of its mandate through the Secretary General to the Council, the first such report to be made within 14 days of the adoption of this resolution;

(13)   Decides to remain actively seized of the matter.[268]

The Deployment of INTERFET

Following passage of Security Council resolution 1264 (1999), the International Force, East Timor (INTERFET), an Australian-led multinational force of 8,000 troops from 17 countries was deployed in East Timor to begin enforcing the mandate contained in resolution 1264 (1999). Although INTERFET was deployed with the consent of the government of Indonesia, the Security Council authorized the deployment under its Chapter VII powers, which gave

INTERFET enforcement powers if necessary to enforce the United Nations mandate.[269] In its initial deployment, INTERFET encountered little resistance from Indonesian troops or Indonesian-backed militias.[270] The Indonesian military cooperated fully with INTERFET and subsequently began withdrawing its forces in compliance with resolution 1264 (1999). Indonesian-backed militias retreated into neighboring West Timor and temporarily halted their violence. Within days of its deployment, INTERFET established control over the capital, Dili, and proceeded to extend its control over the rest of the province.

With a gradual improvement in the security situation, refugees began to emerge from hiding in search of food and to reclaim what was left of their homes, which had been destroyed by fires set by Indonesian-backed militias. INTERFET assisted in the resettlement process and in the distribution of humanitarian assistance. The Secretary General proposed the establishment of a three-year United Nations interim administration in East Timor to prepare the territory for independence.[271] On October 19 the Indonesian Parliament formally ratified the result of the popular consultation of the East Timorese people and their desire to sever ties with Indonesia. Indonesia's legal rights over East Timor thereafter ceased to exist.[272]

The United Nations Transitional Administration in East Timor (UNTAET)

On October 25, 1999 the Security Council adopted resolution 1272 (1999) by which it accepted the recommendations contained in the Secretary General's report to the Security Council on the situation in East Timor. The Security Council determined that the continuing situation in East Timor constituted a threat to peace and security. Acting under Chapter VII of the Charter of the United Nations, the Security Council decided to establish a United Nations Transitional Administration in East Timor (UNTAET). UNTAET was granted overall responsibility for the administration of East Timor, and empowered to exercise all legislative and executive authority, including the administration of justice.[273] The Security Council also decided that the mandate of UNTAET would consist of the following elements:

(1)   To provide security and maintain law and order throughout the territory of East Timor;
(2)   To establish an effective administration;
(3)   To assist in the development of civil and social services;
(4)   To ensure the coordination and delivery of humanitarian assistance, rehabilitation and development assistance;
(5)   To support capacity-building for self-government;
(6)   To assist in the establishment of conditions for sustainable development.[274]

The Security Council further decided that UNTAET would comprise the following units:

(1)   A governance and public administration component, including an international police element, with a strength of up to 1,640 officers;

(2)   A humanitarian assistance and emergency rehabilitation component;

(3)   A military component, with a strength of up to 8,950 troops and up to 200 military observers. UNTAET was given the authorization to take all necessary measures to fulfill its mandates. The Security Council established UNTAET for an initial period until January 31, 2001.[275]

The crisis in East Timor once again underscored the institutional weakness in the United Nations crisis management system. The United Nations was a spectator to another humanitarian crisis that came immediately after the crisis in Kosovo. Although United Nations officials had anticipated the violence in East Timor, the Security Council had no contingency plan to protect United Nations officials in the field or the people of East Timor, who were being massacred in the presence of United Nations civilian police. The Security Council refused to heed calls from international human rights observers and from Portugal itself, the legitimate colonial authority in East Timor, for immediate United Nations intervention to stop the violence.[276]

In his address to the 51st Session of the General Assembly, Secretary General Kofi Annan acknowledged the failure of the United Nations to respond to pleas for help from the victims of such atrocities as had occurred in Kosovo and East Timor.[277] He called for greater United Nations involvement in conflicts within states. The United Nations' failure to respond to the crisis in East Timor, like in previous crises in Rwanda, Bosnia, Sierra Leone, and Kosovo, was contingent on its lack of a standing army, its exclusive reliance on the goodwill of the major powers, and the division within the Security Council over the right of the United Nations to intervene in internal conflicts. China and Russia generally opposed United Nations intervention in humanitarian situations, whereas the United States, Britain, and France supported such interventions when the crisis had implications for their geopolitical interests, or when international public opinion and media coverage was overwhelmingly pro-intervention.

The United Nations' reputation was severely damaged during the East Timor crisis. The United Nations' failure to respond quickly to the crisis left doubts about the organization's ability to manage future regional conflicts. The debate over the proper role the United Nations should play in regional conflicts is certain to continue. The United Nations' problem is institutional; the organization needs to rethink its conflict management scheme in light of the nature of conflicts in the post-Cold War era. Many of these conflicts affect the civilian population disproportionately. United Nations responses to ethnic conflicts need to be proactive and rapid. In both Kosovo and East Timor, the United Nations responded to the violence only after it had escalated to the level of a full-scale humanitarian catastrophe. The United Nations needs to put in place a structure that allows it to respond to conflicts before they degenerate into serious humanitarian crises, as both Kosovo and East Timor demonstrated. An emergency United Nations brigade would deter atrocities, and allow the United Nations to respond sooner to humanitarian emergencies.

The United Nations Interim Administration in East Timor was very successful in implementing its mandate. This was by far one of the most ambitious undertakings for the United Nations. When the United Nations assumed responsibility in East Timor, it had to start from scratch. There were very few trained professionals in East Timor, and much of the country's institutions had been destroyed. The United Nations was required to build all the basic pillars of statehood in East Timor in order to prepare the territory for independence. East Timor was a major accomplishment for the United Nations.[278]

CHAPTER V

THE SECURITY COUNCIL AND SMALL-SCALE TRANSNATIONAL ARMED CONFLICTS

The Security Council has been involved in the resolution of a number of small-scale conflicts which did not receive the international media spotlight like some of the more protracted conflicts discussed above. These small-scale conflicts are less severe, and do not have the same violent impact on the civilian populations as their counterparts in neighboring countries. However, they do have the potential to escalate into more violent conflicts; hence, the Security Council has found it necessary to intervene to contain these conflicts to prevent them from spilling over into neighboring states. These small-scale conflicts usually involve opposition groups fighting for greater autonomy or fighting for independence; disputes between two neighboring states over one state's support for rebel groups; rival ethnic groups vying for control of state power; or rebel groups fighting to overthrow the government. Many of these conflicts are strictly internal, but occasionally involve external forces. This chapter focuses on conflicts in Western Sahara, Macedonia, Georgia, Prevlaka, Tajikistan, Eastern Slavonia, Baranja and Western Sirmium, the Central African Republic, and Guinea-Bissau.

The Situation in Western Sahara

The Western Sahara dispute has been on the agenda of the United Nations since 1975, after Spain abandoned the territory to Morocco, which had previously disputed Spain's claim to the territory.[1] Morocco immediately seized control of the territory and formally annexed it to the Kingdom of Morocco. The United Nations refused to recognize Morocco's sovereignty over Western Sahara.[2] On October 22, 1975 the Security Council adopted resolution 377 (1975) in which it reaffirmed the terms of General Assembly resolution 1514 of December 14, 1960, and all other relevant resolutions on the Territory. The Security Council requested that the Secretary General enter into immediate consultations with the parties concerned and interested, and to report to the Security Council as soon as possible on the results of the consultations in order to enable the Council to adopt the appropriate measures to deal with the situation concerning Western Sahara. On November 2 the Security Council adopted resolution 379 (1975), by which it reaffirmed the provisions of resolution 377 (1975). The Security Council urged all the parties concerned and interested to avoid any unilateral or other action which might further escalate the tension in the area.

Following the commencement of the deployment of Moroccan troops into Western Sahara, the President of the Security Council issued a statement on behalf of the Security Council in which he called on Morocco to put an end forthwith to the declared march into Western Sahara. On November 6 the Security Council adopted resolution 380 (1975), by which it noted with grave concern the deteriorating situation in Western Sahara. The Security Council deplored the holding of the march, and called upon Morocco to immediately withdraw from the Territory of Western Sahara all the participants of the march.

In 1975 the General Assembly requested an Advisory Opinion from the International Court of Justice (ICJ), in which it asked the Court to determine: (1) whether Western Sahara at the time of colonization by Spain was a territory belonging to no one (*terra nullius*); and (2) whether there were legal ties between Western Sahara, the Kingdom of Morocco, and the Mauritanian entity. In its ruling on the first question, the court denied that the territory was *terra nullius*. On the second question, the court ruled that there were legal ties between Western Sahara, the Kingdom of Morocco, and the Mauritanian entity.[3] Morocco disregarded the court's ruling and consolidated its rule over Western Sahara. In response, the POLISARIO Front began an armed struggle against Moroccan forces. The Secretary General continued his consultations with the parties involved, and in 1988 negotiated a ceasefire agreement between Moroccan troops and the POLISARIO Front.[4]

In September 1988 the Security Council reviewed the Secretary General's report on his good offices mission pursued jointly with the Chairman of the Organization of African Unity (OAU), in conformity with General Assembly resolution 40/50 of December 2, 1985.[5] The Security Council adopted resolution 621 (1988), by which it endorsed the recommendations of the Secretary General for the holding of a referendum on self-determination for the people of Western Sahara, organized and supervised by the United Nations and the OAU.[6] The Security Council supported the Secretary General's request for the appointment of a Special Envoy for Western Sahara. The Security Council noted that both Morocco and the POLISARIO Front had agreed in principle to the proposals of the Secretary General and the Chairman of the OAU.

In June 1990 the Security Council adopted resolution 658 (1990) by which it approved the Secretary General's peace proposal. The Security Council called on the parties to cooperate fully with the Secretary General and the Chairman of the OAU in their efforts to find a solution to the Western Sahara problem.[7] In April 1991 the Security Council adopted resolution 690 (1991), by which it accepted the Secretary General's implementation plan.[8] The Security Council authorized the establishment of the United Nations Mission for the Referendum in Western Sahara (MINURSO) to monitor the ceasefire between Moroccan troops and POLISARIO troops, verify the reduction of Moroccan troops in the Territory, monitor the confinement of Moroccan and POLISARIO troops to designated locations, ensure the release of all Western Saharan political prisoners or detainees, oversee the exchange of prisoners of war, implement a repatriation program, identify and register qualified voters, and organize and ensure a free referendum and proclaim the results.[9]

Soon after its adoption, the peace plan ran into difficulties due to the parties' divergent views on various aspects of the plan. The two sides disagreed on the criteria for eligibility of voters.[10] Morocco wanted all Moroccans born and living in the territory to participate in the referendum, whereas the POLISARIO Front wanted only the indigenous population, both inside and outside the territory, to participate in the referendum. The status of the three tribal groups remained a major obstacle to the completion of the identification process for eligible voters. The parties also failed to reconcile their views regarding the appeals process, and the repatriation of refugees by UNHCR. With neither side willing to comprise on the registration formula, it became impossible to implement the plan in conformity with the repeatedly revised timetable.[11] MINURSO was therefore limited to complementing the identification process, verifying the ceasefire and cessation of hostilities, monitoring local police, and ensuring the security and order at identification and registration sites. In May 1996 the Security Council suspended the identification process, authorized the withdrawal of the civilian police unit, and decided to reduce the size of the military component of MINURSO by 20 per cent.[12] The Security Council supported the Secretary General's intention to maintain a political office in Laayoune, with a liaison office in Tindouf, to continue a dialogue with the parties and the two neighboring countries.

More than a decade after the Security Council adopted the settlement plan for Western Sahara, the deadlock over the issue of eligibility of voters remained a sticking point, and continued to delay a possible final settlement to the dispute. Both Morocco and the POLISARIO continued to refuse to compromise on the issue of who was eligible to participate in the referendum. The Security Council continued to renew MINURSO's mandate and reaffirm its commitment to a permanent settlement of the dispute; however, patience began to run out. In an effort to revive the peace process, Secretary General Kofi Annan appointed former US Secretary of State James Baker as his Special Representative to Western Sahara. Baker held several rounds of talks between all the parties, but the talks failed to break the impasse.

In his report to the Security Council for June 20, 2001, the Secretary General accepted a proposed framework agreement for Western Sahara recommended by James Baker. The plan would abandon the referendum and instead grant local autonomy to Western Sahara. The Western Saharan people would have exclusive competence over local governmental administration, budget, taxation, law enforcement, and internal security. Morocco in turn would have exclusive competence over foreign relations, national security, and external defense.[13] The future status of Western Sahara would be determined within five years of adoption of the plan by qualified voters from the territory. The POLISARIO rejected the Baker proposal and threatened to resume the war. The plan clearly favored Morocco at the expense of the right of self-determination for the people of Western Sahara.

The presence of MINURSO has prevented a resumption of full-scale fighting between the two parties. However, other sensitive issues, such as a reduction of Moroccan troop presence in the territory and the repatriation of POLISARIO prisoners of war remained unresolved. Efforts to resolve the conflict have continued, but a final settlement has yet to be reached.

The Situation in Macedonia

Macedonia was one of the last former Yugoslav republics to secede from the Yugoslav Federation. However, unlike Bosnia and Croatia, Macedonia was threatened by both Serbia and Greece.[14] Serbia objected to Macedonia leaving the Yugoslav Federation for fear that the federation would cease to exist. Greece objected to Macedonia using the name 'Macedonia' as its official name for fear that Macedonia might use the name to make territorial claims over the Greek province of Macedonia.[15] Greece retaliated by threatening war, and by blocking Macedonia's application for membership in the United Nations and for recognition from the European Union.

In December 1992 the Security Council deployed a small unit from UNPROFOR to Macedonia to monitor and report on developments in the republic's border areas which could undermine confidence and stability in the region and threaten Macedonia's sovereignty.[16] Following a restructuring of UNPROFOR into three separate units in March 1995, the Security Council adopted resolution 983 (1995) by which it changed the name of the UNPROFOR unit in Macedonia to the United Nations Preventive Deployment Force (UNPREDEP).[17] UNPREDEP was to deter possible threats to Macedonia's sovereignty from the Federal Republic of Yugoslavia and its other neighbors. The Security Council affirmed its commitment to search for an overall settlement to the conflicts in the former Yugoslavia by ensuring the sovereignty and territorial integrity of all states within their internationally recognized borders. UNPREDEP's mandate would expire on November 30, 1995. The Security Council urged UNPREDEP to continue the cooperation between UNPROFOR and the OSCE mission.

For the next three years the Security Council periodically reviewed the situation in Macedonia and extended UNPREDEP's mandate each time for an additional six months.[18] On July 21, 1998 the Security Council adopted resolution 1186 (1998), by which it reiterated its call for the governments of the former Yugoslav Republic of Macedonia and the Federal Republic of Yugoslavia to implement in full their agreement of April 8, 1996, in particular regarding the demarcation of their mutual border.[19] The Security Council authorized an increase in the troop strength of UNPREDEP up to 1,050 and extended the mandate of UNPREDEP for a period of six months until February 28, 1999. UNPREDEP was to continue to deter threats and prevent clashes, monitor the border areas, and report to the Secretary General any developments which could pose a threat to the former Yugoslav Republic of Macedonia.[20]

The presence of UNPREDEP in Macedonia certainly helped prevent the wars in the former Yugoslavia from spreading into neighboring Macedonia. UNPREDEP demonstrated how preventive measures can save the United Nations from the more costly large-scale deployments which are needed after a conflict has escalated. UNPREDEP helped defuse tensions in Macedonia's border regions and prevented a potential conflict between Macedonia and Greece, or Macedonia and the Federal Republic of Yugoslavia.

On February 25, 1999 the Security Council reviewed the mandate of UNPREDEP with the goal of renewing its mandate for an additional six months. The draft resolution was vetoed by China in protest at Macedonia's diplomatic recognition of Taiwan.[21] Taiwan provided a substantial aid package to Macedonia in exchange for Macedonia's recognition of Taiwan as the legitimate government of China. The move infuriated Beijing, which had been seeking to have Taiwan's diplomatic recognition revoked by all states. The Security Council was faced with the possibility of withdrawing UNPREDEP, which had been so successful in keeping peace in the region. NATO and OSCE forces replaced the United Nations mission and continued its mandate, but outside of the United Nations framework.[22]

The continuing presence of OSCE peacekeepers in Macedonia insulated the republic temporarily from the conflicts in Kosovo and other parts of the Balkans. The security situation changed dramatically in February 2001, when ethnic Albanians launched an invasion of Macedonia from Kosovo.[23] The National Liberation Army (NLA), made up of ethnic Albanians who were remnants of the Kosovo Liberation Army (KLA), said they were fighting for greater recognition of the rights of ethnic Albanians in Macedonia.[24] The conflict escalated in spring 2001, after the government of Macedonia refused to negotiate with the rebels. Diplomatic efforts to resolve the war intensified. NATO proposed a series of measures to defuse the war, but the Macedonian government continued to resist meeting the demands of the rebels. The rebels called for greater autonomy, and for constitutional changes that would grant ethnic Albanians greater political rights, including recognition of their language.

Macedonia's attempt to get the Security Council to intervene directly in the conflict was rejected by a number of Council members. The Security Council called for all sides in the conflict to seek a peaceful solution and to cooperate with NATO to find a peaceful settlement, but it did not adopt a resolution on the issue. Instead, the Security Council deferred to NATO and the EU to resolve the conflict. NATO and the EU negotiated a peace agreement between the government of Macedonia and the ethnic Albanians, which they both signed on August 13, 2001. The agreement called for recognition of the Albanian language in areas with an ethnic Albanian population of 20 per cent or more, the recruitment of 1,000 ethnic Albanian police officers, and an amendment to the Macedonian constitution to make it more inclusive.[25] In exchange for agreeing to the terms of the agreement, NATO agreed to deploy a peacekeeping force in Macedonia to disarm the ethnic Albanian rebels. NATO's mission was to conclude within 30 days, and was limited solely to collecting the weapons of members of the NLA. NATO's mission was contingent on passage of the constitutional changes by the Macedonian Parliament.

The Macedonia peace agreement demonstrated NATO's cautious approach to dealing with situations in the Balkans. The agreement was a victory for ethnic Albanians, who made political gains that could not have been realized on the battlefield. Despite NATO's plan to withdraw its forces at the end of the 30-day period, there was no guarantee that the agreement would hold once NATO forces withdrew. Macedonian Slavs protested the terms of the agreement, which they say made too many concessions to ethnic Albanians. They felt betrayed by the international community, who pressured a democratic government to make concessions to terrorists. Neither NATO nor the Bush administration wanted to be drawn into another Balkan war.

Macedonians felt the West had betrayed them, despite the critical support they gave to NATO during the Kosovo war. Macedonia provided safe haven for Kosovo Albanians seeking refuge from the war in Kosovo, and was crucial for NATO's overall war strategy against Yugoslavia. Confronted with its own ethnic Albanian rebellion, Macedonia received no military support from NATO or the international community. The conflict in Macedonia was a security challenge to the democratically elected government of Macedonia, and to stability in the entire Balkans region. The NATO-brokered ceasefire was observed by both sides despite some sporadic incidents, although the situation in Macedonia remained volatile for some time.

The Conflict in Abkhazia, Georgia

Following the breakup of the Soviet Union, the ethnic Russian population in the Republic of Georgia found themselves in the minority. In 1992, civil war broke out between Georgian troops and Abkhazian rebels who were seeking to secede from the Republic of Georgia.[26] More than ten thousand people died in the conflict, and thousands were internally displaced. Fearing a Russian intervention, the Security Council called for a ceasefire and for a negotiated settlement. On July 27, 1993, the government of Georgia and the Abkhaz leadership signed a ceasefire agreement. On August 6, 1993, the Security Council adopted resolution 854 (1993), by which it established the United Nations Observer Mission in Georgia (UNOMIG) to verify compliance with the ceasefire.[27] UNOMIG's mandate called for it to investigate reports of ceasefire violations and to attempt to resolve such incidents with the involved parties, and to report to the Secretary General on the implementation of its mandate, including, in particular, violations of the ceasefire agreement.[28] In September 1993, fighting resumed and intensified, and the original mandate was invalidated, but UNOMIG was given an interim mandate to maintain contacts with the two parties to the conflict and with Russian military contingents, and to monitor and report on the situation, with particular reference to developments relevant to United Nations efforts to promote a comprehensive political settlement.[29]

Following the signing of the Agreement on a Ceasefire and Separation of Forces between the government of Georgia and the Abkhaz leadership in May 1994, the Security Council adopted resolution 934 (1994), by which it authorized UNOMIG to:

(1)   Monitor and verify the implementation of the Agreement;
(2)   Observe the operation of the peacekeeping force for the Commonwealth of Independent States;

(3)   Verify that troops do not remain in or re-enter the security zone and that heavy military equipment does not remain or is not reintroduced in the security zone or the restricted weapons zone;

(4)   Monitor the storage areas for heavy military equipment withdrawn from the security zone and restricted weapons zone;

(5)   Monitor the withdrawal of Georgian troops from the Kodori valley to places beyond the frontiers of Abkhazia;

(6)   Patrol regularly the Kodori valley;

(7)   Investigate reported or alleged violations of the Agreement and attempt to resolve such incidents.

After 1994 the Security Council voted to extend the mandate of UNOMIG several times. In 1999, the Security Council held four meetings on the situation in Georgia. On January 28, the Security Council adopted resolution 1225 (1999), by which it demanded that the Georgian and Abkhaz parties expand their commitment to the United Nations-led peace process.[30] The Security Council underlined the necessity for an early and comprehensive political settlement, including the political status of Abkhazia, and full respect for the sovereignty and territorial integrity of Georgia within its internationally recognized borders. Similarly, in 2000 the Security Council voted twice to expand the mandate of UNOMIG. In both resolutions 1287 and 1311 (2000), the Security Council called on the parties to deepen their commitment to the United Nations-led peace process.[31] On January 31, 2001, the Security Council adopted resolution 1339 (2001) by which it extended the mandate of UNOMIG for an additional six months and called on the parties to expedite the peace process.[32]

The situation in Abkhazia remained deadlocked, with the Abkhaz rebels insisting on total independence from Georgia. Georgia saw the conflict as a challenge by ethnic Russians to incorporate Abkhazia into Russia. UNOMIG's presence helped to maintain the ceasefire, but other issues, such as the return of thousands of ethnic Georgians to their homes in Abkhazia, or a final political settlement, remained outstanding.

The Situation in Prevlaka, Croatia

The United Nations has been involved in the dispute in Prevlaka since 1992. On October 6, 1992 the Security Council adopted resolution 779 (1992) by which it authorized UNPROFOR to resume responsibility for monitoring the demilitarization of the Prevlaka peninsula, claimed by both Croatia and the Federal Republic of Yugoslavia.[33] In March 1995, following the restructuring of UNPROFOR, those functions were undertaken by UNCRO. However, with the termination of UNCRO's mandate in January 1996, the Security Council adopted resolution 1038 (1996) by which it authorized the deployment of the United Nations Mission of Observers in Prevlaka (UNMOP) to continue to monitor the demilitarization of the peninsula for a period of three months, to be extended for an additional three months upon a report of the Secretary General that an extension would continue to help decrease tension in the area.[34] After January 1996, the Security Council voted periodically to extend UNMOP's mandate for additional six-month intervals.

In 1999 the Security Council endorsed the improved cooperation between the Republic of Croatia and the Federal Republic of Yugoslavia and the United Nations military observers, and the decrease in the number of serious incidents in the peninsula. In resolution 1222 (1999) the Security Council reiterated its call for the two parties to cease violations of the demilitarization regime in the United Nations designated zones; take steps to further reduce tension and improve safety and security in the area; and cooperate fully with United Nations military observers and ensure their safety and unrestricted freedom of movement.[35] The Security Council also asked the Secretary General to consider reducing the number of military observers to as few as 22 (from 28), to reflect the improved cooperation and reduction in tension. On July 15, 2000 the Security Council adopted resolution 1252 (1999) by which it extended the mandate of UNMOP for another six months, until January 15, 2001.[36]

On January 15, 2001 the Security Council unanimously adopted resolution 1335 (2001) to extend the mandate of UNMOP for a further six months.[37] The Security Council called upon the two parties to cooperate fully with the United Nations military observers and to ensure their safety and full, unrestricted freedom of movement. The Security Council welcomed the commitments of the democratic governments of Croatia and the Federal Republic of Yugoslavia to resume bilateral talks on the dispute as soon as possible, and it encouraged them to make use of the recommendations and options on developing confidence-building measures provided for in resolution 1252 (1992).[38] Those measures were aimed at further facilitating the freedom of movement of the civilian population. Under resolution 1335 (2001), the Security Council urged the two parties to abide by their mutual commitments and implement fully the Agreement on Normalization of Relations.[39] The Security Council stressed the urgent need for the parties to fulfill rapidly, and in good faith, their commitment to reach a negotiated solution to the dispute in accordance with Article 4 of the Agreement. The Security Council also reiterated its call for a comprehensive demining program to be put in place in the identified minefields in UNMOP's area of responsibility, and for UNMOP and SFOR to cooperate fully with each other.[40]

In his report to the Security Council on the situation in Prevlaka, the Secretary General stated that the situation had not changed from his last reporting. The situation remained calm and stable, and in general, both parties continued to respect the zone. UNMOP observers, he said, had freedom of movement on the Yugoslav side of the zone, but were still required by Croatia to provide advance written notice before patrolling in the northern area.[41] The Secretary General called for lifting those restrictions, for Montenegrin and Croatian police to withdraw from the United Nations-controlled zone, and for resolution of the continued operation of checkpoints at Cape Kobila. On July 11, 2001 the Security Council adopted resolution 1362 (2001) by which it authorized UNMOP to continue monitoring the demilitarization of the

Prevlaka peninsula in accordance with its previous resolutions. On January 15, 2002 the Security Council adopted resolution 1387 (2002), by which it again authorized the United Nations military observers to continue monitoring the demilitarization of the Prevlaka peninsula, in accordance with resolutions 779 (1992) and 981 (1995), and the situation in the Prevlaka peninsula remained on the agenda of the Security Council.

The Situation in Tajikistan

On December 16, 1994 the Security Council adopted resolution 968 (1994) by which it authorized the deployment of the United Nations Mission of Observers in Tajikistan (UNMOT). The Security Council called for a process of national reconciliation between Tajikistan troops and forces of the United Tajik Opposition (UTO). Since 1994 the Security Council has periodically renewed the mandate of UNMOT. In 1999 the Security Council held four meetings on the situation in Tajikistan, and on February 23, 1999 the President of the Security Council issued a statement on behalf of the Security Council. The statement called upon the government and the UTO to intensify efforts to create conditions for holding a constitutional referendum and presidential elections in 1999, as well as the timely holding of parliamentary elections.[42] The statement said the Security Council regretted the slow progress of the last three months and emphasized the need for the parties to speed up the full and sequential implementation of the General Agreement on the Establishment of Peace and National Accord in Tajikistan, especially the Protocol on military issues.[43]

On May 15 the Security Council adopted resolution 1240 (1999) by which it extended the mandate of UNMOT by six months, until November 15. The Security Council called on the parties to speed up the full and sequential implementation, in a balanced manner, of the General Agreement. On August 19 the Security Council met on Tajikistan, and in a statement, the President of the Council welcomed the significant progress made in the implementation of the General Agreement on the Establishment of Peace and National Accord in Tajikistan, achieved to a great extent due to renewed efforts of the President of the country and the leadership of the Commission on National Reconciliation.[44] The Security Council welcomed the official declaration of the UTO to disband its armed units, and the decision by Tajikistan's Supreme Court to lift bans and restrictions on activities by political parties and movements of the UTO as important steps in the democratic development of Tajik society.[45]

On November 15 the Security Council held a meeting to review the situation in Tajikistan. The Security Council adopted resolution 1274 (1999) by which it extended UNMOT's mandate for an additional six months.[46] The Security Council expressed its deep concern at the precarious humanitarian situation in Tajikistan, and it called on the parties to co-operate in ensuring the security and freedom of movement of personnel of the United Nations, the Commonwealth of Independent States (CIS) Peacekeeping Forces, and other international personnel.[47] The Security Council reminded the parties that the international community's ability to assist Tajikistan was linked to the security of those personnel.

Although modest progress was made in settling the conflict in Tajikistan, the situation remained volatile. The Security Council extended UNMOT's mandate in May 2000, and it called on the parties to continue to work toward the implementation of the General Agreement.[48] UNMOT's mission concluded after its May 15 expiration date. The Security Council met twice prior to the expiration of the mandate, and on both occasions issued presidential statements welcoming the success achieved by the parties in the peace process.[49] On November 21 the Security Council was able to welcome decisive progress in the implementation of the General Agreement on the Establishment of Peace and National Accord in Tajikistan, and emphasized the continuing support of the international community in the post-conflict phase to sustain and build on the achievements of the peace process.[50]

The Situation in the Central African Republic

Following attempts to overthrow the government of the Central African Republic by a small group of soldiers, the Security Council adopted resolution 1159 (1998) on March 27 to establish United Nations Mission in the Central African Republic (MINURCA), to take effect on April 15, 1998.[51] On October 15 the Security Council adopted resolution 1201 (1998) to extend the mandate of the mission. MINURCA was originally deployed to replace an inter-African force, which had been established on January 31, 1997 by the heads of state of Gabon, Burkina Faso, Chad, and Mali to monitor the implementation of the Bangui Agreements.[52] MINURCA's mandate called for it to disarm mutineers, militias, and other unlawfully armed people in the country.

On February 26, 1999 the Security Council adopted resolution 1230 (1999) by which it expressed its intention to commence reduction of MINURCA personnel 15 days after the conclusion of presidential elections, with a view to the mission's termination on November 15. However, 10 days prior to the expiration of the mandate, the Security Council expressed its concern about the consequences of then-current political tensions for stability and the functioning of institutions. The Security Council called on the government of the Central African Republic to take concrete measures to implement political, economic, social, and security reforms.[53]

On October 22 the Security Council adopted resolution 1271 (1999) by which it extended the mandate of MINURCA until February 15, 2000, with a view to ensuring a gradual transition from United Nations peacekeepers' involvement in the Central African Republic to a post-conflict peace-building presence, with the aid of UN agencies and the Bretton Woods institutions.[54] The Security Council strongly encouraged the government of the Central

African Republic to coordinate closely with the mission in the progressive transfer of MINURCA's security functions to local security and police forces.

MINURCA's mandate expired on February 15, 2000; however, the Security Council endorsed the decision of the Secretary General to establish a United Nations Peace-Building Office in the Central African Republic (BONUCA) for one year, beginning immediately.[55] The mandate of BONUCA called for it to support the government's efforts to consolidate peace and national reconciliation, strengthen democratic institutions, and facilitate the mobilization at the international level of political support and resources for national reconstruction and economic recovery in the country.[56]

In a report submitted to the Security Council in January 2001, the Secretary General described the Central African Republic as a country gripped in political crisis, mired in social tension, and underpinned by a fragile economy. He urged dialogue between the ruling party and the opposition, who he blamed for causing the crisis, due to attempts 'by every possible means to seize the power that it was unable to win through the ballot box'. The Secretary General's report also painted a mixed picture of human rights in the Central African Republic, where the practice of summary and extra-judicial executions 'seems to have diminished'. On the other hand, he deplored living conditions endured by prisoners in the country. Representatives from the United Nations Peace-building Support Office in the Central African Republic reported on the deplorable conditions in the country's jails. The Secretary General also drew attention to the situation facing approximately 800,000 refugees from the Democratic Republic of the Congo residing in makeshift camps along the southern border of the Central African Republic, who he said, 'live in precarious conditions, involving lack of food, poor or inappropriate medical care and lack of medicines and pitiful accommodation'. The Secretary General called on governments to make good on pledges of funding for the country so it could meet the many-faceted challenges confronting it.[57]

The Situation in Guinea-Bissau

The Security Council established a United Nations presence in Guinea-Bissau in 1998, following an agreement between the government and rebel troops from the Guinea-Bissau Army. On April 6 the Security Council adopted resolution 1216 (1998) by which it created the United Nation Peace-building Support Office (UNOGBIS) in Guinea Bissau to monitor the peace agreement.[58] On January 6, 1999 the Security Council unanimously adopted resolution 1233 (1999) by which it strongly urged the parties in Guinea-Bissau to ensure the smooth functioning of the National Unity government, including measures to build confidence, as well as to encourage the early return of refugees and internally displaced persons.[59] The Security Council called on the government of President João Bernardo Vieira and the self-proclaimed military junta to implement the provisions of the Abuja Agreement of November 1, 1998, which, among other things, called for the holding of national elections.

Peaceful legislative and presidential elections were held on November 28, 1999, but none of the 12 presidential candidates won a majority. A run-off election was held on January 16, 2000, and a new government was sworn in in February.

On March 29, 2000 the Security Council reviewed the situation in Guinea-Bissau and later issued a presidential statement in which it welcomed the return of peace, democracy and constitutional order in Guinea-Bissau.[60] The Security Council stressed the importance of continued cooperation by all parties toward the consolidation of a sustainable peace, and expressed support for the country's newly elected government. The Security Council encouraged the new authorities to develop and implement programs devised to consolidate peace and national reconciliation. Despite these measures, the situation in Guinea-Bissau remained unpredictable, and the conflict caused massive destruction of the country's economy and infrastructure.

The Situation in Eastern Slavonia, Baranja and Western Sirmium

The Basic Agreement signed on November 12, 1995 on the Region of Eastern Slavonia, Baranja and Western Sirmium provided for the peaceful integration of that region into Croatia. The Agreement called on the Security Council to establish a transitional administration to govern the region during the transitional period of 12 months, which might be extended for a further 12 months, and to authorize an international force to maintain peace and security during the said period to assist in the implementation of the Agreement.[61] On January 15, 1996 the Security Council adopted resolution 1037 (1996) by which it established the United Nations Transitional Administration for Eastern Slavonia, Baranja and Western Sirmium (UNTAES) for an initial period of 12 months, with both military and civilian components. The military unit was to supervise and facilitate the demilitarization of the region, monitor the voluntary and safe repatriation of refugees and displaced persons to their places of residence, contribute to the maintenance of peace and security in the region, and assist in implementing the Basic Agreement.[62]

UNTAES's mandate called for the civilian unit to establish a temporary police force, define its structure and size, develop a training program and oversee its implementation, and monitor treatment of offenders and the prison system; undertake tasks relating to civil administration and to the functioning of public services; facilitate the return of refugees; and organize elections, assist in their conduct, and certify the results. In addition, the civilian unit was to assist in the coordination of plans for the development and economic reconstruction of the region; to monitor the parties' compliance with their commitments to respect the highest standards of human rights and fundamental freedoms; promote an atmosphere of confidence among all local residents irrespective of their ethnicity; monitor and facilitate the demining of land within the region; and to maintain an active public affairs element.[63] Furthermore, UNTAES was required to cooperate with the International Criminal Tribunal for the Former

Yugoslavia (ICTY) in performing its task. Member states, acting nationally or through regional organizations, were authorized to take all necessary measures, including close air support, in order to defend or help withdraw UNTAES. However, any such action would be based on request by UNTAES through a process communicating through the United Nations.[64]

The presence of UNTAES in the region helped to reduce tension and a possible escalation of the conflict. UNTAES carried out its mandate successfully, with the cooperation of all the parties involved. The Security Council continued to extend the mandate for UNTAES, pending a final settlement of the conflict.

Conclusion

The early intervention by the Security Council in managing these small-scale conflicts prevented the conflicts from escalating into major wars. The Report of the Panel on United Nations Peace Operations made a case for effective conflict prevention as a means of reducing peacekeeping operations. The Secretary General's report on Prevention of Armed Conflict also articulated a vision for greater emphasis on conflict prevention. The Secretary General also called on the international community to address the root causes of conflicts, such as poverty, gross violations of human rights, economic decay, and political corruption. According to the Carnegie Commission on Deadly Conflict, the international community spent $200 billion on conflict management in seven major interventions in the 1990s, but could have saved $130 billion through a more effective preventive approach. The United Nations continues to invest more in peace operations, which are generally deployed after a conflict has begun, and less in conflict prevention. Similarly, states with the resources spend more in preparing for wars, than in strengthening the capacity of countries to prevent wars. A reversal of that trend is imperative if the United Nations is to succeed in containing the next generation of conflicts. The examples of conflict prevention by the Security Council cited above demonstrate the success of this strategy when applied effectively.

CHAPTER VI

THE SECURITY COUNCIL AND THE MANAGEMENT OF INTER-STATE CONFLICTS

Since the creation of the United Nations in 1945, the world has witnessed several inter-state wars. However, most were either resolved bilaterally, or through the diplomatic efforts of the major powers. The Security Council played a limited role in solving these wars, and when it did, it was because the major powers requested it to do so. States have generally chosen to resolve inter-state disputes involving resort to arms bilaterally or through third-party mediation. During the Cold War the practice was more commonly used for fear that the involvement of the United Nations could complicate the process and draw the conflict unnecessarily into the Cold War dispute between the United States and the Soviet Union. In many instances, the United Nations was unable to intervene to solve conflicts because one or more of the Permanent Members of the Security Council or their allies were parties to these conflicts and used their veto to block any effort by the Security Council to intervene.[1]

Inter-state conflicts have been relatively rare since 1945. The majority of wars have been internal, with little or no significant threat to international peace and security. The few inter-state conflicts that have occurred since 1945 have been relatively small, and were generally contained within a particular geographic area or within the territory of a state. Many of these conflicts were acts of intervention by one great power against a client state, or a border dispute between two developing countries.[2] By nature these conflicts provided for a quick victory and little opportunity for the Security Council to get involved. In some of the other conflicts the parties had an equal but insignificant military balance, and therefore the continuation of the conflict had only a limited impact on international peace and security.

This chapter examines a selected number of the inter-state conflicts that have occurred since 1945, and the role played by the United Nations Security Council in resolving them. The chapter looks at how the Security Council carried out its responsibility, whether that responsibility was delegated, or whether the Security Council resorted to an alternative method rather than invoking Chapter VII to resolve the conflict. The wars selected for review are the Korean War (1950), the Suez Canal Crisis and the Soviet invasion of Hungary (1956), the United States invasion of the Dominican Republic (1965), the Arab-Israel war (1967), the Soviet invasion of Czechoslovakia (1968), the Arab-Israel war (1973), the 1978 and 1982 Israeli invasions of Lebanon and the Israeli-Palestinian conflict, the Soviet invasion of Afghanistan (1979), Vietnam's invasion of Cambodia (1979), the Iran-Iraq War (1980-1988), the Falkland Islands War (1982), the United States invasion of Grenada (1983), United States invasion of Panama (1989), Iraq's invasion of Kuwait (1990), the Eritrea-Ethiopia War (1998-2000), and the war in the Democratic Republic of the Congo (from 1999).

The Korean War

The first challenge to the Security Council's responsibility for managing international peace and security came in 1950 with North Korea's invasion of South Korea. The Security Council convened an emergency meeting to discuss the situation in the Korean Peninsula. The Security Council thereafter adopted resolution 82 (1950) by which it determined that the action of North Korea constituted a breach of the peace. The Security Council called for the immediate cessation of hostilities; and called upon the authorities of North Korea to withdraw forthwith their armed forces to the 38th parallel. The Security Council also called upon all members to render every assistance to the United Nations in the execution of this resolution, and to refrain from giving assistance to the North Korean authorities.[3]

On June 27, 1950 the Security Council adopted resolution 83 (1950) in which it took note of North Korea's failure to withdraw to the 38th parallel and said that urgent military measures were needed to restore international peace and security. The Security Council further acknowledged the appeal from the Republic of Korea to the United Nations for immediate and effective steps to secure peace and security. The Security Council recommended that members of the United Nations furnish such assistance to the Republic of Korea as might be necessary to repel the armed attack and to restore international peace and security in the region.[4]

On July 7, 1950 the Security Council adopted yet another resolution on the situation in the Korean Peninsula. Under resolution 84 (1950), the Security Council recommended that members providing military forces and other assistance pursuant to resolutions 82 (1950) and 83 (1950) make such forces and other assistance available to a unified command under the United States of America. It also asked the United States to designate the commander of these forces, and it authorized the unified command at its discretion to use the United Nations flag in the course of operations against North Korean forces concurrently with flags of the various nations participating.[5]

The Security Council's authorization against North Korea was significantly different from the provision of Article 42 of the Charter of the United Nations. In the Korean conflict the Security Council did not follow the procedures under Chapter VII of the Charter, which calls for imposing non-military measures, such as diplomatic and economic sanctions, on an aggressor before authorizing the use of collective enforcement measures. The Security Council did not impose economic or diplomatic sanctions on North Korea; instead, it authorized enforcement measures, but did not specify under what article it was authorizing such measures.[6] It also delegated the authority to carry out these enforcement measures to the United States without retaining oversight authority over the activities of United States forces.[7]

The Security Council took this unusual action against North Korea in the absence of the Soviet Union, which was boycotting the Security Council in protest over the Council's decision to seat Nationalist China as the legitimate representative of China.[8] Following the Soviet Union's return in August, it vetoed further action by the Security Council to extend the operation. The Soviet action led to the adoption of the 'Uniting for Peace' resolution by the General Assembly. The resolution granted the General Assembly emergency powers to address threats to international peace and security and to recommend collective measures in situations where the Security Council is unable carry out its responsibility because of the use of the veto by one or more Permanent Members.[9] On February 1, 1951, following China's intervention in the conflict on behalf of North Korea, the General Assembly invoked the United for Peace Resolution to condemn China's aggression and to recommend that all states lend every assistance to the United Nations action in Korea.[10]

Legal Issues

Several scholars have questioned the legitimacy of Security Council resolution 84 (1950), which authorized enforcement measures against North Korea in the absence of the Soviet Union. It is questionable whether the Security Council can authorize enforcement measures under Charter VII without the full participation of all the Permanent Members of the Council. According to the voting procedures for the Security Council spelled out in Article 27 of the Charter of the United Nations:

(1)   Each member of the Security Council shall have one vote.

(2)   Decisions of the Security Council on procedural matters shall be made by an affirmed vote of seven members [Changed to nine, following the amendment of the Charter in 1965].

(3)   Decisions of the Security Council on all other matters shall be made by an affirmative vote of seven members [Changed to nine, following amendment of the Charter in 1965] including the concurring votes of the permanent members; provided that, in decisions under Chapter VI, and under paragraph 3 of Article 52, a party to a dispute shall abstain from voting.[11]

The Charter gives special privileges to the major powers to maintain international peace and security and requires their participation in all such matters to have an effective collective security system. Since the Soviet Union was not present and did not vote on the Security Council enforcement measure provision against North Korea, Article 27 (3) would throw into doubt the legality of the Council's decision.[12] More importantly, the delegation by the Security Council of its authority to maintain international peace and security to one member state, the United States, raised further doubts about the legality of the measure. The United States operated in Korea with an unlimited degree of freedom and may have taken action unintended by the Security Council. However, once the Security Council gave the authorization it was difficult for it to retract it. The United States basically used the United Nations flag to give international legitimacy to an operation that was completely national in character. Finally, the decision to grant the General Assembly emergency powers to recommend collective enforcement measures may have been a rushed measure to amend the Charter for political reasons.

The controversy surrounding the Korean operation made it difficult for the Security Council to authorize similar measures in the future. The Security Council did not authorize such large-scale collective military measures again until 1990, when it authorized a Korean-type operation against Iraq to eject it from Kuwait.

The Suez Canal Invasion

Following a decision by President Nasser of Egypt to nationalize the Suez Canal in 1956, Britain, France, and Israel invaded Egypt to prevent such a move. Both British and French nationals owned majority shares in the Canal, and they justified their action on grounds of protecting their nationals. Israel, which was still in a state of war with Egypt, took advantage of the Anglo-French invasion to reduce the future military threat Egypt posed.[13]

The Security Council convened an emergency session to discuss the situation in the Middle East; however, with Britain and France threatening to exercise their veto, the Security Council was unable to condemn the invasion. In a compromise measure, the three invading states agreed to withdraw their forces in exchange for the deployment of a peacekeeping force to interpose between Egyptian and Israel troops in the Sinai Peninsula. The peacekeeping formula was a novel concept in response to a unique challenge facing the Security Council. The deployment of a United Nations Emergency Force was authorized not by the Security Council, but by the General Assembly, and on the consent of all involved parties.[14] The authority to oversee the daily activities of the force was granted to the Secretary General. The legal requirements for the deployment of the force were completely different from those specified in Chapter VII of the Charter. The Suez compromise does not provide for the identification of the aggressor, and it imposes no blame or sanctions on those responsible for the invasion.[15] Instead, it provides for the United Nations to take a neutral stand on the issue and to only go as far as the parties are willing to accept. Under the Suez formula, the United Nations can only remain on the territory of the host state for as long as the host state gives its consent. When that consent is withdrawn, as was the case in Egypt, the United Nations must withdraw its forces.

Legal Issues

The legal status of peacekeeping under the Charter of the United Nations is ambiguous. The Charter does not specifically mention peacekeeping as a peaceful means of settling disputes. However, some scholars consider peacekeeping a Chapter VI measure because of its reliance on the consent of the parties involved and its emphasis on non-enforcement measures.[16]

Although Chapter VI does not specifically mention peacekeeping as one of the peaceful means for settling disputes, it can be inferred that Chapter VI does not limit the list of peaceful means solely to those mentioned.[17] Given the emphasis on peaceful settlement of disputes and reconciliation in peacekeeping, the measure can be considered a Chapter VI measure (See discussion in Chapter I).

Some observers criticized the United Nations for withdrawing its forces from Egypt, even when it was evident that the withdrawal would lead to an outbreak of war between Egypt and Israel. However, that criticism was dismissed, as the United Nations was legally bound by the agreement to withdraw on the request of the government of Egypt.[18] In the absence of further consent from the government of Egypt, the United Nations could not remain on Egyptian territory.

In light of the circumstances surrounding the Suez situation, the Security Council has attempted to address the issue of continuing consent of the parties. The Security Council now deploys many peacekeeping missions under Chapter VII authority with a different mandate than traditional peacekeeping operations. This gives the mission a different legal status that allows it to take all necessary means to implement its mandate. The Security Council also authorizes the creation of an international force under the command of a member state, with authority to use force to implement its mandate. Peacekeeping remains a very attractive alternative for managing regional conflicts. However, the nature of conflicts has changed, and so has the peacekeeping formula that came out of the Suez crisis. The formula has been very successful in resolving disputes between states. Its legal status is no longer in doubt, especially when adopted by the Security Council.

The Hungarian Crisis

On October 23, 1956 demonstrators took to the streets in Budapest in protest against the Hungarian government for its refusal to bring Mr Nagy into the government. The demonstrations turned violent, and at 2.00 a.m. on October 24, Russian tanks rolled into Budapest. At 8.00 a.m. it was announced that Nagy would form a new government. At 9.00 a.m. it was further announced that 'the government had applied for help from the Soviet formation stationed in Hungary (under the Warsaw Pact).'[19] It is not clear who made the request or when it was made. On November 1, following an unsuccessful appeal for Soviet troops to withdraw, Nagy denounced the intervention and declared Hungary neutral. He also called for international assistance to defend against the Soviet intervention.

On November 4 Soviet troops re-entered Budapest and put down the uprising within days. That same day Mr Kadar announced that he had requested the second Soviet intervention. A Special United Nations Committee sent to investigate the situation in Hungary was prevented from entering the country. The Soviet Union later argued that the rebellion was the work of ex-Nazi supporters and of the Western powers, who had sent in arms. The Security Council debated the issue but failed to adopt a resolution because of the Soviet veto.[20] The Security Council took no further action on the Hungarian issue.

Legal Issues

Did the Soviet Union deny the Hungarian people their right to self-determination? When is intervention by invitation legal? Given the chaotic situation in Hungary at the time of the uprising, was it possible to determine who was the legitimate authority of the country? Was the failure of the Security Council to act a tacit approval of great power intervention within their own spheres of influence? The Soviet invasion of Hungary began a process that later became known as the Brezhnev Doctrine, which gave the Soviet Union the right to use military force to defend socialism and to shield Soviet conduct from international legal scrutiny.[21]

The United States Invasion of the Dominican Republic

On April 24, 1965 the Cabral government was overthrown by a group of young military officers and members of the Dominican Revolutionary Party. Fighting erupted and the situation deteriorated to the point where the military junta, which had replaced the Cabral government in opposition to the rebels, informed the United States Embassy that it was not able to guarantee the safety of Americans on the island.[22] In response to a request from the junta, 400 United States Marines landed on the island on April 28 in order, as President Johnson stated, to protect Americans and other foreign nationals.[23] President Johnson later increased the number of American troops to 20,000.

On May 20 President Johnson addressed the nation and gave a different reason for the United States intervention. He said the rebellion in the Dominican Republic, which had started out as a popular revolt, was taken over by communists, and that the United States would not tolerate the establishment of another communist government in the western hemisphere.[24] The United States later secured a resolution from the OAS which appealed for a ceasefire and the establishment of an international neutral zone of refuge, comprising the section of the city of Santo Domingo immediately adjoining the embassies of foreign governments, the inviolability of the said zone to be respected by all hostile factions, and the nationals of all countries to be guaranteed suitable protection and safety within the zone.[25] On May 2 the OAS Committee of Five arrived in the Dominican Republic and began to mediate between the factions. On May 5 the various factions signed the Act of Santo Domingo in which the parties accepted the establishment of a safe zone and bound themselves to respect it. On May 6 the Meeting of Consultation decided to create an Inter-American Force for the Dominican Republic. The various factions in the Dominican Republic later consented to the deployment of a peacekeeping force, which comprised the American troops already in the Dominican Republic, and a few other participating Latin American states.[26]

On May 1 the Soviet Union requested an emergency meeting of the Security Council to discuss the situation in the Dominican Republic. The Security Council discussed the situation in the Dominican Republic from May 3-25, again from June 3-21, and once more between July 21-26.[27] Most member states were critical of the United States action. However, the United States defended its action as a legitimate humanitarian mission on the invitation of the lawful authority of the Dominican Republic.[28] The United States also defended the Inter-American Force created by the OAS as lawful under Article 53 of the Charter of the United Nations.

The United States maintained that the force was like any other peacekeeping force established by the United Nations in Cyprus, Egypt, or the Congo.[29] The United States also argued that the OAS did not need the approval of the Security Council to establish such a force, as its actions were not an enforcement action, but peacekeeping. Other states, including the Soviet Union, said the OAS was involved in an enforcement action without the authorization of the Security Council, thus its action was in violation of Article 53 of the Charter of the United Nations. On May 14 the Security Council adopted by unanimous vote resolution 203 (1965), by which it called for a ceasefire and invited the Secretary General to send a representative to the Dominican Republic for the purpose of reporting to the Security Council on the situation.[30] On May 22 the Security Council adopted resolution 205 (1965), by which it called for the suspension of hostilities in Santo Domingo to be transformed into a permanent ceasefire. The United States abstained because the resolution did not acknowledge the work of the OAS.[31]

On the request of the Security Council, the Secretary General dispatched to the Dominican Republic the Mission of the Representative of the Secretary General in the Dominican Republic (DOMREP), consisting of a three-man delegation to report on the situation. DOMREP operated alongside the Inter-American Force in a subordinate position.[32] It was the first time the United Nations was carrying out such an operation. DOMREP's presence legitimized the United States' view that the OAS had acted legally. However, the situation would have long-term implications for cooperation between the United Nations and regional organizations.

Legal Issues

Serious questions were raised regarding the United States' intervention in the Dominican Republic. Could the United States legally justify its intervention in the Dominican Republic on humanitarian grounds? Was there a right to democratic government in the western hemisphere? Was the OAS entitled to authorize the deployment of the Inter-American Force without the authorization of the Security Council? Was the OAS action in the Dominican Republic peacekeeping, or an enforcement action? Assuming it was enforcement action, had the OAS violated the Charter of the United Nations? Are there any parallels between the position taken by the United States, and that taken by the Soviet Union during the Hungarian crisis?

Under Chapter VIII of the Charter of the United Nations regional arrangements are authorized to carry out non-enforcement measures, which include peacekeeping. However, any enforcement measures must be authorized by the Security Council. The question is how does one differentiate between peacekeeping and enforcement actions in a situation of continuing hostilities? The United States' intervention was a clear violation of Charter rules. Subsequent efforts to legitimize the United States' invasion through the creation of an OAS Inter-American Force also violated the Charter of the United Nations. The Inter-American Force engaged in both peacekeeping and enforcement action. The decision by the Security Council to authorize the Secretary General to dispatch a United Nations mission to Santo Domingo subordinated the authority of the United Nations to a regional organization.

Regional organizations are currently engaged in peacekeeping activities, and are increasingly being called upon by the United Nations to participate in such operations. Given their closeness to the conflicts and their understanding of the situation, regional organizations are better placed to assume greater responsibility in resolving regional conflicts.

Arab-Israeli Conflict of 1967

In 1967 Israel invaded Egypt and Syria after President Nasser prematurely called for the withdrawal of United Nations peacekeepers (UNEF) from the Suez Canal. Israel's invasion was a pre-emptive action to prevent Egyptian and Syrian forces from launching an attack on Israel. Fighting went on for six days before a ceasefire was agreed upon by all sides. Israel occupied a part of the Sinai Peninsula, and the Golan Heights in Syria. The Security Council adopted a number of resolutions in the interim which called on the parties to cease fighting and settle their dispute by peaceful means. Following the signing of a formal ceasefire the Security Council adopted resolution 242 (1967) in which it called for: (1) a withdrawal of Israeli armed forces from territories occupied in the recent conflict; and (2) termination of all claims or states of belligerency and respect for and acknowledgement of the sovereignty, territorial integrity and political independence of every state in the area and their right to live in peace within secure and recognized boundaries free from threats or acts of force.[33] This resolution became the basis for a permanent peace between Israel and its Arab neighbors. However, realizing the goals of the resolution were extremely difficult, given the ambiguity contained in the document.

Legal Issues

Among the many concerns raised by legal scholars and observers is whether Israel acted lawfully by launching a pre-emptive attack against Egypt and Syria on the grounds that it was acting in anticipatory self-defense. There is no legal basis for anticipatory self-defense under Article 51 of the Charter of the United Nations. However, a state facing an imminent threat of an attack can take defensive measures to protect its territory from such an attack. The issue is how to determine when an attack is imminent, and what is the appropriate response. Could Israel have resolved this issue without resorting to war? What was Egypt's intention for asking the United Nations to withdraw its peacekeeping force from Egyptian territory? Did the United Nations have a legal obligation to comply with the Egyptian request to withdraw its forces, even though doing so would lead to war? Does Israel have a legal right to continue the occupation of Arab territories in light of the resolution of the Security Council? These issues have complicated efforts to find a permanent peace in the region.

The Soviet Invasion of Czechoslovakia

In 1968 the Czechoslovakian government initiated a series of reforms under the leadership of President Dubček that ushered in a new era in Czechoslovak politics. The new reform measures provided for press freedom and the liberalization of the political system.[34] The measures departed sharply from the policies of the previous regime or that of other communist regimes in the Soviet bloc. The Soviet Union opposed the reform measures of the Czech communist government and stopped Czechoslovakia from implementing them. In August 1968 Warsaw Pact troops intervened in Czechoslovakia. The reformists were removed from power and a more hard-line communist regime was installed. The Soviet Union claimed it was invited to intervene by the legitimate authority of Czechoslovakia; however, that claim was denied by the Czechoslovak government.[35] President Brezhnev later justified the intervention on the basis of the Brezhnev Doctrine, which he said justified a Warsaw Pact intervention in a socialist state threatened by bourgeois ideology.

In a meeting in the Security Council, the Soviet Foreign Minister Andrea Gromyko said the Czechoslovak situation was an internal matter within the socialist states, to be settled by socialist law. Gromyko went on to say that within the Socialist Community of Nations international law did not apply. The Soviet Union vetoed the Security Council resolution which condemned the action of the Warsaw Pact. The Soviet veto made it virtually impossible for the Security Council to further consider the crisis in Czechoslovakia.

Legal Issues

Was the Warsaw Pact intervention in Czechoslovakia legally justified? Does regional customary law supersede general principles of international law and United Nations law? Was the Brezhnev Doctrine, like the Johnson Doctrine, valid under international law? Are major powers above the rules? What remedies can the United Nations provide for small states against major powers in such circumstances?

Regional bloc rules do not supersede general principles of international law or principles of the Charter of the United Nations, such as sovereign equality and non-intervention. Czechoslovakia did not threaten its neighbors, nor was there an outside threat to Czechoslovakia or to member states of the Warsaw Pact. The Warsaw Pact was a collective defense alliance governed under Article 51 of the Charter. For individual or collective self-defense to be legal under Article 51, there must be an armed attack on a state. The state must also request assistance from its allies. Czechoslovakia was neither attacked, nor did it request assistance from the Warsaw Pact. The Warsaw Pact states had therefore violated Charter laws. The Brezhnev Doctrine, like the Johnson Doctrine, was contrary to principles of international law and Articles 2 (1) and 2 (4) of the Charter of the United Nations. Unfortunately, the United Nations is unable to act when a major power is party to a conflict.

The Arab-Israel Conflict of 1973

In 1973 Egypt and Syria launched simultaneous military attacks on Israel in an attempt to recapture territories lost to Israel in the 1967 war. The Security Council adopted resolution 338 (1973) by which it: (1) called on all the parties to the present fighting to cease all firing and terminate all military activity immediately, no later than 12 hours after the moment of the adoption of this decision, in the positions they then occupied; (2) called upon the parties concerned to immediately after the ceasefire start the implementation of Security Council resolution 242 (1967) in all of its parts; (3) decided that, immediately and concurrently with the ceasefire, negotiations were to start between the parties concerned under appropriate auspices, aimed at establishing a just and durable peace in the Middle East.

On May 31 the Security Council adopted resolution 350 (1974) by which it established the United Nations Disengagement Observer Force (UNDOF) to maintain the ceasefire between Israel and Syria, to supervise the disengagement of Israeli and Syrian forces, and to supervise the areas of separation and limitation, as provided for in the Agreement on Disengagement. The mandate of UNDOF was then renewed every six months. UNDOF stabilized the *status quo* between Israel and Syria and has successfully prevented the resumption of war between two hostile enemies.

The 1978 Israeli Invasion of Lebanon

In 1978 Israel invaded Lebanon in response to a PLO commando attack on Israel that left several Israeli civilians dead. Within days, Israel had occupied the entire southern part of Lebanon. On March 19 the Security Council adopted resolutions 425 (1978) and 426 (1978), in which it called upon Israel to immediately cease its military action and withdraw its forces from all Lebanese territory. The Security Council also decided to establish immediately the United Nations Interim Force for Lebanon (UNIFIL). UNIFIL's mandate called for it to confirm the withdrawal of Israeli forces; restore international peace and security; and assist the government of Lebanon in ensuring the return of its effective authority in the area. UNIFIL was prevented from implementing its mandate due to sporadic fighting in the area between Israeli forces and the Southern Lebanese Army, which resisted Israeli occupation. UNIFIL remained in the region and helped in distributing humanitarian assistance to the civilian population and protecting the civilian pollution from the worst effects of the violence. On April 17, 2000, Israel informed the Secretary General that it was formally withdrawing its forces from southern Lebanon by July 2000 in full compliance with resolutions 425 (1978) and 426 (1978). The Security Council continued to renew UNIFIL's mandate thereafter.

Legal Issues

Was Israel's invasion of Lebanon justified? Did Lebanon have a responsibility to stop the PLO from using bases inside Lebanon to launch attacks on Israel? Was the PLO fighting a legitimate war of liberation? Was the Israeli occupation of Lebanese territory justified? Is a terrorist attack an armed attack within the context of the right to self-defense?

The 1982 Israeli Invasion of Lebanon and the Israeli-Palestinian Conflict

In 1982 Israel invaded Lebanon again, this time to destroy PLO bases in Lebanon and to permanently stop PLO attacks on Israel. Israel's massive bombing campaign quickly overwhelmed PLO fighters. Hundreds of Palestinian refugees were killed, and the Israeli army cornered the PLO in a siege that lasted several days. To avoid an escalation of the conflict, the Reagan Administration negotiated a safe exit to Tunisia for Yasser Arafat and his aides. On June 5 the Security Council adopted resolution 508 (1982) by which it called on the parties to cease immediately and simultaneously all military activities within Lebanon and across the Lebanese-Israeli border. On June 6 the Security Council adopted a second resolution, resolution 509 (1982), in which it demanded that Israel withdraw all its military forces forthwith and unconditionally to the internationally recognized boundaries of Lebanon. It also called on all parties to observe strictly the terms of paragraph 1 of resolution 508 (1982). On June 18 the Security Council adopted resolution 511 (1982), by which it extended the mandate of UNIFIL until August 19, 1982.

Following an incursion by Israeli forces into Beirut, the Security Council adopted resolution 520 (1982), in which it condemned the Israeli incursions and its violation of the ceasefire agreements and of Security Council resolutions. The Security Council further called for the return of Israeli forces to positions occupied before September 15, and for strict respect for the sovereignty, territorial integrity, unity, and political independence of Lebanon under the sole and exclusive authority of the government of Lebanon through the Lebanese Army throughout Lebanon. After Israeli forces massacred hundreds of Palestinian civilians in refugee camps in Beirut, the Security Council adopted resolution 521 (1982), in which it condemned as criminal the massacre of Palestinian civilians in Beirut. The Security Council authorized the Secretary General to increase United Nations observers in and around Beirut from ten to fifty, and insisted on no interference with the deployment and that they enjoy full freedom of movement. Despite the nature of the war crimes committed by Israeli forces, the Security Council did not invoke Chapter VII of the Charter of the United Nations; hence resolution 521 (1982) was not legally binding. The PLO was evacuated to Tunis, and Israel subsequently withdrew its forces with assurances from the United States that a United States-led multinational force would be deployed in Lebanon to restore Lebanese sovereignty and prevent the PLO from regrouping. The Reagan administration bypassed the United Nations Security Council and established a multinational force in Lebanon. However, within months of its deployment, the force suffered huge casualties from a terrorist bombing, which forced the Reagan administration to withdraw the force prematurely. President Reagan's anti-communist military engagements in Africa and the Caribbean and his rhetoric about the Soviet Union made the multinational force very unpopular in the region and compromised its neutrality.

Up until the signing of the Oslo Accords in 1993, Israel and the Palestinians engaged in a continuous low-intensity conflict that resulted in the death of a number of civilians, but for years seemed to be indecisive and going nowhere. Prime Minister Rabin of Israel and Yasser Arafat, the PLO leader, were persuaded by the Foreign Minister of Norway to negotiate an agreement that would end the violence and bring about a mutual recognition. The Oslo Accords were later approved by the United States at a White House ceremony in which Israel and the PLO agreed to work together and with the United States to bring about a permanent peace. Israel gradually withdrew from parts of the West Bank and the Gaza Strip and began final status talks with the PLO. The Oslo Accords suffered a serious setback in 1994, following the assassination of Prime Minister Rabin by a Jewish extremist opposed to the agreement. A new Prime Minister, Benjamin Netanyahu, from the Likud Party, won the next general election vowing to reverse the Oslo Accords. In response to the stalemate, Palestinians in the occupied territories began an intense two-year violent uprising against Israel in what became known as the first *Intifada*.

Following the election of Ariel Sharon in 2000 as the new Prime Minister of Israel, the Palestinians resumed their uprising. Sharon opposed the peace process during his campaign, and soon after taking office he started cracking down on Palestinian militants. He confiscated Palestinian land to expand existing Jewish settlements and to build new ones. Palestinian suicide bombings against Israeli civilians intensified, resulting in further retaliations by the Israeli government. The conflict has continued, despite Israel's targeted assassination of suspected Palestinian militants, forced deportations of Palestinians, demolitions of suspected terrorists' homes, and indiscriminate bombing of civilian areas. Israel has also reoccupied areas previously returned to the Palestinian Authority, and imposed curfews on many Palestinian towns. Israel's policies have infuriated Palestinian militants, who have in turn intensified their campaign against Israel. The cycle of violence on both sides shows no signs of abating.

The role of the Security Council in the Israeli-Palestinian conflict has been limited to passing a few non-binding resolutions. The United States has exercised its veto to prevent the Security Council from condemning Israel or from playing a more active role in finding a solution to the conflict. The United States has protected Israel from international scrutiny and blocked efforts by the Arab League to get the Security Council more involved in the Israeli-Palestinian conflict. Israel has exploited its special relationship with the United States by relying on American Jewish organizations to lobby the US government to support Israel's causes. Successive American presidents have staunchly defended Israel's position at the United Nations, in exchange for support for their re-election efforts. The pro-Israeli lobby in the United States contributes millions of dollars to the political campaigns of both parties. This, in turn, makes it difficult for candidates of either party to be perceived as anti-Israel.

The influence of the Jewish vote in American domestic politics is extremely important, and candidates for political office must demonstrate they are pro-Israel in order to receive the Jewish vote, which is very important to win political office in many key states. Given the connection between Israel and American domestic politics, it is extremely difficult for the United States to play the role of an honest broker in the Israeli-Palestinian conflict. Recent efforts to negotiate a peace agreement have excluded the Security Council. Although the Secretary General is part of the so-called 'Quartet', the United Nations has played a limited role in the implementation of the 'road map'.

To move the peace process forward the United States must give an appearance of fairness in its Middle East policy, which the Arabs view as favoring Israel. Both parties must recognize each other's rights to live within secure boundaries. Israel must comply with Security Council resolution 242 (1967) and withdraw from land it occupied during the 1967 war. Israel must also be willing to compromise on the status of Jerusalem. A permanent peace agreement between Israel and the Palestinians will only happen if the Permanent Members of the Security Council are willing to use the authority of the Security Council to enforce its decisions on all parties to a dispute.

The Soviet Invasion of Afghanistan

In 1978 the non-aligned government of President Dauod was overthrown by force by a more radical government which established close ties with the USSR. In 1979, that government was overthrown by a new Soviet-backed government led by Babrak Karmal, who was flown by Moscow from Eastern Europe to assume the presidency. The change of government was followed by an airlift of 400 Soviet troops into Kabul. The USSR claimed that the Afghan government requested its assistance under a 1978 bilateral Treaty of Friendship to protect Afghanistan from 'armed incursions and provocations from outside'.[36] About 10,000 troops from the USSR were later sent into Afghanistan to help the Afghan Army fight Muslim guerrillas opposed to the government led by Karmal (and later by Najibullah).

Following the Soviet invasion, the Security Council convened an emergency session to debate the situation in Afghanistan. A draft resolution deploring the Soviet intervention and calling for the withdrawal of Soviet troops from Afghanistan was vetoed by the USSR. The vote was 13 to 2 (with USSR and East Germany against).[37] On January 14, the General Assembly adopted resolution ES-6/2 by a vote of 104 to 18, with 18 abstentions. The resolution reaffirmed that 'respect for the sovereignty, territorial integrity and political independence of every state is a fundamental principle of the Charter,' and it strongly deplored 'the recent armed intervention in Afghanistan, which is inconsistent with that principle'.[38] The resolution appealed to all states 'to refrain from any interference in the internal affairs of that country' and called for the 'immediate, unconditional and total withdrawal of the foreign troops from Afghanistan.'[39] The General Assembly resolution was phrased in the language of both the Non-use of Force and Non-Intervention Principles in the 1970 Declaration on Friendly Relations Resolution.

The United States saw the Soviet intervention in Afghanistan as a violation of the understanding between the two superpowers which expected them to refrain from intervening in non-aligned states, or states outside their traditional spheres of influence. The United States and Pakistan provided massive military aid to the Afghan rebels to help them fight a guerrilla war against the Soviet Union. The Soviet Union suffered heavy casualties, but maintained its troops in Afghanistan until 1989. On assuming the presidency of the USSR, President Gorbachev called on the Secretary General to broker a peace agreement with all parties. The General Accord, signed in 1988, provided for the withdrawal of Soviet troops and an end to the guerrilla war.[40] Soviet troops withdrew from Afghanistan on schedule, but the civil war in Afghanistan continued. (For a more detailed analysis of developments in Afghanistan after the withdrawal of Soviet troops see the section on Afghanistan in Chapter II).

Legal Issues

Was the Soviet intervention in Afghanistan justified under the Charter of the United Nations? When is intervention by invitation legal? Was the Soviet-backed regime in Afghanistan legitimate? Was United States support for the Afghan rebels a violation of international law? When is support for a rebel organization fighting government forces legal?

The votes in both the Security Council and the General Assembly indicate that the international community saw the Soviet invasion as a flagrant violation of international law and the Charter of the United Nations. There is no evidence that the government of Afghanistan invited the Soviet Union to intervene on its behalf. Given Soviet support for the illegal Afghan regime, the United States support for the Afghan rebels was perfectly legal under international law.

Vietnam's Invasion of Cambodia

In 1979, Vietnamese forces invaded Cambodia and ousted the Khmer Rouge regime led by Pol Pot. From 1975 to 1979, the Khmer Rouge had carried out a reign of terror in Cambodia, killing over one million Cambodian civilians. The international community criticized the policy of the Khmer Rouge but did nothing to stop the atrocities, which went on for five years. After much international outcry from human rights organizations, Vietnam invaded Cambodia and ousted the Khmer Rouge.[41] Vietnam installed a new government in Cambodia, and its troops remained in the country to defend the new government against a Khmer Rouge guerrilla war. The Khmer Rouge was supported by China.

The international community condemned Vietnam's invasion of Cambodia as a gross violation of the Charter of the United Nations, and called on Vietnam to withdraw its forces from Cambodia. Vietnam justified its action on humanitarian grounds, claiming that it had intervened in Cambodia to save the people of Cambodia from further genocide. The Khmer Rouge retreated to the jungles and carried out a guerrilla war for the next decade, in an attempt to oust the Vietnamese-backed regime.

In 1989 the parties to the conflict in Cambodia, along with the United States, China, the USSR, France, and Japan, signed a framework for a comprehensive political settlement in Paris. The Accords called for the withdrawal of Vietnamese troops from Cambodia, an end to the civil war, and the deployment of a United Nations interim administration and peacekeeping force in Cambodia to monitor the ceasefire and to assume governmental responsibility for Cambodia until a new national government was elected.[42] (For further detail of United Nations operations in Cambodia, see Chapter III).

The Security Council refused to recognize the Vietnamese-backed regime and allowed the Khmer Rouge regime to continue to occupy Cambodia's seat at the United Nations, despite the regime's history of genocide. The Security Council had ignored calls from human rights groups to investigate claims of genocide that were taking place in Cambodia. The situation in Cambodia was not an agenda priority for the Security Council because of Cambodia's extreme communist ideology, and the secrecy under which the regime carried out its activities. Cambodia was a very closed society, and independent observers had little means of verifying the atrocities that were taking place in the country.

Legal Issues

Was Vietnam's invasion of Cambodia legal under the Charter of the United Nations and international law? When can a state use force to oust a regime that is responsible for committing serious acts of genocide? Is the current effort by the United Nations to bring those responsible for acts of genocide in Cambodia a vindication of Vietnam's action? Did the international community acquiesce to the genocide in Cambodia by not doing anything to stop it? Did the Cold War overshadow Cambodia's chances for fair treatment in the Security Council? Did the Security Council violate the Charter by not recognizing the Vietnamese-backed government in Cambodia as the legitimate government of Cambodia, hence denying it the Cambodian seat in the General Assembly?

Vietnam's invasion of Cambodia was a responsible act to protect innocent civilians victimized by their own government. Under international law and the Genocide Convention, states have a responsibility to protect civilians from acts of genocide. By not intervening in Cambodia, the Security Council abdicated its responsibility for maintaining international peace and security. The Security Council's failure to recognize the Vietnamese-backed government of Han Sen, and its decision to allow the Khmer Rouge to continue to occupy the Cambodian seat at the United Nations, was a tacit approval of the actions of the Khmer Rouge.

Argentina's Invasion of the Falkland Islands and the British Response

On April 2, 1982, Argentine forces invaded and took possession of the Falkland Islands. Argentine forces also took control of South Georgia Island some 800 miles east of the Falkland Islands. The small British force on the Falkland Islands and on South Georgia Island was no match for the well-armed Argentine military and surrendered immediately. Argentina justified its invasion of the Falkland Islands on claims of sovereignty over the islands, and on the basis of self-defense against what it called permanent British aggression.

On April 1, 1982 the President of the Security Council had issued a call for Britain and Argentina 'to refrain from the use or threat of force in the region'. On April 3, following Argentina's invasion, the Security Council adopted resolution 502 (1982), by which it determined that there existed a breach of the peace in the region of the Falkland Islands.[43] The resolution:

(1)   Demands an immediate cessation of hostilities;

(2)   Demands an immediate withdrawal of all Argentine forces from the Falkland Islands;

(3)   Calls on the governments of Argentina and the United Kingdom to seek a diplomatic solution to their differences and to fully respect the Purposes and Principles of the Charter of the United Nations.[44]

On April 5 a British military expedition sailed for the South Atlantic to retake control of the islands by force, following Argentina's refusal to withdraw its forces. The European Community supported Britain's position and imposed sanctions on Argentina. The United States also supported Britain and tried to mediate between Britain and Argentina. The OAS supported Argentina's claim but did not invoke its collective defense agreement. The United States was placed in an awkward position in which it had to determine whether to support Argentina in compliance with its OAS treaty obligations, or support Britain on the broader legal principle of non-use of force in international relations or to settle territorial disputes.

British forces arrived in the region on April 25 and shortly thereafter recovered South Georgia Island. After diplomatic efforts by the United States to achieve a peaceful solution to the dispute failed, the British Task Force landed on the Falkland Islands on May 25, and following a brief period of fighting regained control of the islands. Argentine troops surrendered on June 14.

Legal Issues

Security Council resolution 502 (1982) is interesting for what it did not do. Resolution 502 (1982) was not adopted under Chapter VII of the Charter of the United Nations, and it did not condemn Argentina's action. The resolution did not issue a ruling on Argentina's claim to the islands or recognize Britain's right to self-defense in the event Argentina failed to comply with the demands of the Security Council. Britain insisted that it had a right to self-defense, since Argentina did not withdraw its troops as required by Security Council resolution 502 (1982). The Security Council did not condemn Britain's use of force to regain control of the islands, nor did it adopt another resolution to condemn Argentina for its refusal to withdraw from the Falklands Islands.

Under customary international law states have an inherent right to self-defense, but such a right can only be exercised immediately.[45] Given Britain's month-long delay in getting to the South Atlantic, some scholars argued that Britain had forfeited its right to self-defense.[46] Under Article 51 of the Charter of the United Nations states have a right to self-defense if an armed attack occurs and up until the Security Council has taken the necessary measures to maintain international peace and security. Although the Security Council had adopted resolution 502 (1982), Argentina did not comply with its demands, and the Security Council took no further measures. Should Britain have waited for the Security Council to act while Argentina continued to defy the Council's orders? Britain had a responsibility to protect its citizens, who were now under Argentine occupation. Britain had an obligation to attend to the safety of its nationals. Given Argentina's refusal to withdraw its forces from the Falkland Islands and its determination to take the islands by force, Britain had a legitimate right to self-defense under customary international law and the Charter of the United Nations, to use military force to expel Argentine forces from the islands.

The United States' Invasion of Grenada

On October 19, 1983, a radical wing of Prime Minister Maurice Bishop's government placed him under house arrest and moved to replace his government with a more radical regime.[47] Supporters of Bishop took to the streets in protest and later freed him from house arrest. Bishop and several of his cabinet ministers were later executed. A dusk-to-dawn curfew was declared by the regime, and the army was given authority to shoot anyone who violated the curfew.[48] The violence in Grenada was unprecedented and it took neighboring Caribbean governments by surprise. Within days of the disturbances, the United States, which had several hundreds of its citizens at the St. George's Medical School, developed a rescue plan that involved a military invasion of the island. On October 23, United States Marines, along with troops from six Caribbean states, invaded Grenada, and within a few days of fighting had captured the islands and arrested the members of the new revolutionary government.[49]

The United States initially justified its intervention in Grenada on four grounds: (1) to protect and rescue American nationals; (2) collective self-defense under Article 8 of the Treaty of the Organization of East Caribbean States (OECS); (3) an invitation from the Governor General of Grenada, whom it considered the sole authority on the island; and (4) to maintain law and order and to restore democracy in Grenada.[50] All four claims were strongly challenged by a large and diverse group of states. At an emergency session of the Security Council, several states criticized the United States' action in Grenada. A draft Security Council resolution was vetoed by the United States. However, a similar resolution in the General Assembly deploring the United States' action was adopted by a vote of 108 to 9, with 27 abstentions. The Security Council took no further action against the United States. The United States later withdrew the majority of its forces from Grenada, although some troops remained to maintain order and to support the new government.

Legal Issues

Did the United States have a legal right under international law to use force to rescue its nationals in Grenada? Did the United States exhaust all diplomatic avenues before resorting to force to rescue its nationals? Was the action of the OECS legal under Article 8 of the organization Treaty? Did the OECS violate the Charter of the United Nations? Did the Governor General have the constitutional authority to invite foreign forces into Grenada? Did the United States have a legal right under international law to impose its choice of government on Grenada?

The major powers have generally held that they have a right under customary international law to use force to protect their nationals in danger in foreign countries, although it is disputed whether such a right ever existed under customary international law. Although it has been the practice of major powers to intervene in small states for humanitarian reasons, there is no evidence that the practice was accepted as law. Some scholars have called for an exception to be made in situations where the intervening state has exhausted all diplomatic options and resorts to force solely to protect the lives of its nationals who are in imminent danger.[51] The Charter of the United Nations does not make any exception for the use of force to protect or rescue foreign nationals in another state. However, since the coming into force of the Charter, states have resorted to force to protect their nationals in imminent danger in a foreign state, and justified their actions under the self-defense provisions of the Charter. However, all of these cases have been condemned by a majority of members of the General Assembly as a flagrant violation of the Charter and of international law.[52]

The United States did not exhaust all its diplomatic options and the lives of its citizens were not in imminent danger. The United States was given assurances by the revolutionary government that the safety of its nationals would be respected. The United States made no effort to get its nationals out of Grenada through the normal channels. The United States chose not to rely on the assurances of the revolutionary government, because its initial plan was to overthrow the government of Grenada even before the events of October 19.

The second United States justification was based on Article 8 of the OECS Treaty, which provides for collective intervention against external aggression against a member state. There was no external aggression against Grenada, nor did Grenada attack any of its neighbors. It is also questionable whether the Treaty allows for the OECS to invite a non-member to assist in a collective action. The claim is dubious, and was a violation of the Treaty.

The third United States justification depends on whether the Governor General of Grenada had the constitutional authority to invite foreign troops into Grenada. Under the Grenada Constitution, and the People's Law adopted by Bishop's revolutionary government, the Governor General was the ceremonial head of state. He had no executive authority, except for those powers granted to him by the Prime Minister. Grenada had had a change of government, albeit not to the liking of its neighbors or the United States. However, that government was in firm control of the country, and no power vacuum existed in Grenada. The Governor General violated the Constitution and the People's Law by inviting foreign troops to invade Grenada. Presumably, the Governor General could assert residual authority if the country was without a government, but that was not the case.

The fourth justification the United States provided was that it intervened to maintain law and order and to restore democracy. The United Nations Charter makes no exception for intervention to maintain law and order or to restore democracy. The type of government a country chooses is an internal matter which international law does not regulate. A foreign state has no right to impose its choice of government on another state. The intervention thus violated the right of the people of Grenada to self-determination.

The Iran-Iraq War

In September 1980, Iraq invaded Iran in response to Iranian support for Iraqi Kurdish and Shi'ite Muslim opposition groups seeking greater autonomy within Iraq. Iran declared a full-fledged war against Iraq, and fighting ensued for several years. Following the outbreak of hostilities between Iran and Iraq, the President of the Security Council issued a statement indicating the concern of member states regarding the serious deterioration of relations and the escalation in armed activity leading to loss of life and heavy material damage.[53] The statement continued: 'Members of the Security Council are deeply concerned that this conflict can prove increasingly serious and could pose a grave threat to international peace and security.'[54]

On September 26 the Security Council invited the representative of Iraq to participate, without a vote, in the discussion of the agenda item entitled 'The situation between Iran and Iraq.' On September 28, the Security Council adopted resolution 479 (1980), by which it reminded the parties of their obligations under the Charter of the United Nations to settle their international disputes by peaceful means and in such a manner that international peace and security and justice were not endangered.[55] The Security Council resolution also reminded both countries that all 'Member States are obliged to refrain in their international relations from the threat or use of force against the territorial integrity or political independence of any State.'[56] The Security Council called upon Iran and Iraq to refrain immediately from any further use of force, and to settle their dispute by peaceful means and in conformity with principles of justice and international law. The Security Council did not make a determination regarding who was responsible for starting the war, even though the evidence pointed to Iraq as the aggressor.[57] Certain Permanent Members of the Security Council were biased toward Iran because of its recent Islamic Revolution and its decision to sever ties with traditional Western allies. There were concerns about the spread of the Islamic revolution to other states in the Gulf region, and the potential for destabilizing the Islamic world. Some member states on the Security Council saw the war as a way to prevent the Revolution from spreading to other Gulf States. Iran also had very few allies in the Security Council, having previously ignored Security Council resolutions 457 (1979) and 461 (1979) calling on it to release immediately the personnel of the United States being held in Teheran by militant Iranian students.[58] In 1982 the Security Council adopted resolutions 514 (1982) and 522 (1982) by which it called for a ceasefire between Iran and Iraq, and for the withdrawal of forces to internationally recognized boundaries. The Security Council did not revisit the situation in the Persian Gulf until 1984, when it adopted resolution 552 (1984) in response to Iranian attacks on commercial vessels en route to and from the ports of Kuwait and Saudi Arabia.

In February 1986 the Security Council invited a number of states from the Middle East to participate in a discussion on the situation between Iran and Iraq. On February 24 the Security Council adopted resolution 582 (1986), in which it expressed its deep concern about the prolongation of the conflict between the two countries, resulting in the heavy loss of human life and considerable material damage, and endangering international peace and security.[59] Having heard reports of Iraq's use of chemical and biological weapons against Iranian troops, the Security Council noted that both states were parties to the Protocol for the Prohibition of the Use in War of Asphyxiating, Poisonous or Other Gases, and of the Bacteriological Methods of Warfare, of 1925. The Security Council deplored the initial acts which gave rise to the conflict between the two states, and deplored the continuation of the conflict.[60] The Security Council called on Iran and Iraq to observe an immediate ceasefire, a cessation of hostilities, and withdrawal of all forces to the internationally recognized boundaries without delay.

The Security Council met on March 21 to consider the report of the mission dispatched by the Secretary General to investigate allegations of the use of chemical weapons in the conflict between Iran and Iraq. The President of the Security Council issued a statement in which he said that members of the Security Council were profoundly concerned about the unanimous conclusion of the commission that chemical weapons had been used on many occasions by Iraqi forces against Iranian forces.[61] The statement also said that members of the Security Council strongly condemned the continuing use of chemical weapons in clear violation of the Geneva Protocol of 1925, which prohibits such use in war.

On October 8 the Security Council adopted resolution 588 (1986) by which it once again raised concerns about the prolongation of the conflict and reminded the parties of their obligation under the Charter of the United Nations to settle their dispute by peaceful means.[62] The Security Council called on Iran and Iraq to implement fully and without delay resolution 582 (1986), and it requested the Secretary General to intensify his efforts with the parties to give effect to the above-mentioned resolution and to report to the Council no later than November 30.

In 1988 Iran and Iraq reached an agreement with Secretary General Javier Perez de Cuellar to end the war. The agreement was made possible due to a turning point in the conflict. The military balance in the war was significantly tilted in Iraq's favor as a result of a buildup of US forces in the Persian Gulf. The United States became indirectly involved in the war after it decided to re-flag Kuwaiti oil tankers and provide military escort to these vessels through the Persian Gulf.[63] This brought the United States into direct confrontation with Iran, who had previously targeted Kuwaiti oil tankers. The use of chemical weapons against Iranian troops by Iraq also reduced Iran's ability to fight the war. Iran finally capitulated after United States naval vessels bombarded Iranian oil platforms in the Gulf, and an American missile was fired at an Iranian civilian airliner, killing all the passengers and crew.[64] Iran thereafter accepted the United Nations ceasefire agreement.

Prior to the parties' acceptance of the Secretary General's ceasefire proposal, the Security Council adopted resolution 598 (1987) by which it deplored the continuation of the conflict and the bombing of purely civilian population centers, attacks on neutral shipping and civilian aircraft, and the violation of international humanitarian law and other laws of armed conflict, in particular the use of chemical weapons contrary to obligations under the 1925 Geneva Protocol.[65] The Security Council determined that there existed a breach of the peace as regarding the conflict between Iran and Iraq.[66] Acting under Articles 39 and 40 of the Charter of the United Nations, the Security Council:

(1) Demands that, as a first step towards a negotiated settlement, the Islamic Republic of Iran and Iraq observe an immediate ceasefire, discontinue all military actions on land, sea and in the air, and withdraw all forces to the internationally recognized boundaries without delay;

(2) Requests the Secretary General to dispatch a team of United Nations observers to verify, confirm and supervise the ceasefire and withdrawal and further requested the Secretary General to make the necessary arrangements in consultation with the parties and to submit a report thereon to the Security Council;

(3) Urges that prisoners of war be released and repatriated without delay after the cessation of active hostilities in accordance with the Third Geneva Convention of 1949;

(4) Calls upon Iran and Iraq to cooperate with the Secretary General in implementing this resolution and in mediation efforts to achieve a comprehensive, just and honorable settlement, acceptable to both sides, of all outstanding issues, in accordance with the principles contained in the Charter of the United Nations.[67]

On May 9 the Security Council considered the report of the mission dispatched by the Secretary General to investigate allegations of the use of chemical weapons in the conflict. The Security Council adopted resolution 612 (1988) by which it affirmed the urgent necessity of strict observance of the Protocol for the Prohibition of the Use in War of Asphyxiating, Poisonous or Other Gases, and the Bacteriological Methods of Warfare, of 1925. The Security Council further condemned vigorously the continued use of chemical weapons in the conflict between Iran and Iraq, contrary to the Geneva Protocol.[68]

On August 9 the Security Council adopted resolution 619 (1988) by which it approved the report of the Secretary General on the implementation of paragraph 2 of resolution 598 (1987), regarding the deployment of a United Nations observer force to verify, confirm, and supervise the ceasefire and withdrawal of Iranian and Iraqi forces to the internationally recognized boundaries.[69] The Security Council decided to establish immediately, under its authority, a United Nations Iran-Iraq Observer Group (UNIIMOG) for a period of six months to undertake the above mission. UNIIMOG withdrew after the two sides signed a formal peace treaty in 1991.[70]

Legal Issues

Did the Security Council abdicate its responsibility by not condemning Iraq's invasion of Iran and taking stronger action after both Iran and Iraq refused to comply with its demands in resolution 479 (1980)? Did the interests of certain Permanent Members take precedence over compliance with Charter principles? Despite its various resolutions, the Security Council did not take drastic measures against Iran and Iraq to force them to accept a ceasefire. The Security Council did not make a determination regarding Iraq's responsibility for starting the war, nor did it specifically condemn Iraq for using chemical weapons against Iranian forces. Although the Security Council determined the existence of a breach of the peace in resolution 598 (1987), it did not say who was responsible. The Security Council's failure to make such a determination left Iran to believe the Security Council was not impartial. The Security Council was incapable of ending the Iran-Iraq war because certain major powers had a vested interest in the conflict and would not support stronger measures against Iraq.

The United States' Invasion of Panama

On December 20, 1989 United States forces invaded Panama following several weeks of friction between the Bush administration and General Manuel Noriega, Panama's head of state. A few weeks before the invasion, General Noriega had canceled the results of a general election, which his opponent is said to have won, and called on his opponents to challenge him. The United States warned its citizens of their safety in Panama after a United States serviceman and his family were stopped at gunpoint and beaten by Panamanian soldiers. As the war of words between President Bush and Noriega intensified, General Noriega declared that his country was at war with the United States.[71] The United States justified its intervention of Panama on four grounds: (1) to protect American nationals in the Canal Zone; (2) to bring General Noriega to the United States to face charges of drug trafficking; (3) to restore democracy in Panama; and (4) to keep the Panama Canal open to shipping.[72]

On December 21 the Security Council convened an emergency session on the request of Nicaragua to discuss the United States invasion of Panama. Several states voiced concern about the United States' action, and they called for the immediate withdrawal of American forces.[73] A draft Security Council resolution condemning the United States invasion of Panama was vetoed by Britain, France, and the United States.[74] A similar resolution in the General Assembly condemning the United States invasion of Panama as a 'flagrant violation of international law' was adopted by a vote of 75 to 20, with 40 abstentions.[75] The resolution secured fewer votes than in the case of the United States' invasion of Grenada. This could have been a result of General Noriega's unpopularity among the delegates and his conduct during and after the elections. United States forces withdrew from Panama after Noriega was captured and flown to the United States to face charges of drug trafficking. A new government was later installed in Panama by the United States.

Legal Issues

Was the United States' intervention justified under international law and the United Nations Charter? Was the safety of American citizens in danger, and was an invasion warranted to protect them? Is the use of force to apprehend a head of state suspected of drug trafficking in another state legal under the United Nations Charter and customary international law? Was there a threat to the Panama Canal? Was the invitation from Endara legitimate?

The United States' invasion of Panama cannot be justified under the Charter of the United Nations, the Panama Canal Treaties, and international law. Panama had not attacked the United States, nor was the Noriega regime in any way a threat to the United States' interests in the Canal Zone. There is also no indication that the lives of American citizens were in danger. The case of the American serviceman and his family was an isolated incident, which did not amount to a policy of harassment of all Americans. On the drug trafficking charge against General Noriega, there is no independent means of verifying that General Noriega was involved in drug trafficking. The evidence against General Noriega was secret and was gathered by the Central Intelligent Agency, an agency Noriega previously worked for in its efforts to overthrow the government of Nicaragua. The charges against Noriega could have been politically motivated and raised in retaliation against Noriega for his refusal to continue cooperating with the CIA in its secret war against the Sandinistas.

The United States' claims that it intervened in Panama to restore democracy, and on the invitation of president-elect Endara, are not convincing. The United States maintained diplomatic relations with successive military regimes in Panama and may have contributed to prolonging their stay in office. Noriega was a product of the United States military and had worked closely with US military and intelligence agencies. The United States' problem with Panama was not its choice of government, but rather the individual in power, who defied the Bush administration. No state has a right to impose its choice of regime on another state.

The claim that Endara was the elected president and invited the United States to intervene is also not persuasive and does not hold under international law.[76] There is no way of verifying that Endara actually won the elections since the results were not conclusive. Endara did not have the legal authority to invite American troops into Panama when he had no legitimate authority. Finally, the United States claimed that it had intervened in Panama to protect the Panama Canal under the 1978 Panama Canal Treaties. That justification is also not valid. The Treaties provide for intervention only if shipping is interrupted by events in Panama. There was no indication that General Noriega was about to interfere with free navigation through the Canal Zone. The claim is dubious and does not hold under further scrutiny. The Panama invasion was a clear violation of international law and the Charter of the United Nations.[77]

Iraq's Invasion of Kuwait

Iraq's invasion of Kuwait on August 1, 1990 was one of the most blatant acts of aggression by one state against another since 1945. Iraq's invasion of Kuwait came at a particular period in the history of international relations. Within the previous year, the world had witnessed the end of the Cold War, the collapse of the Soviet empire, dramatic changes in relations between the United States and the Soviet Union, and an overall improvement in the international climate. The Security Council had also been revived as a result of President Gorbachev's new policy of *perestroika*, in which he called for a stronger role for the United Nations in settling regional conflicts. Iraq's action was a test for the new consensus that had begun to emerge among the Permanent Members of the Security Council. How the Security Council responded to Iraq's flagrant violation of international law would determine the future course the Security Council would pursue in managing post-Cold War inter-state conflicts.

Following Iraq's invasion of Kuwait, the Security Council convened an emergency meeting on August 2 to discuss the issue. The Security Council adopted resolution 660 (1990), by which it determined that Iraq's invasion of Kuwait was a breach of international peace and security.[78] Acting under Articles 39 and 40 of the Charter of the United Nations, the Security Council:

(1)   Condemns the Iraqi invasion of Kuwait;
(2)   Demands that Iraq withdraw immediately and unconditionally all its forces to the positions in which they were located on August 1, 1990;
(3)   Calls upon Iraq and Kuwait to begin immediately intensive negotiations for the resolution of their differences and supports all efforts in this regard, especially those of the League of Arab States.[79]

Iraq defied the Security Council and did not withdraw its forces. The superior Iraqi army overran Kuwait and captured the country within days. Baghdad subsequently annexed Kuwait as the 29th province of Iraq and installed a puppet regime. On August 6, the Security Council convened another meeting to discuss the situation in the Gulf region. The Security Council acted with unprecedented urgency to adopt resolution 661 (1990), by which it voiced concern that resolution 660 (1990) had not been implemented.[80] The Security Council affirmed under Article 51 of the Charter Kuwait's inherent right of individual and collective self-defense in response to the armed attack by Iraq. Acting under Chapter VII of the Charter of the United Nations, the Security Council:

(1)   Decides… to take the following measures to secure compliance of Iraq with paragraph 2 of resolution 660 and to restore the authority of the legitimate government of Kuwait;
(2)   Decides that all States shall prevent:

(a)   The import into their territories of all commodities and products originating in Iraq or Kuwait or exported there from after the date of the present resolution;

(b)   Any activities by their nationals or in their territories which would promote… the export… of any commodities or products from Iraq or Kuwait…;

(c)   The sale or supply by their nationals or from their territories… of any commodities or products, including weapons or any other military equipment… but not including supplies intended strictly for medical purposes, and in humanitarian circumstances, foodstuffs, to any person or body in Iraq or Kuwait.

(3)   Decides that all States shall not make available to the government of Iraq… any funds…;

(4)   Calls upon all States, including States that are non-members of the United Nations, to act strictly in accordance with the provisions of the present resolution notwithstanding any contract entered into or license granted before the present resolution.[81]

The Security Council followed the adoption of resolution 661 (1990) with a series of other resolutions in the form of declarations or judgments against certain actions taken by Iraq. On August 9 the Security Council unanimously adopted resolution 662 (1990), by which it declared Iraq's merger of Kuwait into Iraq 'null and void',[82] and called upon all states not to recognize the annexation. On August 18, the Security Council adopted resolution 664 (1990), by which it demanded that Iraq release foreign nationals held hostage in Iraq and Kuwait.[83] Iraq defied that resolution and all previous resolutions. In response to Iraq's failure to comply with its demands, the Security Council adopted resolution 665 (1990), by which it:

(1)   Calls upon those Member States co-operating with the government of Kuwait which are deploying maritime forces to the area to use such measures commensurate to the specific circumstances as may be necessary under the authority of the Security Council to halt all inward and outward maritime shipping in order to inspect and verify their cargoes and destinations and to ensure strict implementation of… resolution 661 (1990);

(2)   Further requests the States concerned to co-ordinate their actions… using as appropriate mechanisms of the Military Staff Committee.[84]

In resolution 665 (1990) the Security Council delegated its enforcement powers under Chapter VII to a group of Western states with naval forces in the Gulf to enforce the embargo.[85] The resolution was consistent with resolution 221 (1966), by which the Security Council had authorized Britain to use limited force to enforce the oil embargo against Rhodesia. However, given the concern of some states that the Security Council was authorizing force without Article 43 agreements, the Security Council included reference to the Military Staff Committee.[86] However, the Military Staff Committee exercised no formal control over the operation.

On September 16, the Security Council adopted resolution 667 (1990), by which it unanimously condemned Iraq's 'aggressive acts' against diplomatic premises and personnel in Kuwait and demanded that Iraq comply with the Vienna Conventions on Diplomatic and Consular Relations.[87] On October 29, the Security Council adopted resolution 674 (1990) by which it reminded Iraq 'that under international law it is liable for any loss, damage or injury arising in regard to Kuwait and third States, and their nationals and corporations, as a result of the invasion and illegal occupation of Kuwait by Iraq.'[88] The Security Council also adopted unanimously resolution 677 (1990) on November 28, by which it condemned Iraq's attempt to alter the demographic composition of Kuwait by deporting thousands of Kuwaiti citizens to Iraq.[89]

Despite these measures, Iraq continued to defy the international community. All diplomatic efforts to end the crisis failed. On November 29, the Security Council adopted resolution 678 (1990), by which it authorized states to use all necessary means to eject Iraqi forces from Kuwait.[90] The Security Council resolution 678 (1990) recalled and reaffirmed all previous resolutions on the Gulf. Acting under Chapter VII of the Charter of the United Nations, the Security Council:

(1) Demands that Iraq comply fully with resolution 660 (1990) and all subsequent resolutions and decides, while maintaining all its decisions, to allow Iraq one final opportunity, as a pause of goodwill, to do so;
(2) Authorizes Member States co-operating with the government of Kuwait, unless Iraq on or before January 15, 1991 fully implements, as set forth in paragraph 1 above, the foregoing resolutions, to use all necessary means to uphold and implement Security Council resolution 660 (1990) and all subsequent relevant resolutions and to restore international peace and security in the area;
(3) Requests all States to provide appropriate support for the actions undertaken in pursuance of paragraph 2 of this resolution;
(4) Requests the States concerned to keep the Council regularly informed on the progress of actions undertaken pursuant to paragraphs 2 and 3 of this resolution.[91]

Last-minute diplomatic efforts to secure Iraq's withdrawal from Kuwait failed. On January 15, 1991, on the day the deadline was to expire, the Coalition, made up of forces from 29 countries, began air attacks against Iraqi targets. The air strikes were followed by a ground invasion, which went on for several weeks. Iraq was ejected from Kuwait in approximately 43 days.[92] On March 2, 1991, Iraq accepted a temporary ceasefire, which the Security Council approved under resolution 686 (1991). Iraq accepted liability for damages caused by its invasion and agreed to rescind its annexation of Kuwait.[93] On April 3, the Security Council adopted resolution 687 (1991), by which it formally approved a permanent ceasefire agreement between Iraq and Coalition forces.[94] Resolution 687 (1991), which was adopted under Chapter VII of the Charter of the United Nations, imposed a series of punitive measures on Iraq that were reminiscent of the measures imposed on Germany after World War I. The resolution required Iraq to:

(1) Permit the destruction of Iraqi chemical and biological weapons and all ballistic missiles with a range greater than 150 kilometers;

(2) Submit to on-site inspections of weapon making facilities;

(3) Provide details of locations and amounts of weaponry and undertake not to use, acquire, etc., weapons of mass destruction;

(4) Return all Kuwaiti property that had been seized during the invasion; and

(5) Compensate those who suffered loss or injury because of the invasion.[95]

Resolution 687 (1991) also demanded that Iraq and Kuwait respect the inviolability of the international boundary in accordance with the 1963 demarcation agreement, and called on the Secretary General to make the necessary arrangements with Iraq and Kuwait to demarcate the common boundary between the two states.[96] Resolution 678 (1991) established the United Nations Special Commission (UNSCOM) to inspect and destroy Iraq's weapons of mass destruction and to ensure Iraqi's compliance with its obligations under the ceasefire agreement. A Compensation Commission and a Compensation Fund were established, to be financed out of Iraq's oil sales, in order to pay compensation to victims of Iraq's invasion. The sanctions adopted under resolution 661 (1990) were to remain in place until Iraq complied fully with the terms of all relevant resolutions of the Security Council.[97]

Following the outbreak of fighting between Iraqi forces and Kurdish rebels in the north and Shi'ites in the south, the Security Council adopted resolution 688 (1991), by which it determined that Iraq's military activities against the Kurds had created a humanitarian crisis which constituted a threat to international peace and security.[98] The United States, Britain, and France used the resolution to launch air strikes against Iraq and to justify the imposition of no-fly zones in northern and southern Iraq.[99]

On April 9 the Security Council adopted resolution 689 (1991), by which it authorized the deployment of the United Nations Iraq-Kuwait Observer Mission (UNIKOM) along the common border of Iraq and Kuwait, to replace Coalition forces.[100] The Security Council also created a Boundary Commission to demarcate the boundary between Iraq and Kuwait. Both missions were established under Chapter VII of the Charter, which made them legally binding under Article 25. The Security Council had the authority to determine when to terminate the missions. The Boundary Commission completed its task and submitted its recommendations to the Security Council, which the Security Council approved. Iraq refused to accept the recommendations of the Commission. Iraq also stopped co-operating with UNSCOM, accusing it of working on behalf of the United States.[101]

On December 17, 1999 the Security Council adopted resolution 1284 (1999) by a vote of 11 to 0, with 4 abstentions (China, France, Malaysia, and Russia) to replace UNSCOM with a new inspection unit.[102] Acting under Chapter VII of the Charter of the United Nations, the Security Council established the United Nations Monitoring, Verification and Inspection Commission (UNMOVIC), as a subsidiary organ of the Council, to inspect Iraq's weapons program and to verify Iraq's compliance with the terms of resolution 687 (1991).[103] The new Commission would assume the responsibilities, liabilities and assets of UNSCOM. It was mandated to establish and operate a reinforced, ongoing monitoring and verification system, address unresolved disarmament issues, and identify additional sites to be covered by the new monitoring system.[104]

Iraq did not allow UNMOVIC to enter the country to carry out its mandate. Iraq also rejected the changes made to the 'oil for food program' adopted by the Security Council under resolution 1330 (2000)[105]; however, Iraq soon after indicated its willingness to resume cooperation with the United Nations, but asked the Secretary General for clarification on a series of questions before it gave its consent. Iraq also wanted a definitive date for the removal of the sanctions regime.

Legality of Security Council Resolution 678 (1990)

Was resolution 678 (1990) legal? Can the Security Council delegate its authority to a member state or a group of states? Is the right of a state to self-defense suspended during the period the matter is on the agenda of the Security Council? Iraq challenged the legality of resolution 678 (1990) on the grounds that the Security Council could only authorize the use of force under Articles 42 and 43 of the Charter.[106] Some legal scholars also took a similar view, that the Security Council had violated Articles 42 and 43 of the Charter of the United Nations by not specifically invoking those articles to authorize enforcement measures against Iraq.[107] They cited the fact that no Article 43 agreement was reached with the participating states to place their forces under the command of the United Nations, and that the operational command was not placed under the Military Staff Committee as required by Article 47.[108] For these critics, resolution 678 (1990) authorized a collective self-defense operation under Article 51 of the Charter, not a collective security measure under Article 42 of the Charter of the United Nations.[109]

Resolution 678 (1990) legitimized a self-defense measure that would have been perfectly legal under Article 51 of the Charter.[110] However, certain member states felt it was necessary to have a resolution from the Security Council to give a degree of international legitimacy to the operation and to neutralize domestic opposition to the war.[111] Resolution 678 (1990) authorized the Coalition forces already gathered in the Gulf to use all necessary means, including armed force, to enforce the decisions of the Security Council. The resolution did not impose legally binding obligations under Article 25 of the Charter.[112] Resolution 678 (1990) made no reference to the Military Staff Committee. Nor did it give the Security Council oversight authority over the day-to-day conduct of the operation. The resolution gave the

Coalition *carte blanche* to wage war against Iraq by whatever means.[113] The only obligation the resolution imposed on Coalition forces was to keep the Security Council regularly informed of the progress of the operation. Resolution 678 (1990) was similar to resolution 84 (1950), which authorized enforcement measures against North Korea, and resolution 221 (1966), which authorized enforcement measures against Rhodesia. In both instances the Security Council delegated its authority to a member state. Although the Security Council did not follow the procedures specified in Chapter VII for carrying out enforcement measures, resolution 678 (1990) was consistent with the authority of the Security Council and the operation was perfectly legal under the Charter of the United Nations.[114]

The second question concerns the authority of the Security Council to delegate its authority to a state or a group of states.[115] Nothing in the United Nations Charter prohibits the Security Council from delegating its Chapter VII authority to a member state or a group of states. In the absence of a standing army, and due to the difficulty of getting states to sign an Article 43 agreement to place their troops under the command of the United Nations, the Security Council has no alternative but to delegate some of its authority under Chapter VII to a state or a group of states.

During the early phase of the crisis, Britain and the United States insisted that their forces were in the Gulf on the invitation of the government of Saudi Arabia in order to protect the Kingdom from further Iraqi expansionism and for the collective self-defense of Kuwait, if the government of Kuwait requested such assistance.[116] Both Britain and the United States had maintained that Kuwait's right to individual and collective self-defense under Article 51 of the Charter of the United Nations was affirmed in resolution 660 (1990), and that no additional Security Council authorization was necessary to initiate military action against Iraq.[117] The United Nations also continued to recognize the Kuwaiti government-in-exile as the legitimate government of Kuwait. It is safe to say that Kuwait, having been a victim of an armed attack, had a legitimate right to individual and collective self-defense. By its very nature, resolution 678 (1990) recognized Kuwait's right to collective self-defense by simply calling on states with forces in the Gulf to cooperate with the government of Kuwait to eject Iraqi forces from its territory.[118]

Other concerns raised by the measures imposed on Iraq have to do with the sanctions imposed under resolutions 661 (1990) and 687 (1991). The measures have been deemed excessively harsh and unfair, causing undue hardship for the Iraqi people. The ceasefire resolution – resolution 687 (1991) – also imposed severe restrictions on Iraq's sovereignty. The punitive measures imposed on Iraq in resolution 687 (1991) were adopted under Chapter VII of the Charter, which made them legally binding. The Security Council further invoked Chapter VII to force Iraq to comply with its international treaty obligations, some of which the Iraqi Parliament had not ratified.[119] The Security Council also invoked Chapter VII to deploy an observer force to monitor the demilitarized zone between Iraq and Kuwait. Finally, the Security Council invoked Chapter VII to force Iraq to accept the decision of the Iraq-Kuwait

Boundary Commission.[120] The actions taken by the Security Council against Iraq showed a willingness on the part of certain members of the Security Council to stretch the definition of a threat to international peace and security to include any matter they deem remotely threatening.

The manner in which the Security Council handled the Iraqi situation was the closest the Security Council came to functioning like the Framers of the Charter of the United Nations intended. This was only the third time in the history of the United Nations that the Security Council had authorized Chapter VII military measures against another state.[121] Despite the nature of the authorization, 'Operation Desert Storm' showed that the Security Council is capable of acting swiftly against aggression when it is in the interest of certain Permanent Members for the Security Council to do so. The success of the operation against Iraq gave a boost to the United Nations' role in conflict management, and renewed hope in the ability of the Security Council to respond effectively to future threats to peace.

The Security Council's response to Iraq's invasion of Kuwait may be an exception, rather than the general rule. There is no likelihood the Security Council will act in a similar manner in the future. Kuwait is a small oil-rich kingdom, whose uninterrupted flow of oil is vital for the continuing growth of the world economy. The Western industrial powers simply could not have Iraq controlling such a huge reserve of a critical resource like oil, or a strategic waterway like the Persian Gulf, upon which the economic success of the Western world is so heavily dependent.

Security Council Resolution 688 (1991)

In the wake of Iraq's defeat in Kuwait, Kurdish rebels in the north and Shi'ites in the south of Iraq began a simultaneous rebellion against the Iraqi army. The Iraqi army used excessive force to crush the rebellions. Thousand of Kurdish refugees fled into neighboring Turkey and Iran. The Security Council held an emergency meeting on April 3 to discuss the humanitarian situation in northern Iraq. The Security Council later adopted resolution 688 (1991), by which it determined that the humanitarian situation in northern Iraq constituted a threat to international peace and security.[122] The Security Council voiced concern at Iraq's repression of the civilian population in many parts of Iraq, including in Kurdish-populated areas, which led to a massive flow of refugees toward international frontiers, and to cross-border incursions, which threatened international peace and security in the region. Saying that it was deeply disturbed by the magnitude of the human suffering involved, the Security Council resolution:

(1)   Condemns the repression of the Iraqi civilian population in many parts of Iraq, including in Kurdish populated areas, the consequences of which threaten international peace and security in the region;

(2)   Demands that Iraq, as a contribution to removing the threat to international peace and security in the region, immediately end this repression and expresses the hope in the same context that an open dialogue will take place to ensure that human and political rights of all Iraqi citizens are respected;

(3)   Insists that Iraq allow immediate access by international humanitarian organizations to all those in need of assistance in all parts of Iraq and to make available all necessary facilities for their operation;

(4)   Requests further the Secretary General to use all the resources at his disposal, including those of the relevant United Nations agencies, to address urgently the critical needs of the refugees and displaced Iraqi population;

(5)   Appeals to all Member States and to all humanitarian organizations to contribute to these humanitarian relief efforts.[123]

Following adoption of resolution 688 (1991), the United States, Britain, and France used the resolution to justify an invasion of northern Iraq to establish 'safe havens' for Kurdish civilians, to protect them from further violence and to ensure the delivery of food and other humanitarian assistance.[124] To further protect Kurds in the north and Shi'ites in the south from Iraqi attack, Britain, France, and the United States established 'no-fly zones' north of the 38th parallel and south of the 32nd parallel over Iraq, and banned Iraqi aircraft from entering the air space. Coalition troops were subsequently replaced, with Iraqi consent, by United Nations guards. The Secretary General reacted cautiously to the Security Council request to deploy United Nations peacekeepers in northern Iraq. He felt resolution 688 (1991) had violated Article 2 (7) of the Charter of the United Nations and was not legally binding since it was not adopted under Chapter VII of the Charter of the United Nations. The Secretary General secured an agreement with Iraq for unarmed United Nations policemen to be deployed in northern Iraq to help with the distribution of humanitarian aid.[125]

Legal Issues

Security Council resolution 688 (1991) was unprecedented in nature. It was the first time the Security Council had made the determination that a humanitarian situation threatened international peace and security. The Security Council did not invoke Chapter VII of the Charter of the United Nations to adopt resolution 688 (1991). The language of the resolution was also vague, and it allowed for different interpretations. Several states felt the Security Council had violated Article 2 (7) of the Charter. The precedent established under resolution 688 (1991) became the basis for the Security Council to deploy troops in several humanitarian situations after 1991.[126]

The Eritrea-Ethiopian War

In May 1998 Eritrea and Ethiopia went to war over a disputed strip of land on the countries' common border. Sporadic fighting continued for the next two years, with temporary lulls allowing for the two sides to rearm. The war left hundreds of soldiers and thousands of civilians dead on both sides, and displaced thousands of civilians. The war also devastated the economies and infrastructure of both countries. The war made worse an already-serious food shortage in both countries, brought on by a severe drought that was already affecting the region. The war and drought created a serious humanitarian situation in the region, leading to the deaths of thousands of civilians and leaving millions at risk of starvation. As a province of Ethiopia, Eritrea had fought a bitter thirty-year guerrilla war against the government of Ethiopia. In 1990, Ethiopian rebels overthrew the regime of Haile Mariam Mengistu and established a new government. The new government, whose members were partners in arms with the Eritrean rebels, quickly agreed to grant Eritrea independence.

Relations between the leaders of Eritrea and Ethiopia gradually deteriorated after Eritrea began asserting its sovereignty. Eritrea abandoned use of the Ethiopian currency for its own national currency and took a series of measures that Ethiopia perceived as hostile and provocative. A personal feud between the leaders of the two countries further fueled the conflict. Fighting intensified after Eritrean troops crossed into Ethiopia and occupied several border villages in the disputed zone.

The Ethiopian-Eritrean war is one of the relatively few inter-state conflicts to have occurred since the end of the Cold War. It was a classic inter-state war in which both states enjoyed relative parity in military power. Both the Organization of African Unity (OAU) and the United Nations called on the leaders of Ethiopia and Eritrea to end the fighting and to seek a peaceful solution to their dispute, but the warning went unheeded. After making significant territorial gains, Eritrea accepted the OAU peace proposal, but Ethiopia rejected the plan and vowed to continue the war until it had recaptured the territory taken by Eritrea by force.

The Role of the Security Council

On June 26, 1998 the Security Council held an emergency meeting to discuss the situation between Eritrea and Ethiopia. Following the debate, in which both sides presented their case, the Security Council adopted resolution 1177 (1998), by which it expressed its grave concern at the situation between Eritrea and Ethiopia, and its political, humanitarian, and security implications for the region and for the civilian population.[127] The Security Council reaffirmed the principle of peaceful settlement of disputes enshrined in the Charter and stressed that the use of force is unacceptable as a means of addressing territorial disputes.[128] The Security Council endorsed the OAU peace initiative, but took no action of its own. Security Council resolution 1177 (1998) condemned the use of force and demanded that both sides immediately cease hostilities and refrain from further use of force.[129] The resolution was not adopted under Chapter VII; hence, neither side saw it as legally binding.

Following a renewed outbreak of hostilities between Eritrean and Ethiopian troops in January 1999, the Security Council adopted resolution 1226 (1999) by which it reaffirmed the demands made in resolution 1177 (1998). The Security Council expressed grave concern over the risk of armed conflict between Eritrea and Ethiopia and the escalating arms build-up along their common border. The Security Council once again expressed its strong support for the OAU peace initiative and endorsed the decision of the Secretary General of the United Nations to send a special envoy to the region to support the OAU efforts. The Security Council further welcomed Ethiopia's acceptance of the OAU Framework Agreement and urged Eritrea to do the same. The Security Council called on the parties to maintain their commitment to a peaceful resolution of the border dispute.[130]

On February 10, the Security Council adopted resolution 1227 (1999), by which it determined that the situation between Eritrea and Ethiopia constituted a threat to peace and security.[131] Without invoking Chapter VII of the Charter of the United Nations, the Security Council's resolution:

(1)   Condemns the recourse to the use of force between Eritrea and Ethiopia;

(2)   Demands an immediate halt to the hostilities, in particular the use of air strikes;

(3)   Demands that Ethiopian and Eritrea resume diplomatic efforts to find a peaceful resolution to the conflict;

(4)   Stressed that the Framework Agreement as approved by the Central Organ Summit of the OAU Mechanism for Conflict Prevention, Management, and Resolution on December 17, 1998 remains a viable and sound basis for a peaceful resolution of the conflict;

(5)   Expresses its full support for the efforts of the OAU, the Secretary General and his Special Envoy for Africa, and concerned Member States to find a peaceful resolution to the present hostilities;

(6)   Calls upon Ethiopia and Eritrea to ensure the safety of the civilian population and respect for human rights and international humanitarian law;

(7)   Strongly urges all states to end immediately all sales of arms and munitions to Ethiopia and Eritrea;

(8)   Decides to remain actively seized of the matter.[132]

The Ethiopian representative objected to the Security Council's ban on arms sales, saying that it would have a discriminatory effect on a landlocked country like his, as opposed to one with a long coastline, such as Eritrea. The representative of Ethiopia accused Eritrea of using provocative military actions to divert attention from the core issue, the need for Eritrea to withdraw from Ethiopia. He had strong reservations about the Security Council's call to end arms sales to both countries, which he said did not differentiate between the victim and the aggressor. Eritrea's representative said his country had consistently called for a renunciation of force, a commitment to a peaceful, legal solution, and a ceasefire, but such an approach had been rejected by Ethiopia.[133]

Following a fresh outbreak of fighting between Ethiopia and Eritrea, the President of the Security Council issued a statement on February 27 which demanded an immediate halt to all hostilities between the two countries. The statement welcomed the acceptance by Eritrea of the OUA Framework Agreement, and recalled Ethiopia's prior acceptance of the Agreement as well. The statement reaffirmed the sovereignty and territorial integrity of Ethiopia and Eritrea, and expressed the Security Council's willingness to consider all appropriate support to implement a peace agreement between the two parties.[134]

In May 2000 fighting intensified between Ethiopia and Eritrea. Both sides suffered heavy casualties, but Ethiopia made significant military gains as it recaptured territory previously held by Eritrea. Both sides ignored calls from the Security Council and the OAU for a ceasefire. However, following a series of military setbacks and heavy casualties, Eritrea accepted the ceasefire and agreed to participate in OAU-sponsored peace talks in Algeria. Ethiopia also agreed to join the talks, but decided to continue its military offensive until it had accomplished its strategic objectives.[135]

The Security Council Imposes an Arms Embargo

The Security Council met in emergency session on May 12 to discuss the situation between Ethiopia and Eritrea. Following the debate, the Security Council adopted resolution 1297 (2000), by which it stressed the need for both parties to achieve a peaceful resolution of the conflict. The Security Council expressed strong support for the OAU's peace efforts. The Security Council further stressed that the situation between Ethiopia and Eritrea constituted a threat to peace and security.[136] The Security Council strongly condemned the renewed fighting between the two countries and demanded that both sides immediately cease all military action and refrain from further use of force.[137] Both sides ignored the Security Council's demands. On May 17 the Security Council adopted resolution 1298 (2000) by which it imposed an arms embargo on the parties. Acting under Chapter VII of the Charter of the United Nations, the Security Council:

(1)   Strongly condemns the continuing fighting between Eritrea and Ethiopia;
(2)   Demands that both parties immediately cease all military action and refrain from further use of force;
(3)   Demands further that both parties withdraw their forces from military engagement and take no action that would aggravate tension;
(4)   Decides that all States shall prevent:
          (a) The sale or supply to Eritrea and Ethiopia, by their nationals or from their territories, using their flag vessels or aircraft, of arms and related military

materiel of all types, including weapons and ammunition, military vehicles, equipment, paramilitary equipment and spare parts for the aforementioned, whether or not originating in their territory;

(b) Any provision to Eritrea and Ethiopia by their national or from their territories of technical assistance or training related to the provision, manufacture, maintenance or use of the items in (a) above.[138]

Unfortunately, the Security Council's arms embargo came too late to have any immediate impact on the war. Eritrea and Ethiopia had previously purchased and stockpiled huge quantities of weapons and ammunition that made the embargo irrelevant. However, realizing it could not reverse Ethiopia's military gains, Eritrea reluctantly accepted the OAU Framework Agreement. Ethiopia, on the other hand, continued to press for more concessions from Eritrea before it accepted the Agreement. After Ethiopian troops recaptured all territory previously occupied by Eritrea, Ethiopia accepted the OAU Framework Agreement. On June 14 Ethiopia's Parliament approved the Agreement. On June 18 the governments of Eritrea and Ethiopia signed the OAU ceasefire agreement in Algiers.[139] The accord ended one of the bloodiest and most senseless conflicts in modern African history.

Security Council Establishes UNMEE

On July 31, the Security Council adopted resolution 1312 (2000), by which it acknowledged the role of the OAU in facilitating the Agreement on the Cessation of Hostilities between the government of the Democratic Republic of Ethiopia and the government of the State of Eritrea.[140] The Security Council endorsed the Secretary General's decision to dispatch reconnaissance and liaison teams to the region. The Security Council further decided to establish the United Nations Mission in Ethiopia and Eritrea (UNMEE), consisting of up to 100 military observers and the necessary civilian support staff until January 31, 2001, in anticipation of a peacekeeping operation subject to future Security Council authorization, and to undertake the following mandate:

(1)   To establish and maintain liaison with the parties;

(2)   To visit the parties' military headquarters and other units in all areas of operation of the mission deemed necessary by the Secretary General;

(3)   To establish and put into operation the mechanism for verifying the cessation of hostilities;

(4)   To prepare for the establishment of the Military Coordination Commission provided for in the Cessation of Hostilities Agreement;

(5)   To assist in planning for a future peacekeeping operation as necessary.[141]

On September 15 the Security Council adopted resolution 1320 (2000) by which it authorized the deployment within UNMEE of up to 4,200 troops, including up to 220 military observers.[142] UNMEE was given the following mandate, which required it to:

(1)   Monitor the cessation of hostilities;

(2)   Assist in ensuring the observance of the security commitments agreed by the parties;

(3)   Monitor and verify the redeployment of Ethiopian forces from positions taken after February 6, 1999, which were not under Ethiopian administration before May 6, 1998;

(4)   Monitor the positions of Ethiopian forces once redeployed;

(5)   Simultaneously, monitor the positions of Eritrean forces that are to redeploy in order to remain at a distance of 25 kilometers from positions to which Ethiopian forces shall redeploy;

(6)   Monitor the temporary security zone (TSZ) to assist in ensuring compliance with the Agreement on Cessation of Hostilities;

(7)   Chair the Military Coordination Commission (MCM) to be established by the United Nations and the OAU in accordance with the Agreement on Cessation of Hostilities;

(8)   Coordinate and provide technical assistance for humanitarian mine-action activities in the TSZ and areas adjacent to it; and

(9)   Coordinate the Mission's activities in the TSZ and areas adjacent to it with humanitarian and human rights activities of the United Nations and other organizations in those areas.[143]

The Security Council emphasized that the Agreement on Cessation of Hostilities linked the termination of the United Nations peacekeeping mission with the completion of the process of delimitation and demarcation of the Ethiopia-Eritrea border.

On December 12 the presidents of Ethiopia and Eritrea signed a permanent peace treaty in Algiers. The peace agreement paved the way for the United Nations to deploy UNMEE to monitor implementation of, and compliance with, the peace agreement, and to patrol the demilitarized zone between the two countries. On December 18, UNMEE opened the first air corridor between Ethiopia and Eritrea to serve the logistical and medical needs of the troops being deployed between the two countries. The route was for the sole use of the United Nations mission and international personnel.

The role the Security Council played in the Ethiopia-Eritrea conflict is quite similar to the way the Council has generally responded to inter-state conflicts. The Security Council was never effective in managing inter-state conflicts, and since the end of the Cold war its power to do so has further diminished. The Security Council made no determination in the Ethiopia-Eritrea war regarding which state had breached the peace or committed an act of aggression. The Security Council gave its tacit support to the OAU mediation efforts between the parties, but did not directly intervene until the conflict had escalated into a full-scale war. The Security Council's arms embargo had no impact on the parties or the conduct of the war, as both parties had previously acquired large quantities of weapons sufficient to keep them fighting indefinitely. More importantly, arms embargoes have proved ineffective in post-Cold War conflicts. The amount of arms available on the international weapons market is far greater than the demand. This makes the purchase of arms much easier now than during the Cold War era, and makes it more difficult for the Security Council to regulate.

Legal Issues

The war between Ethiopia and Eritrea raised a number of legal issues that were not addressed by the Security Council. Who was actually responsible for starting the war? Did Eritrea and Ethiopia violate the Charter of the United Nations by using force to settle a territorial dispute? Assuming Eritrea used force first, did Ethiopia have a right to self-defense? Did the parties violate international humanitarian law, and if so, should they be held responsible? Should any of the parties be held liable for property damage caused by their indiscriminate bombing?

It is not clear who had a legitimate claim to the disputed territory since the border was never clearly demarcated after Eritrea gained independence from Ethiopia. However, it is a fundamental norm of international law that states should settle their disputes by peaceful means. The Security Council reaffirmed the parties' obligation under the Charter of the United Nations in its various resolutions. Assuming the disputed territory belonged to Eritrea, Eritrea's attempt to acquire the territory by force violated Articles 2 (3) and 33 of the Charter of the United Nations, which calls on Member States to settle their disputes by peaceful means. Ethiopia had a right to self-defense under Article 51 of the Charter of the United Nations, if it was a victim of an armed attacked by Eritrea. However, Ethiopia also had an obligation under Article 2 (3) to settle its dispute by peaceful means. Neither state attempted to submit the dispute to binding arbitration or to the International Court of Justice for adjudication before resorting to force. Both states committed serious violations of international humanitarian law by indiscriminately bombing civilian areas and mistreating each other's nationals and prisoners of war. Both states were liable for property damage, caused as a result of their indiscriminate bombing and targeting of civilian areas.

The War in the Democratic Republic of the Congo (DRC)

The war in the DRC has been dubbed Africa's 'First World War' as a result of the number of states and rebel groups involved in the conflict: six states and three principal rebel movements were involved in the war. The war started in 1998, after President Mobutu was overthrown in May 1997 by a rebel movement led by Laurent Kabila and backed by Uganda and Rwanda.[144] Mobutu's departure was a welcome relief for both Rwanda and Angola; Mobutu helped fuel the conflict in Rwanda by providing safe haven to remnants of the Hutu army responsible for the genocide in Rwanda, and he allowed his country to be used as a transit point for shipping weapons to the UNITA rebels of Angola. Mobutu ruled Zaire, as the country was called, for thirty years, and his sudden departure left a leadership vacuum that several groups attempted to fill. In the post-Mobutu era various factions scrambled for control. Laurent Kabila, with the help of Rwanda and Uganda, and the backing of the international community, immediately established himself as president and consolidated his power base. He renamed the country the Democratic Republic of the Congo (DRC) and established a virtual one-party state.

Relations between Kabila and Paul Kagame of Rwanda became strained. Kabila expelled Rwandan forces from the DRC in an attempt to legitimize his domestic base. The move prompted army mutinies in the capital Kinshasa, and in Kivu province in the east. The mutiny in Kinshasa was quickly quelled, but the situation in Kivu escalated into a drive to topple the Kabila regime. Opposing the Kabila government were factions of the Rally for Congolese Democracy (RCD), supported by Rwanda and Uganda. Another rebel group, the Movement for the Liberation of Congo (MLC), later emerged. Defending Kabila's government were troops from the former Rwandan army (FAR) and the Interahamwe militia, and the armies of Angola, Namibia, Chad, and Zimbabwe. Relations between Kabila and Paul Kagame further deteriorated as a result of Kabila's relations with the ex-FAR militias, who Rwanda accused of carrying out the genocide in Rwanda. Rwandan troops later intervened in the DRC in pursuit of ex-FAR forces. Rwanda also launched an offensive against the ex-FAR forces in camps in Goma in order to curtail their incursions into Rwanda, and to repatriate genuine Rwandan refugees. Ugandan troops also intervened in the DRC to repel rebel attacks against Uganda.

Forces from Angola, Chad, Namibia, and Zimbabwe intervened in the war on behalf of Kabila for various reasons. Each state had a vested interest in the DRC and its resources, and they intervened not to save Kabila, but for their own political and economic interests. Zimbabwe had an economic stake in the diamond industry in the DRC; Angola wanted to cut off the supplies of weapons to UNITA; and Namibia intervened in order to find jobs for its huge army of unemployed ex-combatants. The intervention of Zimbabwe, Angola, and Namibia led to an escalation of the conflict and hardened the resolve of Rwanda and Uganda to pursue their objectives. The difficult geographic terrain of the DRC, coupled with poor communications, made a quick military victory for any one of the parties extremely difficult.

The Lusaka Ceasefire Agreement

Efforts to mediate an end to the conflict were initiated by the Southern African Development Community (SADC). On July 10, 1999, the DRC, along with Angola, Rwanda, Uganda, and Zimbabwe signed the Lusaka Ceasefire Agreement for the cessation of hostilities between all belligerent forces in the DRC.[145] The MLC signed the Agreement on August 1, but the RCD refused. The Lusaka peace accord called for a ceasefire, followed by the deployment of an international peacekeeping force to monitor implementation of the accord, and for the beginning of a 'national dialogue' on the political future of the DRC. None of the signatories to the Lusaka accord ever lived up to their commitments under the agreement, and numerous violations of the Lusaka Agreement have been reported. Although the Lusaka Agreement continued to be seen as the basis for a settlement of the conflict in the DRC, Rwanda and Uganda questioned its effectiveness in guaranteeing their own security and failed to comply fully with the various provisions of the agreement.

In January 2001, members of his security apparatus assassinated President Kabila. His death provided a window of opportunity to resume the peace process. While still alive, President Kabila had become an obstacle to the peace process. He had become increasing autocratic and banned all political opposition. He stopped cooperating with former President Sir Ketumile Masire of Botswana, the facilitator of the inter-Congolese dialogue, and accused him of not being neutral. The distrust between Kabila, Kagame, and Museveni also made it difficult for the three men to find a consensus to settle the conflict in the DRC. Joseph Kabila, who succeeded his father, immediately appealed to all parties to the conflict to accept the Lusaka Ceasefire Agreement as the basis for a permanent peace in the DRC. The international community welcomed Joseph Kabila's peace overtures and invited him to address the Security Council and to meet United States and EU officials to discuss ways to implement the Lusaka Accord. Joseph Kabila also met with the leaders of Rwanda and Uganda to discuss the withdrawal of their forces from the DRC.

Rwanda and Uganda continued to occupy large parts of Congolese territory in violation of the Lusaka Agreement and Security Council resolutions. Both Rwanda and Uganda maintained that their forces remained in the DRC because the Lusaka Accord did not guarantee their countries' security from attacks by rebels operating from the DRC. Rwanda and Uganda may also have become involved in the DRC for other reasons. A United Nations Committee established by the Security Council to investigate the illegal exploitation of the mineral resources of the DRC accused Rwanda and Uganda of exploiting the natural resources of the DRC for personal gain. The Security Council has begun playing a more active role in resolving the conflict in the DRC, but the situation has proved intractable and a peaceful solution is not likely in the immediate future.

Role of the Security Council

On April 9, 1999 the Security Council discussed the situation in the DRC and thereafter adopted resolution 1234 (1999) by which it expressed its concern over the further deterioration of the situation in the DRC.[146] The Security Council also expressed its firm commitment to preserving the territorial integrity and political independence of the DRC, and it warned against measures taken by forces opposing the government in the eastern part of the DRC in violation of the sovereignty of the country.[147] The Security Council voiced concern at the illicit flow of arms in the Great Lakes region.

On August 15 the Security Council adopted resolution 1258 (1999) by which it approved the July 15 report of the Secretary General and endorsed the recommendation of the Secretary General for the preliminary deployment of United Nations personnel to the DRC. The Security Council also welcomed the signing of the Lusaka Agreement by the parties to the conflict, and it called on all rebel groups to sign the agreement. The Security Council authorized the Secretary General to deploy 90 United Nations military liaison personnel and other staff to the capitals of the signatory states for a period of three month.[148] The mandate for the United Nations mission called for it to:

(1)   Establish contacts and maintain liaison with the Joint Military Commission (JMC) and all parties to the Agreement;
(2)   Assist the JMC and the parties in developing modalities for the Implementation of the Agreement;
(3)   Provide technical assistance, as requested to the JMC;
(4)   Provide information to the Secretary General regarding the situation on the ground, and to assist in refining a concept of operations for a possible further role for the United Nations in the implementation of the Agreement once it is signed by all the parties; and
(5)   Ensure from the parties guarantees of cooperation and assurances of security for possible deployment in country of military observers.[149]

On November 5 the Security Council adopted resolution 1273 (1999) by which it extended the mandate of the military liaison personnel until January 15, 2000.[150] The Security Council expressed concern at alleged violations of the Ceasefire Agreement. The Security Council authorized the establishment of the United Nations Organization Mission in the DRC (MONUC) until March 1, 2000, to assist the Special Representative of the Secretary General. MONUC would comprise a multi-disciplinary staff of personnel in the fields of human rights, humanitarian affairs, public information, medical support, child protection, political affairs, and administrative support. Its mandate included the following tasks:

(1)   To establish contacts with the signatories of the Ceasefire Agreement at their headquarters level, as well as in the capitals of the states signatories;
(2)   To liaise with the JMC and provide technical assistance in the implementation of its functions under the Ceasefire Agreement, including in the investigation of cease fire violations;
(3)   To provide information on security conditions in all areas of its operation, with emphasis on local conditions affecting future decisions on the introduction of United Nations personnel;
(4)   To plan for the observation of the cease fire and disengagement of forces;
(5)   To maintain liaison with all parties to the Ceasefire Agreement to facilitate the delivery of humanitarian assistance to displaced persons, refugees, children, and other

affected persons, and assist in the protection of human rights, including the rights of children.[151]

The resolution called on the Secretary General to take immediate administrative steps for equipping up to 500 United Nations military observers, with the view to facilitating future rapid United Nations deployments, as authorized by the Security Council.

On February 24 the Security Council adopted resolution 1291 (2000) by which it authorized the deployment of phase II of MONUC. The Security Council extended the mandate of MONUC to August 31 and authorized an expansion of up to 5,537 military personnel, including up to 500 observers.[152] The Security Council reaffirmed the purposes and principles of the Charter of the United Nations and its primary role in the maintenance of international peace and security. It reminded all states of their obligation to refrain from the threat or use of force against the territorial integrity or political independence of any state, or in any other manner inconsistent with the purposes of the United Nations. The Security Council also reaffirmed the sovereignty, territorial integrity and political independence of the DRC and all states in the region. The Security Council further reaffirmed the sovereignty of the DRC over its natural resources, and noted with concern reports of the illegal exploitation of the country's assets and the potential consequences of these actions on security conditions and the continuation of hostilities. The Security Council expressed its strong support for the Lusaka Ceasefire Agreement, and it called for the orderly withdrawal of all foreign forces from the DRC in accordance with the Ceasefire Agreement.

According to the Security Council, the deployment of MONUC was to be contingent on the following conditions:

(1)   That the parties respect and uphold the Ceasefire Agreement and the relevant Security Council resolutions;

(2)   That a valid plan for the disengagement of the parties' forces and their redeployment to JMC-approved positions is developed;

(3)   That the parties provide firm and credible assurances, prior to the deployment on MONUC forces, for the security and freedom of movement of United Nations and related personnel.[153]

The Security Council insisted that MONUC would only be deployed after the Security Council received assurances from the Secretary General that the above conditions were fulfilled. The Security Council also recognized efforts by the United Nations to sensitize all its peacekeepers about the dangers of AIDS and called for the United Nations to distribute condoms to all its forces as a precautionary measure against sexually transmitted diseases.

Without invoking Chapter VII of the United Nations Charter, the Security Council determined that the situation in the DRC constituted a threat to international peace and security in the region. The Security Council extended the mandate of MONUC until August 31, 2000, and it authorized expanding MONUC to consist of up to 5,537 military personnel, including 500 observers. MONUC, in cooperation with the JMC, was given the following mandate:

(1) To monitor the implementation of the Ceasefire Agreement and investigate violations of the ceasefire;

(2) To establish and maintain continuous liaison with the field headquarters of all the parties' military forces;

(3) To develop, within 45 days of adoption of this resolution, an action plan for the overall implementation of the Ceasefire Agreement by all concerned with particular emphasis on the following objectives: the collection and verification of military information on the parties' forces, maintenance of the cessation of hostilities and the disengagement and redeployment of the parties' forces, the comprehensive disarmament, demobilization, resettlement and reintegration of all members of the armed groups referred to in annex A, Chapter 9.1 of the Ceasefire Agreement, and the orderly withdrawal of all foreign forces;

(4) To work with the parties to obtain the release of all prisoners of war, military captives and remains in cooperation with international humanitarian agencies;

(5) To supervise and verify the disengagement and deployment of the parties' forces;

(6) Within its capabilities and areas of deployment, to monitor compliance with the provisions of the Ceasefire Agreement on the supply of ammunition, weaponry and other war-related materiel to the field, including to all armed groups referred to in Annex A, Chapter 9.1;

(7) To facilitate humanitarian assistance and human rights monitoring with particular attention to vulnerable groups including, women, children and demobilized child soldiers, as MONUC deems within its capabilities and under acceptable security conditions, in close cooperation with other United Nations agencies, related organizations and non-governmental organizations;

(8) To cooperate closely with the Facilitator of the National Dialogue, provide support and technical assistance to him, coordinate other United Nations agencies' activities to that effect;

(9) To deploy mine action experts to assess the scope of the mine and unexploded ordnance problems, coordinate the initiation of mine action activities, develop a mine action plan, carry out emergency mine action activities as required in support of its mandate.[154]

Acting under Chapter VII of the Charter of the United Nations, the Security Council authorized MONUC to take the necessary action in areas of deployment of its infantry battalions, and as it deemed within its capabilities, to protect United Nations personnel, facilities and equipment, ensure the security and freedom of movement of its personnel, and protect civilians under imminent threat of physical violence.[155] The Security Council condemned all massacres carried out in the DRC, and called for an international investigation into all such events with a view to bringing those responsible to justice.[156] The Security Council further called on all the parties to the conflict in the DRC to respect human rights, international humanitarian law, and the Genocide Convention of 1948.

In early June 2000, forces from Rwanda and Uganda clashed on the territory of the DRC. The Security Council expressed outrage at the continuation of hostilities in the DRC, in particular the renewed fighting between Rwanda and Uganda in Kisangani. On June 16 the Security Council adopted resolution 1304 (2000) by which it criticized Rwanda and Uganda for their failure to comply with their commitment to cease hostilities and withdraw from Kisangani.[157] The Security Council deplored the loss of civilian lives, the threat to the civilian population, and the damage to property inflicted by the forces of Rwanda and Uganda on the Congolese population. The Security Council determined that the situation in the DRC continued to constitute a threat to international peace and security in the region. Acting under Chapter VII of the Charter of the United Nations, the Security Council:

(1)   Calls on all parties to cease hostilities throughout the territory of the DRC and fulfill their obligations under the Ceasefire Agreement and the relevant provisions of the April 8 Kampala disengagement plan;

(2)   Reiterates its unreserved condemnation of the fighting between Ugandan and Rwandan forces in Kisangani in violation of the sovereignty and territorial integrity of the DRC, and demands that these forces and those allied to them desist from further fighting;

(3)   Demands that Ugandan and Rwandan forces as well as the forces of the Congolese armed opposition and other armed groups immediately and completely withdraw from Kisangani, and calls on all parties to the Ceasefire Agreement to respect the demilitarization of the city and its environs;

(4)   The Security Council further demands:

   (a)   That Uganda and Rwanda, which have violated the sovereignty and territorial integrity of DRC, withdraw all their forces from the territory of the DRC without further delay, in conformity with the timetable of the Cease fire Agreement and the April 8 Kampala disengagement plan;

   (b)   That each phase of the withdrawal completed by Ugandan and Rwandan forces be reciprocated by the other parties in conformity with the same timetable;

   (c)   That all other foreign military presence and activity, direct and indirect, in the territory of the DRC be brought to an end in conformity with the provisions of the Ceasefire Agreement;

(5)   In this context the Security Council demands that all parties abstain from any offensive action during the process of disengagement and of withdrawal of foreign forces.[158]

The conflict in the DRC is a complicated one, due to the number of parties involved and the rugged geography of the country. The international community faces a daunting task trying to get all the parties to the conflict to accept the terms of the Lusaka Accord, which many consider flawed. The various rebel groups saw the Lusaka Accord as taking away what they gained on the battlefield without providing them with an alternative. The various rebel groups, backed by Rwanda and Uganda, continued to control huge portions of the DRC. Relinquishing control, as required by the Lusaka Accord, would leave them with an uncertain future and no political leverage. Both Rwanda and Uganda continued to occupy DRC territory in violation of relevant Security Council resolutions, the Lusaka Ceasefire Agreement, the Kampala agreement and the Harare sub-plans.

The DRC brought three cases before the International Court of Justice (ICJ) against Burundi, Rwanda, and Uganda for violating the territorial integrity and political independence of the DRC. Laurent Kabila may have initiated the proceedings in an attempt to delay full implementation of the Lusaka Accord. The situation in the DRC in the post-Kabila era continued to fluctuate. Sporadic fighting continues in various parts of the country, and the central government has not been able to wrest control of all DRC territories occupied by foreign forces and the various rebel groups. All efforts to revive the peace process have failed.

MONUC was deployed in 2001, and as of June 8, MONUC had a total of 2,366 military personnel, including 497 liaison officers and military observers. The two main rebel groups continued to hold out in hopes of winning greater concessions from the central government. Foreign troops, particularly Ugandan and Rwandan forces, continued their occupation of areas of the DRC they captured during the early phases of the conflict. Rwanda and Uganda have not withdrawn all their forces in accordance with their commitments under the Lusaka Ceasefire Agreement and subsequent agreements. A Security Council mission visited the Great Lakes region between May 15 and 26 and held consultations with the heads of state and leaders of the two main rebel groups involved in the conflict in the DRC. The mission called for the withdrawal of all foreign troops from the DRC in accordance with their commitments under the various agreements. On June 15 the Security Council adopted resolution 1355 (2001) by which it endorsed the Secretary General's report of June 8 and its recommendations.[159] The Security Council determined that the situation in the DRC continued to pose a threat to international peace and security in the region.[160] Acting under Chapter VII of the Charter of the United Nations, the Security Council demanded the disengagement and redeployment of rebel forces and the withdrawal of all foreign troops from the DRC. The Security Council decided to extend the mandate of MONUC until June 15, 2002, and to continue to review the situation at least every four months based on reporting by the Secretary General.[161]

Legal Issues

The conflict in the DRC has given rise to several legal issues. Does the DRC have a right of collective self-defense? Do neighboring states have a right to hot pursuit to stop attacks on their territory by rebel groups supported by the government of the DRC? Did Rwanda and Uganda violate international law and the Charter of the United Nations by backing rebel groups seeking to overthrow the government of the DRC? Did the DRC and Rwanda violate international humanitarian law? Do rebel groups have a right to use force to unseat an undemocratic government?

The right of a state to individual and collective self-defense is a well-established right under customary international law and Article 51 of the Charter of the United Nations. The DRC has such a right if its territory is attacked by outside forces, or if rebel groups within its territory are receiving support from external sources. The DRC's right to invite Angolan, Namibian, and Zimbabwean troops onto its soil before or after an external invasion by Ugandan and Rwandan-backed rebels is legal under international law. Rebel groups do not have rights under international law to receive support from external sources, unless they are fighting a legitimate war of self-determination.[162] Rwanda and Uganda violated international law by supporting rebels to overthrow the government of the DRC and invading the DRC. Rwanda and Uganda may have a right to hot pursuit onto DRC territory to stop rebel attacks on their territories if the government of the DRC is supporting the rebels or is unable or unwilling to stop the attacks. However, Rwanda and Uganda would be in violation of the sovereignty and territorial integrity of the DRC if their troops continued to occupy DRC territory, as they have, long after the attacks ceased.

The DRC, like every other state, has an obligation to respect international humanitarian law during armed conflicts, whether internal or international. The DRC is alleged to have participated in the killing and disappearance of thousands of Hutu civilians who took refuge in the DRC after the Rwandan genocide. The actions of the DRC violated the Geneva Conventions of 1949, and the Genocide Convention of 1948. The DRC has blocked efforts by United Nations human rights monitors to investigate the alleged atrocities. The DRC's failure to comply with Security Council demands to respect humanitarian law, and specifically the targeting of the civilian population, is a violation of its obligation under Article 25 of the Charter of the United Nations.

Customary international law does not recognize the rights of rebel organizations to use force to overthrow a dictatorial regime. However, given the growing emphasis on regime legitimacy and democratic government, rebel attempts to overthrow an undemocratic regime seem perfectly legal under contemporary international law. In recent years, states and the United Nations have withheld recognition of regimes based on the manner in which they came into power.[163] Rebels have a right of self-determination, and their exclusion from participation in their government may be considered a denial of such a right. The use of force in pursuit of the right of self-determination is perfectly legal under international law and General Assembly resolution.[164] However, the international community has not articulated the criteria for determining what ethnic or political groups are entitled to the right of self-determination. Current state practice gives no indication of an emerging norm.[165]

The United States' Invasion of Afghanistan

Following the terrorist attacks on the United States on September 11, 2001, the United States vowed to retaliate against any state found responsible for harboring those responsible for the attacks. After it was determined that al Qaeda was responsible, the United States called on the Taliban regime of Afghanistan to surrender Osama bin Laden or face a military attack. The Security Council condemned the attacks on the United States and called for those responsible to be brought to justice.[166] The Security Council also imposed sanctions on the Taliban and called on member states to freeze al Qaeda's assets, in resolution 1373 (2001).[167] The Security Council recognized the inherent right of states to self-defense, but did not specifically acknowledge that the United States had a right to self-defense in this case.

On October 7, 2001 the United States informed the President of the Security Council that it had began a military operation against Afghanistan in exercise of its right of self-defense under Article 51 of the United Nations Charter in response to the September 11 attacks.[168] The Security Council convened an emergency meeting in which it discussed the military operation, but it did not condemn the United States' action. Several member states voiced support for the United States, including the President of the Security Council, who issued a statement affirming the United States' right to self-defense. Following the debate, the Security Council adopted resolution 1383 (2001), in which it endorsed international efforts to root out terrorism.[169]

Both NATO and the Organization of American States (OAS) invoked their collective self-defense arrangements in support of the United States prior to commencement of the military operation in Afghanistan.[170] The Taliban regime was overthrown within weeks of the operation and a new interim government was installed in Afghanistan. At a conference in Bonn, the various parties with an interest in Afghanistan agreed to a timetable to return Afghanistan to democratic rule. The parties also agreed to establish an international stabilization force in the capital, Kabul, to protect the new government and to maintain security within the city limits. The Security Council subsequently adopted resolution 1386 (2001) by which it approved the Bonn Agreement, including the establishment of the international stabilization force. The status of US forces, which remained in the country to battle Taliban and al Qaeda fighters, was not clarified under the resolution.

The situation in Afghanistan has improved significantly, but sporadic fighting between various factions continues. United States forces continue to attack Taliban and al Qaeda hideouts on the Pakistani border. The Karzai government is barely in control of the entire country. On October 13, the Security Council adopted resolution 1510 (2003) by which it authorized an expansion of the mandate of the International Security Assistance Force (ISAF) to allow it to support the Afghan Transitional Authority and its successors in the maintenance of security in areas of Afghanistan outside Kabul and its environs.[171] The Security Council further extended the authorization of the ISAF for a period of twelve months.

The United States Invasion of Iraq (2003)

On March 19 the United States, Britain and over three dozen countries (the so-called 'Coalition of the Willing') began a massive military invasion of Iraq under the banner of 'Iraqi Freedom.' The United States defied the United Nations Security Council and overwhelming international opposition to carry out an invasion of Iraq with the goal of 'regime change.'

In September 2002, President Bush addressed the United Nations General Assembly, at which time he called on the United Nations to enforce its resolutions against Iraq, or the United States would do so. He further went on to say that the United Nations risked becoming irrelevant if it cannot enforce its resolutions.[172] Bush later pressured the Security Council to adopt a resolution that gave Iraq one last chance to comply with its international obligations to disarm, or to face serious consequences.[173] Resolution 1441 (2002) was adopted after several weeks of diplomatic wrangling between the United States and Britain on one side, and France, Russia, and China on the other, over the language of the text and the role of the Security Council if Iraq was found in material breach of its obligations.[174]

Even while going to the Security Council for adoption of resolution 1441 (2002), the United States was insisting that it had the legal authority under existing resolutions, namely resolutions 678 (1990) and 687 (1991), to use force against Iraq if Iraq failed to implement the measures it agreed to under resolution 687 (1991).[175] Security Council resolution 1441 (2002), which was adopted unanimously, called for the return of United Nations weapons inspectors and for full Iraqi cooperation. Both UNMOVIC and the IAEA resumed their work in Iraq promptly, and despite some false statements by Iraqi officials and Iraq's failure to disclose all its weapons programs, the heads of UNMOVIC and the IAEA, Hans Blix and Mohammed El Baradei, respectively, found no evidence that Iraq was in possession of or manufacturing banned weapons of mass destruction.[176]

The Bush administration was convinced that Iraq had not disarmed and that it would require a direct military intervention to force Iraq to disarm. Prime Minister Blair pursued Bush to return to the United Nations Security Council for a second resolution before using force against Iraq. Britain, the United States, and Spain sponsored a draft resolution that would give Iraq a period of one week to disarm or face the threat of force. France and Germany, along with several non-Permanent Members of the Security Council opposed the rush to war, and called for the inspection process to be extended. Failing to convince a majority of the Security Council to support the resolution, the United States withdrew the resolution. President Bush subsequently gave Hussein 48 hours to leave Iraq or face the threat of force.[177]

Without legal justification or authorization from the Security Council, President Bush announced the invasion of Iraq. The president's rationale for war with Iraq contained in a report to Congress were: (1) to protect the national security of the United States, as well as the security of other countries, against the continuing threat posed by Iraqi weapons of mass destruction, and (2) to obtain Iraqi compliance with all relevant United Nations Security Council resolutions regarding Iraq.[178] The president also gave several reasons for invading Iraq: (1) to destroy Iraq's weapons of mass destruction; (2) to liberate the Iraqi people from tyranny; (3) to bring democracy to the region; and (4) to prevent future terrorist attacks against the United States.[179]

President Bush stated that his legal authority to attack Iraq derived from his authority under the United States Constitution as Commander-in-Chief of the armed forces, supported by explicit statutory authorization contained in the Authorization for Use of Military Force Against Iraq Resolution (Public Law 102-1) and the Authorization for Use of Military Force Against Iraq Resolution of 2002 (Public Law 107-243).[180] In addition, the president maintained that the action of the United States was consistent with the United Nations Charter, and Security Council resolution 678 (1990), which authorized the use of force against Iraq in 1990. The United States also relied on resolution 1441 (2002), which it said unanimously decided that Iraq had been and remained in material breach of its obligations under the relevant resolutions and would face serious consequences if it failed immediately to disarm.[181] Finally, the United States said that based on the nature of the threats posed by Iraq that the United States could exercise its inherent right of self-defense, recognized in Article 51 of the United Nations Charter. [182]

On April 9, United States Marines rolled into the center of Baghdad and declared that the regime of Saddam Hussein was no longer in control. On May 1, President Bush declared an end to major hostilities, even though sporadic fighting was still going on in various parts of the country. A number of members of Saddam Hussein's regime were captured and held in detention for war crimes trials. Hussein's two sons were assassinated in July by United States forces in a raid on a house in Mosul, where they were hiding. Six months after President Bush declared an end to major hostilities, Iraq was in a state of chaos and instability. More American soldiers died since the end of major combat operations than during the actual initial invasion. A guerrilla war against American forces quickly intensified. A transition administration handpicked by the Coalition had little authority and did not make much headway in establishing its authority over the country or winning the trust of the Iraqi people.

The Role of the Security Council

The Security Council for the first time may have acted with a degree of independence unseen in the Council since the end of the Cold War. In the pass the Security Council had acted solely as a rubber stamp for issues agreed upon outside the Council chamber, and between the United States, Britain and France. Debates on draft resolutions were procedural instead of substantive. In the Iraq situation three of the permanent members opposed the United States, and the United States could not persuade a majority of non-permanent members to support the resolution.[183] At the end the Security Council did not authorize the use of force against Iraq, as many members felt it was a violation of the United Nations Charter and international law for the Security Council to authorize the removal of a government.[184] Secondly, many members felt that diplomacy had not been given enough time to succeed.[185] The refusal of a majority of members of the Security Council to approve the United States request for military measures against Iraq may have saved the Security Council from being labeled an instrument of United States foreign policy ant to be declared an irrelevant body.[186]

In attacking Iraq the United States maintained that it was enforcing the resolutions of the Security Council. This raises the issue the legality of unilateral force to enforce resolutions of the Security Council without prior Security Council authorization.[187] In 1998 the United States and its allies used force to enforce the no-fly zones in Iraq, and intervened in Yugoslavia to stop Serb atrocities of ethnic Albanian in the Yugoslav province of Kosovo. The United States and its allies did not seek the prior authorization of the Security Council.[188] The Security Council in turn did not condemn these acts as a violation of the Charter. In the recent attack on Iraq the Security Council failed to carry out its responsibility under Chapter VII of the Charter. The Security Council did not meet in emergency session, as expect in a situation of armed conflict, to determine whether the United States attack on Iraq was a threat to the peace or a breach of the peace.[189] Nor did the United States inform the Security Council of its actions against Iraq, as is required when a state uses force in self-defense.[190] The absence of any meaningful debate in the Security Council on the blatant use of force by the United States in violation of Charter norms is likely to damage the credibility of the Security Council in the management of future armed conflict.

Legal Issues

Was the United States' invasion of Iraq legal? The United States claimed that it had the authority under existing Security Council resolutions to attack Iraq. The United States invoked resolutions 678 (1990) and 1441 (2002) in its report to the United States Congress as the legal bases for its attack against Iraq.[191] The United States also said that it was enforcing resolutions of the Security Council.

Security Council resolution 678 (1990) authorized the states cooperation with the government of Kuwait 'to use all necessary means to uphold and implement resolution 660 (1990) and all subsequent relevant resolutions and to restore international peace and security in the area.'[192] The Security Council gave broad authority to the coalition not only to execute the 1991 war against Iraq but also to determine when peace and security had been restored in the Gulf region. The resolution gave extraordinary discretionary authority to the United States-led coalition to wage war against Iraq without imposing a timetable as to when the war should conclude.[193] The United States can claim that peace and security was never fully restored in the Gulf area, as required by resolution 678 (1990); that Iraq's conduct and its failure to comply with resolution 687 (1991), which called on Iraq to disarm, put it in material breach of the relevant resolutions of the Security Council, and as such in violation of resolution 1441 (2002).[194] However, the United States would face a legal hurdle. Subsequent resolutions of the Security Council may have invalidated the authority granted under resolution 678 (1990). Indeed, resolution 687 (1991), which formally approved the ceasefire between Iraq and the coalition, supersedes all previous resolutions. Given that resolution 687 (1991) does not authorize the use of force in the event Iraq failed to comply with its international obligations, any new military action against Iraq would have to be approved by the Security Council under a new resolution. Although the United States did not fully subscribe to that view, it sought a new resolution from the Security Council that warned Iraq of 'serious consequences' if it did not disarm immediately. That resolution, Security Council resolution 1441 (2002), does not provide any explicit authorization to use force against Iraq.[195]

In justifying its invasion of Iraq the United States claimed that it had the authority under resolution 1441 (2002) because Iraq had failed to disarm. The legal basis to attack Iraq under resolution 1441(2002) is less tenuous. Although the resolution warned Iraq of serious consequences if it failed to comply with its international obligations, it does not specifically authorize the use of force. The majority of the states who voted for the resolution did so because they believed a second resolution would be required for the United States to take military action against Iraq.[196] The United States believed that the warning given to Iraq under resolution 1441 (2002) was sufficient to take military action against Iraq. Prime Minister Tony Blair persuaded President Bush to seek a second Security Council resolution in order to win over a skeptical British public who was overwhelmingly opposed to war. The United States withdrew the draft resolution after France and Russia threatened to veto any new resolution to authorize force, and the United States failed to win the backing of a majority of non-permanent members of the Council.[197] The United States subsequently bypassed the Security Council and decided to attack Iraq.

The United States invasion of Iraq was a serious breach of United Nations Charter norms and a significant violation of fundamental principles of international law.[198] The United States invasion is likely to have a profound impact on the rules governing armed conflicts. The United States action did not satisfy the traditional requirements for the use of force, such as self-defense, or more recent requirements, such as gross and systematic violations of human rights and state-sponsored terrorism.[199] A limited military strike to destroy Iraq's weapons of mass destruction could certainly be justified under resolution 687 (1991) if Iraq failed to cooperate fully with the weapons inspectors or was in material breach of its international obligations under other relevant Security Council resolutions. However, even a limited military strike should be authorized by the Security Council to be considered legitimate under international law. Resolution 1441 (2002) required Iraq to disarm but did not give the United States the legal basis to attack Iraq.

Security Council Endorsement of the United States-led Invasion of Iraq

Following President Bush's announcement of a suspension of major combat, the administration began a diplomatic offensive to get the sanctions regime lifted and to seek United Nations legitimacy for the United States' occupation of Iraq. The United States subsequently introduced a draft resolution in the Security Council that was later approved by an overwhelmingly majority of Security Council members. Resolution 1483 (2003) resolved that the United Nations should play a vital role in humanitarian relief, the reconstruction of Iraq, and the restoration and establishment of national and local institutions for representative governance.[200] The resolution further recognized the specific authorities, responsibilities, and obligations under applicable international law of Britain and the United States as occupying powers under unified command, which it called the 'Authority.' Resolution 1483 (2003) also called on the Secretary General to appoint a Special Representative for Iraq whose independent responsibilities would involve reporting regularly to the Council on his activities under this resolution, coordinating activities of the United Nations in post-conflict processes in Iraq, coordinating among United Nations and international agencies engaged in humanitarian assistance and reconstruction activities in Iraq, and, in coordination with the Authority, assisting the people of Iraq in a number of tasks. The resolution terminated the sanctions regime on Iraq and gave broad authority to the Coalition Provisional Authority (CPA) to administer Iraq's oil revenues and to control Iraq's political future.

The Security Council did not address the unilateral United States-led invasion of Iraq, nor did the Council call for an immediate withdrawal of foreign forces and the return of Iraqi sovereignty to the Iraqi people. By failing to do so, the Security Council gave a *post facto* endorsement of the United States' invasion of Iraq and exposed the United Nations to complicity in the United States operation in Iraq. The Security Council's failure to condemn the United States' invasion of Iraq and its subsequent endorsement of the occupation was a clear violation of United Nations Charter norms. It underscores the influence of the United States in the Security Council, and it confirms the assertion that the United Nations is an instrument of the major powers, particularly the United States, Britain, and France. Consequently, the United Nations became the target of guerrilla attacks, which resulted in the death of the United Nations Special Representative and a number of his staff. The United Nations withdrew the majority of its staff in Iraq following a second attack on the United Nations headquarters.

On September 23 President Bush returned to the United Nations to seek support from the international community for rebuilding and stabilizing Iraq. President Bush called on members of the United Nations to provide troops and financial assistance to help stabilize Iraq and help in the reconstruction of the country. President Bush's new request called for the United Nations to play a greater role in post-conflict Iraq, but the precise role for the United Nations remained unclear. The President was seeking a new Security Council resolution that would place US troops under United Nations command but overall control of Iraq would remain in the hands of the Coalition Provisional Authority (CPA). The cost of rebuilding Iraq was estimated at $55 billion; with the United States economy still in recession and the deficit expected to reach $500 billion (it has since reaced much higher), it was difficult for the United States to assume the entire cost of the reconstruction. The United States would also have liked more states to contribute troops to relieve US troops, but many countries would only participate in the stabilization of Iraq under a clear United Nations mandate.

Disagreement between France and Germany on one hand, and the United States and Britain on the other, over the degree of United Nations control, and the timetable for turning over sovereign control of Iraq to the Iraqi people delayed adoption of a new Security Council resolution. More importantly, France and Germany wanted the United Nations to play a greater role than what the United States was willing to give. The United States wanted to turn over control of Iraq to the Governing Council after a constitution had been drafted, with a time scale of two to three years later. The Secretary General wanted a broader transitional government to be appointed within three months and then given the task of drafting a new constitution. The Secretary General rejected any formula that would that would place the United Nations in a subordinate position to the CPA.

After threatening to withdraw the resolution, the United States submitted a revised draft on October 13, which was adopted unanimously by the Security Council on October 16. Security Council resolution 1511 (2003), which was adopted under Chapter VII of the United Nations:

(6) Calls upon the Authority, in this context, to return governing responsibilities and authorities to the people of Iraq as soon as practicable and requests the Authority, in cooperation as appropriate with the government Council and the Secretary General, to report to the Council on the progress being made;

(7) Invites the Governing Council to provide to the Security Council, for its review, no later than 15 December 2003, in cooperation with the Authority and, as circumstances permit, the Special Representative of the Secretary General, a timetable and a program for the drafting of a new constitution for Iraq and for the holding of democratic elections under that constitution;

(8) Resolves that the United Nations, acting through the Secretary General, his Special Representative, and the United Nations Assistance Mission in Iraq, should strengthen its vital role in Iraq, including by providing humanitarian relief, promoting the economic reconstruction of and conditions for sustainable development in Iraq, and advancing efforts to restore and establish national and local institutions for representative government;

(13) Determines that the provision of security and stability is essential to the successful completion of the political process as outlined in paragraph 7 above and to the ability of the United Nations to contribute effectively to that process and the implementation of restoration 1483 (2003), and authorizes a multinational force under unified command to take all necessary measures to contribute to the maintenance and stability

in Iraq, including for the purpose of ensuring necessary conditions for the implementation of the timetable and program as well as to contribute to the security of the United Nations Assistance Mission for Iraq, the Governing Council of Iraq and other institutions of the Iraqi interim administration, and key humanitarian and economic infrastructure;

(14) Urges Member States to contribute assistance under this United Nations mandate, including military forces, to the multinational force referred to in paragraph 13 above.

Resolution 1511 (2003), which was adopted after a great deal of negotiation over its language, did not change the situation on the ground in Iraq. It legitimized the status of United States' and British forces in Iraq and it provided a cover for those countries reluctant to provide troops under the previous status. However, the resolution made no major changes in the role of the United Nations or the status of the CPA and the Governing Council. Although the resolution called for the Security Council to review the requirements and mission of the multinational force, it provided little by way of Security Council oversight of the activities of the multinational force.[201] The resolution finally called on the United States, on behalf of the multinational force, to report to the Security Council on efforts and progress of this force as appropriate and not less than every six months.[202]

Germany, France, and Russia, although they voted for resolution 1511 (2003), indicated they would not participate in the multinational force and would not contribute any additional funding for Iraq than what they had already agreed to. The three countries had fundamental disagreements with the United States over the timetable for handing over authority to the Iraqi people and the precise role the United Nations should play in Iraq. In the end they agreed to vote in favor of the resolution more for expediency than anything else. Under resolution 1511 (2003) the United States would continue to be the occupying power in Iraq for an indefinite period of time, and any troop-contributing state would be viewed as associating with the occupation power.

The war in Iraq has undermined the authority of the Security Council and it has called into question the validity of the United Nations ban on the use of force. Some observers have been quick to dismiss the United Nations ban on the use of force as irrelevant and no longer valid in light of the post-September 11, 2001 security environment and the United States war against Iraq. This is certainly not the case. The United Nations continues to provide the collective legitimacy that nations need to validate their actions in the eyes of their citizens and international public opinion. More and more nations continue to make claims of legitimate use of force based on the United Nations framework. The Charter of the United Nations has faced numerous breaches in the past and the Security Council has experienced greater challenges, which it survived. The United Nations Charter is likely to survive this crisis, but the need to redefine the role of the United Nations in a changed international environment is likely to be taken more seriously now.

Conclusion

From the above cases, it is evident that the Security Council has not been very effective in managing inter-state conflicts. The Security Council has rarely invoked its Chapter VII powers to coerce states to cease hostilities, and even when it did, the parties did not comply promptly. During the Cold War, the Security Council authorized full-scale military measures only against North Korea. In other inter-state conflicts the Security Council could not arrive at a consensus because one or more of the permanent members of the Security Council were parties to the dispute. Since the end of the Cold War the Security Council has authorized military measures in one inter-state conflict and in a number of internal conflicts.[203] During the Cold War the Security Council made very few determinations of the existence of a threat to the peace, breach of the peace or an act of aggression. Whereas the Security Council has imposed Chapter VII measures on state and non-state actors more frequently in the post-Cold War era, the Council has had less success in enforcing Chapter VII measures against these actors. The ability of the Security Council to police its sanctions significantly diminished. Given that many post-Cold War conflicts are internal, usually between national governments and rebel groups seeking to overthrow the government, it is extremely difficult for the Security Council to enforce its resolutions in such situations.

Increasingly, inter-state conflicts are of a limited duration, and that gives the Security Council little time to respond appropriately. Even when the war is an ongoing, the Security Council tends not to intervene unless the conflict poses a serious threat to the interests of Britain, France, or the United States. The role of the Security Council in inter-state conflicts, both during and after the Cold War has been very inconsistent. In many of these inter-state conflicts cited above the Security Council failed to carry out its primary responsibility under the Charter of the United Nations. The role of the Security Council in inter-state conflicts has been limited to calling for a ceasefire or imposing an arms embargo. The Council has also delegated enforcement authority to an individual state or a group of states in some situations.

The conflict in Iraq underscored the problem with the Security Council. Although the Council acted correctly in rejecting the United States' request for authorization to invade Iraq, the Council took no action to censure the United States for breach of its Charter obligations. The failure of the Security Council to condemn the invasion of Iraq and the overthrow of the Iraqi government sets a dangerous precedent, which is likely to undermine the legitimacy of the Council in future armed conflict situations.

CHAPTER VII

THE USE OF NON-MILITARY MEASURES BY THE SECURITY COUNCIL IN RESPONSE TO TRANSNATIONAL ARMED CONFLICTS

Chapter VII of the Charter of the United Nations gives the Security Council exclusive authority to maintain international peace and security. The Security Council is granted authority to invoke Article 41, non-military measures, and only after such measures have failed can the Security Council invoke Article 42 (military measures). In order for the Security Council to invoke either Articles 41 or 42, it must first determine under Article 39 that there exists a threat to the peace, a breach of the peace, or an act of aggression. During the Cold War the Security Council had great difficulty making such a determination because of the inability of the great powers to arrive at a consensus on the existence of a threat to the peace, a breach of the peace, or act of aggression. Until 1990, the Security Council had only authorized non-military sanctions against Rhodesia and South Africa.

Since the end of the Cold War the Security Council has imposed Chapter VII measures in a number of situations, some of which have been very controversial. Many of these instances have raised questions about the legitimacy and fairness of the measures and the severe hardship the sanctions regimes imposed on the civilian population. The Security Council imposed these sanctions without specifying a date for their termination. The duration of the sanctions were at the discretion of each individual member of the Security Council, particularly the Permanent Five.[1] The sanctions regimes were imposed under questionable circumstances that the Security Council determined constituted a threat to international peace and security, although many of these situations fell exclusively within what was once considered the domestic jurisdiction of states.

In August 1990 the Security Council authorized comprehensive sanctions against Iraq under Article 41 of the Charter of the United Nations, for its invasion of Kuwait. In 1991 the Security Council authorized arms embargoes against all the states of the former Yugoslavia and Somalia, and economic sanctions against the Federal Republic of Yugoslavia (Serbia and Montenegro). In 1993 the Security Council established safe havens in Bosnia and a no-fly zone over Bosnia's airspace. The Security Council also authorized the use of force to enforce the safe havens and the no-fly zone. In 1992 the Security Council imposed an arms embargo on Somalia and subsequently authorized the deployment of a multinational force in Somalia in response to a deteriorating humanitarian situation in the country that the Security Council determined constituted a threat to international peace and security. In 1993 the Security Council imposed economic sanctions again the Haitian military regime for the junta's refusal to relinquish power to the democratically-elected government of President Aristide. The Security Council later expanded the sanctions to include an oil embargo, and it invoked Chapter VII to authorize member states with naval forces in the region to use force to ensure the embargo was being complied with. In late 1994 the Security Council authorized the use of military force in removing the Haitian military junta from power and to reinstate the democratically-elected government of President Aristide.

In 1992 the Security Council imposed an arms embargo on the National Patriotic Front of Liberia (NPFL) for its refusal to comply with a ceasefire ordered by the Economic Community of West African States (ECOWAS). The Security Council also imposed military and economic sanctions on Libya for Libya's failure to surrender two suspected terrorists wanted by Britain and the United States for their involvement in the destruction of Pan Am flight 103 over Lockerbie, Scotland. In 1993 the Security Council imposed Article 41 measures on UNITA of Angola for its failure to comply with the results of a United Nations supervised election. The Security Council also imposed an arms embargo on Rwanda after the collapse of the Arusha peace process.

In 1996 the Security Council imposed sanctions on Sudan for its failure to surrender suspected terrorists responsible for the attempted assassination of President Mubarak of Egypt. In 1997 the Security Council imposed military and economic sanctions on the military junta and the Revolutionary United Front (RUF) rebels of Sierra Leone. The Security Council also authorized ECOWAS to use force to enforce the embargo. Following an escalation of the violence in Kosovo in 1998, between Yugoslav security forces and the Kosovo Liberation Army, the Security Council imposed an arms embargo on the Federal Republic of Yugoslavia. The Security Council also imposed an arms embargo on Afghanistan in 1998, and in 2000 it imposed comprehensive economic sanctions on the Taliban regime for its refusal to surrender suspected terrorist, Osama bin Laden. Finally, in 2000 the Security Council imposed an arms embargo on Eritrea and Ethiopia for their refusal to agree to a ceasefire. The Security Council also took the extraordinary measures by invoking Article 41 to establish the International Criminal Tribunal for the former Yugoslavia (ICTY) and the International Criminal Tribunal for Rwanda (ICTR).

Measures against Rhodesia

Following Rhodesia's unilateral declaration of independence (UDI) in 1965, the Security Council adopted resolution 217 (1965) by which it called on all states to refrain from any action which would assist and encourage the illegal regime, to desist from providing it with arms and military materiel and to do their utmost to break all economic relations with southern Rhodesia, including an embargo on oil and petroleum products.[2] In April 1966 the Security Council adopted resolution 221(1966) by which it determined that the situation in Southern Rhodesia constituted a threat to international peace and security.[3] Acting under Chapter VII of the Charter of the United Nations the Security Council replaced the voluntary sanctions it previously imposed on Southern Rhodesia under resolution 217 (1966) with mandatory sanctions under resolution 221 (1966). The Security Council also authorized the

United Kingdom to use force if necessary to check vessels entering the port of Beira, Mozambique, to make sure they did not violate the oil embargo.[4]

On December 12, 1966 the Security Council adopted resolution 232 (1966) by which it determined that the situation in Southern Rhodesia constituted a threat to international peace and security. Acting under Chapter VII of the Charter of the United Nations, the Security Council ordered member states to suspend trade in certain commodities with Rhodesia. The sanctions had limited effect on the white minority regime of Rhodesia. Both Britain and the United States continued to import strategic minerals from Rhodesia, in violation of the United Nations sanctions. The sanctions were terminated under resolution 460 (1979) after the formation of a multi-racial government and the granting of independence to Zimbabwe in 1979. The Security Council sanctions had a psychological effect on the regime and led to its international isolation. The sanctions hurt the economy of Rhodesia and made doing business more costly for the white-minority regime.

Measures against South Africa

After repeated efforts by the General Assembly to get South Africa to abandon its policies of apartheid, the General Assembly imposed a voluntary embargo on the white minority regime.[5] In 1976 the General Assembly intensified its effort to isolate South Africa. The General Assembly called for international support for the armed struggle against the white minority regime, and it urged member states to sever all political and economic ties with South Africa. The General Assembly called on the Security Council to impose mandatory sanctions. The Security Council, however, was more cautious in imposing sanctions on South Africa. Both Britain and the United States maintained close military and economic ties with South Africa and were opposed to imposing mandatory sanctions.

On August 7, 1963 the Security Council adopted resolution 181 (1963) by which it called on the government of South Africa to abandon its policies of apartheid and racial discrimination, as called for in Security Council resolution 134 (1960), and to liberate all persons imprisoned, interned, or subjected to other restrictions for having opposed the policy of apartheid.[6] The Security Council called on all states to cease forthwith the sale and shipment of arms, ammunition of all types and military vehicles to South Africa.[7] The embargo had no immediate effect on the conduct of the regime. On December 4, 1963 the Security Council adopted resolution 182 (1963) by which it deplored the refusal of the government of South Africa to comply with Security Council resolution 181 (1963) and to accept the repeated recommendations of other United Nations organs.[8] The Security Council reaffirmed its call for all states to cease trade in arms with South Africa. In 1977 the Security Council adopted resolution 418 (1977) by which it authorized Article 41 measures against South Africa. The resolution called for a mandatory arms embargo on South Africa, and a ban on nuclear cooperation with South Africa. Many Western states, including the United States and Israel, continued security and economic cooperation with South Africa, in violation of the Security Council sanctions. In 1985 the United States and Britain vetoed a draft Security Council resolution recommending non-mandatory economic sanctions against South Africa.

United Nations efforts to eliminate racial discrimination in South Africa failed because certain Permanent Members of the Security Council refused to go along with more stringent measures against South Africa. Both the United States and Britain viewed South Africa as an important strategic partner and refused to support more punitive sanctions against it. However, a combination of grassroots efforts within the United States, Britain, and other Western European states to force multinational companies to divest their assets from South Africa, and repeated condemnation of South Africa by the General Assembly, convinced the South African regime to reconsider its policies of apartheid racial discrimination, and to agree to multi-racial elections. Following multi-racial elections in 1994, the Security Council adopted resolution 919 (1994) by which it terminated the sanctions again South Africa. South Africa was also allowed to resume its membership in the General Assembly in June 1994.

The sanctions against South Africa had limited impact on the apartheid policies of the white minority regime because of the country's strong economy and industrial base. South Africa also had close ties with some permanent members on the Security Council who refused to impose mandatory sanctions. The Security Council sanctions helped isolate South Africa and forced the white minority regime to accept United Nations demands to abolish its racial policies.

Measures against Iraq

Following Iraq's invasion of Kuwait on August 2, 1990, the Security Council adopted resolution 660 (1990) by which it condemned Iraq's action, and called for Iraq's immediate and unconditional withdrawal from Kuwaiti territory.[9] Within days of Iraq's failure to comply with resolution 660 (1990), the Security Council adopted resolution 661 (1990), by which it imposed mandatory economic sanctions on Iraq under Article 41.[10] Acting under Chapter VII of the Charter of the United Nations, the Security Council also vowed to take further action if Iraq did not comply with its demands. On August 25, 1990 the Security Council adopted resolution 665 (1990) by which it reinforced the sanctions imposed on Iraq in resolution 661 (1990). Acting under Chapter VII of the Charter of the United Nations, the Security Council authorized a naval blockade against Iraq to ensure strict compliance with the embargo. The sanctions against Iraq were further tightened under resolution 670 (1990).

The Security Council adopted several additional resolutions to condemn Iraq for other illegal activities in Kuwait. The non-military measures imposed on Iraq did not lead to Iraq's withdrawal from Kuwait. In fact, it did the opposite. Iraq continued to defy the international community and its conduct in Kuwait became even more alarming. Given Iraq's behavior it became increasingly apparent that non-military sanctions alone would not force Iraq to withdraw from Kuwait. On November 29 the Security Council adopted resolution 678 (1990) by which it authorized military measures against Iraq if it did not withdraw from Kuwait by January 15, 1991.[11]

Resolution 678 (1990) was the first authorization for collective enforcement measures adopted by the Security Council under Chapter VII since the Korean War. Security Council resolution 678 (1990) fell short of the requirements for collective security required under Articles 42 and 43 of the Charter. Resolution 678 (1990) did not invoke Article 43, which requires states to sign agreements with the United Nations before placing their forces under the command of the United Nations for collective action. Instead, resolution 678 (1990) called on member states cooperating with the government of Kuwait to use all necessary means to uphold and implement Security Council resolution 660 (1990) and to restore international peace and security in the area.[12] Following an air campaign and ground offensive, Iraq was ejected from Kuwait within 100 days. Iraq later accepted the terms of a ceasefire agreement, which the Security Council ratified by passage of resolution 687 (1991).[13]

Security Council resolution 687 (1991) imposed a series of Chapter VII restrictive measures on Iraq, including the destruction of Iraq's biological and chemical weapon stockpiles and long-range ballistic missiles. It required Iraq to cooperate fully with United Nations weapons inspectors, and to open its military facilities for inspection by the International Atomic Energy Agency (IAEA) and the United Nations Special Commission (UNSCOM). Resolution 687 (1991) further restricted Iraq's sale of oil and other petroleum products and it gave the United Nations legal authority to supervise Iraq's sale of oil and to use part of the proceeds to pay compensation to war victims, to purchase food and medicine for Iraqi civilians, and to cover all cost incurred by UNSCOM.[14]

Resolution 687 (1991) also required Iraq and Kuwait to respect the inviolability of the international boundary demarcated by the United Nations. Acting under Chapter VII of the Charter of the United Nations, the Security Council authorized the deployment of the United Nations Iraq-Kuwait Observation Mission (UNIKOM) to patrol the demilitarized zone between Iraq and Kuwait. The Security Council's action was unprecedented; in the past the Security Council has always relied on the consent of the parties before deploying a peacekeeping force. The sanctions against Iraq and the measures adopted under resolution 687 (1991) were to remain in place until the Security Council was satisfied that Iraq had complied fully with all previous resolutions.[15]

In the immediate aftermath of the Gulf War, Iraq moved to crush rebellions against the government by Shiites in the south and Kurds in the north of the country. The Iraqi army used excessive force to put down the uprisings and it led to a massive exodus of refugees into Iran and Turkey. In response to this new emergency situation, the Security Council adopted resolution 688 (1991) by which it condemned Iraq's repression and determined that the humanitarian situation constitutes a 'threat to international peace and security.'[16] The Security

Council insisted that Iraq allow immediate access by international humanitarian organizations to those in the country. Concerned about the pending humanitarian crisis in northern Iraq, the United States, Britain, and France invoked resolution 688 (1991) to send troops into northern Iraq to establish a 'safe haven' for Kurdish refugees. Allied troops were later replaced by a small contingent of unarmed United Nations policemen with the consent of the Iraqi government. The United States, Britain and France also invoked resolution 688 (1991) to establish 'no-fly' zones over northern Iraq in 1991, and over southern Iraq in 1992.

The use of force by the United States, Britain, and France in northern Iraq was not explicitly authorized by resolution 688 (1991); however, when one reads resolution 688 (1991) in conjunction with the resolutions 678 (1990) and 687 (1991), the action of the allies can be considered legally justified. A decade after the Gulf War ended, Iraq remained under the sanctions regime because of its refusal to cooperate with United Nations weapons inspectors and to implement fully all previous Security Council resolutions. The United States and Britain had publicly called for regime change in Iraq and were unlikely to support an immediate termination of the sanctions against Iraq. United States proposals to modify the sanctions regime to make it more responsive to the humanitarian needs of the civilian population were rejected by a number of members of the Security Council, including China, France, and Russia; Iraq also rejected the modifications.

Developments in Iraq following the United States-led intervention and subsequent occupation of that country would radically alter the debate in the Security Council and would bring to an end the sanctions regime imposed on the Baghdad government in 1990. The Security Council did not authorize the United States-led invasion of Iraq, neither did it condemn it. The Security Council did not even convene a meeting to address the breach of the peace brought about by the United States-led invasion of Iraq. Given the acrimony that had divided the Security Council, some members may have felt it was not wise to revive the pre-war animosity. However, the failure of the Security Council to address the United States invasion of Iraq shows how much influence the United States wields in the Security Council and how the Security Council is incapable of acting independently of the wishes of its permanent members.

On May 1, 2003 President Bush announced an end to major hostilities in Iraq and proceeded to seek a suspension of the sanctions regime against Iraq. Despite misgivings about the United States unilateral intervention in Iraq, the Security Council acquiesced to the United States' demand and adopted resolution 1483 (2003) by which it lifted the economic sanctions against Iraq, but maintained the ban on weapons contained in resolution 687 (1991).[17] Resolution 1483 (2003) called for the United Nations to play a vital role in humanitarian relief, the reconstruction of Iraq, and the restoration and establishment of national and local institutions for representative government, but it deferred to the Coalition Provisional Authority the major responsibilities for governing Iraq and administering Iraq's economy.[18] Resolution 1483 (2003) did not address the legality of the United States-led invasion and occupation and it made no mention of a return to Iraqi sovereignty.[19] By adopting resolution 1483 (2003) the Security Council legitimized the United States invasion and occupation of Iraq and it failed to exercise its responsibility for maintaining international peace and security as specified in Charter VII of the Charter of the United Nations. It has become obvious to critics of the Security Council that the sanctions against Iraq were maintained at the behest of the United States and Britain. The sanctions were lifted only because the United States so desired.

Measures against the Former Yugoslavia

On September 25, 1991 the Security Council convened a session at the request of the Permanent Representative of Yugoslavia to consider the situation in the Former Yugoslavia. Following the debate, the Security Council adopted resolution 713 (1991) by which it determined that the continuing situation in the Former Yugoslavia constituted a threat to international peace and security.[20] The Security Council urged all the parties to the conflict in the former Yugoslavia to settle their disputes peacefully and through negotiation at the Conference on Yugoslavia. Acting under Chapter VII of the Charter of the United Nations, the Security Council decided that all states should, for the purpose of establishing peace and stability in Yugoslavia, immediately implement a general and complete embargo on all deliveries of weapons and military equipment to Yugoslavia until the Security Council decided otherwise, following consultation between the Secretary General and the government of Yugoslavia.[21] Between November 1991 and April 1992 the Security Council adopted six additional resolutions of various kinds in an attempt to halt the conflict in Bosnia, to no avail.

Following an escalation of the conflict and the rapid deterioration of the situation in Bosnia, the Security Council adopted resolution 752 (1992) by which it demanded that all the parties and others concerned in Bosnia stop the fighting immediately, respect immediately and fully the ceasefire signed on April 12, and cooperate with the European Community to bring about urgently a negotiated political solution respecting the principle that any change of borders by force is not acceptable.[22] The Security Council also called for all forms of interference by units of the Yugoslav People's Army as well as elements of the Croatian Army to cease immediately, and for them to withdraw immediately or be subject to the authority of the government of Bosnia. Finally, the Security Council called for all irregular forces in Bosnia to be disbanded and disarmed.[23]

On May 30, 1992, the Security Council adopted resolution 757 (1992) by which it deplored the fact that its demands in resolution 752 (1992) had not been complied with. Acting under Chapter VII of the Charter of the United Nations, the Security Council condemned the failure of the authorities in the FRY, including the Yugoslav National Army (JNA), to take effective measures to fulfill the requirements of resolutions 752 (1992).[24] The Security Council further demanded that any elements of the Croatian Army still present in Bosnia and Herzegovina to act in accordance with paragraph 4 of resolution 752 (1992) without further delay.[25] The Security Council decided that all states were to prevent:

(1)   The import into their territories of all commodities and products originating in the Federal Republic of Yugoslavia (Serbia and Montenegro) exported therefrom after the date of this present resolution;

(2)   Any activities by their nationals or in their territories which would promote or are calculated to promote the export or trans-shipment of any commodities or products originating in the FRY; and any dealings by their nationals or their flag vessels or aircraft or in their territories in any commodities or products originating in the FRY and exported therefrom after the date of the present resolution, including in Yugoslavia for the purposes of such activities or dealings;

(3)   The sale or supply by their nationals or from their territories or using their flag vessels or aircraft of any commodities or products, whether or not originating in their territories, but not including supplies intended strictly for medical purposes and foodstuffs notified to the Committee established pursuant to resolution 724 (1991), to any person or body in the FRY or to any person or body for the purpose of any business carried on in or operated from the FRY, and any activities by their nationals or in their territories which promote or are calculated to promote such sale or supply of such commodities or products.[26]

The Security Council further decided that all states shall not make available to the authorities in the FRY or to any commercial, industrial or public utility undertaking in the FRY, any funds or any other financial or economic resources. The Security Council further called on states to prevent their nationals and any persons within their territories from removing from their territories or otherwise making available to those authorities or to any such undertaking any such funds or resources and from remitting any other funds to persons or bodies within the FRY, except payments exclusively for strictly medical or humanitarian purposes and foodstuffs.[27]

The Security Council also decided that all states were to:

(1)   Deny permission to any aircraft to take off from, land in or fly over their territory if it is destined to land or had taken off from the territory of the FRY, unless the particular flight has been approved, for humanitarian or other purposes consistent with the relevant resolutions of the Council, by the Committee established by resolution 724 (1991);

(2)   Prohibit, by their nationals or from their territory, the provision of engineering and maintenance servicing of aircraft registered in the FRY or operated by or on behalf of entities in the FRY or components for such aircraft, the certification of airworthiness for such aircraft, and the payment of new claims against existing insurance contracts and the provision of new direct insurance for such aircraft.[28]

In addition, the Security Council decided that all states were to:

(1)   Reduce the level of the staff at diplomatic missions and consular posts in the FRY;
(2)   Take the necessary steps to prevent the participation in sporting events on their territory of persons or groups representing the FRY;
(3)   Suspend scientific and technical cooperation and cultural exchanges and visits involving persons or groups officially sponsored by or representing the FRY.[29]

In resolutions 770 (1992) the Security Council invoked Chapter VII by which it authorized states to take nationally or through regional organizations all necessary measures to facilitate delivery of humanitarian assistance to Sarajevo and other parts of Bosnia and Herzegovina. Pursuant to resolution 770 (1992), the Security Council adopted resolution 781 (1992) by which it decided to establish a ban on military flights in the airspace of Bosnia and Herzegovina, and it requested UNPROFOR to monitor compliance with the ban on military flights.[30] On November 10 the Security Council adopted resolution 786 (1992) by which it reaffirmed the ban on military flights over Bosnia and Herzegovina, and it extended the ban to both fixed wing and rotary-wing aircraft.[31]

On November 16, 1992, the Security Council voted to further expand the existing sanctions against Yugoslavia to include an oil embargo. Resolution 787 (1992) prohibited the trans-shipment of crude oil, petroleum products, coal, energy-related equipment, iron, steel, other metals, chemicals, rubber, tires, vehicles, aircraft and motors of all types unless such trans-shipment were specifically authorized on a case-by-case basis by the Committee established by resolution 724 (1991) under its no-objection procedure.[32] Acting under Chapter VII of the Charter of the United Nations, the Security Council decided that any vessel in which a majority or controlling interest was held by a person or undertaking in or operating from the FRY would be considered, for the purpose of implementation of the relevant resolutions of the Security Council, a vessel of the FRY regardless of the flag under which the vessel sails.[33]

The Security Council also authorized measures to enforce the sanctions. Acting under Chapters VII and VIII of the Charter of the United Nations, the Security Council called upon states, acting nationally or through regional agencies or arrangements, to use such measures commensurate with the specific circumstances as may be necessary under the authority of the Security Council to halt all inward and outward maritime shipping in order to inspect and verify their cargoes and destinations and to ensure strict implementation of the provisions of resolutions 713 (1991) and 757 (1992).[34] The Security Council also invoked Chapter VII to establish several 'safe areas', and a no-fly zone over the airspace of Bosnia and Herzegovina.

Finally, on May 25, 1993 the Security Council adopted resolution 827 (1993) by which it decided to establish the International Criminal Tribunal for the Former Yugoslavia (ICTY) to prosecute the individuals criminally responsible for violation of international humanitarian law in the Former Yugoslavia. Acting under Chapter VII of the Charter of the United Nations, the Security Council determined that the situation in the Former Yugoslavia constituted a threat to international peace and security.[35] The Security Council then approved the recommendation of the Secretary General contained in his report to the Security Council, which called for establishing a war crimes tribunal under Article 41 of the Charter of the United Nations.[36] The establishment of the tribunal was an extraordinary measure by the Security Council. Although Article 41 does not explicitly provide for the establishment of war crimes tribunals as a non-military measure, it does not prevent it either. However, the manner in which the tribunal was established raised questions about its legitimacy and the authority of the Security Council to create such mechanisms for maintaining international peace and security.[37]

During the ICTY's first trial of a Bosnian Serb war crimes suspect, Dusko Tadic, his attorneys challenged the legal authority of the Security Council to establish a war crimes tribunal and the legitimacy of the tribunal itself to try the defendant. The ICTY Trial Chamber felt it would be inappropriate for it to decide on the issue and referred the matter to the ICTY Appeals Chamber. The Appeals Chamber upheld the authority of the Security Council to establish the ICTY under its Chapter VII powers.[38] Tadic was subsequently convicted and sentenced to prison.

The non-military measures adopted by the Security Council against Yugoslavia were not enough to stop the war in Bosnia or to protect the civilian safe areas. On the contrary, the arms embargo may have prolonged the war it prevented the Bosnian Muslims from defending themselves against a well-armed Yugoslav Army. In response to the Serbs continuing bombardment of civilian areas, the Security Council approved resolution 998 (1995) by which it authorized NATO to use air strikes to enforce the no-fly ban and to protect the civilian safe areas.[39] The use of force by NATO would ultimately force the Bosnian Serbs to accept a ceasefire. In November 1995 the United States invited the parties to the Bosnian conflict to peace talks in Dayton, Ohio. After several weeks of negotiations the parties signed the Dayton Peace Accord.[40] The Security Council later approved the accord, including the deployment of a NATO-led peacekeeping force to guarantee implementation of the accord.[41]

The non-military sanctions imposed on the Federal Republic of Yugoslavia (Serbia and Montenegro) had no immediate effect on the policies of the Yugoslav government. However, the sanctions may have contributed to Milošević's downfall several years later. The sanctions destroyed Yugoslavia's economy and brought undue hardship on the civilian population. The economic hardship led to growing opposition against the regime of President Milošević. In November 2000 Milošević was rejected in Yugoslavia's first democratic elections. His refusal to accept defeat led to mass protest, which forced him to capitulate. The Security Council sanctions against Yugoslavia may not have been adequate to force Milošević out of power, but the sanctions in part contributed to his dilemma and his ultimate downfall. In April 2001 Milošević was arrested on corruption charges and placed under house arrest. He was later extradited to the ICTY to stand trial for genocide and war crimes committed during the Bosnia and Kosovo wars.

Measures against Somalia

In 1992 Somalia faced a serious humanitarian crisis caused by a severe drought. The situation was compounded as a result of the breakdown of legitimate governmental authority in Somalia, and an ongoing civil war. After efforts to deliver humanitarian assistance failed due to an escalation in fighting, the Security Council adopted resolution 733 (1992) by which it called on the parties to agree to a cease fire and to cooperate with aid agencies in the distribution of humanitarian assistance to the civilian population.[42] Acting under Chapter VII of the Charter of the United Nations, the Security Council imposed an arms embargo on Somalia.[43] The Security Council subsequently adopted resolution 746 (1992) by which it authorized the Secretary General to dispatch a team of technical experts to Somalia to establish mechanisms to ensure the unimpeded delivery of humanitarian assistance.[44]

On April 24 the Security Council adopted resolution 751(1992) by which it established the United Nations Operation in Somalia I (UNOSOM I).[45] The Security Council authorized the immediate deployment of 50 observers to Somalia to monitor the ceasefire in the capital, Mogadishu, and to establish a security force to facilitate the distribution of food and other humanitarian assistance. Disagreement between the United Nations and the warring factions over the modalities of the force delayed the deployment of UNSOM I and complicated the United Nations mission. Meanwhile, the humanitarian situation in Somalia continued to deteriorate. On July 27 the Security Council adopted resolution 767 (1992) by which it authorized an emergency airlift to deliver humanitarian assistance and to call for the cooperation of the warring factions in the deployment of the security force.[46]

By late November 1992 the measures adopted by the Security Council had so far failed to alleviate the humanitarian crisis or end the war in Somalia. The arms embargo had no effect on a country flooded with weapons. In the absence of a legitimate governmental authority in Somalia to restore order or to negotiate with, the Security Council had to find an alternative by which it could facilitate the delivery of humanitarian assistance to the civilian population. On December 3 the Security Council adopted resolution 794 (1992) to authorize the distribution of humanitarian assistance. Acting under Chapter VII of the Charter of the United Nations, the Security Council determined that the 'magnitude of the humanitarian tragedy caused by the conflict in Somalia, further exacerbated by the obstacles being created to the distribution of humanitarian assistance, constitutes a threat to international peace and security.'[47] The Security Council authorized Member States to use all necessary means to establish as soon as possible a secure environment for humanitarian relief operations in Somalia. The United States agreed to lead the international force to undertake the mission. The United States-led United Task Force (UNTAF) was required to coordinate the mission with UNOSOM I and keep the Secretary General informed of its actions.[48] After establishing a safe environment for the distribution of humanitarian assistance, UNTAF withdrew and was replaced by UNOSOM II. UNOSOM II was established under Chapter VII of the Charter with an enlarged mandate and the authority to use force to establish throughout Somalia a secure environment for the distribution of humanitarian assistance.[49]

UNOSOM II assumed the mandate of UNITAF, and was given additional 'responsibility for consolidation, expansion and maintenance of a secure environment throughout Somalia' and the provision of security to assist the repatriation of refugees and assist in the resettlement of displaced persons. UNOSOM II was also responsible for completing the disarmament of factions, enforcing the Addis Ababa Agreement of January 1993, and to assist in rebuilding the country's economy, social and political institutions and achieving national political reconciliation. Following a series of attacks on UNOSOM II forces by the warring factions, including the death of scores of Pakistani peacekeepers and 18 American servicemen, the Security Council adopted resolution 954 (1994) by which it decided to terminate the mission of UNOSOM II by March 31, 1995.[50]

The humanitarian mission in Somalia was helpful in getting much needed humanitarian assistance to the starving civilian population. However, the United Nations attempt to broker a political settlement and its engagement in nation-building complicated the goals of the mission. UNOSOM failed because the Security Council took the wrong approach to the management of a humanitarian situation. A Chapter VII authorization was inappropriate for resolving the Somalia crisis.

Measures against Haiti

Haiti became the target of Security Council sanctions in June 1993, after regional sanctions imposed by the OAS failed to resolve the political crisis. The Security Council was previously asked by the deposed President of Haiti, Jean Bertrand Aristide, to take action against the military junta, which overthrew his democratically-elected government, but the Security Council declined. On June 16, 1993 the Security Council adopted resolution 841 (1993) by which it determined that the situation in Haiti constituted a threat to international peace and security.[51] Acting under Chapter VII of the Charter of the United Nations, the Security Council converted the OAS sanctions into mandatory United Nations sanctions. The Security Council also imposed an embargo on petroleum and petroleum-related products on Haiti, until the Secretary General determined that significant progress had been made to resolve the political stalemate in country.[52] Fearing further sanctions, the military regime agreed to United Nations sponsored talks on Governors Island, New York. The junta signed the proposed comprise agreement, which called for it to leave office.

Following conclusion of the Governors Island Agreement in August 1993, the Security Council adopted resolution 861(1993) by which it endorsed the agreement. The Security Council also lifted the sanctions on Haiti imposed in resolution 841 (1993).[53] After the military regime reneged on its commitments under the Governors Island Agreement to relinquish power in September 1993 the Security Council adopted resolution 867 (1993) to impose additional sanction, including an oil embargo. In October 1993 the Security Council adopted resolution 875 (1993) by which it authorized the United States to use its naval vessels in the region to enforce the oil embargo.[54] Despite these measures the regime continued to defy the international community. On July 31, 1994 the Security Council adopted resolution 940 (1994) by which it determined that the deteriorating human rights situation in Haiti and the military regime's refusal to comply with the Governors Island Agreement constituted a threat to international peace and security.[55]

Acting under Charter VII of the Charter of the United Nations, the Security Council authorized states to form a multinational force (MNF) under unified command and control and to use all necessary means to restore the legitimately elected President and authorities of the government of Haiti.[56] On the eve of a full-scale military invasion of Haiti by United States forces, former President Jimmy Carter led a three-man delegation to Haiti to negotiate the regime's exit. The Carter agreement provided for a peaceful landing of United States forces in Haiti with the full cooperation of the military junta. In exchange for their cooperation, members of the military junta were granted amnesty and asylum in Panama.[57] President Aristide was reinstated as Haiti's president in October 1994 and he ruled until his term in office expired in 1996. The United Nations Mission in Haiti (UNMIH) resumed its full peacekeeping function in March 1995. The multinational force thereafter withdrew its forces from Haiti after it had established stability in Haiti. The non-military sanctions were not enough to force the Haitian military junta to relinquish office. The authorization to use force was a necessary and important requirement to the Haiti equation. The non-military sanctions were counter-productive; the regime profited from the lucrative illegal trade in goods.

Measures against Rwanda

Following the signing of a ceasefire agreement in Arusha, Tanzania, between the government of Rwanda and the Uganda-based Rwanda Patriotic Front (RPF) rebel movement in 1993, the Security Council adopted resolution 846 (1993) on June 22 by which it authorized the deployment of the UN Observer Mission Uganda Rwanda (UNOMUR) peacekeeping force on the Uganda side of the border to monitor the ceasefire agreement. However, the tragic events of April 1994 prevented UNOMUR from fully implementing its mandate.

In October 1993 the Security Council adopted resolution 872 (1993) by which it authorized the establishment of the United Nations Assistance Mission for Rwanda (UNAMIR).

UNAMIR's mandate called for it to ensure the security of the capital, Kigali, monitor the ceasefire agreement and the security situation in general, until a new government of national unity was installed.[58] On January 6, 1994 the Security Council adopted resolution 893 (1994) by which it authorized the deployment of UNAMIR.[59] However, the transitional institutions were not established as planned and the security situation quickly deteriorated.

On April 5, 1994 the situation in Rwanda took a turn for the worse, after the presidents of Rwanda and Burundi were killed in a plane crash on approaching the Kigali airport. Immediately following the death of the two presidents, Hutu extremists from the Rwandan Army and civilians began a campaign of massacring Tutsis. Within a hundred days over half a million Tutsis and moderate Hutus were killed.[60] Hutu extremists also attacked and killed several members of the Belgian contingent of UNAMIR. The incident led Belgium to withdraw the remainder of its troops from the United Nations mission. Belgium's decision forced the United Nations to reduce the mandate of UNAMIR.[61]

On May 17 the Security Council adopted resolution 918 (1994) by which it condemned the violence against innocent civilians. Acting under Charter VII of the Charter of the United Nations, the Security Council imposed an arms embargo on Rwanda.[62] The embargo was useless; those committing the violence were armed with machetes rather than guns. The embargo therefore had no significant effect on the violence. The Security Council later substantially reduced the troop level of UNAMIR and modified its mandate to prevent it from protecting innocent civilians who had taken refuge in UNAMIR's headquarters.[63] After much international condemnation, the Security Council accepted a French proposal to establish a temporary multinational operation for humanitarian purposes in Rwanda until the deployment of an expanded UNAMIR.

On June 22 the Security Council adopted resolution 929 (1994) by which it authorized the French proposal. Acting under Chapter VII of the Charter of the United Nations, the Secretary Council determined that the situation in Rwanda constituted a threat to international peace and security.[64] The Security Council authorized member states to use all necessary means to achieve the humanitarian objectives set out in subparagraphs 4 (a) and (b) of resolution 925 (1994). The Council's authorization came too late to stop the genocide, and was basically an authorization given to France to protect its Hutu allies who were fleeing Rwanda after their defeat in the civil war.

On the recommendation of the Secretary General, the Security Council adopted resolution 955 (1994) by which it determined that the situation in Rwanda constituted a threat to international peace and security. The Security Council went on to invoke Chapter VII of the Charter of the United Nations to establish the International Criminal Tribunal for Rwanda (ICTR) for the sole purpose of prosecuting persons responsible for genocide and other serious violations of international humanitarian law committed in the territory of Rwanda and Rwandan citizens responsible for genocide and other such violations committed in the territory of neighboring states, between January 1, 1994 and December 31, 1994.[65] The establishment of the Rwanda tribunal was based on the precedent established in Yugoslavia, in which the Security Council established the International Criminal Tribunal for the Former Yugoslavia to prosecute those responsible for serious violations of humanitarian law. The creation of the ICTR was a clear demonstration of the failure of the Security Council to act early enough to stop the Rwanda genocide.[66]

Measures against Libya

After repeated efforts by Britain and the United States to get Libya to cooperate in the investigation of the bombing of Pan Am flight 103 over Lockerbie, Scotland, in 1989, they co-sponsored a resolution in the Security Council calling on Libya to cooperate fully and effectively with Britain and the United States and to provide a full and effective response to their requests.[67] On January 21, 1992, the Security Council adopted resolution 731 (1992) by which it said it was deeply disturbed by the world-wide persistence of acts of international terrorism in all its forms, including those in which states were directly or indirectly involved, which endanger or take innocent lives and have a deleterious effect on international relations and jeopardize the security of states.[68] The Security Council also said it was deeply concerned by all illegal activities directed against international civil aviation, and it affirmed the right of all states, in accordance with the Charter of the United Nations and relevant principles of international law, to protect their nationals from acts of international terrorism that constitute threats to international peace and security.[69]

The Security Council went on to say that it was deeply concerned over the results of investigations which implicated officials of the Libyan government and which were contained in Security Council documents that included the requests addressed to the Libyan authorities by France, the United Kingdom, and the United States in connection with the legal procedures related to the attacks carried out against Pan Am flight 103 and UTA flight 772.[70]

The Security Council further stated in resolution 731 (1992) that was it was determined to eliminate international terrorism, and to this end, condemned the destruction of Pan Am flight 103 and UTA flight 772 and the resultant loss of hundreds of lives. The Security Council strongly deplored the fact that the Libyan government had not responded effectively to the above requests to cooperate fully in establishing responsibility for the terrorist acts. It urged the Libyan government immediately to provide a full and effective response to those requests so as to contribute to the elimination of international terrorism. Finally, the Security Council requested the Secretary General to seek the cooperation of the Libyan government to respond fully and effectively to those requests, and it called on all states individually and collectively to encourage the Libyan government to respond fully and effectively to those requests.

Libya insisted that Britain and the United States provide it with proof that its nationals were involved in the bombing of Pan Am flight 103, which they declined to do. Libya also launched a legal challenge against Britain and the United States before the International Court of Justice. Libya accused both states of violating the Montreal Convention of 1971.[71] Libya called on the ICJ to issue interim measures of protection to delay the imposition of sanctions by the Security Council. While the ICJ was deliberating on Libya's request, the Security Council adopted resolution 748 (1992), by which it imposed Chapter VII sanctions on Libya.[72] The ICJ, as a result, determined that Libya's obligations under Article 103 of the Charter of the United Nations take precedence over all its other international obligations. Hence, the Court denied Libya's request for interim measures.[73]

The ICJ was criticized by some legal scholars for not addressing Libya's request directly.[74] The court indicated that it had no authority to render judicial review of Security Council decisions adopted under Chapter VII of the Charter of the United Nations for maintaining international peace and security.[75] The measures against Libya were a clear demonstration of the extent to which the Security Council can exercise its discretionary authority under Chapter VII without its actions being reviewed by another organ of the United Nations.[76]

Security Council resolution 748 (1992) reaffirmed demands made in resolution 731 (1992). The Security Council said it was deeply concerned that the Libyan government had not provided a full and effective response to the requests in resolution 731 (1992). The Security Council also stated that it was convinced that the suppression of acts of international terrorism, including those in which states are directly or indirectly involved, is essential for the maintenance of international peace and security.[77] Acting under Chapter VII of the Charter, the Security Council decided that:

(1)   The Libyan government must now comply without any further delay with paragraph 3 of resolution 731 (1992) regarding the requests addressed to the Libyan authorities by France, the United Kingdom and the United States;

(2)   The Libyan government must commit itself definitively to cease all forms of terrorist action and all assistance to terrorist groups and that it must promptly, by concrete actions, demonstrate its renunciation of terrorism;

(3)   On April 15, 1992, all states shall adopt the measures set out below, which shall apply until the Security Council decides that the Libyan government has complied with paragraphs 1 and 2 above;

(4)   Decides also that all states shall:

(a)   Deny permission to any aircraft to take off from, land in or over-fly their territory if it is destined to land in or has taken off from the territory of Libya, unless the particular flight has been approved on grounds of significant humanitarian need by the Security Council Committee established by paragraph 9 of this resolution;

(b)   Prohibit, by their nationals or from their territory, the supply of any aircraft components to Libya, the provision of engineering and maintenance servicing of Libyan aircraft or aircraft components, the certification of airworthiness for Libyan aircraft, the payment of new claims against existing insurance contracts and the provision of new direct insurance for Libyan aircraft;[78]

(5)   Decides further that all states shall:

(a)   Prohibit any provision to Libya by their nationals or from their territory of arms and related materiel of all types, including the sale or transfer of weapons and ammunition, military vehicles and equipment, paramilitary police equipment and spare parts for the aforementioned, as well as the provision of any types of equipment, supplies and grants of licensing arrangements, for the manufacture or maintenance;

(b)   Prohibit any provision to Libya by their nationals or from their territory of technical advice, assistance or training related to the provision, manufacture, maintenance, or use of the items in subparagraph (a) above;

(c)   Withdraw any of their officials or agents present in Libya to advice the Libyan authorities on military matters.[79]

Finally the Security Council decided that all states were to:

(1)   Significantly reduce the number and level of the staff at Libya diplomatic missions and consular posts and restrict or control the movement within their territory of all such staff who remain;

(2)   Prevent the operation of all Libyan Arab Airlines offices;

(3)   Take all appropriate steps to deny entry or expel Libyan nationals who have been denied entry to or expelled from other states because of their involvement in terrorist activities.[80]

The measures against Libya were adopted by a vote of ten to none, with five abstentions (Cape Verde, China, India, Morocco, and Zimbabwe). The Security Council agreed to review Libya's cooperation with its demands every 120 days. It called on the Secretary General to continue his role in trying to secure Libya's cooperation, as spelled out in resolution 731 (1992).[81]

On November 11, 1993 the Security Council reviewed Libya's compliance with resolutions 731 (1992) and 748 (1992) and it adopted resolution 883 (1993) by which it determined that Libya's continued failure to demonstrate by concrete actions its renunciation of terrorism, and in particular its continued failure to respond fully and effectively to the requests and decisions in resolutions 731 (1992) and 748 (1992), constituted a threat to international peace and security.[82] Acting under Chapter VII of the Charter, the Security Council:

(1)   Demands once again that the Libyan government comply without any further delay with resolution 731 (1992) and 748 (1992);

(2)   Decides, in order to secure compliance by the Libyan government with the decisions of the Council, to take the following measures, which shall come into force at 00.01 EST on December 1, 1993 unless the Secretary General has reported to the Council in the terms set out in paragraph 16 of this resolution;

(3)   Decides that all states in which there are funds or other financial resources (including funds derived or generated from property) owned or controlled, directly or indirectly, by:

(a)   The government of Libya or public authorities of Libya, or

(b)   any Libyan undertaking;

shall freeze such funds and financial resources and ensure that neither they nor any other funds and financial resources are made available, by their nationals or by any persons within their territory, directly or indirectly, to or for the benefit of the government or public authorities of Libya or any Libyan undertaking, which for the purposes of this paragraph, means any commercial, industrial or public utility undertaking which is owned or controlled, directly or indirectly, by the government or public authorities of Libya or any entity owned or controlled by the government or public authorities of Libya.[83]

The Security Council further decided that all states were to prohibit any provision to Libya by their nationals or from their territory of the items listed in the annex to this resolution, as well as the provision of any type of equipment, supplies, and grants of licensing arrangements for the manufacture or maintenance of such items. In addition, the Security Council decided that in order to make fully effective the provisions of resolution 748 (1992), all states were to:

(1)   Require the immediate and complete closure of all Libyan Arab Airlines offices within their territories;

(2)   Prohibit any commercial transactions with Libyan Arab Airlines by their nationals or from their territory, including the honoring or endorsement of any tickets or other documents issued by that airline;

(3)   Prohibit, by their nationals or from their territory, the entering into or renewal of arrangements for (i) the making available, for operation within Libya, of any aircraft or aircraft components, or (ii) the provision of engineering or maintenance servicing of any aircraft components within Libya.

(4)   Prohibit, by their nationals or from their territory, the supply of any materials destined for the construction, improvement or maintenance of Libyan civilian or military airfields and associated facilities and equipment, or of any engineering or other services or components destined for the maintenance of any Libyan civil or military airfields or associated facilities and equipment, except emergency equipment and equipment and services directly related to civilian air traffic control;

(5)   Prohibit, by their nationals or from their territory, any provision of advice, assistance, or training to Libyan pilots, flight engineers, or aircraft and ground maintenance personnel associated with the operation of aircraft and airfields within Libya;

(6)   Prohibit, by their nationals or from their territory, any renewal of any direct insurance
        for Libyan aircraft.[84]

Following intense diplomatic negotiations between Libyan officials and the Secretary
General, and between Libyan officials and Saudi Arabia's Ambassador to the United States,
and Libyan officials and former President Nelson Mandela of South Africa, Libya accepted a
compromise proposal from the Secretary General of the United Nations in 1999. The proposal
called for the two suspects to be transferred to the Netherlands for trial by a special court
under Scottish law.[85] After receiving confirmation that the two Libyan suspects had arrived in
the Netherlands, the Security Council adopted resolution 1192 (1998), by which it suspended
the sanctions against Libya. In January 2001 the special court convicted one suspect and
found the other not guilty.[86] However, the United States and Britain continued to oppose
lifting the sanctions completely until they were confident that Libya would no longer support
international terrorism. The attacks of September 11 on the United States also delayed any
action on lifting the sanctions against Libya. Both President Bush and Prime Minister Tony
Blair wanted Libya to take full responsibility for the bombing of Pan Am flight 103 and pay
compensation to the victims before the lifting of sanctions could be considered.

Some observers questioned the actions of the Security Council against Libya, and voiced
concern that the Security Council was expanding its authority under Chapter VII to include
matters that are essentially within the domestic jurisdiction of states. It is questionable
whether Libya's refusal to surrender its nationals for trial in the United States or Britain
constitutes a threat to international peace and security.[87] An extradition request is a bilateral
agreement that two states negotiate in good faith. The Security Council was calling on Libya
to violate its own domestic laws in order to comply with its demands. The issue was not the
threat of terrorism but whether Libya had an obligation to extradite its citizens in violation of
its constitution. The Security Council's action showed complete disrespect for the judicial
branch given that the International Court of Justice was deliberating Libya's request for
interim measures.

The sanctions against Libya brought economic hardship and international isolation on the
civilian population. Libya was motivated to accept the Secretary General's proposal in part
because Gaddafi wanted the sanctions lifted in order to attract Western investment in Libya's
oil sector. Although the OAU and the Arab League had voted to disregard the sanctions, and
several African leaders had violated the ban on air travel to Tripoli, the psychological impact
of labeling Libya a terrorist nation was beginning to have an effect on President Gaddafi, who
wanted to improve his international image as a great African statesman. The sanctions
influenced Libya's decision to extradite the suspects, but lingering questions about the
fairness of the sanctions remained.

In August 2003 Libya reached an agreement with the families of the victims of Pan Am flight
103 and UTA flight 772. The agreement paved the way for the Security Council to lift the

sanctions against Libya. On September 12 the Security Council adopted resolution 1506 (2003) by which it decided to lift the measures set forth in paragraphs 4, 5, and 6 of its resolution 748 (1992) and paragraphs 3, 4, 5, 6, and 7 of its resolution 883 (1993). The Security Council also dissolved the Committee established by paragraph 9 of resolution 748 (1993).[88]

Measures against Liberia

The Security Council ignored the conflict in Liberia for well over a year, and remained silent after ECOWAS intervened without its prior authorization. However, following the death of six American nuns in November 1992, the Security Council adopted resolution 788 (1992) by which it condemned the killing of innocent civilians and called for an end to the fighting.[89] Acting under Chapter VII of the United Nations, the Security Council determined that the situation in Liberia constituted a threat to international peace and security. The Security Council decided that all states, for the purpose of establishing peace and stability in Liberia, were to immediately implement a general and complete embargo on deliveries of weapons and military equipment to Liberia until the Security Council decided otherwise. The Security Council exempted ECOWAS from the embargo and called on member states to cooperate with ECOWAS to bring about a peaceful end to the conflict.[90]

The arms embargo had no immediate effect on the conflict. In fact, after the arms embargo took effect, the National Patriotic Front of Liberia (NPFL) intensified its military campaign and made significant territorial gains. Weapons continued to flow into rebel-controlled areas from Côte d'Ivoire and Sierra Leone. The NPFL agreed to a negotiated settlement only after they had gained control of much of the country and were given assurances that they would be part of any new government in Liberia. The war had reached a stalemate, and both ECOMOG and the NPFL were battle-fatigued, with neither side likely to prevail militarily. The NPFL accepted an ECOWAS peace proposal, which provided for a ceasefire and the holding of national elections. The NPFL later won those elections and Charles Taylor, the NPFL leader, became the country's new president.[91]

The war ended in Liberia, but it did not bring peace to the region. Soon after the conflict ended in Liberia, rebels in Sierra Leone began using bases in Liberia to launch attacks in Sierra Leone. The connection between Taylor and rebels in Sierra Leone raised serious concerns for the international community. Liberia became a conduit for the traffic in illegal diamonds extracted from Sierra Leone. The rebels used the proceeds from the sale of diamonds to purchase weapons on the black market. Taylor's conduct became so destabilizing that the Security Council imposed new sanctions on Liberia in 2001.[92]

On March 7, 2001 the Security Council adopted resolution 1343 (2001) by which it determined that the active support provided by the government of Liberia for armed rebel groups in neighboring countries, and in particular its support for the RUF in Sierra Leone, constituted a threat to international peace and security in the region.[93] Acting under Chapter VII of the Charter of the United Nations, the Security Council lifted the arms embargo imposed on Liberia in resolution 788 (1992) and dissolved the Committee established under resolution 985 (1995).[94] The Security Council further demanded that the government of Liberia immediately cease its support for the RUF in Sierra Leone and for other armed rebel groups in the region, and in particular take the following concrete steps:

(1)   Expel all RUF members from Liberia, including such individuals as are listed by the Committee established by paragraph 14 of this resolution, and prohibit all RUF activities on its territory, provided that nothing in this paragraph shall oblige Liberia to expel its own nationals from its territory;

(2)   Cease all financial and, in accordance with resolution 1171 (1998), military support to the RUF, including all transfers of arms and ammunition, all military training and the provision of logistical and communications support, and take the necessary steps to ensure that such support is provided from the territory of Liberia by its nationals;

(3)   Cease all direct or indirect import of Sierra Leone rough diamonds which are not controlled through the Certificate of Origin regime of the government of Sierra Leone, in accordance with resolution 1306 (2000);

(4)   Freeze funds or financial resources or assets that are made available by its nationals or within its territory directly or indirectly for the benefit of the RUF or entities owned or controlled directly or indirectly by the RUF;

(5)   Ground all Liberia-registered aircraft operating within its jurisdiction until it updates its register of aircraft pursuant to Annex VII to the Chicago Convention on International Civil Aviation of 1944 and provides to the Council the updated information concerning the registration and ownership of each aircraft registered in Liberia.[95]

The Security Council stressed that the demands in paragraph 2 were intended to lead to further progress in the peace process in Sierra Leone, and, in that regard, called upon the President of Liberia to help ensure that the RUF meet the following objectives:

(1)   Allow the United Nations Mission in Sierra Leone (UNAMSIL) free access throughout Sierra Leone;

(2)   Release all abductees;

(3)   Enter their fighters in the disarmament, demobilization and reintegration process;

(4)   Return all weapons and other equipment seized from UNAMSIL.[96]

The Security Council demanded that all states in the region take action to prevent armed individuals and groups from using their territory to prepare and commit attacks on neighboring countries, and refrain from any action that might contribute to further destabilization of the situation on the borders between Guinea, Liberia, and Sierra Leone.[97] In addition, the Security Council decided that:

(1)   All states shall take the necessary measures to prevent the sale or supply to Liberia, by their nationals or from their territories or using their flag vessels or aircraft, of arms and related materiel of all types, including weapons and ammunition, military vehicles and equipment, paramilitary equipment and spare parts for the aforementioned, whether or not originating in their territories;

(2)   All states shall take the necessary measures to prevent any provision to Liberia by their nationals or from their territories of technical training or assistance related to the provision, manufacture, maintenance or use of items in subparagraph 1.[98]

Finally, the Security Council decided that all states were to take the necessary measures to prevent the direct or indirect import of all rough diamonds from Liberia, whether or not such diamonds originated in Liberia.[99] It further demanded that all states take the necessary measures to prevent the entry into or transit through their territories of senior members of the government of Liberia and its armed forces and their spouses and any other individuals providing financial and military support to armed rebel groups in countries neighboring Liberia, in particular the RUF in Sierra Leone, as designated by the Committee established by this resolution.[100] The sanctions imposed on Liberia took effect on May 7 and were to continue for fourteen months, at which time the Security Council would review whether the government of Liberia had complied with its demands.

Measures against Angola (UNITA)

The Angolan situation was one of the most difficult cases for the Security Council. In January 1989 the Security Council authorized the deployment of the United Nations Angola Verification Mission I (UNAVEM I) to supervise the withdrawal of Cuban troops from Angola.[101] That mission was successfully completed in 1991. However, prior to the end of UNAVEM I's mandate, the Security Council extended the mandate of the mission to assist in the implementation of the 'Acordos de Paz' between the government of Angola and the UNITA rebel movement.[102] The agreement called for UNAVEM I to monitor the ceasefire and assist in organizing the first democratic elections in Angola. The elections which took place in September 1993 had a turnout of 90 percent. The determination of the Angolan people for peace led to a demonstration of civic responsibility unseen in many parts of Africa. UNITA lost the elections and as a result refused to honor the outcome. UNITA also abandoned the peace process and decided to resume the war.

Following the signing of the Lusaka Protocol in 1994, the Security Council adopted resolutions 952 (1994) and 966 (1994), which authorized the deployment of UNAVEM II to verify the initial stages of the agreement.[103] UNITA also refused to cooperate with UNAVEM

II in implementing the main provisions of the accord. UNITA's failure to comply with the accord brought a strong condemnation from the Security Council. On September 15, 1993, the Security Council also adopted its longest and strongest resolution on the Angola situation. In resolution 864 (1993), the Security Council condemned UNITA for its failure to comply with its commitments under the various agreements and reiterated the urgent need for it to return to the peace process and agree to a ceasefire. Acting under Chapter VII of the Charter of the United Nations, the Security Council determined that the situation in Angola constituted a threat to international peace and security.[104] The Security Council imposed sanctions on the sale to UNITA of arms and petroleum within ten days, unless the Secretary General informed the Security Council within that time that an effective ceasefire and a return to the peace process had taken place and that UNITA was implementing the previous Security Council resolutions.[105] The Security Council also threatened to impose further sanctions on UNITA in November, unless it agreed to a ceasefire and returned to the peace process.

On August 28, 1997 the Security Council revisited the situation in Angola. At the end of the debate the Security Council adopted resolution 1127 (1997) by which it called on UNITA and the government of Angola to complete the remaining aspects of the peace process.[106] Acting under Chapter VII of the Charter of the United Nations, the Security Council determined that the situation in Angola constituted a threat to international peace and security in the region.[107] The Security Council also decided that all states were to take the necessary measures to prevent the entry into or transit through their territories of all senior officials of UNITA or of adult members of their immediate families; suspend or cancel all travel documents, visas or residence permits issued to senior UNITA officials and adult members of their immediate families; require the immediate and complete closure of all UNITA offices in their territories, with a view to prohibiting flights of aircraft by or for UNITA, the supply of any aircraft or aircraft components to UNITA and the insurance, engineering and servicing of UNITA aircraft; deny permission to any aircraft to take off from, land in, or overfly their territories if it had taken off from or was destined to land at a place in the territory of Angola other than one on a list supplied by the government of Angola to the Committee created pursuant to resolution 864 (1993); prohibit, by their nationals or from their territories or using their flag vessels or aircraft, the supply of or making available in any form, any aircraft or aircraft components to the territory of Angola other than through named points of entry on the list to be supplied by the government of Angola; prohibit, by their nationals or from their territories, the provision of engineering and maintenance servicing, the certification of airworthiness, the payment of new claims against existing insurance contracts, or the provision or renewal of direct insurance with respect to any aircraft registered in Angola other than those on the list to be provided by the government of Angola to the Committee.[108]

On June 12, 1998, the Security Council adopted resolution 1173 (1998) by which it expressed its grave concern at the critical situation in the peace process as a result of UNITA's failure to implement its obligations under the 'Acordos de Paz' and the Lusaka Protocol.[109] The Security Council condemned UNITA and held its leadership responsible for its failure to implement fully its obligations contained in the Lusaka Protocol, relevant Security Council resolutions, in particular resolution 1127 (1997) and the plan submitted by the Special Representative of the Secretary General to the Joint Commission.[110] The Security Council determined that the situation in Angola constituted a threat to international peace and security in the region.[111] Acting under Chapter VII of the Charter of the United Nations, the Security Council called on all states to freeze the financial resources, including any funds derived or generated from property of UNITA as an organization or of senior officials of UNITA or adult members of their immediate families designated pursuant to paragraph 11 of resolution 1127 (1997).[112] The Security Council also decided that all states shall take the necessary measures to prevent all contacts with the leadership of UNITA in areas of Angola to which state administration had not been extended; prohibit the direct or indirect import from Angola to their territory of all diamonds that were not controlled through the Certification of Origin regime of the Government of Unity and National Reconciliation (GURN); prohibit the sale or supply to persons or entities in areas of Angola under UNITA control, by the nationals or from their territory, or using their flag vessels or aircraft, of equipment used in mining or mining services; prohibit the sale of motorized vehicles or watercraft or spare parts for such vehicles, or ground or waterborne transportation services.[113]

The sanction measures imposed on UNITA had little effect on the rebel movement. UNITA did not return to the negotiating table or accept the terms of the Lusaka Protocol. UNITA continued to sell illicit diamonds through accomplices in Burkina Faso, Liberia, and Togo. Although the sanctions isolated UNITA, it also made UNITA more determined to press ahead with its war aims, which were to impose hardship on the civilian population and to destabilize the central government. UNITA continued to control a significant part of Angolan territory and continued exporting the resources under its control to buy weapons to fuel its war effort.

Efforts by the Security Council to bring peace to Angola through non-military sanctions were a complete failure. The sanctions were a piecemeal and inadequate measure to deal with the longest ongoing conflict in Africa. The failure of the Security Council to authorize more aggressive measures against UNITA, such as military intervention, showed a lack of political will on the part of certain members of the Security Council to do more when conflict threatened peace and security in Africa.

Measures against Sierra Leone

Following the ousting of the democratically-elected government of Sierra Leone by the Sierra Leone military, the Economic Commission of West African States (ECOWAS) intervened to restore the democratically-elected government to power. On October 8, 1997 the Security Council adopted resolution 1132 (1997) by which it deplored the refusal of the military junta to restore the democratic government of Sierra Leone to power.[114] Acting under Chapter VII of the Charter of the United Nations, the Security Council determined that the situation in

Sierra Leone constitutes a threat to international peace and security in the region.[115] The
Security Council imposed a ban on the sale of arms and petroleum products to the military
regime, and placed a travel ban on members of the military regime and their immediate family
members.[116] The Security Council also authorized ECOWAS to ensure strict implementation
of the provisions of resolution 1132 (1997). The military junta defied the Security Council
and ECOWAS and reneged on its commitments to relinquish power.

On March 10, 1998, President Kabbah returned to Sierra Leone and was reinstated by the
direct military intervention of ECOWAS. In April 1998 the Security Council adopted
resolution 1162 (1998) by which it welcomed the return of democracy to Sierra Leone. Acting
under Chapter VII of the Charter of the United Nations, the Security Council voted to lift the
petroleum embargo imposed on Sierra Leone under resolution 1132 (1997).[117] The Security
Council also authorized the deployment of a team of ten United Nations military liaison and
security advisory personnel to Sierra Leone to report on the military situation in the country,
to ascertain the state of and to assist in the finalization of planning by ECOMOG for future
tasks, such as identification of former combatant elements to be disarmed and the design of a
disarmament plan, as well as to perform other related security tasks.[118]

On June 5, 1998, the Security Council met to consider the situation in Sierra Leone and at the
end of the debate adopted resolution 1171 (1998). Acting under Chapter VII of the Charter of
the United Nations, the Security Council voted to terminate the remaining sanctions imposed
on Sierra Leone under resolution 1132 (1997).[119] In July the Security Council authorized the
deployment of the United Nations Observer Mission in Sierra Leone (UNOMSIL) for a six-
month period, to monitor the military and security situation in Sierra Leone, the disarmament
and demobilization of former combatants, and to assist in monitoring respect for international
humanitarian law.[120]

In June 1999, the government of Sierra Leone and the Revolutionary United Front (RUF)
signed the Lome Peace Agreement, which called for a power-sharing national government
and an end to the civil war.[121] The United Nations was called upon to monitor implementation
of the accord. The RUF refused to disarm or to give up territory under its control, and
continued the illicit trade in diamonds through the government of Liberia, using the proceeds
to purchase additional weapons. In October 1999 the Security Council adopted resolution
1270 (1999) by which it authorized the deployment of the United Nations Mission in Sierra
Leone (UNAMSIL) for a period of six months.[122] However, the force was not adequately
trained and was ill-equipped for the security situation on the ground. Dozens of peacekeepers
were taken hostage by RUF rebels and their weapons confiscated.

In response to the deteriorating security situation in Sierra Leone the Security Council
adopted resolution 1299 (2000) on May 19 to reinforce the military component of UNAMSIL
and to provide the mission with additional resources to fulfill its mandate. The military
component of UNAMSIL was expanded to a maximum of 13,000 military personnel,

including the 260 military observers already deployed. The Security Council also exempted states cooperating with UNAMSIL from the restrictions imposed in resolution 1171 (1998).[123] The Security Council continued to renew the mandate of UNAMSIL every six months.

On August 14, 2000 the Security Council took steps to address the very serious crimes committed in Sierra Leone against the people of that country and against United Nations and associated personnel by members of RUF and the security forces. The Security Council adopted resolution 1315 (2000), by which it deplored the atrocities committed against innocent civilians and international protected persons. The Security Council requested the Secretary General to negotiate an agreement with the government of Sierra Leone to create an independent special court consistent with this resolution, and expressed its readiness to take further steps expeditiously upon receiving and reviewing the report of the Secretary General.[124] On October 4, the Secretary General submitted his report to the Security Council, with the recommendation for the establishment of a Special Court for Sierra Leone. The report detailed the nature of the Special Court and its competences, its subject-matter jurisdiction, personal jurisdiction, and organizational structure, among other matters.[125]

The establishment of the Special Court for Sierra Leone departed significantly from the two *ad hoc* tribunals established by the Security Council for the former Yugoslavia and Rwanda. The Special Court has a mixed jurisdiction and will apply both international humanitarian laws and the national laws of Sierra Leone. The Special Court began its investigation of atrocities committed during the civil war in 2002, and issued indictments of several senior RUF and Kamajor officials. The Special Court was watched as a model for other countries, such as Cambodia and Iraq. The situation in Sierra Leone gradually stabilized, but destabilizing events in neighboring Liberia and Guinea probably had an adverse effect on the fragile peace process.

Measures against Afghanistan

On August 28, 1998 the Security Council adopted resolution 1193 (1998), by which it expressed its grave concern at the continuing conflict which had escalated recently due to the Taliban's offensives in the northern parts of the country.[126] The Security Council further deplored the terrorist activities taking place in Afghanistan and called on the various Afghan factions to refrain from harboring and training terrorists and their organizations, and to halt illegal drug activities.[127] On December 8, 1998, the Security Council adopted resolution 1214 (1998), by which it once again expressed grave concern at the continuing conflict in Afghanistan, which had sharply escalated as a result of the offensive by the Taliban forces.[128] The Security Council demanded that the Taliban, as well as the other Afghan factions, stop fighting, conclude a ceasefire, and resume negotiations without delay or preconditions under United Nations auspices.[129] The Security Council further demanded that the Taliban stop providing sanctuary and training for international terrorists and their organizations, and that all Afghan factions cooperate with efforts to bring indicted terrorists to justice. The Security Council resolutions had no influence on the situation in Afghanistan. Fighting among the various Afghan factions intensified, and the Taliban regime showed no interest in expelling suspected terrorists from its territory.

Following the Taliban's failure to comply with Security Council resolutions 1193 (1998) and 1214 (1998), the Security Council adopted resolution 1267 (1999) on October 15, 1999, by which it strongly condemned the continuing use of Afghan territory, especially areas controlled by the Taliban, for the sheltering and training of terrorists and planning of terrorist acts, and reaffirmed its conviction that the suppression of international terrorism was essential for the maintenance of international peace and security. The Security Council deplored the fact that the Taliban continued to provide safe haven to Osama bin Laden and allow him and others associated with him to operate a network of terrorist training camps from Taliban-controlled territory and use Afghanistan as a base from which to sponsor international terrorist operations.[130] Acting under Chapter VII of the Charter of the United Nations, the Security Council called on the Taliban to comply promptly with its previous resolutions, and in particular cease the provision of sanctuary and training for international terrorists and their organizations.[131] The Security Council also demanded that the Taliban turn over Osama bin Laden immediately to the appropriate authorities in a country where he had been indicted. The Security Council further decided that in order to enforce its demands, all states were to:

(1)   Deny permission for any aircraft to take off from or land in their territory if it is owned, leased or operated by or on behalf of the Taliban as designated by the Committee of the Security Council in accordance with rule 28 of its provisional rules;

(2)   Freeze funds and other financial resources, including funds derived or generated from property owned or controlled directly or indirectly by the Taliban, or by any undertaking owned or controlled by the Taliban, as designed by the Committee, and ensure that neither they nor any other funds or financial resources so designated or made available, by their nationals or by any persons within their territory, to or for the benefit of the Taliban or any undertaking owned or controlled, directly or indirectly, by the Taliban.[132]

On October 22 the Security Council issued a statement, following a review of the Secretary General's report on the situation in Afghanistan, in which it condemned the Taliban for its July military offensive and for sheltering terrorists.[133] The Security Council expressed grave concern about outside interference in the Afghan conflict, and called for immediate steps to improve the human rights situation and to halt the significant increase in the cultivation and trafficking of illegal drugs.[134] In the statement, the President of the Security Council said that the Taliban's July offensive undermined international efforts to facilitate peace in Afghanistan.[135] That offensive was launched just one week after the 'six plus two' group of China, Iran, Pakistan, Tajikistan, Turkmenistan, and Uzbekistan, and the Russian Federation and the United States, adopted the 'Declaration on Fundamental Principles for a Peaceful Settlement of the Conflict in Afghanistan' in Tashkent, Uzbekistan.

Under the Tashkent Declaration, members of the group agreed not to provide military support to any Afghan party, and to prevent the use of the group's territories for such purposes. The Security Council urged members of the group and the Afghan factions to implement the principles in the Declaration in support of the efforts of the United Nations toward a peaceful resolution of the conflict. The Security Council deplored the worsening human rights situation in Afghanistan, and expressed alarm at the Taliban's disregard for the international community's concerns. It called on the Taliban to adhere to international norms and standards, improve the human rights situation and, as an immediate first step, ensure the protection of civilians. Finally, the Security Council demanded that the Taliban turn over Osama bin Laden to appropriate authorities, and for the Taliban to cooperate with the United Nations in investigating the occupation of the Consulate General of Iran and the murder of Iranian diplomats and a journalist in Mazar-e-Sharif, with a view to prosecuting those responsible. [136]

Despite the threat of further sanctions, the Taliban refused to comply with the key demands of the Security Council. On December 19, 2000 the Security Council adopted resolution 1333 (2000) by a vote of 13 to 0 with 2 abstentions (China and Malaysia), and thereby tightened the previous sanctions imposed on Afghanistan under resolution 1267 (1999) and imposed additional sanctions on the Taliban.[137] Security Council resolution 1333 (2000) strongly condemned the continuing use of the areas of Afghanistan under the control of the Afghan faction known as the Taliban, also calling itself the Islamic Emirate of Afghanistan, for the sheltering and training of terrorists and planning of terrorist acts.[138] The Security Council reaffirmed its conviction that the suppression of international terrorism was essential for the maintenance of international peace and security. The resolution further deplored the fact that the Taliban continued to provide safe haven to Osama bin Laden and allow him and others associated with him to operate a network of terrorist training camps from Taliban-controlled territory, and to use Afghanistan as a base from which to sponsor international terrorist operations.[139] The Security Council took note of the indictment of Osama bin Laden and his associates in the United States for the August 7, 1998 bombing of the United States embassies in Nairobi and Dar-es-Salaam, and for conspiring to kill Americans outside the United States.[140] The Security Council further took note of the direct benefits the Taliban derived from illicit opium cultivation, reiterated its deep concern over the continuing violations of international humanitarian law, and reiterated its view that the murder of Iranian diplomats and journalists at the country's Consulate General constituted flagrant violations of established international law.[141]

Acting under Chapter VII of the Charter of the United Nations, the Security Council made the following demands:

(1)   Demands that the Taliban comply with resolution 1267 (1999) and, in particular, cease the provision of sanctuary and training for international terrorists and their organizations, take appropriate effective measures to ensure that the territory under its control is not used for terrorist installations and camps, or for the preparation or organization of terrorist acts against other states or their citizens, and cooperate with international efforts to bring indicted terrorists to justice;

(2)   Demands also that the Taliban comply without further delay with the demand of the security Council in paragraph 2 of resolution 1267 (1999) that requires the Taliban to turn over Usama bin Laden to appropriate authorities in a country where he has been indicted, or to appropriate authorities in a country where he will be returned to such a country, or to appropriate authorities in a country where he will be arrested and effectively brought to justice;

(3)   Demands further that the Taliban should act swiftly to close all camps where terrorists are trained within the territory under its control, and call for the confirmation of such closures by the United Nations, inter alia, through information made available to the United Nations by Member States in compliance with this resolution;

(4)   Reminds all states of their obligation to implement strictly the measures imposed by paragraph 4 of resolution 1267 (1999);

(5)   Decides that all States shall:

    (a)   Prevent the direct or indirect supply, sale and transfer to the territory of Afghanistan under Taliban control as designated by the Committee established pursuant to resolution 1267 (1999), hereinafter known as the Committee, by their nationals or from their territories, or using their flag vessels or aircraft, of arms and related materiel of all types including weapons and ammunition, military vehicles and equipment, paramilitary equipment, and spare parts for the aforementioned;

    (b)   Prevent the direct or indirect sale, supply and transfer to the territory of Afghanistan under Taliban control, as designated by the Committee, by their nationals or from their territories, of technical advice, assistance, or training related to the military activities of the armed personnel under the control of the Taliban;

    (c)   Withdraw any of their officials, agents, advisers, and military personnel employed by contract or other arrangement present in Afghanistan to advise the Taliban on military or related security matters, and urge other nationals in this context to leave the country;

(6)   Decides that the measures imposed by paragraph 5 above shall not apply to supplies of non-lethal military equipment intended solely for humanitarian or protective use, and related technical assistance or training, as approved in advance by the Committee, and affirmed that the measures imposed by paragraph 5 above do not apply to protective clothing, including flak jackets and military helmets, exported to Afghanistan by United Nations personnel, representatives of the media, and humanitarian workers for their personal use only;

(7)   Urges all States that maintain diplomatic relations with the Taliban to reduce significantly the number and level of the staff at Taliban missions and posts and restrict or control the movement within their territory of all such staff who remain; in the case of Taliban missions to international organizations, the host State may, as it deems necessary, consult the organization concerned on the measures required to implement this paragraph;

(8)   Decides that all States shall take further measures:

    (a)   To close immediately and completely all Taliban offices in their territories;

    (b)   To close immediately all offices of Arian Afghan Airlines in their territories;

    (c)   To freeze without delay funds and other financial assets of Usama bin Laden and individuals and entities associated with him as designated by the Committee, including those in the Al-Qaida organization, and including funds derived or generated from property owned or controlled directly or indirectly by Usama bin Laden and individuals and entities associated with him, and to ensure that neither they nor any other funds or financial resources are made available, by their nationals or by any person within their territory, directly or indirectly for the benefit of Usama bin Laden, his associates or any entities associated with him including the Al-Qaida organization and requests the Committee to maintain an updated list, based on information provided by States and regional organizations, of the individuals and entities designated as being associated with Usama bin Laden, including those in the Al-Qaida organization;

(9)   Demands that the Taliban, as well as others, halt all illegal drugs activities and work to virtually eliminate the illicit cultivation of opium poppy, the proceeds of which finance Taliban terrorist activities;

(10)   Decides that all States shall prevent the sale, supply or transfer, by their nationals or from their territories, of the chemical acetic anhydride to any person in the territory of Afghanistan under Taliban control as designated by the Committee or to any person for the purpose of any activity carried on in, or operated from, the territory under Taliban control as designated by the Committee;

(11)   Decides also that all States are required to deny any aircraft permission to take off from, land in or over-fly their territories if that aircraft has taken off from, or is destined to land at, a place in the territory of Afghanistan designated by the Committee as being under Taliban control, unless the particular flight has been approved in advance by the Committee on the grounds of humanitarian needs, including religious obligations such as the performance of Hajj, or on the grounds that the flight promotes discussion of a peaceful resolution of the conflict in Afghanistan, or is likely to promote Taliban compliance with this resolution or with resolution 1267 (1999);

(12)   Urges States to take steps to restrict the entry into or transit through their territory of all senior officials of the rank of Deputy Minister or higher in the Taliban, the equivalent rank of armed personnel under the control of the Taliban, and other senior advisers and dignitaries of the Taliban, unless those officials are traveling for

humanitarian purposes, including religious obligation such as the performance of the Hajj, or where travel promotes discussion of a peaceful resolution of the conflict in Afghanistan or involves compliance with this resolution or resolution 1267 (1999).[142]

These new sanctions were to take effect one month after the adoption of resolution 1333 (2000). The new sanction measures were opposed by the Secretary General, humanitarian aid agencies, and a number of states, including Pakistan, which was one of only three states to recognize the Taliban's Emirate. Many of those who opposed the new sanction measures were concerned about the humanitarian impact on the civilian population and the difficulty it would pose for the work of United Nations aid agencies in Afghanistan. The Taliban also voiced its opposition to the sanctions, and said it would not surrender Osama bin Laden to the United States. The sanctions made the Taliban more defiant and less willing to cooperate with the international community to improve the human rights of women in the country and negotiate an end to the civil war. The Taliban regime was ultimately overthrown by United States forces in response to the September 11, 2001 terrorist attacks on the United States.

Security Council Measures against Sudan

Sudan became the target of Security Council sanctions in January 1996 after it refused to turn over two men suspected of attempting to assassinate President Hosni Mubarak of Egypt in the Ethiopian capital Addis Ababa on June 26, 1995. In January 1996 the Security Council adopted resolution 1044 (1996) by which it condemned the terrorist assassination attempt on the life of President Mubarak, and strongly deplored the flagrant violation of the sovereignty and territorial integrity of Ethiopia and the attempt to disturb the peace and security of Ethiopia and the region as a whole.[143] The Security Council called upon the government of Sudan to comply with the requests of the OAU, and without further delay to:

(1) Undertake immediate action to extradite to Ethiopia for prosecution the three suspects sheltered in the Sudan and wanted in connection with the assassination attempt on the basis of the 1964 Extradition Treaty between Ethiopia and the Sudan;

(2) Desist from engaging in activities of assisting, supporting and facilitating terrorist activities and from giving shelter and sanctuaries to terrorist elements and act in its relations with its neighbors and with others in full conformity with the Charter of the United Nations and with the Charter of the OAU.[144]

On March 11 the Secretary General informed the Security Council that Sudan had not complied with its demands in resolution 1044 (1996). The Security Council adopted resolution 1054 (1996), by which it reaffirmed that the suppression of international terrorism, including state-sponsored terrorism, was essential for the maintenance of international peace and security. The Security Council also determined that the non-compliance by the government of Sudan with the requests set out in paragraph 4 of resolution 1044 (1996) constituted a threat to international peace and security.[145] Acting under Chapter VII of the Charter of the United Nations, the Security Council demanded that the government of Sudan comply without further delay with the requests set out in paragraph 4 of resolution 1044 (1996). The Security Council decided that all states were to:

(1) Significantly reduce the number and level of the staff at Sudanese diplomatic missions and consular posts and restrict or control the movement within their territory of all such staff who remain;

(2) Take steps to restrict the entry into or transit through their territory of members of the government of Sudan, officials of that government and members of the Sudanese armed forces.[146]

These measures were to take effect at 00.01 Eastern Standard Time on May 10, 1996. The Security Council said it would re-examine the matter in 60 days to determine whether to adopt additional measures against Sudan to ensure its compliance. On August 16, 1996, the Security Council reviewed the sanctions imposed on Sudan and adopted resolution 1070 (1996), by which it determined that Sudan had not complied with the requests of the OAU.[147] Acting under Chapter VII of the Charter of the United Nations, the Security Council decided that all States deny aircraft permission to take off from, land in, or overfly their territories if the aircraft were registered in Sudan, or owned, leased or operated by or on behalf of Sudan Airways, or by any undertaking, wherever located or organized, which was substantially owned or controlled by Sudan Airways, or owned, leased or operated by the government or public authorities of Sudan.[148]

The sanctions against Sudan remain in place despite assurances from the government of Ethiopia and the Secretary General of the OAU that the suspected terrorists were no longer in Sudan. Ethiopia and the OAU also called on the Security Council to lift the sanctions against Sudan. The United States opposed lifting the sanctions until Sudan did more to stop terrorism. The United States also accused Sudan of collaboration with individuals suspected of bombing the United States embassies in Nairobi and Dar-es-Salam. Since September 11, 2001, Sudan began to make efforts to improve its image. It provided information to the United States on the activities of Osama bin Laden, and cooperated with the United States in trying to end the civil war in the southern part of the country.

Measures against Yugoslavia (Kosovo)

In 1998 Yugoslavia carried out a violent campaign against the ethnic Albanian civilian population in Kosovo, which caught the attention of the international community. The massive flow of ethnic Albanian refugees from the province into neighboring Albania and Macedonia gave rise to a serious humanitarian crisis. On March 31, 1998, the Security Council adopted resolution 1160 (1998) by which it condemned the use of excessive force by

Serbian police against civilians and peaceful demonstrators in Kosovo, as well as acts of terrorism by the Kosovo Liberation Army (KLA).[149] The Security Council also called on Yugoslavia to take the necessary measures immediately to achieve a political settlement to the conflict in Kosovo. Acting under Chapter VII of the Charter of the United Nations, the Security Council imposed an arms embargo on the Federal Republic of Yugoslavia.[150] The Security Council called on all states to 'prevent the sale or supply to the FRY, including Kosovo, by their nationals or from their territories or using their flag vessels and aircraft, of arms and related materiel of all types, such as weapons and ammunition, military vehicles and equipment and spare parts for the aforementioned, and shall prevent arming and training for terrorist activities there.'

The Security Council arms embargo had no impact on the conflict in Kosovo. The conflict escalated and the violence against Albanian civilians by the Yugoslav Army increased. On September 23, the Security Council met in emergency session to discuss the situation in Kosovo. Following the debate, the Council adopted resolution 1199 (1998) by which it voiced concern at the recent escalation in fighting in Kosovo, particularly the excessive and indiscriminate use of force by Serbian security forces and the Yugoslav Army.[151] The fighting led to the displacement of over 23,000 civilians from their homes, and another 50,000 took refuge in other parts of the FRY. Resolution 1199 (1998) imposed a ban on all external support for military activities in Kosovo, including the supply of arms and training for terrorist activities in Kosovo. The Security Council also determined that the deteriorating humanitarian situation in Kosovo constituted a threat to international peace and security in the region.[152] Acting under Chapter VII of the Charter of the United Nations, the Security Council demanded that all parties, groups and individuals immediately cease hostilities and observe a ceasefire in Kosovo.[153]

The Security Council resolutions had no immediate effect on Yugoslavia's policy in Kosovo. Fearing a further escalation in the conflict, and a deterioration of the human rights situation in Kosovo, NATO threatened to intervene if President Milošević declined its request to participate in peace talks in Rambouillet, France, under the auspices of the EU. Milošević initially refused to attend the peace talks but later agreed to send a low-level delegation. After three weeks of difficult negotiations the parties reached an accord, which they took back to their respected constituencies for approval. The Kosovo Albanians accepted the accord, but the Yugoslav Parliament rejected it. Milošević objected to certain provisions in the Rambouillet Agreement, in particular, the deployment of a NATO-led peacekeeping force on Yugoslav soil. After Milošević rejected repeated warnings from NATO to accept the accord, NATO began an unauthorized bombing campaign against Yugoslavia.[154] NATO did not consult the United Nations Security Council for authorization to carry out its military attacks on Yugoslavia, which many observers felt was a violation of the Charter of the United Nations.[155] The bombing campaign destroyed much of Yugoslavia's infrastructure and communication system and precipitated a humanitarian crisis. The bombing also intensified the flow of refugees from Kosovo into neighboring Albania.

Yugoslavia later agreed to a ceasefire and a peace deal for Kosovo on NATO's terms.[156] The new agreement called for the deployment of a NATO-led international force (KFOR) to guarantee the safety of the people of Kosovo, and for Kosovo to be placed under a United Nations interim administration. On June 10, the Security Council adopted resolution 1244 (1999), by which it approved the Kosovo peace agreement.[157] The future political status of Kosovo was not addressed at the time. Both Serbia and the Kosovo government rejected the various proposals on Kosovo's future status. Serbia saw Kosovo as an integral part of its sovereign territory and the seat of its religious faith. It refused to grant Kosovo independence, as demanded by the Albanian majority. With the backing of the United States and several EU states, the Kosovo leadership declared Kosovo an independent state against opposition from Serbia and Russia. In response to a request from the General Assembly for an Advisory Opinion on Kosovo's unilateral declaration of independence, the International Court of Justice (ICJ) ruled that the declaration in and of itself was not a violation of international law. The ICJ skirted the issue of whether the declaration did in fact violate Serbia's sovereignty and territorial integrity. [158] However, Kosovo has not been admitted to the United Nations.

Measures against Eritrea and Ethiopia

Following the outbreak of hostilities between Eritrea and Ethiopia in June 1998 over a disputed border region, the Security Council adopted resolution 1177 (1998) by which it expressed grave concern over the humanitarian implications of the conflict. The Security Council condemned the use of force and called on the two states to immediately cease hostilities and refrain from further use of force.[159] After a fresh outbreak of fighting in early 1999, the Security Council adopted resolution 1227 (1999) by which it again condemned the fighting between Eritrea and Ethiopia, and determined that the conflict constituted a threat to international peace and security.[160] Fighting intensified in May 2000, after a brief lull. On May 10 the Security Council adopted resolution 1297 (2000) by which it called on the parties to seek a peaceful solution to the dispute. The Security Council resolved to meet again within 72 hours of adoption of resolution 1297 (2000) to take immediate steps to ensure compliance with this resolution in the event hostilities continued.[161]

On May 17, the Security Council revisited the situation between Eritrea and Ethiopia. The Security Council decided that both states had failed to comply with its demand to stop fighting. The Security Council adopted resolution 1298 (2000) by which it imposed an arms embargo on Eritrea and Ethiopia.[162] Acting under Chapter VII of the Charter of the United Nations, the Security Council decided that all states were to prevent:

(a)   The sale or supply to Eritrea and Ethiopia, by their nationals or from their territories, or using their flag vessels or aircraft, of arms and related materiel of all types, including weapons and ammunition, military vehicles and equipment, paramilitary equipment and spare parts of the aforementioned, whether or not originating in their territory;

(b)   Any provision to Eritrea and Ethiopia by their nationals of from their territories of technical assistance or training related to the provision, manufacture, maintenance or use of the items in (a) above.[163]

The sanctions were to remain in place for a twelve-month period, after which time the Security Council would review whether the governments of Eritrea and Ethiopia had complied with its demands.

The sanctions imposed on Eritrea and Ethiopia under resolution 1298 (2000) did nothing to halt the war. Eritrea and Ethiopia had purchased and stockpiled large quantities of weapons during the lull in fighting. The Security Council embargo came too late to have any impact on the war. On June 18 Eritrea and Ethiopia signed the OAU Framework Agreement, which provided for a ceasefire and the suspension of the state of hostilities.[164]

Conclusion

The Security Council's use of non-military sanctions to maintain international peace and security has, overall, not been very successful. Sanctions, as an instrument of coercion, have seldom worked in the past, and are not likely to have any significant impact on the parties to a conflict. Both target states and their allies have found ways to circumvent the sanctions regimes. Economic sanctions tend to have adverse effects on the civilian population. In fact, many of the regimes targeted for sanctions ended up profiting from them by engaging in lucrative smuggling operations that netted them millions of dollars from the sale of illegally imported goods.[165] Arms embargoes are generally ineffective because of the fluid nature of the international arms market and the ready availability of small arms. The Security Council has no system in place to enforce its sanctions regimes, and it rarely authorizes military measures to guarantee compliance with the sanctions imposed on states or rebel organizations.

The Security Council will continue to invoke Chapter VII non-military sanctions even though they have failed to accomplish their intended objectives. However, the imposition of non-military sanctions is the first step the Security Council can take in a list of measures designed to maintain international peace and security. Non-military sanctions have had little impact in solving international conflicts and the Security Council should consider alternative measures such as limited demonstration of military force.

CHAPTER VIII: CONCLUSION

ENHANCING THE CAPACITY OF THE SECURITY COUNCIL TO RESPOND TO TRANSNATIONAL ARMED CONFLICTS

The Security Council's performance in the management of regional conflicts has been mixed. The Security Council was successful in some conflicts, but failed in too many. In some cases the Security Council waited too long to act, leaving the conflict to escalate to the point where the measures imposed by the Security Council were too little and too late, and hence ineffective. One of the fundamental flaws of the Security Council conflict management approach is its over-reliance on the goodwill of the major powers and the need for a consensus among the five Permanent Members (the 'P5'). The Security Council has no clearly-defined guidelines by which it could determine what conflicts constitute a threat to international peace and security. What constitutes a threat to international peace and security is determined on a case-by-case basis. In many of the cases examined in this book, the Security Council could not make a determination, or it made a determination regarding a threat to the peace after the fact. Even when a determination was made by the Security Council under Article 39 of the Charter, the Security Council failed to follow through on the necessary enforcement measures.[1] In some cases the Security Council rushed to judgment, and in other cases it did not act quickly enough. The Security Council also adopted resolutions in which it threatened to impose sanctions on the parties if they did not comply with its demands, but failed to take more drastic measures against non-complying states.[2]

Of the many cases examined in this book, the Security Council was successful in discharging its responsibility in only a few instances. In those cases, the Security Council had the support of key permanent members of the Council, particularly Britain, France, and the United States.[3] The Security Council was also successful in cases where the parties to a conflict were willing to cooperate with the Council to find a peaceful solution to the conflict. The evidence suggests that the Security Council will get involved in a conflict when the conflict directly affects the interests of one or all three Western Permanent Members (the 'P3') on the Security Council. In many of the cases examined in this book, one finds the Security Council deferring to regional organizations or delegating its authority to individual states or a group of states, instead of acting as a body in the manner specified in Chapter VII. Although the end of the Cold War led to a more active and assertive Security Council, it has not created a stronger entity with the capacity to act collectively. The ability of the Security Council to resolve regional conflicts has diminished to the extent that states can no longer rely on the Security Council to intervene on their behalf.

In the remainder of this chapter, I group the various conflicts into two categories: successes and failures. I look at how the Security Council performed in each category and whether it complied with the provisions of the Charter of the United Nations which granted it authority to maintain international peace and security. I also make some recommendations for enhancing the capacity of the Security Council to respond more effectively to threats to international peace and security. Some of my observations have been discussed in recent reports on the role of the Security Council, and the United Nations in general, in maintaining international peace and security. Special reference will be made of the Brahmi Report and the Report of the Secretary General on Enhancing the Capacity of the United Nations in the Maintenance of International Peace and Security.

Security Council Successes

The collapse of the grand alliance a few years after the creation of United Nations, coupled with the different goals of the major powers, prevented the organization from becoming an effective instrument for maintaining international peace and security. The conflicts the United Nations confronted in its formative years involved one or more major powers, which automatically barred the United Nations from intervening in the conflict. The United Nations soon came up with peacekeeping as a compromise mechanism for maintaining international peace. The single most important military challenge for the United Nations came when North Korea invaded South Korea in 1950. The situation was a test for the Security Council, but its task was made easy by the absence of the Soviet Union, which was boycotting the Security Council. The Security Council was able to reach an agreement to authorize military action against North Korea, but slightly different from what the Framers of the Charter had anticipated. The Security Council delegated its authority to the United States, instead of waiting for an Article 43 agreement to be signed by the participating states. After Korea, the Security Council was only able to authorize enforcement action in two other instances, Rhodesia and South Africa.

In 1965 the Security Council imposed mandatory sanctions against Rhodesia, and subsequently authorized Britain to use force to enforce the oil embargo. In 1977 the Security Council imposed an arms embargo on South Africa, but did not authorize the use of force to enforce compliance with the embargo. The Security Council's experience with sanctions during the Cold War was very limited. However, in the post-Cold War era, the Security Council invoked Chapter VII with greater frequency.

Beginning with Iraq's invasion of Kuwait, the Security Council enjoyed a brief period of success. The Security Council resolved conflicts in Cambodia, Namibia, Angola (Cuban troop withdrawal), Mozambique, Central America, and Haiti. The Security Council succeeded because it had the backing of the permanent members, particularly the United States, Britain, and France, and the cooperation of the parties to the conflicts. In many of these conflicts the parties either voluntarily called on the United Nations for assistance, or the Security Council imposed its will on the parties. These conflicts were holdovers from the Cold War, and the major powers were eager to see them resolved. The conflicts were draining the resources of the parties, and it was unlikely that any one party would prevail on the battle field. The Security Council became involved after the parties had negotiated and signed ceasefires and peace agreements, and invited the United Nations to monitor the ceasefires or help with the implementation of these agreements. In Cambodia, Namibia, Angola, Mozambique, and Central America, the parties reached a settlement through the mediation efforts of one or more of the permanent members of the Security Council, and turned to the United Nations for assistance in overseeing the implementation of the agreements. That strategy worked very well, because the permanent members had a vested interest in the successful implementation of the agreements. The parties also acted responsibly and carried out their obligations under the agreements in good faith.

In the Haiti situation, for example, the Security Council succeeded because the United States successfully convinced other members of the Security Council that the overthrow of a democratically elected government in the Western Hemisphere constituted a threat to international peace and security in the region and therefore President Aristide, who was elected to office in a United Nations-organized election, should be reinstated, by force if necessary.[4] The Haitian situation was a unique event in Security Council history. Never before had the Security Council decided that a military regime was a threat to international peace and security and authorized the use of force to restore the democratically elected government. The Security Council was careful not to establish a precedent in the Haitian situation by declaring the military junta a threat to international peace and security. Instead, the Security Council relied on the more plausible arguments of being invited by President Aristide to intervene in Haiti, and the deteriorating human rights situation in the country, to justify imposing Chapter VII measures against the Haitian military regime.[5] The military measures authorized by resolution 940 (1994) were never carried out due to the last-minute diplomatic efforts of former US President Jimmy Carter. The Security Council's action did raise some concerns in the international legal community about what constitutes a threat to international peace and security, and whether the Security Council was not venturing into areas traditionally considered to be within the domestic jurisdiction of member states.[6]

Security Council Failures

The climate of cooperation that followed the end of the Cold War did not lead to stability in all parts of the globe. The end of the Cold War created power vacuums in many weak states and gave rise to long subdued ethnic and religious nationalism that could not be contained by the intervention of the Security Council. In the post-Cold War, the character of regional conflicts as well as the nature of the participants changed dramatically. Many post-Cold War regional conflicts were within states, and between government forces and rebel organizations. The reason behind many of these wars was to overthrow the central government or to secede from the existing state. The conflicts were often brutal, and the parties did not often comply with international humanitarian law or respect human rights.[7]

Serious atrocities were committed against civilian populations. The groups fighting these conflicts had no unified command structure, and acted in total disregard for international law or international agreements negotiated on their behalf. The ability of the United Nations to intervene in so many regional conflicts was beginning to decline, as some permanent members of the Security Council were not inclined to authorize any new peacekeeping missions in the absence of a vital strategic or economic interest. The Security Council initially deferred to regional organizations or simply ignored these conflicts with the hopes that they would go away. When the Security Council finally decided to intervene, its involvement was limited to imposing arms embargoes or economic sanctions on the parties.

Finding a peaceful solution to these conflicts became increasingly difficult because the parties had no defined goals, or their goals conflicted with the objectives of the international community. The involvement of the Security Council did not always produce the desired results. In fact, Security Council involvement sometimes complicated efforts to find a peaceful solution. The inability of the Security Council to act expeditiously in Bosnia, Somalia, Rwanda, Liberia, and Sierra Leone helped prolong these conflicts and contributed to the perception that the Security Council was unable or unwilling to resolve certain regional conflicts.

The conflicts in Bosnia, Somalia, and Rwanda represent three failures of the Security Council. The Security Council intervened in these conflicts reluctantly, and only after regional organizations had tried and failed in their efforts to find a peaceful solution. In all three conflicts the Security Council approved mandates that were inadequate and ill-conceived. The United Nations also failed in these situations because the permanent members of the Security Council did not want to authorize military intervention for geopolitical and domestic political reasons.

The United Nations suffered a humiliating defeat in Bosnia because of the failure of the Security Council to act more decisively. The Security Council adopted a number of resolutions that it was unwilling to enforce with military force when necessary.[8] When the Security Council did authorize NATO to use air strikes to enforce the no-fly zones created over Bosnia, or to protect the civilian safe havens, it did so under a complicated scheme that placed the decision to use force in the hands of the Secretary General's Special Representative. UNPROFOR was initially established as a peacekeeping force, but its mandate was constantly adjusted as the situation on the ground changed. UNPROFOR's multiple tasks complicated its mission and compromised its neutrality. UNPROFOR's inadequate military hardware also prevented it from defending the safe havens against a superior Bosnian Serb army. The Serb army overran the safe havens and massacred thousands of Bosnian civilians. The Serb army also repeatedly violated the airspace over Bosnia. The failure of the Security Council to authorize additional military strikes against the Serb army placed UNPROFOR in a precarious position and prevented it from protecting the civilian population. The United Nations mission in Bosnia failed because of the lack of political will on the part of some of the permanent members of the Security Council to support military intervention in Bosnia.[9]

The situation in Somalia was unlike any other conflict the Security Council had attempted to resolve. In its early stages, the Security Council overlooked the gravity of the humanitarian situation in Somalia and ignored appeals from the Secretary General and aid agencies for United Nations intervention to facilitate the distribution of humanitarian assistance and to protect aid workers. Some permanent members of the Security Council were reluctant to authorize United Nations intervention in Somalia because of the domestic nature of the conflict and the precedent the Security Council would set if it authorized United Nations intervention in a situation considered within the domestic jurisdiction of a state. However, as the humanitarian and security situations deteriorated, the Security Council adopted resolution 733 (1992) by which it imposed an arms embargo on Somalia.[10] The arms embargo did nothing to stop the fighting or to improve the humanitarian situation in Somalia. Against mounting international criticism, the Security Council reluctantly adopted resolution 751 (1992) to authorize the deployment of a peacekeeping force to Somalia. The United Nations Operation in Somalia (UNOSOM I), which comprised a contingent of inadequately trained, ill-equipped Pakistani troops, was responsible for monitoring the ceasefire between the warring factions, providing security and protection for United Nations personnel, equipment, and supplies at the seaports and airports in Mogadishu, and escort deliveries of humanitarian supplies from there to distribution centers in the city and immediate surroundings.[11] The Pakistanis were quickly overrun by Somali warlords.

In December 1992 the Security Council accepted a request from the United States to deploy a US-led multinational force to Somalia. The Security Council adopted resolution 794 (1992), by which it authorized the deployment of the United Task Force (UNITAF).[12] Acting under Chapter VII of the Charter, the Security Council authorized UNITAF to use all necessary means to create a secure environment for the delivery of humanitarian aid in Somalia.[13] In March 1993, the Security Council adopted resolution 814 (1993) to establish UNOSOM II to take over from UNITAF.[14] The deployment of UNOSOM II was authorized under Chapter VII of the Charter, and UNOSOM II was given the authority to use all necessary means to implement its mandate.[15] The nature of UNOSOM's mandate brought it directly into the conflict. UNOSOM II engaged in combat after some of its members were killed, and a warrant was issued by the Security Council for the arrest of General Aidid. Several American and Pakistani peacekeepers were later killed. This event led to a dramatic change in the United Nations presence in Somalia. The United States Congress called for the withdrawal of American troops, and criticized the United Nations for the death of American military personnel. The United Nations withdrew from Somalia in March 1995 without successfully completing its mission. The Somalia fiasco led to a change in the attitudes of some of the permanent members towards future United Nations involvement in regional conflicts.

Contrary to popular belief, the United Nations mission in Somalia was not a complete failure. The humanitarian aspect of the United Nations operation was successful, but the United Nations' role in nation-building and in trying to impose a political solution on the Somalis failed miserably. UNOSOM II's mandate, which included nation-building and the establishment of political institutions, put the United Nations into direct confrontation with some of the warring factions. UNOSOM II's mandate compromised the neutrality of the United Nations and contributed to the failure of the mission. UNOSOM II was viewed by some elements in Somalia as a hostile occupying army that favored one warring faction over others.

The Security Council first became involved in Rwanda in 1993 when it adopted resolution 846 (1993) to authorize the deployment of a peacekeeping force to Rwanda to monitor a ceasefire between Ugandan-backed rebels and government troops.[16] The United Nations Observer Mission Uganda Rwanda (UNOMUR) was deployed on the Uganda side of the border to monitor a ceasefire agreement between government troops and rebels of the Patriotic Front. In October 1993 the Security Council adopted resolution 872 (1993) by which it authorized the deployment of the United Nations Assistance Mission for Rwanda (UNAMIR). UNAMIR was responsible for security of the capital, Kigali, monitoring the ceasefire, and investigating allegations of non-compliance with the Arusha Peace Agreement.[17]

Following the outbreak of violence in Rwanda in 1994, in the wake of the death of the presidents of Rwanda and Burundi, the Security Council initially ignored calls from human rights organizations to intervene to stop violence. The Security Council deliberately refused to recognize the extent of the violence in Rwanda to avoid authorizing United Nations intervention.[18] Some permanent members of the Security Council, particularly the United States, opposed United Nations intervention for fear of a repeat of the Somalia experience. The Clinton Administration was concerned that the United States Congress would not support the participation of American troops in another United Nations peacekeeping mission in Africa in the aftermath of the Somalia debacle. In fact, the United States advised its diplomats to refrain from calling the violence in Rwanda genocide for fear that the United States would have been legally obligated to intervene as a party to the 1948 Genocide Convention. The Security Council later determined that genocide had in fact occurred in Rwanda, but only after the violence had stopped.

As the scale of the violence in Rwanda increased, the Security Council voted to reduce the troop level of UNAMIR and barred the peacekeepers from protecting civilians who had taken refuge in UNAMIR's headquarters.[19] Many of those who sought refuge in UNAMIR's headquarters were subsequently killed. After the killing subsided the Security Council authorized member states to use all necessary means to accomplish their humanitarian objectives in Rwanda. The French-led multinational force (Operation Turquoise) established a humanitarian protective zone for the Hutu refugees fleeing the conflict in Rwanda after the

Tutsi-led Patriotic Front rebels captured the capital, Kigali, and established a new Tutsi-dominated government.[20] The Rwanda genocide will go down as one of the tragic failures of the Security Council. Early intervention by the Security Council could have averted the death of thousands of civilians. The Security Council ignored reports of a pending massacre from the commander of UNAMIR for fear of getting involved in another African conflict that was not viewed as a priority for many of the Security Council.

The Security Council also responded too late to requests for United Nations intervention in the conflicts in Liberia and Sierra Leone. Both conflicts were allowed to escalate before the Security Council decided to intervene. In the initial stages of the conflict the Security Council deferred to ECOWAS to find a peaceful solution to both conflicts. Although the ECOWAS involvement in the conflict violated the principles of the Charter of the United Nations, the Security Council did not condemn it.[21] The Security Council endorsed the actions of ECOWAS in both conflicts, and exempted ECOMOG, the military wing of ECOWAS, from the arms embargoes imposed on the Liberian and Sierra Leonean rebels.[22] The Security Council played no direct role in the peace negotiations for Liberia and Sierra Leone. After the parties signed their peace agreements, the Security Council authorized the deployment of United Nations peacekeepers to assist in implementing the agreements. The war in Liberia ended in 1997 after the peace agreement took effect and free elections were held, which Charles Taylor won. The parties to the conflict in Sierra Leone signed a peace agreement in Lome in 1999 and invited the United Nations to monitor compliance with the accord. After a series of setbacks, the Security Council voted to enlarge UNAMSIL, which became one of the largest United Nations peacekeeping missions deployed in a conflict zone.

The role of the Security Council in Angola after the withdrawal of Cuban forces also raised questions about the commitment of the United Nations to resolving regional conflicts. Following completion of UNAVEM I's mandate, the Security Council first approved the deployment of the United Nations Angola Verification Mission (UNAVEM II) to verify implementation of the peace accord signed between the government of Angola and the UNITA rebel movement.[23] UNAVEM II was also authorized to assist in organizing democratic elections in Angola. Although Angola is a much bigger country than Cambodia or Namibia, the Security Council approved a force far fewer than the ones it authorized for the other two two countries.[24] The Security Council also invested fewer resources in the Angola peace process than it did for Namibia and Cambodia. UNAVEM II failed because some permanent members of the Security Council were not committed to the peace process in Angola. Economic sanctions were imposed against UNITA, but no further actions were ever considered. The war ended, in the end, as a result of the death of Jonas Savimbi.

The Security Council and Inter-State Conflicts

The success of the Security Council in managing inter-state conflicts has been mixed. Until 1990 the Security Council had authorized military measures against states only on two occasions: North Korea in 1950 and Rhodesia in 1966. In both cases the Security Council delegated its Chapter VII authority to individual states, without retaining the right to monitor the actual day-to-day conduct of the operations. In the Korean situation the Security Council authorized enforcement measures in the absence of a permanent member, the Soviet Union. This raised serious questions about the legality of the operation. Article 27 calls for decisions of the Security Council on substantive matters to be made by an affirmative vote of nine members, including the concurrent votes of all five permanent members. Since the USSR did not participate in the deliberations and did not vote on the issue, it would appear that the measure against North Korea was illegal. In the Rhodesia situation, all five permanent members participated in the deliberations and either voted or abstained on the measure.

During the Iran-Iraq War the Security Council called for the parties to cease fighting and to settle their dispute by peaceful means in accordance with their obligations under the Charter of the United Nations, but it did not condemn Iraq, or impose sanctions on the parties for their failure to comply with its demands. Iraq violated international humanitarian laws by using chemical and biological weapons against Iranian soldiers and civilians. Given Iran's pariah status, members of the Security Council did not want to appear to be siding with a state that had previous defied international law. Certain permanent members of the Security Council wanted to punish Iran for violating international law and defying the will of the international community. There was no pressing desire in the Security Council to take punitive measures against Iraq. No sanctions were imposed on Iraq and Iran, and the war was allowed to continue until 1988. Iraq was not immediately sanctioned for using poisonous gases against Iranian soldiers and its own civilian population until the end of the Iraq-Kuwait conflict. The Security Council imposed a sanctions regime on Iraq that required the destruction of all Iraq's stockpiles of chemical and biological weapons and the means to manufacture weapons of mass destruction.[25]

In the Falkland Islands War, both Britain and Argentina failed to comply with Security Council resolution calling on them to cease fighting and to settle their dispute by peaceful means. Argentina also refused to withdraw its troops from the Falkland Islands in violation of the same Security Council resolution. Britain in turn defied the Security Council by using force to retake the islands from Argentina. Britain justified its action as self-defense under Article 51 of the Charter of the United Nations, and claimed that since Argentina had not complied with the demands of the Security Council, it therefore retained a legitimate right to self-defense to protect its nationals held hostage by Argentine forces. The fact that Britain could exercise its veto in the Security Council prevented the Security Council from adopting any new resolution condemning Britain's use of force to retake the islands from Argentina.

Argentina withdrew its forces from the Falkland Islands after British forces defeated the Argentines and recaptured the islands.

Iraq's invasion and subsequent annexation of Kuwait was handled quite differently by the Security Council. The Cold War had ended, the United States and the USSR were enjoying a new spirit of cooperation, and for the first time in its history, the Security Council was able to reach a consensus decision. The Security Council acted immediately to condemn Iraq for invading Kuwait and threatened to take additional measures, including both non-military and military measures to force Iraq to comply with its demands. The Security Council's reponse to Iraq's aggression was unprecedented. Twenty-four hours after Iraq invaded Kuwait, the Security Council condemned Iraq's action and called for an immediate withdrawal. Within a matter of days after adoption of resolution 660 (1990), the Security Council adopted resolution 661 (1990) by which it imposed sanctions on Iraq. The Security Council thereafter authorized military states with naval vessels in the region to use all necessary means to enforce the embargo. The Security Council subsequently authorized military measures to eject Iraqi forces from Kuwait.[26] The Security Council's successful handling of Iraq's aggression against Kuwait gave rise to hopes that the United Nations collective security regime was finally functional. It gave the United Nations the reassurance necessary to tackle more complex regional conflicts that were to confront the international community as the Cold War shield that had once provided cover for these conflicts began to disappear. However, the combination of factors that gave rise to the collective actions against Iraq did not exist in other conflicts, and this suddenly led to a change in attitude by the permanent members of the Security Council toward certain regional conflicts.

The Security Council did not do well in its handling of the war between Eritrea and Ethiopia, or the conflict in the Democratic Republic of the Congo (DRC). The Security Council imposed an arms embargo against Eritrea and Ethiopia, but it had no impact on the parties. The Security Council had very few options to stop the Eritrea-Ethiopia war. None of the permanent members of the Security Council had enough of a vital interest in the region to sacrifice a direct military intervention. The ghost of Somalia was too fresh in the minds of American policymakers to risk another intervention in the Horn of Africa. The Security Council could not impose more drastic measures to stop the war because it would have had no way of enforcing the measures. Ethiopia scored a military victory against Eritrea and ended the war on its own terms without the Security Council forcing it to do so.

The conflict in the DRC involving six African states, which began in 1998, took the Security Council by surprise. The Security Council adopted several resolutions to call on the parties to respect the territorial integrity of the DRC and to withdraw their forces from the DRC in accordance with their obligations under the Lusaka Ceasefire Agreement. However, none of the parties complied with the demands of the Security Council. The Security Council has taken no further measures against the parties to force them to comply with its demands.

The Security Council has not demonstrated the political will necessary for managing inter-state conflicts. The interstate conflicts that have been waged since the end of the Cold War, except for Iraq's invasion of Kuwait, had little impact on international peace and security. The Security Council took a 'wait and see' attitude toward most of the conflicts, except for Kuwait. The Security Council had little influence in ending these wars. The wars posed no major challenge to international or regional peace and security, and had no significant impact on the vital interests of the major powers. The Security Council has not played a more vigorous role in managing inter-state conflicts because no consensus exist among the permanent members of the Security Council on how to deal with every situation that may give rise to a threat to the peace. As in other conflict situations, the Security Council is only willing to take military measures to maintain international peace and security when the outcome of the conflict has a direct imapct one one or more of the permanent members on the Security Council, particularly the United States, Britain, and France. The influence of the Security Council in inter-state conflicts has waned, and it is likely to continue to decline as more and more nations question the legitimacy of the Security Council. The United States' decision to bypass the Security Council to go to war with Iraq in 2003 underscores the concerns of many nations that the Security Council regime for international peace and security needs to be reformed.

Recommendations for Enhancing the Capacity of the Security Council to Respond to Transnational Armed Conflicts

With the end of the Cold War came many unexpected conflicts within states. These conflicts had serious implications for international peace and security. The line between domestic and international conflicts has blurred, and increasingly, internal disputes are posing the greatest threats to international peace and security. This has made it more likely for the Security Council to have a say in these disputes. The Security Council cannot avoid these conflicts because of their humanitarian impact and their potential for spreading into neighboring states. The humanitarian dimension and the level of violence against the civilian population give these conflicts an international dimension unforeseen when the Charter was negotiated. The inability of regional organizations to substitute for the United Nations in most instances makes it absolutely essential that the Security Council play a greater role in resolving these conflicts.

The number of regional conflicts has grown at such an alarming rate that the Security Council has not been able to attend to every conflict without delegating some of the authority to individual member states or regional organizations. The increasing number of regional conflicts has strained the financial resources of the United Nations, and member states are increasingly reluctant to spend more on new United Nations peacekeeping operations. The Security Council, therefore, must be more selective about which conflicts it will attempt to resolve, and which ones it will defer to individual member states or regional organizations. In so doing the Security Council must be careful that it authorizes United Nations intervention only in conflicts that the United Nations is capable of resolving successfully, and to defer to certain member states or regional organizations those conflicts the United Nations believes regional organizations can resolve successfully.

In order for the United Nations to respond more effectively to threats to international peace and security, the Security Council must first determine which conflicts are priorities to the international community and which ones are not. The Security Council must establish certain guidelines by which it decides when the United Nations can and cannot intervene in a conflict situation. The Security Council should participate directly in all peace negotiations to make sure that the responsibility assigned to the United Nations is attainable. The Security Council should also create a security advisory committee as a permanent body within the Security Council to advise members of the Council on situations that constitute a threat to international peace and security, and how to respond appropriately. Where necessary, the Security Council should initiate its own diplomatic measures to find a peaceful solution to the conflict before it authorizes Chapter VII measures.

In too many instances, the Security Council authorized Chapter VII measures without calculating the political fallout and the economic hardship these measures would impose on the civilian population. These sanction measures have proven counter-productive and led to anti-United Nations sentiment in the conflict zones and among many nations. In many of the cases in which the Security Council imposed Chapter VII measures, they failed to accomplish the objectives of the international community. The target regimes exploited the loopholes in the sanctions and profited from the shortage of imported items by controlling the illegal flow of goods into the country.

The Security Council should also reactivate the Military Staff Committee to advise it and the Secretariat on peace and security matters. The MSC should play a more active role in managing United Nations peacekeeping and peacemaking operations. Military missions should only be deployed if the MSC approves of the deployment after sound miltary decisions are made. The practice of placing United Nations forces under the command of the Secretary General is no longer a working formula for the kinds of conflicts afflicting the international community. The Secretary General should coordinate the political and diplomatic aspects of peacekeeping missions and defer to the MSC for overseeing the day-to-day activities of peacekeeping operations. The United Nations needs to establish a military structure to deal with serious security situations such as Sierra Leone, Kosovo, East Timor, and Bosnia. The Security Council should only adopt resolutions relating to a particular threat to the peace if it follows through in enforcing the resolutions. The Security Council must see to it that the will of the international community is respected by rebel groups and irregular militias, in order for its demands to be credible.

Most post-Cold War conflicts are a result of deep-rooted internal structural imbalances in the political processes, distribution of economic benefits, human rights abuses, political repression, corruption, and mass poverty. The Security Council must address these issues as serious threats to international peace and security and take preventive measures to prevent these problems from escalating into full-scale conflicts. The Security Council should deny recognition to any regime that comes into power through undemocratic or unconstitutional means, or through an electoral process that was not certified by international observers as free and fair. The Security Council should also call for greater respect for human rights, equitable distribution of wealth, and social and economic development that benefits those most likely to resort to violence, to redress political exclusion or repression.

Measures to maintain international peace and security require a comprehensive plan that includes the total rehabilitation of a state. Maintaining peace and security is no longer disengaging hostile armies; it requires a complete package that includes human rights monitoring, establishing democratic institutions and the rule of law, restoring people's faith in government, mine clearing, disengaging and demobilization of rebel armies and reintegrating them into civilian life, resettling large numbers of displaced civilians, organizing and monitoring democratic elections, promoting economic development and resource management, and post-conflict monitoring of the situation to prevent a resumption of war. Measures to maintain international peace and security also require the United Nations to commit itself to the long-term monitoring of the country's political development, its human rights record, and economic and social conditions. The United Nations needs additional resources for conflict prevention and such efforts should be coordinated with international financial institutions, the private sector, and NGOs.

The Security Council must enhance the capacity of regional organizations and provide them with the tools to maintain regional peace and security. The Security Council must also help these organizations establish permanent security infrastructures to respond more effectively to threats to regional peace and security. The Security Council should establish guidelines by which regional organizations can resort to enforcement measures to avoid situations like Liberia, Sierra Leone, and Kosovo. The current arrangement in which regional organizations take it on themselves to determine when to intervene in a regional conflict is a dangerous mechanism that has serious repercussions for international peace and security.

The 1999 NATO military strikes against Yugoslavia to stop the violence against ethnic Albanians in Kosovo, and the ECOWAS intervention in Sierra Leone to restore the democratically elected government raise serious legal questions with respect to the world order precedent that is being established. The Security Council cannot abdicate its responsibility by failing to act and acquiescing to regional organizations that use force without Security Council authorization. Given the fierce nature of regional conflicts, and the unpredictable manner in which they occur, it seems likely that regional organizations can respond quicker than the Security Council. The nature of regional conflicts calls for a new security partnership between the United Nations and regional organizations, as was demonstrated in Bosnia between the United Nations and NATO, in Haiti between the United Nations and the OAS, and in Liberia, Sierra Leone, and Eritrea and Ethiopia between the United Nations and ECOWAS and the OAU. More importantly, the Security Council should encourage the establishment of United Nations liaison offices within the secretariat of regional organizations in conflict-prone zones.

The increasing reliance of the United Nations on the 'P3' members of the Security Council – the United States, Britain, and France – to decide when the United Nations should intervene in a conflict is not a working formula for maintaining international peace and security. All five permanent members should participate equally in all Security Council deliberations and initiatives. China seldom supports Security Council initiatives and rarely participates in United Nations peacekeeping activities. China has shown a lack of interest in strengthening the capacity of the United Nations. Russia has shown a greater commitment to the efforts of the United Nations, but has not contributed personnel or the financial resources for peacekeeping operations. Reliance on the United States, Britain, and France leaves the United Nations vulnerable to the domestic policies of these states. However, without their support the United Nations could not function.

The P3 nations' support for United Nations missions is too closely identified with their own national interest and their domestic politics and public opinion. This arrangement makes it extremely difficult for the United Nations to establish clear guidelines on what constitutes a threat to international peace and security, and how to respond appropriately to such threats. The practice of informal consultation among the P3 has raised questions about the legitimacy of the Security Council's actions, and complicated its efforts to win the cooperation of all member states and the parties to a conflict.

The United Nations must also establish a new formula for funding peacekeeping operations. The current method for assessing peacekeeping dues, which is done only after the Security Council has approved the deployment of a mission, can delay the process and complicate efforts to expedite the deployment. Many states, including the Permanent Members of the Security Council, do not pay their dues on time. This seriously handicaps the United Nations' ability to respond to crisis situations. The current outstanding peacekeeping dues are estimated at $2.32 billion; the United States alone owes over $1 billion. Funding for peacekeeping operations has not kept up with the growing number of conflicts. There is too much reliance on the goodwill of some states and the voluntary contributions they make. Peacekeeping dues should be included in the annual budget of the United Nations, and should be placed in a separate category as funds for maintaining international peace and security. The United Nations should also require that host countries contribute more for peacekeeping missions stationed on their territory, providing these states are in a position to pay.

Finally, the Security Council must establish better guidelines for withdrawing United Nations peacekeeping missions from a conflict zone. The United Nations should not withdraw its troops due to losses suffered or where the parties failed to fully implement the peace agreement. United Nations forces should only withdraw when it has the assurance that its withdrawal will not create a security vacuum and lead to a resumption of war. A United Nations withdrawal should be contingent on the parties reaching a permanent peace that is fully implemented. All exit strategies should be linked to a thorough military assessment by the MSC before the Security Council can approve such a withdrawal. A decision to withdraw from a conflict should be a military decision, and should not be done for political expediency.

APPENDIX

1945 Charter of the United Nations

Adopted in San Francisco, USA, on 26 June 1945

APPENDIX

WE THE PEOPLES OF THE UNITED NATIONS DETERMINED

to save succeeding generations from the scourge of war, which twice in our lifetime has brought untold sorrow to mankind, and

to reaffirm faith in fundamental human rights, in the dignity and worth of the human person, in the equal rights of men and women and of nations large and small, and

to establish conditions under which justice and respect for the obligations arising from treaties and other sources of international law can be maintained, and

to promote social progress and better standards of life in larger freedom,

AND FOR THESE ENDS

to practice tolerance and live together in peace with one another as good neighbors, and

to unite our strength to maintain international peace and security, and

to ensure, by the acceptance of principles and the institution of methods, that armed force shall not be used, save in the common interest, and

to employ international machinery for the promotion of the economic and social advancement of all peoples,

HAVE RESOLVED TO COMBINE OUR EFFORTS TO ACCOMPLISH THESE AIMS.

Accordingly, our respective governments, through representatives assembled in the city of San Francisco, who have exhibited their full powers found to be in good and due form, have agreed to the present Charter of the United Nations and do hereby establish an international organization to be known as the United Nations.

CHAPTER I - PURPOSES AND PRINCIPLES

Article 1

The Purposes of the United Nations are:

1. To maintain international peace and security, and to that end: to take effective collective measures for the prevention and removal of threats to the peace, and for the suppression of acts of aggression or other breaches of the peace, and to bring about by peaceful means, and in conformity with the principles of justice and international law, adjustment or settlement of international disputes or situations which might lead to a breach of the peace;

2. To develop friendly relations among nations based on respect for the principle of equal rights and self-determination of peoples, and to take other appropriate measures to strengthen universal peace;

3. To achieve international cooperation in solving international problems of an economic, social, cultural, or humanitarian character, and in promoting and encouraging respect for human rights and for fundamental freedoms for all without distinction as to race, sex, language, or religion; and

4. To be a center for harmonizing the actions of nations in the attainment of these common ends.

Article 2

The Organization and its Members, in pursuit of the Purposes stated in Article 1, shall act in accordance with the following Principles.

1. The Organization is based on the principle of the sovereign equality of all its Members.

2. All Members, in order to ensure to all of them the rights and benefits resulting from membership, shall fulfill in good faith the obligations assumed by them in accordance with the present Charter.

3. All Members shall settle their international disputes by peaceful means in such a manner that international peace and security, and justice, are not endangered.

4. All Members shall refrain in their international relations from the threat or use of force against the territorial integrity or political independence of any state, or in any other manner inconsistent with the Purposes of the United Nations.

5. All Members shall give the United Nations every assistance in any action it takes in accordance with the present Charter, and shall refrain from giving assistance to any state against which the United Nations is taking preventive or enforcement action.

6. The Organization shall ensure that states which are not Members of the United Nations act in accordance with these Principles so far as may be necessary for the maintenance of international peace and security.

7. Nothing contained in the present Charter shall authorize the United Nations to intervene in matters which are essentially within the domestic jurisdiction of any state or shall require the Members to submit such matters to settlement under the present Charter; but this principle shall not prejudice the application of enforcement measures under Chapter VII.

CHAPTER II - MEMBERSHIP

Article 3

The original Members of the United Nations shall be the states which, having participated in the United Nations Conference on International Organization at San Francisco, or having previously signed the Declaration by United Nations of 1 January 1942, sign the present Charter and ratify it in accordance with Article 110.

Article 4

1. Membership in the United Nations is open to all other peace-loving states which accept the obligations contained in the present Charter and, in the judgment of the Organization, are able and willing to carry out these obligations.

2. The admission of any such state to membership in the United Nations will be effected by a decision of the General Assembly upon the recommendation of the Security Council.

Article 5

A Member of the United Nations against which preventive or enforcement action has been taken by the Security Council may be suspended from the exercise of the rights and privileges of membership by the General Assembly upon the recommendation of the Security Council. The exercise of these rights and privileges may be restored by the Security Council.

Article 6

A Member of the United Nations which has persistently violated the Principles contained in the present Charter may be expelled from the Organization by the General Assembly upon the recommendation of the Security Council.

CHAPTER III - ORGANS

Article 7

1. There are established as the principal organs of the United Nations: a General Assembly, a Security Council, an Economic and Social Council, a Trusteeship Council, an International Court of Justice, and a Secretariat.

2. Such subsidiary organs as may be found necessary may be established in accordance with the present Charter.

Article 8

The United Nations shall place no restrictions on the eligibility of men and women to participate in any capacity and under conditions of equality in its principal and subsidiary organs.

CHAPTER IV - THE GENERAL ASSEMBLY

COMPOSITION

Article 9

1. The General Assembly shall consist of all the Members of the United Nations.

2. Each Member shall have not more than five representatives in the General Assembly.

FUNCTIONS AND POWERS

Article 10

The General Assembly may discuss any questions or any matters within the scope of the present Charter or relating to the powers and functions of any organs provided for in the present Charter, and, except as provided in Article 12, may make recommendations to the Members of the United Nations or to the Security Council or to both on any such questions or matters.

Article 11

1. The General Assembly may consider the general principles of cooperation in the maintenance of international peace and security, including the principles governing disarmament and the regulation of armaments, and may make recommendations with regard to such principles to the Members or to the Security Council or to both.

2. The General Assembly may discuss any questions relating to the maintenance of international peace and security brought before it by any Member of the United Nations, or by the Security Council, or by a state which is not a Member of the United Nations in accordance with Article 35, paragraph 2, and, except as provided in Article 12, may make recommendations with regard to any such questions to the state or states concerned or to the Security Council or to both. Any such question on which action is necessary shall be referred to the Security Council by the General Assembly either before or after discussion.

3. The General Assembly may call the attention of the Security Council to situations which are likely to endanger international peace and security.

4. The powers of the General Assembly set forth in this Article shall not limit the general scope of Article 10.

Article 12

1. While the Security Council is exercising in respect of any dispute or situation the functions assigned to it in the present Charter, the General Assembly shall not make any recommendation with regard to that dispute or situation unless the Security Council so requests.

2. The Secretary-General, with the consent of the Security Council, shall notify the General Assembly at each session of any matters relative to the maintenance of international peace and security which are being deal with by the Security Council and shall similarly notify the General Assembly, or the Members of the United Nations if the General Assembly is not in session, immediately the Security Council ceases to deal with such matters.

Article 13

1. The General Assembly shall initiate studies and make recommendations for the purpose of:

a. promoting international cooperation in the political field and encouraging the progressive development of international law and its codification;

b. promoting international cooperation in the economic, social, cultural, educational, and health fields, and assisting in the realization of human rights and fundamental freedoms for all without distinction as to race, sex, language, or religion.

2. The further responsibilities, functions, and powers of the General Assembly with respect to matters mentioned in paragraph 1(b) above are set forth in Chapters IX and X.

Article 14

Subject to the provisions of Article 12, the General Assembly may recommend measures for the peaceful adjustment of any situation, regardless of origin, which it deems likely to impair the general welfare or friendly relations among nations, including situations resulting from a violation of the provisions of the present Charter setting forth the Purposes and Principles of the United Nations.

Article 15

1. The General Assembly shall receive and consider annual and special reports from the Security Council; these reports shall include an account of the measures that the Security Council has decided upon or taken to maintain international peace and security.

2. The General Assembly shall receive and consider reports from the other organs of the United Nations.

Article 16

The General Assembly shall perform such functions with respect to the international trusteeship system as are assigned to it under Chapters XII and XIII, including the approval of the trusteeship agreements for areas not designated as strategic.

Article 17

1. The General Assembly shall consider and approve the budget of the Organization.

2. The expenses of the Organization shall be borne by the Members as apportioned by the General Assembly.

3. The General Assembly shall consider and approve any financial and budgetary arrangements with specialized agencies referred to in Article 57 and shall examine the administrative budgets of such specialized agencies with a view to making recommendations to the agencies concerned.

VOTING

Article 18

1. Each member of the General Assembly shall have one vote.

2. Decisions of the General Assembly on important questions shall be made by a two-thirds majority of the members present and voting. These questions shall include: recommendations with respect to the maintenance of international peace and security, the election of the non-

permanent members of the Security Council, the election of the members of the Economic and Social Council, the election of members of the Trusteeship Council in accordance with paragraph l(c) of Article 86, the admission of new Members to the United Nations, the suspension of the rights and privileges of membership, the expulsion of Members, questions relating to the operation of the trusteeship system, and budgetary questions.

3. Decisions on other questions, including the determination of additional categories of questions to be decided by a two-thirds majority, shall be made by a majority of the members present and voting.

Article 19

A Member of the United Nations which is in arrears in the payment of its financial contributions to the Organization shall have no vote in the General Assembly if the amount of its arrears equals or exceeds the amount of the contributions due from it for the preceding two full years. The General Assembly may, nevertheless, permit such a Member to vote if it is satisfied that the failure to pay is due to conditions beyond the control of the Member.

PROCEDURE

Article 20

The General Assembly shall meet in regular annual sessions and in such special sessions as occasion may require. Special sessions shall be convoked by the Secretary-General at the request of the Security Council or of a majority of the Members of the United Nations.

Article 21

The General Assembly shall adopt its own rules of procedure. It shall elect its President for each session.

Article 22

The General Assembly may establish such subsidiary organs as it deems necessary for the performance of its functions.

CHAPTER V - THE SECURITY COUNCIL

COMPOSITION

Article 23

1. The Security Council shall consist of fifteen Members of the United Nations. The Republic of China, France, the Union of Soviet Socialist Republics, the United Kingdom of Great Britain and Northern Ireland, and the United States of America shall be permanent members of the Security Council. The General Assembly shall elect ten other Members of the United Nations to be non-permanent members of the Security Council, due regard being specially paid, in the first instance to the contribution of Members of the United Nations to the maintenance of international peace and security and to the other purposes of the Organization, and also to equitable geographical distribution.

2. The non-permanent members of the Security Council shall be elected for a term of two years. In the first election of the non-permanent members after the increase of the membership of the Security Council from eleven to fifteen, two of the four additional members shall be chosen for a term of one year. A retiring member shall not be eligible for immediate re-election.

3. Each member of the Security Council shall have one representative.

FUNCTIONS AND POWERS

Article 24

1. In order to ensure prompt and effective action by the United Nations, its Members confer on the Security Council primary responsibility for the maintenance of international peace and security, and agree that in carrying out its duties under this responsibility the Security Council acts on their behalf.

2. In discharging these duties the Security Council shall act in accordance with the Purposes and Principles of the United Nations. The specific powers granted to the Security Council for the discharge of these duties are laid down in Chapters VI, VII, VIII, and XII.

3. The Security Council shall submit annual and, when necessary, special reports to the General Assembly for its consideration.

Article 25

The Members of the United Nations agree to accept and carry out the decisions of the Security Council in accordance with the present Charter.

Article 26

In order to promote the establishment and maintenance of international peace and security with the least diversion for armaments of the world's human and economic resources, the Security Council shall be responsible for formulating, with the assistance of the Military Staff Committee referred to in Article 47, plans to be submitted to the Members of the United Nations for the establishment of a system for the regulation of armaments.

VOTING

Article 27

1. Each member of the Security Council shall have one vote.

2. Decisions of the Security Council on procedural matters shall be made by an affirmative vote of nine members.

3. Decisions of the Security Council on all other matters shall be made by an affirmative vote of nine members including the concurring votes of the permanent members; provided that, in decisions under Chapter VI, and under paragraph 3 of Article 52, a party to a dispute shall abstain from voting.

PROCEDURE

Article 28

1. The Security Council shall be so organized as to be able to function continuously. Each member of the Security Council shall for this purpose be represented at all times at the seat of the Organization.

2. The Security Council shall hold periodic meetings at which each of its members may, if it so desires, be represented by a member of the government or by some other specially designated representative.

3. The Security Council may hold meetings at such places other than the seat of the Organization as in its judgment will best facilitate its work.

Article 29

The Security Council may establish such subsidiary organs as it deems necessary for the performance of its functions.

Article 30

The Security Council shall adopt its own rules of procedure, including the method of selecting its President.

Article 31

Any Member of the United Nations which is not a member of the Security Council may participate, without vote, in the discussion of any question brought before the Security Council whenever the latter considers that the interests of that Member are specially affected.

Article 32

Any Member of the United Nations which is not a member of the Security Council or any state which is not a Member of the United Nations, if it is a party to a dispute under consideration by the Security Council, shall be invited to participate, without vote, in the discussion relating to the dispute. The Security Council shall lay down such conditions as it deems just for the participation of a state which is not a Member of the United Nations.

CHAPTER VI - PACIFIC SETTLEMENT OF DISPUTES

Article 33

1. The parties to any dispute, the continuance of which is likely to endanger the maintenance of international peace and security, shall, first of all, seek a solution by negotiation, enquiry, mediation, conciliation, arbitration, judicial settlement, resort to regional agencies or arrangements, or other peaceful means of their own choice.

2. The Security Council shall, when it deems necessary, call upon the parties to settle their dispute by such means.

Article 34

The Security Council may investigate any dispute, or any situation which might lead to international friction or give rise to a dispute, in order to determine whether the continuance of the dispute or situation is likely to endanger the maintenance of international peace and security.

Article 35

1. Any Member of the United Nations may bring any dispute, or any situation of the nature referred to in Article 34, to the attention of the Security Council or of the General Assembly.

2. A state which is not a Member of the United Nations may bring to the attention of the Security Council or of the General Assembly any dispute to which it is a party if it accepts in advance, for the purposes of the dispute, the obligations of pacific settlement provided in the present Charter.

3. The proceedings of the General Assembly in respect to matters brought to its attention under this Article will be subject to the provisions of Articles 11 and 12.

Article 36

1. The Security Council may, at any stage of a dispute of the nature referred to in Article 33 or of a situation of like nature, recommend appropriate procedures or methods of adjustment.

2. The Security Council should take into consideration any procedures for the settlement of the dispute which have already been adopted by the parties.

3. In making recommendations under this Article the Security Council should also take into consideration that legal disputes should as a general rule be referred by the parties to the International Court of Justice in accordance with the provisions of the Statute of the Court.

Article 37

1. Should the parties to a dispute of the nature referred to in Article 33 fail to settle it by the means indicated in that Article, they shall refer it to the Security Council.

2. If the Security Council deems that the continuance of the dispute is in fact likely to endanger the maintenance of international peace and security, it shall decide whether to take action under Article 36 or to recommend such terms of settlement as it may consider appropriate.

Article 38

Without prejudice to the provisions of Article 33 to 37, the Security Council may, if all the parties to any dispute so request, make recommendations to the parties with a view to a pacific settlement of the dispute.

CHAPTER VII - ACTION WITH RESPECT TO THREATS TO THE PEACE, BREACHES OF THE PEACE, AND ACTS OF AGGRESSION

Article 39

The Security Council shall determine the existence of any threat to the peace, breach of the peace, or act of aggression and shall make recommendations, or decide what measures shall be taken in accordance with Articles 41 and 42, to maintain or restore international peace and security.

Article 40

In order to prevent an aggravation of the situation, the Security Council may, before making the recommendations or deciding upon the measures provided for in Article 39, call upon the parties concerned to comply with such provisional measures at it deems necessary or desirable. Such provisional measures shall be without prejudice to the rights, claims, or position of the parties concerned. The Security Council shall duly take account of failure to comply with such provisional measures.

Article 41

The Security Council may decide what measures not involving the use of armed force are to be employed to give effect to its decisions, and it may call upon the Members of the United Nations to apply such measures. These may include complete or partial interruption of economic relations and of rail, sea, air, postal, telegraphic, radio, and other means of communication, and the severance of diplomatic relations.

Article 42

Should the Security Council consider that measures provided for in Article 41 would be inadequate or have proved to be inadequate, it may take such action by air, sea, or land forces as may be necessary to maintain or restore international peace and security. Such action may include demonstrations, blockade, and other operations by air, sea, or land forces of Members of the United Nations.

Article 43

1. All Members of the United Nations, in order to contribute to the maintenance of international peace and security, undertake to make available to the Security Council, on its call and in accordance with a special agreement or agreements, armed forces, assistance, and facilities, including rights of passage, necessary for the purpose of maintaining international peace and security.

2. Such agreement or agreements shall govern the numbers and types of forces, their degree of readiness and general location, and the nature of the facilities and assistance to be provided.

3. The agreement or agreements shall be negotiated as soon as possible on the initiative of the Security Council. They shall be concluded between the Security Council and Members or between the Security Council and groups of Members and shall be subject to ratification by the signatory states in accordance with their respective constitutional processes.

Article 44

When the Security Council has decided to use force it shall, before calling upon a Member not represented on it to provide armed forces in fulfillment of the obligations assumed under Article 43, invite that Member, if the Member so desires, to participate in the decisions of the Security Council concerning the employment of contingents of that Member's armed forces.

Article 45

In order to enable the United Nations to take urgent military measures, Members shall hold immediately available national air-force contingents for combined international enforcement action. The strength and degree of readiness of these contingents and plans for their combined action shall be determined, within the limits laid down in the special agreement or agreements referred to in Article 43, by the Security Council with the assistance of the Military Staff Committee.

Article 46

Plans for the application of armed force shall be made by the Security Council with the assistance of the Military Staff Committee.

Article 47

1. There shall be established a Military Staff Committee to advise and assist the Security Council on all questions relating to the Security Council's military requirements for the maintenance of international peace and security, the employment and command of forces placed at its disposal, the regulation of armaments, and possible disarmament.

2. The Military Staff Committee shall consist of the Chiefs of Staff of the permanent members of the Security Council or their representatives. Any Member of the United Nations not permanently represented on the Committee shall be invited by the Committee to be associated with it when the efficient discharge of the Committee's responsibilities requires the participation of that Member in its work.

3. The Military Staff Committee shall be responsible under the Security Council for the strategic direction of any armed forces placed at the disposal of the Security Council. Questions relating to the command of such forces shall be worked out subsequently.

4. The Military Staff Committee, with the authorization of the Security Council and after consultation with appropriate regional agencies, may establish regional subcommittees.

Article 48

1. The action required to carry out the decisions of the Security Council for the maintenance of international peace and security shall be taken by all the Members of the United Nations or by some of them, as the Security Council may determine.

2. Such decisions shall be carried out by the Members of the United Nations directly and through their action in the appropriate international agencies of which they are members.

Article 49

The Members of the United Nations shall join in affording mutual assistance in carrying out the measures decided upon by the Security Council.

Article 50

If preventive or enforcement measures against any state are taken by the Security Council, any other state, whether a Member of the United Nations or not, which finds itself confronted with special economic problems arising from the carrying out of those measures shall have the right to consult the Security Council with regard to a solution of those problems.

Article 51

Nothing in the present Charter shall impair the inherent right of individual or collective self-defense if an armed attack occurs against a Member of the United Nations, until the Security Council has taken the measures necessary to maintain international peace and security. Measures taken by Members in the exercise of this right of self-defense shall be immediately reported to the Security Council and shall not in any way affect the authority and responsibility of the Security Council under the present Charter to take at any time such action as it deems necessary in order to maintain or restore international peace and security.

CHAPTER VIII - REGIONAL ARRANGEMENTS

Article 52

1. Nothing in the present Charter precludes the existence of regional arrangements or agencies for dealing with such matters relating to the maintenance of international peace and security as are appropriate for regional action, provided that such arrangements or agencies and their activities are consistent with the Purposes and Principles of the United Nations.

2. The Members of the United Nations entering into such arrangements or constituting such agencies shall make every effort to achieve pacific settlement of local disputes through such

regional arrangements or by such regional agencies before referring them to the Security Council.

3. The Security Council shall encourage the development of pacific settlement of local disputes through such regional arrangements or by such regional agencies either on the initiative of the states concerned or by reference from the Security Council.

4. This Article in no way impairs the application of Articles 34 and 35.

Article 53

1. The Security Council shall, where appropriate, utilize such regional arrangements or agencies for enforcement action under its authority. But no enforcement action shall be taken under regional arrangements or by regional agencies without the authorization of the Security Council, with the exception of measures against any enemy state, as defined in paragraph 2 of this Article, provided for pursuant to Article 107 or in regional arrangements directed against renewal of aggressive policy on the part of any such state, until such time as the Organization may, on request of the governments concerned, be charged with the responsibility for preventing further aggression by such a state.

2. The term enemy state as used in paragraph 1 of this Article applies to any state which during the Second World War has been an enemy of any signatory of the present Charter.

Article 54

The Security Council shall at all times be kept fully informed of activities undertaken or in contemplation under regional arrangements or by regional agencies for the maintenance of international peace and security.

CHAPTER IX - INTERNATIONAL ECONOMIC AND SOCIAL COOPERATION

Article 55

With a view to the creation of conditions of stability and well-being which are necessary for peaceful and friendly relations among nations based on respect for the principle of equal rights and self-determination of people, the United Nations shall promote:

a. higher standards of living, full employment, and conditions of economic and social progress and development;

b. solutions of international economic, social, health, and related problems; and international cultural and educational cooperation; and

c. universal respect for; and observance of, human rights and fundamental freedoms for all without distinction as to race, sex, language, or religion.

Article 56

All members pledge themselves to take joint and separate action in cooperation with the Organization for the achievement of the purposes set forth in Article 55.

Article 57

1. The various specialized agencies, established by intergovernmental agreement and having wide international responsibilities, as defined in their basic instruments, in economic, social, cultural, educational, health, and related fields, shall be brought into relationship with the United Nations in accordance with the provisions of Article 63.

2. Such agencies thus brought into relationship with the United Nations are hereinafter referred to as specialized agencies.

Article 58

The Organization shall make recommendations for the coordination of the policies and activities of the specialized agencies.

Article 59

The Organization shall, where appropriate, initiate negotiations among the states concerned for the creation of any new specialized agencies required for the accomplishment of the purposes set forth in Article 55.

Article 60

Responsibility for the discharge of the functions of the Organization set forth in this Chapter shall be vested in the General Assembly and, under the authority of the General Assembly, in the Economic and Social Council, which shall have for this purpose the powers set forth in Chapter X.

CHAPTER X - THE ECONOMIC AND SOCIAL COUNCIL

COMPOSITION

Article 61

1. The Economic and Social Council shall consist of fifty-four Members of the United Nations elected by the General Assembly.

2. Subject to the provisions of paragraph 3, eighteen members of the Economic and Social Council shall be elected each year for a term of three years. A retiring member shall be eligible for immediate re-election.

3. At the first election after the increase in the membership of the Economic and Social Council from twenty-seven to fifty-four members, in addition to the members elected in place of the nine members whose term of office expires at the end of that year, twenty-seven additional members shall be elected. Of these twenty-seven additional members, the term of office of nine members so elected shall expire at the end of one year, and of nine other members at the end of two years, in accordance with arrangements made by the General Assembly.

4. Each member of the Economic and Social Council shall have one representative.

FUNCTIONS AND POWERS

Article 62

1. The Economic and Social Council may make or initiate studies and reports with respect to international economic, social, cultural, educational, health, and related matters and may make recommendations with respect to any such matters to the General Assembly, to the Members of the United Nations, and to the specialized agencies concerned.

2. It may make recommendations for the purpose of promoting respect for, and observance of, human rights and fundamental freedoms for all.

3. It may prepare draft conventions for submission to the General Assembly, with respect to matters falling within its competence.

4. It may call, in accordance with the rules prescribed by the United Nations, international conferences on matters falling within its competence.

Article 63

1. The Economic and Social Council may enter into agreements with any of the agencies referred to in Article 57, defining the terms on which the agency concerned shall be brought into relationship with the United Nations. Such agreements shall be subject to approval by the General Assembly.

2. It may co-ordinate the activities of the specialized agencies through consultation with and recommendations to such agencies and through recommendations to the General Assembly and to the Members of the United Nations.

Article 64

1. The Economic and Social Council may take appropriate steps to obtain regular reports from the specialized agencies. It may make arrangements with the Members of the United Nations and with the specialized agencies to obtain reports on the steps taken to give effect to its own recommendations and to recommendations on matters falling within its competence made by the General Assembly.

2. It may communicate its observations on these reports to the General Assembly.

Article 65

The Economic and Social Council may furnish information to the Security Council and shall assist the Security Council upon its request.

Article 66

1. The Economic and Social Council shall perform such functions as fall within its competence in connection with the carrying out of the recommendations of the General Assembly.

2. It may, with the approval of the General Assembly, perform services at the request of Members of the United Nations and at the request of specialized agencies.

3. It shall perform such other functions as are specified elsewhere in the present Charter or as may be assigned to it by the General Assembly.

VOTING

Article 67

1. Each member of the Economic and Social Council shall have one vote.

2. Decisions of the Economic and Social Council shall be made by a majority of the members present and voting.

PROCEDURE

Article 68

The Economic and Social Council shall set up commissions in economic and social fields and for the promotion of human rights, and such other commissions as may be required for the performance of its functions.

Article 69

The Economic and Social Council shall invite any Member of the United Nations to participate, without vote, in its deliberations on any matter of particular concern to that Member.

Article 70

The Economic and Social Council may make arrangements for representatives of the specialized agencies to participate, without vote, in its deliberations and in those of the commissions established by it, and for its representatives to participate in the deliberations of the specialized agencies.

Article 71

The Economic and Social Council may make suitable arrangements for consultation with non-governmental organizations which are concerned with matters within its competence. Such arrangements may be made with international organizations and, where appropriate, with national organizations after consultation with the Member of the United Nations concerned.

Article 72

1. The Economic and Social Council shall adopt its own rules of procedure, including the method of selecting its President.

2. The Economic and Social Council shall meet as required in accordance with its rules, which shall include provision for the convening of meetings on the request of a majority of its members.

CHAPTER XI - DECLARATION REGARDING NON-SELF-GOVERNING TERRITORIES

Article 73

Members of the United Nations which have or assume responsibilities for the administration of territories whose peoples have not yet attained a full measure of self-government recognize the principle that the interests of the inhabitants of these territories are paramount, and accept as a sacred trust the obligation to promote to the utmost, within the system of international peace and security established by the present Charter, the well-being of the inhabitants of these territories, and, to this end:

a. to ensure, with due respect for the culture of the peoples concerned, their political, economic, social, and educational advancement, their just treatment, and their protection against abuses;

b. to develop self-government, to take due account of the political aspirations of the peoples, and to assist them in the progressive development of their free political institutions, according to the particular circumstances of each territory and its peoples and their varying stages of advancement;

c. to further international peace and security;

d. to promote constructive measures of development, to encourage research, and to cooperate with one another and, when and where appropriate, with specialized international bodies with a view to the practical achievement of the social, economic, and scientific purposes set forth in this Article; and

e. to transmit regularly to the Secretary-General for information purposes, subject to such limitation as security and constitutional considerations may require, statistical and other information of a technical nature relating to economic, social, and educational conditions in the territories for which they are respectively responsible other than those territories to which Chapters XII and XIII apply.

Article 74

Members of the United Nations also agree that their policy in respect of the territories to which this Chapter applies, no less than in respect of their metropolitan areas, must be based on the general principle of good-neighborliness, due account being taken of the interests and well-being of the rest of the world, in social, economic, and commercial matters.

CHAPTER XII - INTERNATIONAL TRUSTEESHIP SYSTEM

Article 75

The United Nations shall establish under its authority an international trusteeship system for the administration and supervision of such territories as may be placed thereunder by subsequent individual agreements. These territories are hereinafter referred to as trust territories.

Article 76

The basic objectives of the trusteeship system, in accordance with the Purposes of the United Nations laid down in Article 1 of the present Charter, shall be:

a. to further international peace and security;

b. to promote the political, economic, social, and educational advancement of the inhabitants of the trust territories, and their progressive development towards self-government or independence as may be appropriate to the particular circumstances of each territory and its peoples and the freely expressed wishes of the peoples concerned, and as may be provided by the terms of each trusteeship agreement;

c. to encourage respect for human rights and for fundamental freedoms for all without distinction as to race, sex, language, or religion, and to encourage recognition of the interdependence of the peoples of the world; and

d. to ensure equal treatment in social, economic, and commercial matters for all Members of the United Nations and their nationals, and also equal treatment for the latter in the administration of justice, without prejudice to the attainment of the foregoing objectives and subject to the provisions of Article 80.

Article 77

1. The trusteeship system shall apply to such territories in the following categories as may be placed thereunder by means of trusteeship agreements:

   a. territories now held under mandate;

   b. territories which may be detached from enemy states as a result of the Second World War; and

   c. territories voluntarily placed under the system by states responsible for their administration.

2. It will be a matter for subsequent agreement as to which territories in the foregoing categories will be brought under the trusteeship system and upon what terms.

Article 78

The trusteeship system shall not apply to territories which have become Members of the United Nations, relationship among which shall be based on respect for the principle of sovereign equality.

Article 79

The terms of trusteeship for each territory to be placed under the trusteeship system, including any alteration or amendment, shall be agreed upon by the states directly concerned, including the mandatory power in the case of territories held under mandate by a Member of the United Nations, and shall be approved as provided for in Articles 83 and 85.

Article 80

1. Except as may be agreed upon in individual trusteeship agreements, made under Articles 77, 79, and 81, placing each territory under the trusteeship system, and until such agreements have been concluded, nothing in this Chapter shall be construed in or of itself to alter in any manner the rights whatsoever of any states or any peoples or the terms of existing international instruments to which Members of the United Nations may respectively be parties.

2. Paragraph 1 of this Article shall not be interpreted as giving grounds for delay or postponement of the negotiation and conclusion of agreements for placing mandated and other territories under the trusteeship system as provided for in Article 77.

Article 81

The trusteeship agreement shall in each case include the terms under which the trust territory will be administered and designate the authority which will exercise the administration of the trust territory. Such authority, hereinafter called the administering authority, may be one or more states or the Organization itself.

Article 82

There may be designated, in any trusteeship agreement, a strategic area or areas which may include part or all of the trust territory to which the agreement applies, without prejudice to any special agreement or agreements made under Article 43.

Article 83

1. All functions of the United Nations relating to strategic areas, including the approval of the terms of the trusteeship agreements and of their alteration or amendment, shall be exercised by the Security Council.

2. The basic objectives set forth in Article 76 shall be applicable to the people of each strategic area.

3. The Security Council shall, subject to the provisions of the trusteeship agreements and without prejudice to security considerations, avail itself of the assistance of the Trusteeship Council to perform those functions of the United Nations under the trusteeship system relating to political, economic, social, and educational matters in the strategic areas.

Article 84

It shall be the duty of the administering authority to ensure that the trust territory shall play its part in the maintenance of international peace and security. To this end the administering authority may make use of volunteer forces, facilities, and assistance from the trust territory in carrying out the obligations towards the Security Council undertaken in this regard by the administering authority, as well as for local defence and the maintenance of law and order within the trust territory.

Article 85

1. The functions of the United Nations with regard to trusteeship agreements for all areas not designated as strategic, including the approval of the terms of the trusteeship agreements and of their alteration or amendment, shall be exercised by the General Assembly.

2. The Trusteeship Council, operating under the authority of the General Assembly, shall assist the General Assembly in carrying out these functions.

CHAPTER XIII - THE TRUSTEESHIP COUNCIL

COMPOSITION

Article 86

1. The Trusteeship Council shall consist of the following Members of the United Nations:

   a. those Members administering trust territories;

   b. such of those Members mentioned by name in Article 23 as are not administering trust territories; and

c. as many other Members elected for three-year terms by the General Assembly as may be necessary to ensure that the total number of members of the Trusteeship Council is equally divided between those Members of the United Nations which administer trust territories and those which do not.

2. Each member of the Trusteeship Council shall designate one specially qualified person to represent it therein.

FUNCTIONS AND POWERS

Article 87

The General Assembly and, under its authority, the Trusteeship Council, in carrying out their functions, may:

a. consider reports submitted by the administering authority;

b. accept petitions and examine them in consultation with the administering authority;

c. provide for periodic visits to the respective trust territories at times agreed upon with the administering authority; and

d. take these and other actions in conformity with the terms of the trusteeship agreements.

Article 88

The Trusteeship Council shall formulate a questionnaire on the political, economic, social, and educational advancement of the inhabitants of each trust territory, and the administering authority for each trust territory within the competence of the General Assembly shall make an annual report to the General Assembly upon the basis of such questionnaire.

VOTING

Article 89

1. Each member of the Trusteeship Council shall have one vote.

2. Decisions of the Trusteeship Council shall be made by a majority of the members present and voting.

PROCEDURE

Article 90

1. The Trusteeship Council shall adopt its own rules of procedure, including the method of selecting its President.

2. The Trusteeship Council shall meet as required in accordance with its rules, which shall include provision for the convening of meetings on the request of a majority of its members.

Article 91

The Trusteeship Council shall, when appropriate, avail itself of the assistance of the Economic and Social Council and of the specialized agencies in regard to matters with which they are respectively concerned.

CHAPTER XIV - THE INTERNATIONAL COURT OF JUSTICE

Article 92

The International Court of Justice shall be the principal judicial organ of the United Nations. It shall function in accordance with the annexed Statute, which is based upon the Statute of the Permanent Court of International Justice and forms an integral part of the present Charter.

Article 93

1. All Members of the United Nations are ipso facto parties to the Statute of the International Court of Justice.

2. A state which is not a Member of the United Nations may become a party to the Statute of the International Court of Justice on conditions to be determined in each case by the General Assembly upon the recommendation of the Security Council.

Article 94

1. Each Member of the United Nations undertakes to comply with the decision of the International Court of Justice in any case to which it is a party.

2. If any party to a case fails to perform the obligations incumbent upon it under a judgment rendered by the Court, the other party may have recourse to the Security Council, which may, if it deems necessary, make recommendations or decide upon measures to be taken to give effect to the judgment.

Article 95

Nothing in the present Charter shall prevent Members of the United Nations from entrusting the solution of their differences to other tribunals by virtue of agreements already in existence or which may be concluded in the future.

Article 96

1. The General Assembly or the Security Council may request the International Court of Justice to give an advisory opinion on any legal question.

2. Other organs of the United Nations and specialized agencies, which may at any time be so authorized by the General Assembly, may also request advisory opinions of the Court on legal questions arising within the scope of their activities.

CHAPTER XV - THE SECRETARIAT

Article 97

The Secretariat shall comprise a Secretary-General and such staff as the Organization may require. The Secretary-General shall be appointed by the General Assembly upon the recommendation of the Security Council. He shall be the chief administrative officer of the Organization.

Article 98

The Secretary-General shall act in that capacity in all meetings of the General Assembly, of the Security Council, of the Economic and Social Council, and of the Trusteeship Council, and shall perform such other functions as are entrusted to him by these organs. The Secretary-General shall make an annual report to the General Assembly on the work of the Organization.

Article 99

The Secretary-General may bring to the attention of the Security Council any matter which in his opinion may threaten the maintenance of international peace and security.

Article 100

1. In the performance of their duties the Secretary-General and the staff shall not seek or receive instructions from any government or from any other authority external to the Organization. They shall refrain from any action which might reflect on their position as international officials responsible only to the Organization.

2. Each Member of the United Nations undertakes to respect the exclusively international character of the responsibilities of the Secretary-General and the staff and not to seek to influence them in the discharge of their responsibilities.

Article 101

1. The staff shall be appointed by the Secretary-General under regulations established by the General Assembly.

2. Appropriate staffs shall be permanently assigned to the Economic and Social Council, the Trusteeship Council, and, as required, to other organs of the United Nations. These staffs shall form a part of the Secretariat.

3. The paramount consideration in the employment of the staff and in the determination of the conditions of service shall be the necessity of securing the highest standards of efficiency, competence, and integrity. Due regard shall be paid to the importance of recruiting the staff on as wide a geographical basis as possible.

CHAPTER XVI - MISCELLANEOUS PROVISIONS

Article 102

1. Every treaty and every international agreement entered into by any Member of the United Nations after the present Charter comes into force shall as soon as possible be registered with the Secretariat and published by it.

2. No party to any such treaty or international agreement which has not been registered in accordance with the provisions of paragraph I of this Article may invoke that treaty or agreement before any organ of the United Nations.

Article 103

In the event of a conflict between the obligations of the Members of the United Nations under the present Charter and their obligations under any other international agreement, their obligations under the present Charter shall prevail.

Article 104

The Organization shall enjoy in the territory of each of its Members such legal capacity as may be necessary for the exercise of its functions and the fulfillment of its purposes.

Article 105

1. The Organization shall enjoy in the territory of each of its Members such privileges and immunities as are necessary for the fulfillment of its purposes.

2. Representatives of the Members of the United Nations and officials of the Organization shall similarly enjoy such privileges and immunities as are necessary for the independent exercise of their functions in connection with the Organization.

3. The General Assembly may make recommendations with a view to determining the details of the application of paragraphs 1 and 2 of this Article or may propose conventions to the Members of the United Nations for this purpose.

CHAPTER XVII - TRANSITIONAL SECURITY ARRANGEMENTS

Article 106

Pending the coming into force of such special agreements referred to in Article 43 as in the opinion of the Security Council enable it to begin the exercise of its responsibilities under Article 42, the parties to the Four-Nation Declaration, signed at Moscow, 30 October 1943, and France, shall, in accordance with the provisions of paragraph 5 of that Declaration, consult with one another and as occasion requires with other Members of the United Nations with a view to such joint action on behalf of the Organization as may be necessary for the purpose of maintaining international peace and security.

Article 107

Nothing in the present Charter shall invalidate or preclude action, in relation to any state which during the Second World War has been an enemy of any signatory to the present Charter, taken or authorized as a result of that war by the governments having responsibility for such action.

CHAPTER XVIII - AMENDMENTS

Article 108

Amendments to the present Charter shall come into force for all Members of the United Nations when they have been adopted by a vote of two thirds of the members of the General Assembly and ratified in accordance with their respective constitutional processes by two thirds of the Members of the United Nations, including all the permanent members of the Security Council.

Article 109

1. A General Conference of the Members of the United Nations for the purpose of reviewing the present Charter may be held at a date and place to be fixed by a two-thirds vote of the members of the General Assembly and by a vote of any nine members of the Security Council. Each Member of the United Nations shall have one vote in the conference.

2. Any alteration of the present Charter recommended by a two-thirds vote of the conference shall take effect when ratified in accordance with their respective constitutional processes by two thirds of the Members of the United Nations including all the permanent members of the Security Council.

3. If such a conference has not been held before the tenth annual session of the General Assembly following the coming into force of the present Charter, the proposal to call such a conference shall be placed on the agenda of that session of the General Assembly, and the conference shall be held if so decided by a majority vote of the members of the General Assembly and by a vote of any seven members of the Security Council.

CHAPTER XIX - RATIFICATION AND SIGNATURE

Article 110

1. The present Charter shall be ratified by the signatory states in accordance with their respective constitutional processes.

2. The ratifications shall be deposited with the government of the United States of America, which shall notify all the signatory states of each deposit as well as the Secretary-General of the Organization when he has been appointed.

3. The present Charter shall come into force upon the deposit of ratifications by the Republic of China, France, the Union of Soviet Socialist Republics, the United Kingdom of Great Britain and Northern Ireland, and the United States of America, and by a majority of the other signatory states. A protocol of the ratifications deposited shall thereupon be drawn up by the government of the United States of America which shall communicate copies thereof to all the signatory states.

4. The states signatory to the present Charter which ratify it after it has come into force will become original Members of the United Nations on the date of the deposit of their respective ratifications.

Article 111

The present Charter, of which the Chinese, French, Russian, English, and Spanish texts are equally authentic, shall remain deposited in the archives of the government of the United

States of America. Duly certified copies thereof shall be transmitted by that government to the governments of the other signatory states.

IN FAITH WHEREOF *the representatives of the governments of the United Nations have signed the present Charter.*

DONE at the city of San Francisco the twenty-sixth day of June, one thousand nine hundred and forty-five.

REFERENCES

INTRODUCTION

[1] Alan James, 'Unit Veto Dominance in United Nations Peace-Keeping', in Lawrence S. Finkelstein (ed.), *Politics in the United Nations System* (1988), p. 79
[2] See L.M. Goodrich & G.L. Rosner, 'The United Nations Emergency Forces', *International Organization* (Summer 1957), p. 3
[3] For a general overview of United Nations peacekeeping activities, see UN Publications, *The Blue Helmets: A Review of United Nations Peacekeeping* (3rd ed. 1996); see also M.R. Berdel, 'The Security Council, Peacekeeping and Internal Conflict after the Cold War', *Duke Journal of Comp. & Int'l Law* (1996), p. 79
[4] See James Traub, 'Who Needs the U.N. Security Council', *The New York Times Magazine*, Nov 17, 2002, at p. 47
[5] Ibid.
[6] See Sir Anthony Parsons, 'The United Nations in the Post-Cold War Era', *International Relations* (Dec 1992), pp. 189-90
[7] Ibid.
[8] See Nicholas J. Wheeler, *Saving Strangers* (2000), Part III, for an excellent analysis of United Nations peacekeeping successes and failures
[9] Christine Gray, *International Law and the Use of Force* (2000), pp. 189-90

CHAPTER I - UNITED NATIONS LAW FOR MAINTAINING INTERNATIONAL PEACE AND SECURITY

[1] See Article 2(3) of the UN Charter, available online at http://www.un.org/aboutun/charter
[2] See Article 2(4), ibid.
[3] See Article 2(6), ibid.
[4] See Article 2(7), ibid.
[5] For an excellent analysis of the authority of the Security Council, see Jose Alvarez, 'Judging the Security Council,' *AJIL* (1996), p. 1
[6] Susan Lamb, 'Legal Limits to United Nations Security Council Powers', in Goodwin-Gill & Talmon (ed.), *The Reality of International Law* (1999), p. 365

The Power of the Security Council under the Charter of the United Nations

[7] Leland Goodrich and Edward Hambro, *Charter of the United Nations* (2nd edition) (1949), p. 204
[8] Ibid.
[9] See Article 39, UN Charter
[10] Goodrich and Hambro (1949), p. 208
[11] Bruno Simma, *The Charter of the United Nations* (1995), p. 619
[12] Article 41, UN Charter, ibid.
[13] Simma, ibid. p. 631
[14] Article 43, UN Charter, ibid.
[15] Article 44, ibid.
[16] Article 45, ibid.
[17] Article 46, ibid.
[18] Article 47, ibid.
[19] Article 48, ibid.
[20] Article 49, ibid.
[21] Article 50, ibid.
[22] Article 51, ibid.
[23] Lamb, Ibid.
[24] Saadia Touval, 'Why the UN Fails', *Foreign Affairs* (Sep/Oct 1994), p. 46-48
[25] Ibid.
[26] Ibid.

The Situation in the Korean Peninsula

[27] S/Res/82(1950)

[28] S/Res/83(1950)

[29] S/Res/84(1950)

[30] See Article 51 of the UN Charter

[31] Goodrich, 'Collective Measures against Aggression', *Int. Conc.*, no. 494 (1953), p. 178

[32] Alan L. Keyes, 'The UN, a Wobbly House of Cards', *Wall Street Journal*, Aug 30, 1990, at A8

[33] Ibid.

[34] Michael Howard, 'The Historical Development of the UN's Role in International Security', in Adam Roberts & Benedict Kingsbury (ed.), *United Nations, Divided World* (1993), p. 66

[35] General Assembly Resolution 377(A) (1950)

[36] David Gibbs, 'Dag Hammarskjold, the United Nations and the Congo Crisis of 1960-61: A Reinterpretation', *The Journal of Modern African Studies* (Mar 1993)

[37] Carole J.L. Collins, 'The Cold War Comes to Africa: Cordier and the 1960 Congo Crisis', *Journal of International Affairs* (Summer 1993), pp. 243-45

[38] *Certain Expenses of the United Nations Advisory Opinion*, ICJ Reports (1962), p. 151

[39] Carole J.L. Collins (1993), ibid.

[40] Joshua Sinai, 'United Nations and non-United Nations, Peacekeeping in the Arab-Israeli Sector: Five Scenarios', *The Middle East Journal* (Autumn 1995)

[41] Saadia Touval (1994), ibid.

The Situation in Rhodesia

[42] S/Res/216(1965)

[43] Ibid.

[44] Ibid.

[45] Ibid.

[46] S/Res/221(1966)

[47] Ibid.

[48] S/Res/232(1966)

[49] S/Res/253(1968)

[50] S/Res/460(1979)

The Situation in South Africa

[51] S/Res/418(1977)

[52] S/Res/181(1963)

[53] S/Res/919(1994)

[54] S/Res/661(1990), Res/665(1990), Res/678(1990)

[55] S/Res/713(1991), 770(1992), 827(1993), 1031(1995), 1088(1996)

[56] S/Res/733(1992), 794(1992), 814(1993)

[57] S/Res/731(1992), 748(1992), 883(1993)

[58] S/Res/788(1992)

[59] S/Res/841(1993), 875(1993), 940(1994)

[60] S/Res/864(1993)

[61] S/Res/929(1994)

[62] S/Res/1054(1996)

[63] S/Res/1080(1996)

[64] S/Res/1162(1998), 1171(1998)

[65] S/Res/1244(1999)

[66] S/Res/1264(1999)

[67] S/Res/1304(2000)

[68] S/Res/1298(2000)

[69] Thomas Franck, *Fairness in International Law and Institutions* (1997), pp. 289-289

[70] Barbara Slavin, 'Iraq's Citizens Starving From U.N. Sanctions', *USA Today*, Nov 19, 1997, at A9

[71] C. Joyner, 'Sanctions, Compliance and International Law: Reflections on the United Nations' Experience against Iraq', *AJIL* (1991), p. 1

[72] Albert Wohlstetter and Fred Hoffman, 'To Break the Deadlock, Reclaim Kuwaiti Airspace', *Wall Street Journal*, Sep 12, 1990, at A18

[73] Eugene Rostow, 'Until What? Enforcement Action or Collective Self Defense?', *AJIL* (1991), p. 510

[74] Franck, ibid., pp. 286-287

[75] Carrole J. Doherty, 'U.N. Command of U.S. Troops Restricted by House Again', *Congressional Quarterly Weekly Report*, no. 36, Sept 7, 1996

[76] Paul Lewis, 'U.N. Plans by U.S. and France Clash,' *New York Times*, Feb 2, 1992, at A17

The Legality of Peacekeeping Operations

[77] Alan L. Keyes (1990), ibid.

[78] Craig R. Whitney, 'The French Aren't Alone in Having Gall', Dec 6, 1998, Sec 4, p. 6

[79] Ahron Bregman and Jihan El-Tahri, *Fifty Years Wars: Israel and the Arabs* (1998)

[80] General Assembly Resolution 998, Nov 1956

[81] Ibid.

[82] See Anthony Nutting, *No End of a Lesson: The Story of Suez* (1967)

[83] Ibid.

[84] Sally Morphet, 'United Nations Peacekeeping and Election-Monitoring', in Roberts and Kingsbury (ed.), ibid., p. 183

[85] See Chapters VI and VII of the UN Charter

[86] T. Weiss, D. Forsythe, R. Coate, *The United Nations and Changing World Politics* (1994), p. 54

[87] See Article 33 of the UN Charter

[88] See Article 34

[89] See Article 35

[90] See Article 36

[91] Ibid.

[92] See Article 37

[93] See Article 38

[94] Louis Sohn, 'The Security Council's Role in the Settlement of International Disputes', *AJIL* (1984), pp. 402-404

[95] Ibid.

[96] Bruno Simma, *The Charter of the United Nations* (1995), pp. 512-13

[97] Ibid.

[98] Ibid., pp. 590-91

The Role of Regional Arrangements and Agencies

[99] Article 52, U.N. Charter, available online at http://www.un.org/aboutun/charter

[100] Ibid.

[101] Ibid.

[102] Article 53, ibid.

[103] Article 54, ibid.

[104] Michael Akehurst, 'Enforcement Action by Regional Agencies with Special Reference to the Organisation of American States', *BYIL* (1967), pp. 175-227

[105] Ibid.

[106] Ibid.

[107] Simma, ibid., pp. 692-94

[108] Akerhurst, ibid.

[109] Ibid.

[110] Ibid.

[111] Ibid.

[112] Ibid.

[113] Ibid.

[114] Weiss, et al, ibid., pp. 60-65

[115] Simma, ibid., pp. 592-93

[116] Ibid.

[117] Ibid.

[118] Ibid., pp. 695-96

[119] Akerhurst, ibid.

[120] Ibid.

[121] Simma, ibid., pp. 694-96

[122] Ibid.

[123] Karsten Nowrot and Emily W. Schabacker, 'The Use of Force to Restore Democracy: International Legal Implications of the ECOWAS Intervention in Sierra Leone', *American University International Review* (1998), p. 321

[124] S/Res/788(1992)

[125] S/Res/1244(1999)

CHAPTER II - THE SECURITY COUNCIL AND TRANSNATIONAL ARMED CONFLICTS

Conflict Management during the Cold War: Phase I

[1] Albrecht Schabel, 'A Future of Peacekeeping?', *Peace Review* (Dec 1997), pp. 563-569

The Suez Canal Crisis

[2] Bregman and El-Tahri (1998)

[3] Ibid.

[4] Ibid.

[5] Ibid.

[6] Ibid.

[7] Nutting (1967), ibid.

The Congo Crisis

[8] Howard French, 'What Goes Around Comes to Zaire', *New York Times*, Mar 23, 1997, at p. 4

[9] David A. Kay, 'The Politics of Decolonization: The New Nations and the United Nations Political Process', in Robert S. Wood (ed.), *The Process of International Organizations*, p. 401

[10] Ibid.

[11] John Stoessinger, *The United Nations and the Superpowers* (1966), p.79

[12] Christine Coleiro, 'Britain and the Congo Crisis, 1960-63', *Peacekeeping & International Relations* (Jul-Oct 1997)

[13] Ibid.

[14] Carole J.L. Collins (1993), ibid.

[15] Franck, ibid., pp. 227-228

[16] Morphet, ibid., pp. 190-92

[17] Ibid.

The Crisis in West Irian

[18] Ibid., p. 194

[19] Ibid.

The Situation in Cyprus

[20] Michael Barletta, 'Mediterranean countdown', *Bulletin of Atomic Scientists* (Nov/Dec 1998), pp. 12-14

[21] Ergun Olgon, 'Recognizing Two States in Cyprus Would Facilitate Co-existence and Stability', *Survival* (Autumn 1998), pp. 35-42

[22] David M. Last, 'Peacekeeping Doctrine and Conflict Resolution Technique', *Armed Forces and Society* (Winter 1995/96)

[23] Michael Barletta (1998), ibid.

[24] Ibid.

[25] Ergun Olgon (1998), ibid.

[26] David M. Last (1998), ibid.

[27] Ibid.

The Conflict in Kashmir

[28] S/Res/39(1948)

[29] S/Res/47(1948)

[30] S/Res/91(1948)

[31] Morphet, ibid, p. 193

[32] Ibid.

The Civil War in Lebanon

[33] Ibid, pp. 188-89

[34] William B. Quandt, 'Notes From the Minefield: United States Intervention in Lebanon and the Middle East, 1945-1958', *Foreign Affairs* (May/Jun 1997), p. 143

[35] Nitza Nachmias, 'The Impossible Peacekeeping Mission: UNIFIL', *Peacekeeping & International Relations* (Sep/Oct 1996), pp. 14-16

[36] Ibid.

[37] Christopher S. Wren, 'U.N. clears way for peacekeepers in Southern Lebanon', *NYT*, Jun 17, 2000, at A6

The Civil War in Yemen

[38] Michael B. Bishku, 'The Kennedy Administration, the U.N. and the Yemini Civil War', *American-Arab Affairs*, no. 4, 1992

[39] Ibid.

The Situation in the Middle East after the 1973 Arab-Israeli War

[40] Weiss, et al, ibid., p. 47

[41] Ibid.

Conflict Management after the Cold War: Phase II

[42] Bruce Russett and James S. Sutterlin, 'The U.N. in a New World Order', *Foreign Affairs* (Spring 1991), pp. 70-72

[43] Ibid.

The Iran-Iraq War

[44] S/Res/619(1988)

[45] Ibid.

The Afghanistan Conflicts

[46] 'Afghanistan Revisited', *National Review* (Aug 1993)

[47] S/Res/622/(1988)

[48] Ibid.

[49] Max Hilaire, 'The Role of the United Nations in the Post Cold war Era', *Revue de Droit International* (2000), p. 106

[50] Ibid.

[51] Serge Schemann, 'U.N.'s Candid Reshaper – Kofi Atta Annan', *NYT*, Oct 13, 2001, at A3

Conflict Management after the Cold War: Phase III

[52] Albrecht Schabel, 'A Future of Peacekeeping?', *Peace Review* (Dec 1997), pp. 563-569

[53] Hilaire, ibid., p. 146

[54] John Tassitore & Susan Woolfson (ed.), *A Global Agenda* (1992), p. 89

[55] S/Res/743(1992)

[56] Ibid.

[57] S/Res/797(1992)

[58] S/Res/794(1992)

[59] John Gerard Ruggie, 'Wandering in the Void: Charting the U.N.'s New Strategic Role', *Foreign Affairs* (Nov/Dec 1993)

[60] Ibid.

The Namibia Conflict

[61] Bicesse Peace Accords, May 31, 1991, UN Doc. S/22609
[62] S/Res/632(1989)
[63] S/Res/435(1978)
[64] 'Southwest Africa Negotiations', *Department of State Bulletin*, no. 2140, Nov 1988
[65] Ibid.

The Angolan Civil War

[66] S/Res/626 (1988)
[67] Ibid.
[68] S/Res/696 (1991)
[69] 'UNAVEM II Created to Verify Peaceful Transition', *UN Chronicle* (Sep 1991), p. 27
[70] Ibid.
[71] Margaret J. Anstee, 'Angola: The Forgotten Tragedy: A Test Case for U.N. Peacekeeping', *International Relations* (1993), p. 497
[72] Ibid.
[73] *UN Chronicle*, ibid.
[74] 'With Pace of Peace Process Slow, Meeting Goals of Lusaka Protocol will Determine UNAVEM's Continuation', *UN Chronicle* (1996), pp. 50-51
[75] S/Res/976 (1995)
[76] *UN Chronicle*, ibid.
[77] S/Res/1127 (1997)
[78] Barbara Crossette, 'UN Puts Strong Sanctions on Angolan Rebel Force', *NYT*, Aug 29, 1997, at A8
[79] S/Res/1118 (1997)
[80] S/Res/1229 (1999)
[81] *Report of the Secretary General on the United Nations Observer Mission in Angola*, S/1999/187, Feb 19, 1999
[82] S/Res/1237 (1999)
[83] Ibid.
[84] S/Res/1268 (1999)
[85] 'Deadline for Angola', *The Economist*, Aug 23, 1997, pp. 34-35
[86] S/Res/1268 (1999)
[87] *The Economist*, ibid.
[88] Anstee, ibid., pp. 498-99

The Situation in Cambodia

[89] Tessitore & Woolfson (ed.), ibid., p. 84
[90] S/Res/717 (1991)
[91] S/res/718 (1991)
[92] Ibid.
[93] S/Res/728 (1991)
[94] Sheri Prasso, 'Cambodia: A $3 Billion Boondoggle', *Bulletin of Atomic Scientists* (Mar 1995)
[95] John-Paul Menu, 'Cambodia Heals its Wounds', *World Health* (Nov/Dec 1996), pp. 18-19
[96] Denise Barricklow, 'Champions of Peace: UN Volunteers in Cambodia', *Choices* (Jun 1994)
[97] Ibid.
[98] Paul Lewis, 'U.N. Curbing Trade with Khmer Rouge', *NYT*, Dec 1, 1992, at A9
[99] Barbara Crossette, 'Outsiders Gone, Cambodia Unravels', *NYT*, Dec 1993, at p.41

The Civil War in Mozambique

[100] S/Res/782 (1992)
[101] Ibid.
[102] S/Res/797 (1992)
[103] Ibid.
[104] 'Continued International Support Needed to Consolidate Peace', *UN Chronicle* (Jun 1995), p. 19
[105] Weiss et al, ibid., pp. 60-68
[106] Ibid.
[107] Ibid.

CHAPTER III - TRANSNATIONAL ARMED CONFLICTS AND THE DELEGATION OF AUTHORITY BY THE SECURITY COUNCIL

[1] Hurst Hannum, 'The Specter of Secession', *Foreign Affairs* (Mar/Apr 1998), pp. 13-18
[2] Weiss et al, Ibid, p. 60-68
[3] Ibid

The Somalia Conflict

[4] See Boutrous Boutrous-Ghali, *An Agenda for Peace*, UN Doc. S/24111 (1992); and *Supplement to An Agenda for Peace*, UN Doc. A/50/60-S/1995/1 (1995)
[5] Guenter Lewy, 'The Case for Humanitarian Intervention', *Orbis* (Fall 1993), pp. 621-23
[6] 'Somalia Rescue Begins', *Africa News*, Aug 3, 1992
[7] See Article 2(7) of the U.N. Charter
[8] S/Res/733(1992)
[9] S/Res/751(1992)
[10] S/Res/775(1992)
[11] Samuel M. Makinda, 'Somalia: From Humanitarian Intervention to Military Offensive?', *The World Today* (Oct 1993)
[12] John R. Bolton, 'Wrong Turn in Somalia', *Foreign Affairs* (Jan/Feb 1994), pp. 56-58
[13] Ibid.
[14] S/Res/794(1992)
[15] 'Operation Restore Hope', *U.S. News & World Report*, no. 23, Dec 14, 1992
[16] Herman J. Cohen, 'Update on Operation Restore Hope', *U.S. Department of State Dispatch*, no. 51 (Dec 1992)
[17] S/Res/814(1993)
[18] Ibid.
[19] Herman J. Cohen (1992), ibid.
[20] 'U.S. Hands Over Somali Mission to New U.N. Peacekeeping Force', *Arms Control Today*, no. 5 (Jun 1993)
[21] Ibid.
[22] S/Res/837(1993)
[23] Joshua Hammer and Douglas Waller, 'A Starring Role in 'The Fugitive'', *Newsweek*, Sep 6, 1993
[24] John H. Cushman, Jr., '5 G.I.'s are Killed as Somalis Down 2 U.S. Helicopters', *NYT*, Oct 4, 1993, at A1
[25] Hilaire, ibid., pp. 121-22
[26] Thomas E. Ricks, 'U.S. Steps up Search for Ways out of Somalia', *WSJ*, Aug 10, 1993, at A1
[27] John R. Bolton (1994), ibid.
[28] Cevic Bir, 'Interoperability and Intervention Operations', *RUSI Journal*, no. 6, Dec 1997, pp. 22-26
[29] Ibid.
[30] Ibid.
[31] Ibid.
[32] Danosh Sarooshi, *The United Nations and the Development of Collective Security* (1999), pp. 187-191
[33] Presidential Decision Directive 25 (PDD 25)

The Conflicts in the Former Yugoslavia

[34] Robert D. Kaplan, 'Why Yugoslavia Exploded', *Reader's Digest*, no. 851, Mar 1993
[35] 'In Defense of the Serbians', *WSJ*, Sep 21, 1993, at A22
[36] 'A World More Scared Than Scary,' *The Economist*, Apr 17, 1993
[37] Xin Bi, 'Yugoslavia: Western Doubts on Armed Intervention', *Beijing Review*, Aug 31, 1992
[38] Paul Lewis, 'Guns vs Talk: U.N. is Pressing for Talks in Bosnia', *NYT*, Jan 1, 1993, at A12
[39] S/Res/713(1991)
[40] S/Res/721(1991)
[41] S/Res/724(1991)
[42] Ibid.
[43] Ibid.
[44] S/Res/727(1992), ibid.
[45] S/Res/740(1992), ibid.
[46] Ibid.
[47] Report of the Secretary General, Feb 15, 1991

[48] S/Res/743(1992), ibid.
[49] Ibid.
[50] S/Res/757(1992), ibid.
[51] Ibid.
[52] Ibid.
[53] Ibid.
[54] Ibid.
[55] S/Res/758(1992)
[56] Ibid.
[57] Nigel White, 'UN Peacekeeping - Development or Destruction', *International Relations* (1994), pp. 151-53
[58] Ibid.
[59] S/Res/777(1992)
[60] Ibid.
[61] S/Res/781(1992)
[62] S/Res/786(1992)
[63] S/Res/787(1992)
[64] Ibid.
[65] S/Res/795(1992)
[66] S/Res/983(1995), ibid.
[67] S/Res/1037(1996), ibid.
[68] S/Res/808 (1993)
[69] Ibid.
[70] Ibid.
[71] Alan Riding, 'NATO Agrees to Enforce Flight Ban Over Bosnia Ordered by U.N.', Apr 3, 1993, at A5
[72] Ibid.
[73] Andrew Giarelli, 'Shame of Srebrenica', *World Press Review* (Jan 1996)
[74] S/Res/781(1992)
[75] Ibid.
[76] S/Res/816(1993), ibid.
[77] Ibid.
[78] Ibid.
[79] S/Res/820(1993), ibid.
[80] Ibid.
[81] S/Res/824 (1993), ibid.
[82] Ibid.
[83] 'Serbs Take U.N. Hostages', *New For You*, no. 22, Jun 1995
[84] Elizabeth Neuffer, *The Key to My Neighbor's House* (2002), pp. 140-41
[85] 'After Owen-Vance', *New Statesman & Society*, May 7, 1993
[86] Paul Lewis, 'U.N. Chief Backing Vance-Owens Plan', *NYT*, Feb 10, 1993, at A7
[87] Steven Greenhouse, 'Dole Again Criticizes Clinton Bosnia Plan', *NYT*, Aug 21, 1995, at A6
[88] S/Res/836(1993)
[89] See S/Res/824(1993), S/Res/836(1993), ibid.
[90] 'Air Strike in Bosnia', *NYT*, May 26, 1995, at A26
[91] Ivo H. Daalder, *Getting to Dayton: The Making of American Foreign Policy* (2000), p. 99
[92] John J. Mearsheirmer, 'The Only Exit From Bosnia', *NYT*, Oct 7, 1997, at A27
[93] *Dayton Peace Accords: General Framework Agreement for Peace in Bosnia & Herzegovina*, U.S. Dept. of State, Dec 14, 1995, Annex I-A.
[94] Ibid.
[95] S/Res/1022(1995)
[96] Ibid.
[97] S/Res/1031(1995)
[98] Ibid.
[99] Ibid.
[100] S/Res/1035(1995)
[101] Ibid.
[102] Carl Bildt, 'Implementing the Civilian Tasks of the Bosnian Peace Agreement', *NATO Review*, no. 5, Sep 1996
[103] Jim Hooper, 'Dayton's Mandate for Apprehending War Criminals', *PBS*
[104] Margaret Neuffer, ibid, p.174

[105] S/Res/713(1991)

The Situation in Haiti

[106] Larry Rohter, 'U.N. Force Takes up Duties in Haiti', *NYT*, Apr 2, 1995, p. 14
[107] Andrew Scobell and Brad Hammitt, 'Goons Gunmen and Gendarmerie: Toward a Reconceptualization of Paramilitary Formations', *Journal of Politics and Military Sociology* (Winter 1998), pp. 213-227
[108] Peter Mckenna, 'Canada and the Haiti Crisis', *Journal of Canadian Studies*, no. 3 (Fall 1997)
[109] Howard W. French, 'Haitian Turmoil Seen as Threat to Vote,' *NYT*, May 15, 1990, p. 12
[110] *Fact on Line*, Vol. 7-20 (1990), p. 665
[111] Robert Pear, 'U.N. Team Reports on Nicaragua Vote', *NYT*, Feb 7, 1990, at A10
[112] A/Res/45/2(1990)
[113] Gregory Fox & Brad Roth (ed.), *Democratic Governance and International Law* (2000), p. 300
[114] Thomas Franck, 'The Emerging Right to Democratic Governance', *AJIL* (1992), p. 81
[115] Domingo Acevedo, 'The Haitian Crisis and the OAS Response', in Lori Fisler Damrosch (ed.), *Enforcing Restraint* (1993), p. 129
[116] Andrew Bilski, 'Final Measures', *Maclean's*, no. 39, Sep 26, 1994
[117] See 'Support for Democratic Government of Haiti', resolution MRE/RES.1/91, Oct 3, 1991
[118] Ibid.
[119] Fox & Roth, ibid., p. 284
[120] A/Res/46/7(1991)
[121] Ibid.
[122] Ibid.
[123] See Amnesty International, *Haiti: Human Rights Violations in the Aftermath of the Coup d'Etat* (Oct 1991)
[124] Franck, ibid., p. 112
[125] S/Res/841(1993)
[126] Ibid.
[127] Sarooshi, ibid., pp. 233-234
[128] Eliane Sciolino, 'On the Brink of War, a Tense Battle of Wills', *NYT*, Sep 20, 1994, at A1
[129] S/Res/873(1994)
[130] S/Res/875(1994), ibid.
[131] S/Res/933(1994), ibid.
[132] See U.N. Secretary General Report S/1994/765
[133] S/Res/940(1994)
[134] Ibid.
[135] Carl Mollins, 'Trust and Respect', *Maclean's*, no. 40, Oct 3, 1994
[136] Ibid.
[137] Bill Clinton (1995), ibid.
[138] Strobe Talbott, 'Promoting democracy and economic growth in Haiti', *U.S. Department of State Dispatch*, Mar 13, 1995, p. 185
[139] Eliane Sciolino, ibid.
[140] S/Res/964(1994)
[141] S/Res/1007(1995)
[142] Barbara Crossette, 'U.N. Mission to Haiti is Reprieved', *NYT*, Mar 1, 1996, at A8
[143] S/Res/1085(1996)
[144] S/Res/1123(1997)
[145] S/Res/1141(1997)
[146] S/Res/1212(1998)
[147] S/Res. 940(1994)
[148] Letter dated Jul 29, 1994, from Permanent Representative of Haiti to the Secretary General, UN Doc. S/1994/905; letter from the Permanent Representative of Haiti Addressed to the President of the Security Council, UN Doc S/1994/910 (1994)
[149] Brad Roth, *Governmental Illegitimacy in International Law* (1999), p. 381
[150] Doswald-Beck, 'The Legal Validity of Military Intervention by Invitation', *BYIL* (1985), p. 189
[151] Ibid.
[152] Richard Falk, 'The Haiti Intervention: A Dangerous World Order Precedent for the United Nations', *Harvard ILJ* (1995), p.342
[153] 'Santiago Commitment to Democracy and the Renewal of the Inter-American System', AG/RES.1080 (XX1-0/91) 5th Plenary Session, Jun 5, 1991; Document of the Copenhagen Meeting of the Conference on the Human

Dimension of the CSCE, Jun 29, 1990, para. 5, in Arie Bloed (ed), *The Conference on Security and Cooperation in Europe: Analysis and Basic Documents, 1972-93* (1993), pp. 441-44

The Conflict in Rwanda

[154] See Richard L. Millett, 'Beyond Sovereignty: International Efforts to Support Latin American Democracy', *Journal of International Studies and World Affairs*, no.3 (Fall 1994)
[155] V. Nanda, T. Muther, Jr., & A. Eckert, 'Tragedies in Somalia, Yugoslavia, Haiti, Rwanda and Liberia - Revisiting the Validity of Humanitarian Intervention Under International Law - Part II', *Denv.J.I.L.* (1998), p. 847-48
[156] Michael Twaddle, 'Africa – The Rwandan Crisis, 1959-1994: History of a Genocide', *International Affairs*, no. 2 (Apr 1997)
[157] Ibid.
[158] Horace Campbell, 'The United Nations & the Genocide in Rwanda', in Napoleon Abdulai (ed), *Genocide in Rwanda: Background and Current Situation* (1994)
[159] Ibid.
[160] Ibid.
[161] S/Res/812(1993)
[162] Ibid.
[163] S/Res/846(1993)
[164] Horace Campbell (1994), ibid.
[165] Nicholas Wheeler, *Saving Strangers* (2000), p. 215
[166] Campbell (1994), ibid.
[167] Ibid.
[168] Ibid.
[169] S/Res/872(1993)
[170] S/Res/893(1993)
[171] Nanda, et al, ibid., p. 848-49
[172] Campbell (1994), ibid.
[173] Ibid.
[174] Ibid.
[175] Wheeler, ibid., p. 217
[176] Campbell (1994), ibid.
[177] Wheeler, ibid., pp. 219-20
[178] S/Res/912 (1994), ibid.
[179] Ibid.
[180] Ibid.
[181] Ibid.
[182] Ibid.
[183] S/Res/918(1994), ibid.
[184] Ibid.
[185] Ibid.
[186] Ibid.
[187] S/Res/918 (1994)
[188] Ibid.
[189] S/Res/925 (1994), ibid.
[190] Ibid.
[191] Ibid.
[192] S/Res/ 929 (1994), ibid.
[193] 'Fleeing Rwanda, Again', *The Economist*, Aug 20, 1994
[194] S/Res/929(1994)
[195] Ibid.
[196] S/Res/935 (1994)
[197] S/Res/955 (1994)
[198] Ibid.
[199] OAU Report, *The International Panel of Eminent Personalities to Investigate the 1994 Genocide in Rwanda and Surrounding Events*, Jul 7, 2000
[200] S/res/965 (1994)
[201] Ibid.

[202] S/Res/997 (1994)

[203] Ibid.

[204] S/Res/1005 (1995)

[205] S/Res/1011 (1995)

[206] Ibid.

[207] Ibid.

[208] Ibid.

[209] S/Res/1029(1995), ibid.

[210] Lawyers' Committee for Human Rights, *Prosecuting Genocide in Rwanda, a Lawyers' Committee Report on the ICTR and National Trials*, Jul 1997

[211] ICTR, Judgment, *Prosecutor v. Jean-Paul Akayesu*, Sep 2, 1998, p. 39

[212] See online at http://www.ictr.org/wwwroot/ENGLISH/cases/Barayagwiza/index

[213] S/Res/1013 (1995)

[214] S.R. Feil, *Preventing Genocide: A Report to the Carnegie Commission on Preventing Deadly Conflict* (1998), p. 27

[215] 'Rwanda Stand Reflects New US Caution', *International Herald Tribune*, May 19, 1994; *Final Report on Rwanda Genocide*, UN Doc. S/1997/1010; and *Addendum* S/1998/63.

[216] Ibid.

CHAPTER IV - REGIONAL ORGANIZATIONS AND TRANSNATIONAL ARMED CONFLICTS

The Conflicts in Central America

[1] Lindsey Gruson, 'Latin Presidents Announce Accord on Contra Bases', *NYT*, Feb 15, 1989, at A1

[2] Sam Vincent Meddis, 'Iran-Contra Report Accuses Reagan, Bush', *USA Today*, Jan 19, 1994, at A1

[3] Mark A. Uhlig, 'U.S. Urges Nicaragua to Forgive Legal Claim', *NYT*, Sep 30, 1990

[4] Jaime Daremblum, 'The Americas: Odd Couple Pushes Central American Parliament', *WSJ*, Jan 2, 1989, at p. 1

[5] Allen Weinstein, 'The Americas: Saving the Nicaraguan Election', *WSJ*, Nov 10, 1989, at p. 1

[6] Robert Pear, 'U.N. Team Reports on Nicaragua Vote', *NYT*, Feb 7, 1990, at A10

[7] S/Res/637(1989)

[8] Ibid.

[9] Ibid.

[10] Paul Berman, 'Why the Sandinistas Lost,' *Dissent*, no. 3 (Summer 1990)

[11] See S/Res/644(1989)

[12] S/Res/693(1991)

[13] 'UN Human Rights Observers for El Salvador', *U.N. Chronicle*, no. 3 (Sep 1991)

[14] Tommy Sue Montgomery, 'Getting to Peace in El Salvador: The Roles of the United Nations Secretariat and ONUSAL', *Journal of Inter-American Studies and World Affairs* (Winter 1995)

[15] Ibid.

[16] Julia Preston, 'In a U.N. Success Story, Guatemalan Abuses Fall', *NYT*, Mar 27, 1996, at A8

[17] Paul Jeffrey, 'Guatemala Army Hires Firm for Image', *National Catholic Reporter*, Jun 2, 1995

The Conflict in Liberia

[18] See 'ECOWAS to Dispatch Intervention Force to Liberia', *XINHUA*, Aug 7, 1990

[19] See 'ECOWAS Head Asks Burkina Faso to Speed Peace in Liberia', *Reuters*, Sep 7, 1990

[20] See, Peter da Costa, 'Liberia: Peacemakers Look to UN as Mediation Runs Out of Steam', *Inter Press Service*, Sep 23, 1992

[21] 'ECOMOG Ordered to Return Fire', *XINHUA General Overseas News Service*, Sep 14, 1990

[22] David Wippman, 'Enforcing the Peace: ECOWAS and the Liberian Civil War', in Lori Fisler Damrosch (ed.), ibid., p. 165

[23] S/Res/788(1992)

[24] Ibid.

[25] See Peter da Costa, 'Liberia: Peacemakers Look to the U.N. as Mediations Runs out of Steam', *Inter Press Service*, Sep 23, 1992

[26] S/Res/813(1992)

[27] Ibid.

[28] Ibid.

[29] Ved P. Nanda, Thomas F. Muther, Jr. and Amy E. Eckert, 'Tragedies in Somalia, Yugoslavia, Haiti, Rwanda and Liberia – Revisiting the Validity of Humanitarian Intervention Under International Law – Part II', *Den. J.I.L & Pol.* (1998)

[30] S/Res/856(1993)

[31] S/Res/866(1993)

[32] Ibid.

[33] Ibid.

[34] S/Res/1001(1995)

[35] See Stephen Riley & Max Sesay, 'Liberia: After Abuja', *Review of African Political Economy*, no.69 (1996)

[36] S/Res/1014(1995)

[37] S/Res/1020(1995)

[38] Ibid.

[39] SC/886 (2000); S/Res/1343 (2001)

The Conflict in Sierra Leone

[40] 'Sierra Leone Military Arrests 5 Cabinet Officials After Coup', *New York Times*, May 27, 1997, at A10

[41] ECOWAS Summit Final Communiqué available online at http://www.sierra-leone.org/documents-subregional.html

[42] 'International: Putting a Country Together Again', *The Economist*, Feb 21, 1998

[43] 'Sierra Leone Reached a Truce', *WSJ*, Apr 24, 1996, at A1

[44] 'Sierra Leone: Peace Agreement a Model', *UN Chronicle*, no. 4, 1996

[45] David Rieff, 'In Sierra Leone, The UN had no Peace to Keep', *WSJ*, May 8, 2000, at A42

[46] See S/PRST/1997/29, S/PRST/1997/36 and S/PRST/1997/42, online at http://www.un.org/Docs/sc/statements/1997/sprst97.htm

[47] S/Res/1132(1997)

[48] Ibid.

[49] Ibid.

[50] Ibid.

[51] Ibid.

[52] 'Peacewatch: Sierra Leone', *UN Chronicle*, no. 1, 1998, pp. 76-77

[53] Ibid.

[54] See S/1998/1176, available online at http://www.un.org/Docs/sc/reports/1998/sgrep98.htm

[55] Margaret Bald, 'Pax Nigeriana', *World Press Review*, May 1998

[56] See S/PRST/1998/5 of 26 Feb 1998, available online at http://www.un.org/Docs/sc/statements/1998/sprst98.htm

[57] S/Res/1156(1998)

[58] S/Res/1162(1998), ibid.

[59] Ibid.

[60] See S/1998/249 of 17 Mar 1998

[61] Ibid.

[62] S/Res/1171(1998)

[63] Ibid.

[64] Ibid.

[65] Ibid.

[66] Barbara Crossette, 'In West Africa, a Grisly Extension of Rebel Terror', *New York Times*, Jul 30, 1998, at A1

[67] S/Res/1181(1998)

[68] Ibid.

[69] Ibid.

[70] Ibid.

[71] S/Res/1220(1999)

[72] S/Res/1231(1999)

[73] Ibid.

[74] Ibid.

[75] S/Res/1245(1999)

[76] Ibid.

[77] Ibid.

[78] Norimitsu Onishi, 'Sierra Leone Victims and Rebels Hear Albright's Message of Peace', *NYT*, Oct 19, 1999, at A1

[79] Paul Lewis, 'Amnesty in Sierra Leone Opposed by Rights Group', *NYT*, Jul 26, 1999, at A7

[80] Ibid.

[81] S/Res/1260(1999)

[82] Ibid.

[83] Ibid.

[84] See S/1999/1003 of 28 Sep 1999, available online at http://www.un.org/Docs/sc/reports/1999/sgrep99.htm.

[85] S/Res/1270(1999)

[86] Ibid.

[87] Ibid.

[88] Ibid.

[89] S/Res/1289(2000)

[90] Ibid.

[91] Ibid.

[92] Ibid.

[93] Secretary General Report S/2000/13 of Jan 11, 2000

[94] Ibid.

[95] Ibid.

[96] Ibid.

[97] See SG Report S/2000/13

[98] Ibid.

[99] 'Rebels Release More Hostages in Sierra Leone', *NYT*, May 27, 2000, at A4

[100] '11 British Soldiers Taken Hostage by Rebels in Sierra Leone,' *NYT*, Aug 27, 2000, at p. 1

[101] Barbara Crossette, 'Curbing Illicit Diamonds', *NYT*, Dec 3, 2000, p. 42

[102] S/Res/1299(2000)

[103] Jane Parlez, 'G.I.s to Arrive in Nigeria This Week to Train Locals', *NYT*, Aug 23, 2000, at A10

[104] Karsten Nowrot and Emily W. Schabacker, 'The Use of Force to Restore Democracy: International Legal Implications of the ECOWAS Intervention in Sierra Leone', *American University International Law Review* (1998), p. 321

[105] Ibid.

[106] Ved P. Nanda, et al, ibid., pp. 862-64

[107] Ibid.

[108] Nowrot and Schabacker (1998), ibid.

[109] Ibid.

[110] See *Military and Paramilitary Activities in and Against Nicaragua (Nicaragua v. US)*, ICJ Reports, 1986

[111] Christine Gray, *International Law and the Use of Force* (2000), p. 57

[112] Ibid.

[113] Nowrot & Schabacker, ibid.

[114] Christine Gray, ibid., pp. 108-09

[115] Gray, ibid., p. 7

[116] Thomas Franck, 'Legitimacy and the Democratic Entitlement', in Fox & Roth (ed.), ibid., pp. 46-47

[117] Santiago Commitment to Democracy and the Renewal of the Inter-American System, AG/Res. 1080, 5th plenary session, Jun 5, 1991; *Document of the Copenhagen Meeting of the Conference on Human Dimension of the CSCE*, Jun 29, 1990, ibid.

[118] Nowrot and Schabacker (1998), ibid.

[119] S/PRST/1997/29

[120] Nowrot and Schabacker (1998), ibid.

[121] See Simon Chesterman, *Just War or Just Peace* (2000) for analysis of humanitarian intervention, pp. 44-87

[122] S/Res/770 (1992)

[123] Ibid.

[124] S/Res/794(1992)

[125] See S/Res/929, Res/940(1998)

[126] David Lipman, ibid., p. 164-65

[127] S/Res/1315

[128] UNAMSIL Press Briefing, Mar 22, 2002

[129] Ilene Cohn, 'The Protection of Children and the Quest for Truth and Justice in Sierra Leone', *Journal of International Affairs* (Fall 2001), pp. 1-34

[130] Ibid.

[131] Ibid.

[132] Ibid.

[133] Ibid.

The Security Council, NATO, and the Situation in Kosovo

[134] *UN Chronicle*, no. 2, 1999, p. 14
[135] Christopher Bennett, 'In Kosovo, Cost of Inaction Is High', *WSJ*, Oct 2, 1998, at A14
[136] Ibid.
[137] Carla Anne Robbins, 'U.S. Allies Resist Tougher Sanctions on Belgrade - Consensus Emerges For Arms Embargo', *WSJ*, Mar 26, 1998, at A16
[138] S/Res/1160(1998)
[139] Ibid.
[140] Ibid.
[141] Ibid.
[142] S/Res/1199 (1999)
[143] Ibid.
[144] Ibid.
[145] Ibid.
[146] Ibid.
[147] Ibid.
[148] Ibid.
[149] S/1998/92 *Report of the Secretary General Prepared Pursuant to Resolutions 1160 (1998) and 1199 (1998) of the Security Council*, Oct 3, 1998
[150] Nicholas Wheeler, *Saving Strangers* (2000), pp. 260-61
[151] Ibid.
[152] Ibid.
[153] B. Simma, 'NATO, the UN and the Use of Force: Legal Aspects', *EJIL* (1999), p. 7
[154] Ibid.
[155] See Tim Judah, *Kosovo: War and Revenge* (2000), p. 227
[156] Ibid.
[157] *Security Council Demands Federal Republic of Yugoslavia Comply with NATO and OSCE Verification Missions in Kosovo*, UN Press Release, SC/6588, Oct 24, 1998
[158] Ibid.
[159] S/Res/1203 (1998)
[160] Ibid.
[161] Ibid.
[162] Ibid.
[163] *UN Chronicle*, no.1 (1999), p. 81
[164] S/Res/1207 (1998)
[165] Ibid.
[166] *UN Chronicle*, no. 1 (1999), p. 81
[167] Jonathan Charney, 'Anticipatory Humanitarian Intervention in Kosovo', *AJIL* (1999), p. 840
[168] M. Weller, 'The Rambouillet Conference on Kosovo', *International Affairs* (1999), p.231
[169] Ibid.
[170] Simon Chesterman, ibid., p. 264
[171] Ibid.
[172] Ibid.
[173] C. Guicherd, 'International Law and the War in Kosovo', *Survival* (1999), pp. 26-27
[174] *Military and Paramilitary Activities in and Against Nicaragua*, ICJ Reports (1986)
[175] Christine Chinkin, 'Kosovo: A 'Good' or 'Bad' War', *AJIL* (1999), p. 841
[176] *Agreement on Principles (Peace Plan) to Move Towards a Resolution of the Kosovo Crisis*, UN doc. S/1999/649, reprinted in SC Res. 1244, Annex II (Jun 10, 1999)
[177] Mary Robinson, UN High Commissioner for Human Rights, *Report on the Human Rights Situation Involving Kosovo*, Apr 30, 1999
[178] Steven Lee Myers, 'Cohen and Other Ministers Size Up Possible Ground Force', *NYT*, May 29, 1999, at A6
[179] S/Res/1239(1999)
[180] Ibid.
[181] 'World Again Displays its Hollow Commitment Against War Crimes', *USA Today*, May 28, 1999, at A14
[182] Indictment, *Prosecutor v. Milosevic, et al*, ICTY (confirmed May 24, 1999)
[183] 'The Case Against Mr. Milosevic', *NYT*, May 28, 1999, at A22

[184] D.S. Cloud, K.A. Robbins, R. Block, and Andrew Higgins, 'Russia and West Agree to Kosovo Deal - Bombing Halt Looks Closer As Serbian Troops Show Preparations for Pullout', *Wall Street Journal*, Jun 9, 1999, at A3

[185] *UN Chronicle*, no.1 (1999), p. 5

[186] 'The Case Against Mr Milosevic', ibid.

[187] Ibid.

[188] 'International Law: Milosevic Arraigned in UN Tribunal, He Challenges its Validity', *International Journal on World Peace*, no. 3 (Sep 2001), pp. 69-71.

[189] *Legality of the Use of Force*, Yugoslavia v. Belgium (Order of Jun 2, 1999)

[190] See Yugoslavia's *Application for Interim Measures* (Apr 9, 1999), ibid.

[191] See ICJ Decision, *Annual Review of United Nations Affairs* (1999), p. 1055

[192] Ibid.

[193] Thomas E. Ricks and Carla Anne Robbins, 'NATO Resists Retargeting Yugoslav Bombs - Some Fear Depopulating Kosovo May Be Prelude to Carving It Up', *WSJ*, Mar 30, 1999, at A18

[194] See Kosovo Peace Plan, reprinted in 38ILM (1999) p. 1217

[195] Leonid Kuchma, 'A Peace Plan for Kosovo', *WSJ*, Apr 23, 1999, at A14

[196] *UN Chronicle*, no. 2 (1999), p. 12

[197] S/Res/1244(1999)

[198] Ibid.

[199] Ibid.

[200] Ibid.

[201] William J. Clinton, 'Letter to Congressional Leaders Reporting on the Deployment of United States Military Personnel as Part of the Kosovo International Security Force', *Weekly Compilation of Presidential Documents*, Jun 26, 2000, pp. 1387-1388

[202] S/Res/1244(1999)

[203] Craig R. Whitney, 'NATO Commander Seeks To Resolve Russian Role', *NYT*, Jun 13, 1999, at A1

[204] Ibid.

[205] Clinton (2000), ibid.

[206] S/Res/1244(1999)

[207] S/Res/1244(1999)

[208] Mayura Koiwai, 'Two New Peacekeeping Missions: Province of Yugoslavia, Kosovo', *Peacekeeping & International Relations*, no. 4 (Jul/Aug 1999)

[209] S/Res/1244(1999)

[210] *UN Chronicle*, no.3 (1999), p. 65

[211] Ibid.

[212] Carlotta Gall, 'In Riot-Torn Kosovo City, Serbs Force Albanians From Homes', *NYT*, Feb 12, 2000, at A6

[213] Ibid.

[214] Steven Erlanger, 'Is Serbia's Victory Kosovo's Loss?', *NYT*, Oct 29, 2000, at A 4

[215] Michael Meyer, 'Tottering on the Edge After Last Week's Bus Blast it's Just a Matter of Time Before Violence Hits NATO Troops: An Insider's View', *Newsweek*, Feb 26, 2001, p. 20

[216] David S. Cloud, 'Albright's Spokesman Helped Shape Kosovo Pact - James Rubin Wooed the Rebels', *WSJ*, Jun 29, 1999, at A 11

[217] Joshua Hammer, '... And Justice for Some', *Newsweek*, Jun 19, 2000, p. 44

[218] Cloud et al (1999), ibid.

[219] Nicholas Wheeler, *Saving Strangers* (2000), p. 269

[220] Address to the Nation on Airstrikes Against Serbian Targets in the Federal Republic of Yugoslavia, *Federal News Service*, Mar 24, 1999

[221] S/Res/1203(1998)

[222] James Rubin, US Department of State Press Briefing, Mar 16, 1999

[223] *UN Chronicle*, no. 2 (1999), p. 13

[224] Judith Miller, 'Russia's Move To End Strikes Loses; Margin Is a Surprise', *NYT*, Mar 27, 1999, at A7

[225] Comment by Fernando Enrique Petrella, Argentina's Representative to the UN, *UN Chronicle*, no. 2 (1999), p.13

[226] Statement by Kofi Annan, *UN Chronicle*, no. 1 (1999), p. 81

[227] Ibid, p. 13

[228] Martin Walker, 'EU Members' Views Differ on NATO Action', *Europe*, Apr 1999, pp. S2-S3; see also Christine Gray, *International Law and the Use of Force* (2000), p. 195

[229] Michael R. Gordon, 'Russian Anger at U.S. Tempered by Need for Cash', NYT, Mar 25, 1999 at A1

[230] *UN Chronicle*, no. 2 (1999), pp. 13-14

[231] See Article 51 of UN Charter

[232] Nanda, Muther, Jr. and Eckert (1998), ibid.

[233] Michael Glennon, 'The Charter: Does it Fit?', *UN Chronicle*, no. 2 (1999), pp. 32-33

The Situation in East Timor

[234] *UN Chronicle*, no. 2 (1999), p. 84

[235] Ibid.

[236] Ibid.

[237] S/Res/384(1975).

[238] GA Res 34/40 (1979), *UN Chronicle*, no. 1 (1980), p. 53

[239] *UN Chronicle*, no. 1 (1999), p. 84

[240] Frank Ching, 'A UN Report on East Timor', *Far Eastern Economic Review*, Apr 6, 1995

[241] 'A Way Out: Indonesia Offers Autonomy to East Timor', *Far East Economic Review*, Aug 20, 1998

[242] Ibid.

[243] 'Mission in East Timor Established to Conduct 'Popular Consultation' on Territory's Status', *UN Chronicle*, no. 2 (1999), pp. 70-71

[244] S/Res/1236(1999)

[245] Ibid.

[246] *Report of the Secretary General on the Situation in East Timor* S/1999/595, May 22, 1999

[247] See Ibid (S/1999/595)

[248] S/Res/1246(1999)

[249] Ibid.

[250] Ibid.

[251] Ibid.

[252] 'Leaders: Terror in Timor', *The Economist,* May 1, 1999

[253] Ron Moreau, 'Militia Violence Disrupts the Referendum: One Thug, One Vote', *Newsweek*, Sep 13, 1999

[254] Seth Mydans, 'Timorese Vote in Prelude to Nationhood', *New York Times,* Aug 31, 2001, at A 8

[255] Seth Mydans, 'Timorese Refugees Tell of Terror by Militias After Foreigners Left', *NYT*, Oct 10, 2000, at A1

[256] Barbara Crossette, 'U.N. Says a Quarter of East Timorese Have Fled', *NYT*, Sep 8, 1999, at A1

[257] Raphael Pura, 'Jakarta Blames Ex-Top General For Mass Violence in East Timor', *WSJ*, Feb 1, 2000, at A23

[258] Seth Mydans, 'Australia Begins Airdrops of Food Aid to East Timor', *NYT,* Sep 18, 1999, at A4

[259] Barbara Crosette (1999), ibid., p. A1

[260] Seth Mydans, 'Militias in Timor Menace Refugees at U.N. Compound', *NYT*, Sep 11, 1999, at A1

[261] 'East Timor: Threshold of Transition Reattained', *UN Chronicle*, no. 3 (1999), p.60

[262] Barabara Crosette, 'A Push to Intervene in East Timor is Gathering Backers at the UN', *NYT*, Sep 7, 1999, at A1

[263] Elizabeth Becker, 'United States and Indonesia Quietly Resume Military Cooperation', *NYT*, May 24, 2000, at A10

[264] Jeremy Wagstaff, Jay Solomon, and Neil King, Jr., 'Indonesia to Permit Peacekeepers in East Timor', *WSJ*, Sep 13, 1999, at p. 33

[265] S/Res/1264(1999)

[266] Ibid.

[267] Ibid.

[268] Ibid.

[269] Jeremy Wagstaff, 'U.N. Passes Plan to Restore Peace in East Timor - Australian-Led Force Will Have Few U.S. Troops', *WSJ*, Sep 16, 1999, at A25

[270] Julie Schmit, 'U.N. Force Meets no Resistance on Arrival', *USA Today*, Sep 21, 1999, at 12A

[271] 'U.N. Governance in East Timor', *NYT*, Oct 7, 1999, at A30

[272] 'East Timor Becomes 191st U.N. Member Today', *NYT*, Sep 27, 2002, at A11

[273] S/Res/1272(1999)

[274] Ibid.

[275] Ibid.

[276] Barbara Crossette, 'A Push to Intervene in East Timor Is Gathering Backers at the U.N', *NYT*, Sep 7, 1999, at A1

[277] Statement by Kofi Annan, UN General Assembly 51st Session, 1999

[278] Corel Bell, 'East Timor, Canberra and Washington: A Case Study in Crisis Management', *Australian Journal of International Affairs* (Jul 2000), pp. 171-177

CHAPTER V - THE SECURITY COUNCIL AND SMALL-SCALE TRANSNATIONAL ARMED CONFLICTS

The Situation in Western Sahara

[1] John F. Burns, 'Sahara Impasse: Line in Sand or National Border?', *New York Times*, Jun 16, 1999, at A10
[2] Yahia H. Zoubir and Anthony G. Pazzanita, 'The United Nations' Failure in Resolving the Western Sahara Conflict', *The Middle East Journal* (Autumn 1995)
[3] Western Sahara Advisory Opinion, Oct 16, 1975
[4] Zoubir and Pazzanita (1995), ibid.
[5] Ibid.
[6] S/Res/621(1988)
[7] S/Res/658(1991)
[8] S/Res/690(1991)
[9] Ibid.
[10] Burns, *NYT* (1999), ibid.
[11] Zoubir and Pazzanita (1995), ibid.
[12] Ibid.
[13] *Report of the Secretary General on Situation Concerning Western Sahara*, S/2001/613, Jun 20, 2001

The Situation in Macedonia

[14] Chuck Sudetic, 'Real Macedonia Issue is Real Estate', *NYT*, Mar12, 1994, at A4
[15] Ibid.
[16] R/Res 795 (1992)
[17] S/Res/983(1995)
[18] S/Res/1082 (1996), S/Res/1105 (1997), S/Res/1110 (1997), S/Res/1140 (1997), S/Res/1142 (1997)
[19] S/Res/1186(1998)
[20] Stuart J. Kaufman, 'Preventive Peacekeeping, Ethnic Violence, and Macedonia', *Studies in Conflict and Terrorism* (Jul 1996)
[21] Mayura Koiwai, 'Veto Ends UN Mission in Macedonia', *Peacekeeping & International Relations* (Mar/Apr 1999)
[22] 'NATO Starts New Mission', *News for You*, Sep 5, 2001
[23] Koiwai, *Peacekeeping & International Relations* (1999), ibid.
[24] 'Interview: The Unlikely Pacifist, Leader of the Macedonian National Liberation Army', *Newsweek*, Sep 3, 2001, at p. 68
[25] Shanda Deziel, 'NATO in Macedonia', *Maclean's*, no. 36, Sep 3, 2001

The Conflict in Abkhazia, Georgia

[26] 'Abkhazia: Small War, Big Risk', *New York Times*, Oct 8, 1992, at A 34
[27] S/Res/854(1993)
[28] Ibid.
[29] 'Fighting Breaks Out in Georgia Buffer Region', *NYT*, May 27, 1998, at A3
[30] S/Res/1225(1999)
[31] S/Res/1287(2000), S/Res/1311(2000)
[32] S/Res/1339(2001)

The Situation in Prevlaka, Croatia

[33] S/Res/779(1992)
[34] S/Res/1038(1996)
[35] S/Res/122(1999)
[36] S/Res/1252(1999)
[37] S/Res/1335(1999)
[38] Ibid.
[39] Ibid.
[40] Ibid.

[41] *Report of the Secretary General on the United Nations Mission of Observers in Prevlaka*, S/2001/661, Jul 3, 2001

The Situation in Tajikistan

[42] Statement by the President of the Security Council on the Situation in Tajikistan and Along the Tajik-Afghan Border, S/PRST/1999/8, Feb 23, 1999
[43] Ibid.
[44] *UN Chronicle*, no. 1 (1999), p. 83
[45] Aleksandr Klimov and Arkady Dubnov, 'Tajik Opposition Disarms', *Current Digest of Post-Soviet Press*, Sep 8, 1999, pp. 19-20
[46] S/Res/1274(1999)
[47] Ibid.
[48] Secretary General's Report on the Situation in Tajikistan, S/2000/387, May 5, 2000
[49] Statement by the President of the Security Council on the Situation in Tajikistan, S/PRST/1999/25, Aug 19, 1999
[50] Statement by the President of the Security Council on the Situation in Tajikistan, S/PRST/2000/17, May 12, 2000

The Situation in the Central African Republic

[51] S/Res/1159(1998)
[52] 'Central African Republic in 3-Way Peace Accord', *NYT*, Jan 26, 1997, at A19
[53] Ibid.
[54] S/Res/1271(1999)
[55] 'Other Peacekeeping Related Actions', *UN Chronicle*, no. 1 (2000), p. 18
[56] Ibid.
[57] *Report of the Secretary General on the Situation in Central African Republic*, S/2001/35 on Jan 11, 2001

The Situation in Guinea-Bissau

[58] S/Res/1216(1998)
[59] S/Res/1233(1999)
[60] Statement by the President of the Security Council on the Situation in Guinea-Bissau, S/PRST/2000/11, Mar 29, 2000

The Situation in Eastern Slavonia, Baranja and Western Sirmium

[61] *Report of the Secretary General on the Situation in Eastern Slavonia, Baranja and Western Sirmium*, S/1995/1028, Dec 13, 1995
[62] S/Res/1037(1996)
[63] Ibid.
[64] Ibid.

CHAPTER VI - THE SECURITY COUNCIL AND THE MANAGEMENT OF INTER-STATE CONFLICTS

[1] See Patil, *The UN Veto in World Affairs* (1992); & Bailey & Daws, *The Procedure of the UN Security Council* (1998), p. 226
[2] Christine Gray, *International Law and the Use of Force* (2000), pp. 144-46

The Korean War

[3] S/Res/82(1950)
[4] S/Res/83(1950)
[5] S/Res 84 (1950)
[6] Ibid.
[7] Richard A. Falk, 'The United Nations and the Rule of Law', *Transnational Law & Contemporary Problems* (1994), p. 613

[8] Ibid.

[9] Ibid.

[10] Uniting for Peace Resolution, G.A. Res. 337 (A)(V), 5; U.N. G.A. GAOR, Supp. (No.20) 10, U.N. Doc.A/1775 (1951)

[11] Ibid.

[12] Ibid.

The Suez Canal Invasion

[13] Bregman and El-Tahri (1998), ibid.

[14] Ibid.

[15] Ibid

[16] Bjorn Hettne, 'The United Nations and Conflict Management: The Role of 'Regionalism' ', *Transnational Law & Contemporary Problems* (1999), p. 644

[17] Falk (1994), ibid.

[18] Nutting (1967), ibid.

The Hungarian Crisis

[19] D.J. Harris, *Cases and Materials on International Law* (1991), p. 843

[20] Ibid.

[21] 'Challenging the Brezhnev Doctrine', *WSJ*, Feb 28, 1985, at p. 1

The United States Invasion of the Dominican Republic

[22] Statement by President Johnson, reprinted in *Department of State Bulletin* (1965), p. 738

[23] Ibid.

[24] David Nicholas, 'US Interventionism in Latin America: Dominican Crisis and the OAS', *International Affairs* (Summer 1988)

[25] Ibid.

[26] Max Hilaire, *International Law and United States Military Intervention in the Western Hemisphere* (1997), pp. 70-71

[27] SCOR (1965), paras 79-80; paras 225-227

[28] Ibid.

[29] Michael Akerhurst, 'Enforcement Action by Regional Agency, with Special Reference to the OAS', *BYIL* (1967), p. 198

[30] S/Res/203(1965)

[31] Akerhurst, ibid.

[32] S/Res/205(1965)

Arab-Israeli Conflict of 1967

[33] S/Res/242 (1967)

The Soviet Invasion of Czechoslovakia

[34] D.J. Harris, ibid, p. 844

[35] SCOR (1968)

The Soviet Invasion of Afghanistan

[36] SCOR (1979)

[37] 'Security Council Fails to Adopt Draft Resolution on Afghanistan', *UN Chronicle*, no. 2 (Mar 1980), p. 9

[38] General Assembly Res. ES-6/2

[39] Ibid.

[40] George Bush, 'Soviets Withdraw from Afghanistan', *Department of State Bulletin* (Apr 1989), p. 48

Vietnam's Invasion of Cambodia

[41] Falk, *The United Nations and the Rule of Law* (1994), ibid.
[42] Ibid.
[43] S/Res/502(1982)
[44] Ibid.
[45] See Caroline Incident, in Harris, ibid, pp. 848-49
[46] Ibid, p. 855; see also, UN Doc. S/PV 2346, p. 7

The United States' Invasion of Grenada

[47] William Gilmore, *Grenada Intervention* (1984), pp. 30-32
[48] Ibid.
[49] Sherri L. Burr, 'The Grenada Invasion: Politics, Law, and Foreign Policy Decisionmaking by Robert J. Beck', *AJIL* (Jul 1995), p. 671
[50] Ibid.
[51] Hettne, *The United Nations and Conflict Management: The Role of the New Regionalism* (1994)
[52] Ibid.

The Iraq-Iran War

[53] Statement by President of the Security Council on Iran-Iraq War, S/14190, Sep 23, 1980
[54] Ibid.
[55] S/Res/479(1980)
[56] Ibid.
[57] Ibid.
[58] S/Res/457 (1979) & S/Res/461 (1979), adopted on Dec 4, 1979 and Dec 31, 1979, respectively
[59] S/Res/582(1986)
[60] Ibid.
[61] Statement by President of the Security Council on Iran-Iraq, S/18538, Dec 22, 1986
[62] S/Res/588(1986)
[63] See De Guttry & Ronzitti (ed.), *The Iran-Iraq War (1980-1988) and the Law of Naval Warfare* (1993), p. 216
[64] Ibid.
[65] S/Res/598(1987)
[66] Ibid.
[67] Ibid.
[68] S/Res/612(1988)
[69] S/Res/619(1988)
[70] 'UNIIMOG Mandate Terminated by Security Council', *UN Chronicle*, no. 1 (1991), p. 18

The United States' Invasion of Panama

[71] Max Hilaire, *International Law and United States Military Intervention in the Western Hemisphere* (1997), pp. 115-123
[72] Statement by President George Bush Justifying United States Invasion of Panama, *New York Times*, Dec 20, 1989, at A1
[73] 'United States Invokes 'Self Defence'', *UN Chronicle*, no. 1 (1990), p. 67
[74] Ibid.
[75] 'Assembly Demands Immediate Halt to United States Intervention in Panama', ibid.
[76] C. Doswald-Beck, 'The Legality of Intervention by Invitation', *BYIL* (1985), p. 189; also, Oscar Schachter, 'The Legality of Pro-Democratic Invasion', *AJIL* (1984), p. 645
[77] See UN General Assembly *Declaration on the Inadmissibility of Intervention in the Domestic Affairs of the State and the Protection of Their Independence and Sovereignty*; G.A. Res. 2131, UN Doc. A/6014 (1966); for an analysis of the legality of the US Invasion of Panama, see Ved Nanda, 'The Validity of United States Intervention in Panama Under International Law', *AJIL* (1990), p. 494

Iraq's Invasion of Kuwait

[78] S/Res/660(1990), adopted by a vote of 14 to 0; Yemen did not participate in the vote
[79] Ibid.
[80] S/Res/661 (1990)

[81] Ibid.

[82] S/Res /662 (1990)

[83] S/Res/664 (1990)

[84] S/Res/665 (1990)

[85] Ibid.

[86] Ibid.

[87] S/Res/667 (1990)

[88] S/Res/674

[89] S/Res/677 (1990)

[90] S/Res/678 (1990)

[91] Ibid.

[92] 'War in Persian Gulf Area Ends', *UN Chronicle*, no. 2 (1991), p. 4

[93] 'Iraq Accept UN Ceasefire, Demand for Reparations, But Calls Council Resolution 'Unjust'', ibid., p. 5

[94] 'Resolution 687: An Unprecedented Text', ibid., p. 6

[95] S/Res/687 (1991)

[96] Ibid.

[97] Ibid.

[98] S/Res/688 (1991)

[99] The no-fly zones forbade Iraqi warplanes from entering airspace over northern and southern Iraq. The zones were not officially sanctioned by the Security Council and were considered illegal by Iraq.

[100] S/Res/689 (1991)

[101] Jules Lobel and Michael Ratner, 'Bypassing the Security Council: Ambiguous Authorizations to Use Force, Ceasefires and the Iraqi Inspection Regime', *AJIL* (1999), p. 124

[102] S/Res/1284 (1999)

[103] Ibid.

[104] Ibid.

[105] S/Res/1330 (2000)

Legality of Security Council Resolution 678 (1990)

[106] Statement by Iraq's Ambassador to the United Nations, Al-Anbari; see a 'Pause of Goodwill - Security Council Enacts 48-Day Waiting Period for Iraqi Compliance With Resolution', *UN Chronicle*, no 1 (1991), p. 46

[107] Burns Weston, 'Security Council Resolution 678 and Persian Gulf Decision Making: Precarious Legitimacy', *AJIL* (1991), pp. 518-20

[108] Oscar Schachter, 'United Nations Law in the Gulf Conflict', *AJIL* (1991), p. 459

[109] Eugene Rostow, 'Until What? Enforcement Action or Collective Self Defense?', *AJIL* (1991), p. 509

[110] Ibid.

[111] Ibid

[112] Michael Glennon, 'The Constitution and Chapter VII of the United Nations Charter', *AJIL* (1991), p.81

[113] Ibid.

[114] Schacter, ibid., p. 60

[115] See Danesh Sarooshi, *The United Nations and the Development of Collective Security* (1999) for detailed discussion on the United Nations Charter

[116] 'U.S. Troops Dispatched to Saudi Arabia for defense of Kingdom', *NYT*, Aug 8, 1990, at A1

[117] See Rostow, who argues that under resolutions 660, 661 and 678 the Security Council conceived of its actions as supplementing the programs of collective self-defense organized by the United States, not as supplanting them, ibid., p.510

[118] S/Res/678 (1991)

[119] Thomas Franck, *Fairness in International Law and Institution* (1999), p.235

[120] Ibid.

[121] North Korea and Rhodesia are the two other cases in which the Security Council authorized enforcement action during the Cold War.

Security Council Resolution 688 (1991)

[122] R/sec 688 (1991)

[123] Ibid.

[124] Franck, ibid., p. 236

[125] Ibid, p. 234-35

[126] The Security Council has invoked the precedent established under resolution 688 (1991) to authorize the deployment of military forces in Somalia, Bosnia, and Rwanda.

The Eritrea-Ethiopia War

[127] S/Res/1177(1998)
[128] Ibid.
[129] Ibid.
[130] Res/1226 (1999)
[131] S/Res/1227 (1997)
[132] Ibid.
[133] See Statement by Eritrean Delegate, Security Council Press Release, SC/6652, Feb 27, 1999
[134] Statement by President of the Security Council on the Situation Between Eritrea and Ethiopia, S/PRST/2000/34, Nov 21, 2000
[135] 'OAU Nations Pledge to End Violent Conflicts in Africa', *News for You*, Aug 4, 1999, p. 2
[136] S/Res/1297 (2000)
[137] Ibid.
[138] S/Res/1298 (2000)
[139] UN Doc. S/2000/601; also see 'Eritreans and Ethiopians Sign Treaty to End Their Border War', *New York Times*, Dec 13, 2000, at A12
[140] S/Res/1312 (2000)
[141] Ibid.
[142] S/Res/1320 (2000)
[143] Ibid.

The War in the DRC

[144] Ian Fisher and Norimitsu Onishi, 'Chaos in Congo: Armies Ravage a Rich Land Creating Africa's 'First World War'', *New York Times*, Feb 6, 2000
[145] Lusaka Ceasefire Agreement, UN Doc. S/1999/815

The Role of the Security Council

[146] S/Res/1234(1999)
[147] Ibid.
[148] S/Res/1258(1999)
[149] Ibid.
[150] S/Res/1273(1999)
[151] Ibid.
[152] S/Res/1291(1999)
[153] Ibid.
[154] Ibid.
[155] Ibid.
[156] Ibid
[157] S/Res/1303(2000)
[158] Ibid.
[159] S/Res/1355(2000)
[160] Ibid.
[161] Ibid.
[162] Robert W. Gomulkiewicz, 'International Law Governing Aid to Opposition Groups in Civil War: Resurrecting the Standards of Belligerency', *Washington Law Review* (1988), p. 43
[163] Brad R. Roth, *Governmental Illegitimacy and International Law* (1999), pp. 246-250
[164] Heather A. Wilson, *International Law and the Use of Force by National Liberation Movements* (1988), pp. 78-88
[165] Brad R. Roth, ibid., p. 251

The United States' Invasion of Afghanistan

[166] S/Res/1368 (2001)

[167] S/Res/1373 (2001)

[168] Letter from US Rep. to President of the SC, Oct 7, 2001

[169] S/Res/1383 (2001)

[170] NATO press release, Sep 12, 2001; and OAS Doc. OEA/Ser.F/II.24/RC.24/Res.1/01, Sep 21, 2001

[171] S/Res/1510 (2003)

The United States' Invasion of Iraq (2003)

[172] President Bush's Address to the General Assembly; reprinted in *Washington Post*, Sep 13, 2002, at A31

[173] Sean Murphy, 'Contemporary Practice of the United States Relating to International Law', *AJIL* (2002), p. 960

[174] Keith Richburg & Sharon Lafraniere, 'No Force Yet, Three Nations Say', Washington Post, Mar 6, 2003, at A19

[175] Peter Slevin, 'U.S. Says War Has Legal Basis', Washington Post, Mar 21, 2003, at A14

[176] Excerpts of Reports of UNMOVIC and IAEA; reprinted in *New York Times*, Jan 28, 2003, at A10-11; see also 'In a Chief Inspector's Words: 'A Substantial Measure of Disarmament'', *NYT*, Mar 8, 2003, at A8

[177] President Bush Address to the Nation, Mar 19, 2003

[178] President Bush Report to Congress; reprinted in *NYT*, Mar 20, 2003, at A18

[179] President Bush Address, ibid.

[180] Report to Congress, ibid.

[181] Ibid.

[182] Ibid.

[183] Memorandum Opposing U.S. Iraq Policy; reprinted in the *NYT*, Feb 25, 2003, at A10

[184] Bob Sherwood, 'Military force: pre-emptive defence or breach of international law?', *Financial Times*, Mar 11, 2003, p. 11

[185] Memorandum, ibid.

[186] Anne-Marie Slaughter, 'The Will That Makes It Work', *Washington Post*, Mar 2, 2003, at B1

[187] Jochen A. Frowein, 'Unilateral Interpretation of Security Council Resolution - A Threat to Collective Security', in Volkmar Gotz, Veter Selmer & Rudiger Wolfrum (ed.), *Liberamicorum Gunther Jaenicke* (1998), p. 97

[188] Helmut Freudenschulss, 'Between Unilateralism and Collective Security: Authorizations of the Use of Force by the UN Security Council', *European Journal of International Law*, no. 4 (1994), pp. 102-141

[189] For an analysis on Article 39, see Good & Hambro, *Charter of the United Nations* (1949), pp. 262-65

[190] Oscar Schachter, *International Law in Theory and Practice* (1991), p. 138; see also Bruno Simma, *Charter of the United Nations* (1995), p. 608, for analysis on Article 51

[191] 'White House Tells Congress Why the Nation Must go to War', *NYT*, Mar 30, 2003, at A18

[192] S/Res/678 (1990), para. 2

[193] Eugene Rostow, 'Until What? Enforcement Action or Collective Self Defense?', *AJIL* (1991), p. 509

[194] S/Res/1441 (2002)

[195] Ibid.

[196] 'The Rationale for the U.N. Resolution on Iraq, in the Diplomat's Own Words', *New York Times*, Nov 9, 2002, at A8

[197] 'In the Delegates' Words: Hawks and Doves Debate at the Security Council', *NYT*, Mar 8, 2003, at A9

[198] Oscar Schachter, ibid., p. 106; see also G.A. Res. 2625 (XV) (1970)

[199] See Secretary General Javier Perez de Cuellar's Address at University of Bordeaux, U.N. Press Release, SG/MS 4560, Apr 24, 1991

[200] S/Res/1483 (2003)

[201] S/Res/1511 (2003), para. 15

[202] Ibid, para. 25

[203] See S/Res/678 (1990)

CHAPTER VII - THE USE OF NON-MILITARY MEASURES BY THE SECURITY COUNCIL IN RESPONSE TO TRANSNATIONAL ARMED CONFLICTS

[1] Bailey and Daws, *The Procedure of the Security Council* (1998), pp. 365-74

Measures against Rhodesia

[2] S/Res/217(1965)

[3] S/Res/221(1966)
[4] Ibid.

Measures against South Africa

[5] General Assembly Res. 2877 (XXVI) (1971); General Assembly Res. 3397 (XXX) (1971)
[6] S/Res/181(1963)
[7] Ibid.
[8] S/Res/182(1963)

Measures against Iraq

[9] S/Res/660(1990)
[10] S/Res/661(1990)
[11] S/Res/678(1990)
[12] Ibid.
[13] S/Res/687(1991)
[14] Ibid.
[15] Ibid.
[16] S/Res/688(1991)
[17] S/Res/1483 (2003)
[18] Ibid.
[19] Ibid.

Measures against the Former Yugoslavia

[20] S/Res/713(1991)
[21] Ibid.
[22] S/Res/752(1992)
[23] Ibid.
[24] S/Res/757(1992)
[25] Ibid.
[26] Ibid.
[27] Ibid.
[28] Ibid.
[29] Ibid.
[30] S/Res/781(1992)
[31] S/Res/786(1992)
[32] S/Res/787(1992)
[33] Ibid.
[34] Ibid.
[35] S/Res/827(1993)
[36] Thomas Franck, *Fairness in International Law and Institutions* (1998)
[37] See *Decision of the Appeals Chamber Decision in Prosecutor v. Tadic Regarding Jurisdiction of ICTY*, No. IT-94-1-AR72 (Oct 1995), reprinted in *ILM* (1996). See also George H. Aldrich, 'Jurisdiction of the International Criminal Tribunal for Yugoslavia', *AJIL* (1996), p. 64
[38] James Podgers, 'A Victory for Process', *ABA Journal*, Jul 1997, p. 30
[39] S/Res/998(1995)
[40] Anthony Borden, 'The Dayton Deal', *The Nation*, Dec 18, 1995, p. 773; Dayton Peace Accords, UN Doc. S/1995/999
[41] S/Res 11031 (1995)

Measures against Somalia

[42] S/Res/733(1992)
[43] Ibid.
[44] S/Res/ 746(1992)
[45] S/Res/751(1992)
[46] S/Res/767(1992)

[47] S/Res/794(1992)

[48] Nanda, Muther, Jr., and Eckert (1998), ibid.

[49] Ibid.

[50] S/Res/954(1994)

Measures against Haiti

[51] S/Res/841(1993)

[52] Nanda et al (1998), ibid.

[53] Ibid.

[54] S/Res/875(1993)

[55] S/Res/940(1994)

[56] Ibid.

[57] Nanda et al, ibid.

Measures against Rwanda

[58] S/Res/872(1993)

[59] S/Res/893(1994)

[60] Nicholas Wheeler, *Saving Strangers* (2000), p. 225

[61] Letter dated April 13, S/1994/430, from the Representative of Belgium Addressed to the President of the Security Council

[62] S/Res/918 (1994)

[63] S/Res/912 (1994); also see 'UN Force Begins Rwanda Pullout', *International Herald Tribune*, Apr 21, 1994

[64] S/Res/929 (1994)

[65] S/Res/Res/955 (1994)

[66] Elizabeth Neuffer, *The Key to My Neighbor's House* (2002), pp. 123-24

Measures against Libya

[67] Vera Gowland-Debbas, 'The Relationship between the International Court of Justice and the Security Council in the Light of the Lockerbie Case', *AJIL* (1994), p. 611

[68] S/Res/731(1992)

[69] Ibid.

[70] Ibid.

[71] Question of Interpretation and Application of the 1971 Montreal Convention Arising from the Aerial Incident at Lockerbie, Libya Arab Jamahiriya v. United Kingdom, and Libya Arab Jamahiriya v. United States of America, filed Mar 3, 1992

[72] S/Res/748 (1992)

[73] *Annual Review of United Nations Affairs* (2001), pp. 3-269

[74] Gowland-Debbas, ibid.

[75] Question of Interpretation and Application of the 1971 Montreal Convention, Libya v. United Kingdom, Order of Apr 14, 1992; *ICJ Reports* (1992), p. 3

[76] Jose Alvarez, 'Judging the Security Council', *AJIL* (1996), pp. 24-28

[77] S/Res/748 (1992)

[78] Ibid.

[79] Ibid.

[80] Ibid.

[81] Ibid

[82] S/Res/883 (1993)

[83] Ibid.

[84] Ibid.

[85] Letter of Secretary General to the President of the Security Council, Apr 5, 1999 (S/1999/378)

[86] Donald G. McNeil, Jr., 'Libyan Convicted by Scottish Court in 88 Pan Am Blast', *NYT*, Feb 1, 2001, at A1

[87] Thomas Franck, *Fairness in International Law and Institutions* (1998), p. 416

[88] S/Res/1506 (2003)

Measures against Liberia

[89] S/Res/788(1992)

[90] Ibid.

[91] Nanda, Muther, Jr., and Eckert (1998), Vol. 26 no. 5, ibid.

[92] Kathleen Huvane, 'U.N. Cracks Down on 'Conflict Diamonds'', *World Watch*, no. 5 (Sep/Oct 2001), p. 9

[93] S/Res/1343(2001)

[94] Ibid.

[95] Ibid.

[96] Ibid.

[97] Ibid.

[98] Ibid.

[99] Ibid.

[100] Ibid.

Measures against Angola (UNITA)

[101] S/Res/626 (1988) of Dec 20, 1989; for a detailed analysis of UNAVEM I's performance, see Margaret J. Anstee, 'Angola: The Forgotten Tragedy - A Test Case for UN Peacekeeping', *International Relations*, no. 6 (Dec 1993)

[102] S/Res/696 (1991)

[103] S/Res/952 (1994) and 966 (1994)

[104] S/Res/864 (1993)

[105] Ibid.

[106] S/Res/1127 (1997)

[107] Ibid.

[108] Ibid.

[109] S/Res/1173(1997)

[110] Ibid.

[111] Ibid.

[112] Ibid.

[113] Ibid.

Measures against Sierra Leone

[114] S/Res/1132(1997)

[115] Ibid.

[116] Ibid.

[117] S/Res/1162(1998)

[118] Ibid.

[119] S/Res/1171(1998)

[120] Barbara Crossette, '6,000 UN Peacekeepers Planned for Sierra Leone', *NYT*, Oct 23, 1999, at A4

[121] Lome Peace Agreement, UN. Doc. S/1999/777); See also 'Sierra Leone 'Peace Accord' Presages an End to Electoral Government', *Defense & Foreign Affairs Strategic Policy*, no. 7 (Jul 1999)

[122] S/Res/1270(1999)

[123] S/Res/1299 (2000)

[124] S/Res/1315 (2000)

[125] *Report of the Secretary General on the Establishment of the Special Court for Sierra Leone*, S/2000/915, Oct 4, 2000

Measures against Afghanistan

[126] S/Res/1193(1998)

[127] Ibid.

[128] S/Res/1214(1998)

[129] Ibid.

[130] S/Res/1267(1999)

[131] Ibid.

[132] Ibid.

[133] Statement by President of the Security Council on the Situation in Afghanistan, S/PRST/1999/29, Oct 22, 1999

[134] Ibid.
[135] Ibid.
[136] Ibid.
[137] S/Res/1333 (2000)
[138] Ibid.
[139] Ibid.
[140] Ibid.
[141] Ibid.
[142] Ibid.

Security Council Measures against Sudan

[143] S/Res/1044(1996)
[144] Ibid.
[145] S/Res/1054(1996)
[146] Ibid.
[147] S/Res/1070(1996)
[148] Ibid.

Measures against Yugoslavia (Kosovo)

[149] S/Res/1160(1998)
[150] Ibid.
[151] S/Res/1199(1998)
[152] Ibid.
[153] Ibid.
[154] 'NATO Attack Serbian Forces After 'Ethnic Cleansing' Begins in Kosovo', *International Journal on World Peace* (Mar 1999)
[155] Bruno Simma, 'NATO, the UN and the Use of Force: Legal Aspects', *European Journal of International Law* (1999), p. 6
[156] Smita P. Nordwall, 'NATO, Yugoslavia Agreement Targets Weapons Smuggling', *USA Today*, Mar 13, 2001, at A9
[157] S/Res/1244(1999)
[158] Accordance with International Law of the Unilateral Declaration of Independence in Respect of Kosovo, Request for Advisory Opinion, Jul 22, 2010

Measures against Eritrea and Ethiopia

[159] S/Res/1177(1998)
[160] S/Res/1227(1999)
[161] S/Res/1297(2000)
[162] S/Res/1298(2000)
[163] Ibid.
[164] Agreement on Cessation of Hostilities Between Federal Democratic Republic of Ethiopia and the State of Eritrea, UN Doc. S/2000/601; see also 'Eritreans and Ethiopians Sign Treaty to End Their Border War', *NYT*, Dec 13, 2000, at A12

Conclusion

[165] *Report of the Secretary General on Impact of Sanctions*, S/50/203, Jul 15, 1995; see also Bailey and Daws, *The Procedure of the Security Council* (1998), p. 366

CHAPTER VIII: CONCLUSION - ENHANCING THE CAPACITY OF THE SECURITY COUNCIL TO RESPOND TO TRANSNATIONAL ARMED CONFLICTS

[1] See Article 39 of UN Charter
[2] Sonnenfeld, *Resolutions of the United Nations Security Council* (1988)
[3] Nigel White, *The United Nations System* (2002), pp. 152-155

Security Council Successes

[4] Richard Falk, 'The United Nations and the Rule of Law', *Transnational Law & Contemporary Problems* (Fall 1994), p. 611
[5] Richard Falk, 'The Haiti Intervention: A Dangerous World Order Precedent for the United Nations', *Harvard International Law Journal* (Spring 1995), p. 342
[6] Thomas Franck, *Fairness in International Law and Institutions* (2000), pp. 224-44

Security Council Failures

[7] Christiane Gray, *International Law and the Use of Force* (2000), p. 155
[8] Nicholas Wheeler, *Saving Strangers* (2000), p. 251-53
[9] Ibid.
[10] S/Res/733 (1992)
[11] S/Res/751 (1992)
[12] S/Res/794 (1992)
[13] Ibid.
[14] S/Res/814 (1993)
[15] Ibid.
[16] S/Res/846 (1993)
[17] S/Res/872 (1993)
[18] Nicholas Wheeler, *Saving Strangers* (2000), p. 215; see also S.R. Feil, *Preventing Genocide: A Report to the Carnegie Commission on Preventing Deadly Conflict* (1998), p. 27
[19] S/Res/912 (1994)
[20] S/Res/ 929 (1994)
[21] Oscar Schachter, 'Authorized Uses of Force by the United Nations and Regional Organizations', in Lori Damrosch & David Scheffer (ed.), *Law and Force in the New International Order* (1991), p. 88
[22] S/Res/788 (1992) & 1132 (1997)
[23] S/Res/952 (1994) & 966 (1994)
[24] See Margaret Anstee, 'Angola: The Forgotten Tragedy', *International Relations* (Dec 1993), p. 501-02

The Security Council and Inter-State Conflicts

[25] S/Res/687 (1991)
[26] S/Res/678 (1990)